# IMAGINARY CONVERSATIONS

Copyright by the National Portrait Gallery

Walter Savage Landor, 1828
(From the bust by John Gibson)

Selected Imaginary Conversations
of
Literary Men and Statesmen

Walter Savage Landor

Edited by
CHARLES L. PROUDFIT

Petrarca. . . . Among the chief pleasures of my life, and among the commonest of my occupations, was the bringing before me such heroes and heroines of antiquity, such poets and sages, such of the prosperous and the unfortunate, as most interested me by their courage, their wisdom, their eloquence, or their adventures. Engaging them in the conversation best suited to their characters, I knew perfectly their manners, their steps, their voices: and often did I moisten with my tears the models I had been forming of the less happy.
—The Pentameron

UNIVERSITY OF NEBRASKA PRESS · LINCOLN

Copyright © 1969 by the University of Nebraska Press
All rights reserved
Library of Congress Catalog Card Number 69-10272

Manufactured in the United States of America

To Sharon

CONTENTS

Acknowledgments	ix
Introduction	xi
Landor Chronology	xxiii
Selected Bibliography	xxviii
Boccaccio and Petrarca	1
Lucullus and Cæsar	15
Mr. Pitt and Mr. Canning	47
John of Gaunt and Joanna of Kent	75
The Lady Lisle and Elizabeth Gaunt	83
Chaucer, Boccaccio, and Petrarca	93
Alexander and the Priest of Hammon	139
Diogenes and Plato	155
Textual Notes	229
Index	255

ACKNOWLEDGMENTS

I would like to express my indebtedness to those scholars of Landor whose efforts have proved invaluable in the preparation of this edition. Foremost among them is Professor R. H. Super, whose numerous writings on Landor, particularly his *Walter Savage Landor: A Biography*, provide the basis for all future critical studies. I am also indebted to John Forster's *Walter Savage Landor* for its preservation of anecdotes and correspondence, to C. G. Crump's six-volume edition of the *Imaginary Conversations* for its useful, though limited, annotations, and to Doris E. Peterson's unpublished doctoral dissertation, "Landor's Treatment of His Source Materials in the 'Imaginary Conversations Greek and Roman.'"

No personal indebtedness is greater than that to Professor R. H. Super, under whose direction I first began my work with Landor as a graduate student, and whose sustained interest and encouragement I have valued. I also acknowledge with gratitude the suggestions and assistance of Professors William A. Coles, Roger A. Pack, and Constance Wright, and of the Reverend H. L. H. Townshend and Miss Diana Landor.

I wish to thank the staffs of The University of Michigan General Library and the University of Colorado Norlin Library for their help in providing materials necessary for preparing this edition. I should also like to thank the Horace H. Rackham School of Graduate Studies of The University of Michigan and the University of Colorado Council on Research and Creative Work, which through grants have provided me with time for continuing my research.

Acknowledgments are due to the National Portrait Gallery of London for permission to reproduce photographs of John Gibson's bust of Walter Savage Landor; to The Belknap Press of Harvard University Press for permission to quote from *The Journals and Miscellaneous Notebooks of Ralph Waldo Emerson*, ed. William H. Gilman (1960–1966); to Cambridge University Press for permission to quote from *Encyclopaedia Britannica*, ed. Hugh Chisholm (11th ed., 1911); to Chapman and Hall Ltd. for permission to quote from *The Complete Works of Walter Savage Landor*, ed. T. Earle Welby and Stephen Wheeler (1927–1936); to Harvard University Press for permission to quote from Douglas Bush, *Mythology and the Romantic Tradition in English Poetry* (1937), and from the Loeb Classical Library; to Methuen and Co. Ltd. for permission to quote from *The Sports and Pastimes of the People of England*, ed. J. C. Cox (2d ed.

rev., 1903), and from A. E. Taylor, *Plato: The Man and His Work* (7th ed., 1960); and to John Murray for permission to quote from Walter Savage Landor, *Charles James Fox: A Commentary on His Life and Character*, ed. Stephen Wheeler (1907).

Finally, to Sharon, my wife, whose cheerful presence and helpful criticism have meant so much, I offer my especial gratitude.

INTRODUCTION

The life of Walter Savage Landor spanned eighty-nine years of English literary history, beginning with the close of the Neoclassical Age and ending with the Victorian Era. Landor, who was born on January 30, 1775, was nine years old when Samuel Johnson died; a lad of fourteen on the day the Bastille fell; and a youth of eighteen when England, under Pitt, declared war on France. A contemporary of Wordsworth, Coleridge, Lamb, and Hazlitt, he outlived the first and second generations of Romantic writers and formed a new circle of friends among such eminent Victorians as Thomas Carlyle, Charles Dickens, and Robert and Elizabeth Barrett Browning. And in March of 1864, six months before Landor's death on September 17, we find a young, unknown poet, Algernon Charles Swinburne, calling at Landor's apartment in Florence to pay his respects to the writer, then in his ninetieth year.

While Landor is frequently regarded as a Victorian, the *Imaginary Conversations*, which he considered his great work, were for the most part completed by 1829, during the period of the great Romantics. Temperamentally, he is not unlike the Romantic poets; indeed, although Landor once declined to meet Shelley while they were both residing at Pisa[1] because of the stories circulating about Shelley's relationship with his first wife, Landor's academic career was no less chaotic than young Shelley's, the women in his life were even more numerous, and his family's displeasure with his behavior and management of his affairs was certainly as intense. The stereotype of the staid Victorian does not reflect Landor's personal life nearly so well as the popularized conception of the "Romantic."

Landor was removed from Rugby at the age of sixteen without completing his academic career because he "was rebellious, and incited others to rebellion."[2] His removal, allowed in lieu of an expulsion, was the result of numerous conflicts between Landor and the headmaster, Thomas James, which culminated, according to the memory of Charles Apperley, a younger classmate, when Dr. James came to Landor's room to speak with him and Landor, in response to Dr. James's identification of himself, replied, "*Get thee* hence, *Satan!*"[3] Landor's career at Trinity College

[1] Kate Field, "Last Days of Walter Savage Landor," *Atlantic Monthly*, XVII (May 1866), 543.
[2] John Forster, *Walter Savage Landor: A Biography* (2 vols.; London, 1869), I, 197. Hereafter referred to as Forster.
[3] Charles Apperley ("Nimrod"), "My Life and Times," *Fraser's Magazine*, XXVI (August 1842), 171.

ended in similar disaster when, during an evening wine party, he fired a gun at the shuttered windows of the room of a classmate, whom he disliked, from his own room across the courtyard.[4] Although he was rusticated with an agreement that he could return to Oxford at the end of two terms, Landor chose not to continue his studies.

All of his life Landor found women attractive, and from his youth they seemed to be attracted to him. His relationships, however, were filled with upheaval. His first love, Nancy Jones, whom he began addressing in his poetry as Iöne in 1793, had died by 1806, eight years after Landor included a memorial to their past romance in *Gebir* in 1798. According to his brother Robert, Nancy bore Landor an illegitimate child, but there is no evidence to prove it.[5] Rose Aylmer, whom Landor immortalized in his verses to her, written after her death, died of cholera in Calcutta in early 1800, just a few years after Landor met her. Jane Sophia Swift, a descendant of Jonathan Swift's Uncle Godwin, whom Landor addressed as Ianthe in his poetry and with whom he assuredly was in love, married Godwin Swift around 1803,[6] presumably by family arrangement. Her return to Ireland for the marriage left young Landor exceedingly disappointed, although they saw much of each other as good friends when she was widowed after a second marriage.

His own marriage to Julia Thuillier, whom he took as a bride when she was only seventeen and he thirty-six, was a failure. He lived faithfully with her for twenty-four years, and they had four children—three sons, Arnold, Walter, and Charles, and a daughter, Julia—but he never found in his wife, who was an extremely handsome woman, the companionship for which he longed. Julia Landor's interests rested in parties and dances, and she could no more have been satisfied with her husband's desire for solitude and his great appetite for reading and conversation than he with her love for an active social life. Further, Landor's inability to manage his finances left the family perpetually in the shadow of threatening domestic insecurity, alleviated only by arrangements between Landor and his brothers to provide for the needs of his family from rent and annuities before Landor's personal income was advanced. But it would be wrong to suppose that Landor was wantonly extravagant; he just was never capable of grasping the rudiments of finance, tended to be generous to a fault

---

[4] Forster, I, 53–56.

[5] R. H. Super, *Walter Savage Landor: A Biography* (New York: New York University Press, 1954), p. 34. Hereafter referred to as Super.

[6] Super, p. 58.

with what he had, and spent a great deal of money on books and paintings, particularly the latter.

The Victorian Landor depended for mature female companionship upon the friendship of Sophia Paynter, a half-sister to Rose Aylmer, Ianthe, and Lady Blessington whom he met in Florence in 1827 and whose wit, grace, and good company were pleasurable to him in spite of the scandalous reputation which rendered her acceptable to unconventional literary circles, but not to high society. Landor was also forever bestowing favors upon young ladies. As is reflected in his writings, he never lost his delight in the opposite sex, and that delight in part accounts for his tendency to idealize and sentimentalize women in both his poems and prose. It is this Victorian Landor who is caricatured as Boythorn in Dickens' *Bleak House*. Dickens captures Landor's affection for dogs in Boythorn's love for his canary, his loud laughter in Boythorn's hearty "Ha, ha, ha," his constant involvement in litigation in Boythorn's right-of-way dispute, and his impetuous nature and humorous rascality in Boythorn's observations and remarks. As amiable as these qualities appear in Boythorn and as they indeed were in Landor, his propensity for legal squabbles and his violent retorts frequently became a burden to family and friends. His legal problems during his years in Italy were numerous, and in fact the Landor family's move from England to Italy was hastened by the court proceedings of his creditors with regard to Llanthony, an estate in Wales owned by Landor.[7] The Landors did not establish a permanent Italian residence until 1829, when a generous loan from Joseph Ablett enabled Landor to purchase the villa in Fiesole owned by Count Gherardesca which was built, Landor told Southey, "upon the spot where Boccaccio led his women to bathe when they had left the first scene of their story-telling."[8]

Landor separated from his wife in 1835 and returned to England. There he encountered a new generation of writers: among his contemporaries only Wordsworth and Southey remained. He began to make the acquaintance of the young literary men of the day—Browning, Dickens, John Forster, and Carlyle—men who stimulated him, even at sixty, to maintain a lively interest in his writing. He remained in England, living primarily at Bath, until 1858, when he became involved in a libel suit. Then in his middle eighties, Landor was unable to cope with it effectively and was encouraged by friends to return to his family in Italy to escape his

[7] Forster, I, 407–409. See also Super, p. 124.
[8] Forster, II, 220.

problems. He soon found life with his family unbearable. In July, 1859, Robert Browning found Landor, a destitute old man, alone, wandering aimlessly the streets of Florence with nowhere to go. Browning took him into his home and cared for him until, through John Forster, he was able to get in touch with Landor's English relatives, who made provision for him during his last years. Those last years were pleasant ones for Landor, spent among the English and Americans in Florence, particularly with the Brownings until Mrs. Browning's death. At the end of his life, Landor was nursed by his sons Walter and Charles. He died on September 17, 1864, and was buried in Florence.

In thinking of this spirited literary figure, it is interesting to reflect that his poem *Gebir* was read attentively by Shelley and De Quincey during their undergraduate years,[9] and that Landor himself was able to read upon first publication the works of both the English Romantics and the Victorians, that he conversed with the youthful Emerson during one of his visits to Italy,[10] and that he read Hawthorne's *The Marble Faun* soon after its appearance.[11] A long life does not merit recognition for that alone, but when that life is one of active involvement with and influence upon important figures, the longevity and resilience assume great significance.

Landor began his career as a poet in 1795 with a volume entitled *The Poems of Walter Savage Landor*, which, like so many youthful efforts, sold poorly—in this case thirty-six out of the one thousand copies printed.[12] He actually received no substantial attention until the publication in 1798 of *Gebir*, which appeared just two months before the *Lyrical Ballads*. This poem, written in the tradition of the Greek pastoral, has Egypt as its locale and concerns the courtship of a shepherd and a nymph. The notice it received was largely due to a favorable assessment made by Robert Southey, then a young poet himself, in the *Critical Review*.[13] It was Southey, moreover, who introduced both Scott and Wordsworth to the work. Landor continued to write poetry all of his life, but the fact that prose was ultimately to be a more successful medium for him is suggested in his early works by his inability to objectify successfully his personal opinions, likes and dislikes, and satirical judgments of prominent people with whom he disagreed or whom he regarded as suitable for ridicule. *Gebir*, for example, expressed both Landor's political idealism and his respect for Napoleon—a dangerous attitude in 1798. Although Landor was later to regard the results of Napoleon's career as reprehensible, he

[9] Super, p. 68.   [10] Super, pp. 235–237.   [11] Super, p. 488.
[12] Super, p. 23.   [13] Super, pp. 45–46.

placed the blame less on the Emperor than on the French, of whom he observed "how incapable was that people of Liberty, and how prone to despotism. Let me never be called inconsistent if I praised the good and true, abhorring and detesting the vicious and the false."[14]

"Abhorring" and "detesting" are strong words, fitting ones for the strength of the convictions expressed by Landor, a lifelong advocate of tyrannicide. So outspoken was he, indeed, that his brief career as a political writer begun at the urging of Dr. Samuel Parr around the turn of the century, came to naught. The very vehemence of Landor's opinions rendered him ill-suited for that profession, since his statements often left him open to charges of libel and were even too radical for the Whig journals most sympathetic to his persuasions.[15] It was the Imaginary Conversation which proved finally to be the literary form best suited to Landor's temperament, for it was malleable enough to absorb and express his attitudes and opinions without necessarily forcing him to accept personal responsibility for the statements uttered by his dramatis personae.

Landor became seriously interested in the prospect of writing dialogues through Southey's experimentation with the form in 1821.[16] By March, 1822, he had completed fifteen Conversations he considered publishable, and by September of that year the number had grown to twenty-three. Largely through the efforts of Julius Hare, acting voluntarily as Landor's London agent, the first two volumes of the *Imaginary Conversations* appeared in 1824. The bulk of his Conversations—eighty-three—were written between 1824 and 1829. Throughout his life he was continually rewriting and revising these works which he considered to be his most serious endeavor, asserting that "poetry was always my amusement, prose my study and business. I have publisht five volumes of *Imaginary Conversations*: cut the worst of them thro the middle, and there will remain in this decimal fraction quite enough to satisfy my appetite for fame. I shall dine late; but the dining-room will be well lighted, the guests few and select."[17] In 1838, writing to Lady Blessington from Bath,

---

[14] MS note dated October 30, 1863, in copy of *Poetry, by the Author of Gebir* (1802) owned by Signora Elfrida Mangioni-Landor, transcribed by M. F. Ashley Montagu and quoted by Super, p. 65.
[15] Malcolm Elwin, *Landor: A Replevin* (London: Macdonald, 1958), p. 75.
[16] Super, p. 158.
[17] "Archdeacon Hare and Landor," *The Complete Works of Walter Savage Landor*, ed. T. Earle Welby and Stephen Wheeler (16 vols.; London: Chapman and Hall, 1927–1936), VI, 37.

Landor confesses that "the revisal of my 'Imaginary Conversations' has cost me more time than the composition. For this, after all, is my great work; the others are but boudoir-tables to lay it on—tables with very slender legs, though fancifully inlaid and pretty well polished."[18]

R. H. Super, in his biography of Landor, remarks that the *Imaginary Conversations* "from the start appeared to Landor as personal essays (political, literary, and of many other sorts) in dialogue form. In a few instances (and generally not in the earlier Conversations) Landor attempted to make his dialogues genuinely dramatic and his characters expressive of emotions and attitudes they actually might have held; for the most part, the Conversations were Landor's own reflections on a wide variety of subjects and their relevance was contemporary, not historical."[19] Landor's earliest reviewers also noted the presence of the author in his dramatis personae, one reviewer observing that Landor speaks through his characters rather than allowing them to speak for themselves:

> He does not employ the real dramatic magic of transforming himself into the character of his selection or creation; he only produces a compound being of which a tenth may be Milton or Marvel, and the remaining nine-tenths are Walter Savage Landor. The result, however, is far more valuable than it would have been had even the most successful imitation been the distinguishing merit of the book.... We may never lose sight of the author, but then we never wish to lose sight of him; nay, we like the company into which he leads us all the better for their bearing evident marks of being animated by his spirit.[20]

A modern reader approaching Landor for the first time is inclined to agree that "we may never lose sight of the author," although the problems this awareness of the author presents may at times render less acceptable the judgment "but then we never wish to lose sight of him." The personal and contemporary in Landor's Conversations abound and can cause numerous difficulties. If general readers do happen to be acquainted with some of Landor's short poems or one of the short dramatic Conversations —"Leofric and Godiva," for instance—one reason is that they require little in the way of specific frame of reference and may be comprehended

---

[18] A. Morrison, *The Blessington Papers* (London: privately printed, 1895), pp. 130–131; quoted by R. H. Super in *The Publication of Landor's Works*, Supplement to the Bibliographical Society's *Transactions*, No. 18 (London: Bibliographical Society, 1954), p. 73.

[19] Super, p. 159.

[20] *Westminster Review*, I (April 1824), 433.

INTRODUCTION xvii

and enjoyed easily upon first reading. Indeed, it may come as a surprise to discover that Landor, whom most of us meet for the first time in a textbook, had so many readers among his contemporaries that by the end of 1824 the first edition of the *Imaginary Conversations* had almost sold out and the publisher had proceeded to print a second, revised edition of one thousand copies.[21] To read Landor today, one needs liberal annotation to provide the political, social, and personal background essential for understanding his allusions. Furthermore, Landor is a man who takes a knowledge of Greek and Roman literature, art, philosophy, and mythology for granted. He was one of those English gentlemen so situated that he could devote his life to letters and the arts without having to worry about steady, remunerative employment. He enjoyed the leisure necessary for immersing himself in the thought and learning of antiquity while maintaining contact with current English and Continental political and social developments. If one has turned to the other Romantic prose writers in preference to Landor, such masters of the personal essay as Hazlitt, Lamb, and De Quincey, who do not make such extensive demands, it is not surprising. But the relative ease of reading them ought not lead us to ignore Landor, whose eccentricities and sense of the past endow him with exceptional interest, and whose vigorous longevity was ever informed and shaped by an irrepressible spirit.

The reception of the *Imaginary Conversations* and the critical attitude toward them have varied since their publication. Although, for instance, the fourth and fifth volumes of the *Conversations*, published in 1829, did not meet the same success at the booksellers' as the first three volumes, the reception of the *Collected Works*, published under the supervision of John Forster in 1846, was exceedingly favorable among Landor's contemporaries. That was in spite of those among the 1846 reviewers who were frequently guilty of reprehensible neglect and misreading because they resented the intensive effort required to read Landor.[22] This difficulty did not deter the large numbers of people who, Super observes, were reading the 1846 edition following its publication: "One need only browse at large among the printed memoirs and correspondence of Landor's contemporaries to see how many people bought and read in these books, not from any friendship for the author, but because the books gave pleasure."[23]

Landor's fellow writers also read him with appreciation. Browning, reminiscing after Landor's death, voices his conviction that Landor "has

[21] Super, p. 181.   [22] Super, pp. 362–363.   [23] Super, pp. 363–364.

written passages not exceeded in beauty and subtlety by any literature that I am acquainted with."[24] Elsewhere Browning acknowledges those qualities which have continued to attract followers to Landor, describing him as "a man who, in spite of strange mistakings, and unfortunate hastinesses of judgment and temper, was gifted with more extraordinary endowments, as well of heart as of head, than ever met in a man before,— so far as my experience goes. The weakness is already past and forgotten, but that royalty of intellect will be increasingly perceived by the world."[25] Swinburne, who dedicated *Atlanta in Calydon* to Landor, immortalized him both in the poem "In Memory of Walter Savage Landor" and in his "Song for the Centenary of Walter Savage Landor," which concludes with this stanza:

> Poet whose large-eyed loyalty of love
>   Was pure toward all high poets, all their kind
> And all bright words and all sweet works thereof;
>   Strong like the sun, and like the sunlight kind;
> Heart that no fear but every grief might move
>   Wherewith men's hearts were bound of powers that bind;
> The purest soul that ever proof could prove
>   From taint of tortuous or of envious mind;
>   Whose eyes elate and clear
>   Nor shame nor ever fear
> But only pity or glorious wrath could blind;
>   Name set for love apart,
>   Held lifelong in my heart,
> Face like a father's toward my face inclined;
>   No gifts like thine are mine to give,
> Who by thine own words only bid thee hail, and live.

This enjoyment of Landor by poets and novelists has continued into the twentieth century. We find allusions to Landor in Pound, Yeats,[26] and

---

[24] *Robert Browning and Julia Wedgwood, a Broken Friendship as Revealed by Their Letters*, ed. Richard Curle (New York: Frederick A. Stokes, 1937), p. 78.

[25] Browning to Robert Landor, November 28, 1864, MS, Yale University Library, quoted by Super, p. 509.

[26] Vivian Mercier deals with the interest of Yeats and Pound in Landor in "The Future of Landor Criticism," *Some British Romantics: A Collection of Essays*, ed. James V. Logan, John E. Jordan, and Northrop Frye (Columbus: Ohio State University Press, 1966), pp. 45–49.

Virginia Woolf; and E. M. Forster in *Howards End* even has Meg Schlegel reading Landor's *Imaginary Conversations* aloud to her brother, Tibby, during an illness.

Landor has not, however, been particularly popular with scholars and critics; his works, especially the prose, have not been so much criticized as neglected.[27] Pierre Vitoux's *L'Œuvre de Walter Savage Landor*[28] is the most satisfactory complete critical study of Landor and his works to appear in this century. Vitoux deals with Landor's prose as only one knowledgeable in the classics and in Landor's background can. Hermann M. Flasdieck's "Walter Savage Landor und seine 'Imaginary Conversations,'"[29] which supports convincingly the thesis that the Conversations are essentially informal essays, is the most important interpretive periodical contribution in many years. One wonders why it is that the reader of Landor must turn to Germany and France for fine published[30] critical works which will assist him with Landor's prose when Landor is, after all, an English writer.

The answer is, in part, that it has been customary to ignore Landor in the twentieth century. This is reflected in F. R. Leavis' assertion that "in a world where there is more literature worth attention than anyone can hope to find time for, it seems worse than pointless to keep up the pretense that Landor is, or should be, current classic, yielding to the elect an elevated delight."[31] Although Landor's prose has, in a sense, been the property of an elect, it is open to question that this has to be a permanent situation, as Leavis' statement implies. Certainly it is my belief that an annotated edition of Landor's prose makes his acquaintance both possible

[27] See R. H. Super, "Walter Savage Landor," *The English Romantic Poets and Essayists: A Review of Research and Criticism*, ed. C. W. Houtchens and L. H. Houtchens (2nd ed. rev.; New York: Modern Language Association of America, 1966), pp. 221–253.

[28] Pierre Vitoux, *L'Œuvre de Walter Savage Landor* (Paris: Presses Universitaires de France, 1964).

[29] Hermann M. Flasdieck, "Walter Savage Landor und seine 'Imaginary Conversations,'" *Englische Studien*, LVIII (1924), 390–431.

[30] Two unpublished doctoral dissertations of particular value are Doris E. Peterson's "Landor's Treatment of His Source Materials in the 'Imaginary Conversations Greek and Roman'" (University of Minnesota, 1942); and Alice LaVonne Prasher's "Walter Savage Landor's *Imaginary Conversations*: A Critical Edition of the First Eight Conversations in Volume One. [with] *Imaginary Conversations of Literary Men and Statesmen*. By Walter Savage Landor, Esq. The First Volume. 1824" (Northwestern University, 1966).

[31] F. R. Leavis, "Landor and the Seasoned Epicure," *Scrutiny*, XI (December 1942), 150.

and pleasurable to a much more extensive audience than he has enjoyed in the past.

Douglas Bush's observation that "Landor's work is mostly of the kind that does not date"[32] also touches upon a critical problem partly responsible for Landor's neglect. Scholars and critics tend to be compulsive categorizers, and Landor is not easily categorized. Like Arnold, he is a classicist; like that of Lamb, Hazlitt, and De Quincey, his prose possesses characteristics of the personal essay; like Shelley, he writes poetry which is frequently idealistic and grounded in the mythological and classical; like Byron, he engages in vituperative satire; like Carlyle, Macaulay, and Mill, he airs his views on contemporary matters in his prose; like Keats, he expresses deep personal feelings in his poetry; and like Browning, he dramatizes a philosophy and ideology through the words of his characters. Where does a scholar place him? How does a scholar attempt to mold, categorize, analyze, and criticize this amorphous mass? But even though other major writers who have produced a quantity of work generally have received sufficient attention from critics and editors to render them accessible to the modern reader, this has not been the case with Landor. In Stephen Wheeler's four-volume edition of Landor's poetry, one does find a definitive work.[33] All of the poems are collected, the text is accurate, useful annotations are provided, and the poems are indexed. But none of the three editions containing Landor's collected prose is definitive,[34] and only that of C. G. Crump, which contains useful but limited explanatory notes, can make a scholarly claim. In anthologies Landor's prose, when it has been included at all, has been represented by short dramatic pieces, often in snippets, which afford the reader only a limited view of his work.

I have endeavored, in selecting Conversations for this volume, to present a broad sampling of the subjects and forms which are found in the *Imaginary Conversations* as a whole. These selections, which were first

---

[32] Douglas Bush, *Mythology and the Romantic Tradition in English Poetry* (Cambridge: Harvard University Press, 1937), p. 229.

[33] Stephen Wheeler, at Welby's death, completed in 1933–1936 the sixteen-volume edition of *The Complete Works of Walter Savage Landor* by editing Volumes XIII–XVI, which contain Landor's poetry. This edition was also issued separately as *The Poetical Works of Walter Savage Landor*, ed. Stephen Wheeler (3 vols.; Oxford: Clarendon Press, 1937).

[34] *The Works and Life of Walter Savage Landor*, ed. John Forster (8 vols.; London, 1876); *Selected Works of Walter Savage Landor*, ed. C. G. Crump (10 vols.; London, 1891–1893); and *The Complete Works of Walter Savage Landor*, ed. T. Earle Welby and Stephen Wheeler (16 vols.; London: Chapman and Hall, 1927–1936).

published in 1829, are arranged in this volume in their original order, and have been chosen from among the dramatic, Italian, English, and classical Conversations. Two of them, "Diogenes and Plato" and "Lucullus and Cæsar," were favorites of the author. The Conversations included may be generally classified into three groups: dramatic, semidramatic, and discursive. "John of Gaunt and Joanna of Kent," "The Lady Lisle and Elizabeth Gaunt," and "Alexander and the Priest of Hammon" are dramatic in that either character or the combination of character and action are of primary interest, and the author's intrusions into the Conversations are kept at a minimum. "Lucullus and Cæsar," "Boccaccio and Petrarca," and "Chaucer, Boccaccio, and Petrarca" are, for the most part, semidramatic; there is a certain interest in action and character, yet the author is also observed speaking through one or more of the characters and at times endowing them with his own personal likes and dislikes. In the two Italian Conversations this semidramatic element constitutes a frame which introduces tales told by the interlocutors in their characteristic manner. One might term "Diogenes and Plato" a discursive dialogue, since it is predominantly an emotional attack against both the person and the philosophy of Plato, whom Landor thoroughly disliked. "Mr. Pitt and Mr. Canning," although possessing both dramatic and discursive elements, can perhaps best be described as a political lampoon in which Landor caricatures two English statesmen whom he despised and discusses through these caricatures the means by which politicians come to power and maintain themselves in it. A careful reading of these Conversations, with annotations, illuminates Landor's ability to move freely from the dramatic to the discursive within the framework of a dialogue form which becomes uniquely his own in its attempt to imitate the informal exchange of actual conversation.

In the annotations and headnotes accompanying each Conversation, I have tried to provide information which may prove helpful to the reader in interpreting Landor's personal, historical, social, political, and literary allusions. Since so much of what is interesting in the Conversations rests in what is interesting about Landor, I have taken particular pains to acquaint the reader with opinions and tastes expressed by Landor which are similar to those expressed by the speakers in the Conversations. It is hoped that this edition will increase the general reader's appreciation of Landor's prose and at the same time provide a workable, definitive text for both students and scholars of Landor's prose. Although I have attempted to annotate the text as thoroughly as possible, the highly allusive and personal nature of the works makes it almost inevitable that certain passages deserving explication will be overlooked. Chaucer's tale in "Chaucer, Boccaccio, and Petrarca," for example, is little more than an extended private joke on Landor's part at the expense of the old Lucy family of Warwickshire. Most certainly personal allusions occur in this tale which were known only to those most intimately involved and are probably beyond the reach of modern scholarship.

The Works of Walter Savage Landor (1846),[35] which generally represents Landor's final revision of the Conversations, has been chosen as the basic text. Since Landor lived eighteen years after the publication of the 1846 *Works*, I have collated that edition with both the first edition (1824–1829) and John Forster's *The Works and Life of Walter Savage Landor* (1876). The results of this collation have shown Landor to be such a painstaking revisionist and conscious prose stylist that I have recorded all the textual variants in language and spelling[36] and all punctuation variants that are not obviously the work of the printer. Printer's errors have been corrected.

Landor frequently appended notes to his Conversations indicating sources or commenting upon his own text. These notes reveal, in some instances, Landor's personality and eccentricities fully as well as his works themselves. They consequently have been retained in the "Critical Notes" and identified accordingly, with the exception of those instances where Landor merely alluded to a source and my annotation provides more complete information.

CHARLES L. PROUDFIT

University of Colorado

---

[35] *The Works of Walter Savage Landor* (2 vols.; London, 1846).

[36] Landor had set orthographical theories which he followed assiduously in his personal spelling and which led his editor, John Forster, to take pains with regularizing his spelling. Spelling variants which do occur in the text are usually significant. For a more detailed study of Landor's orthographic practices see Charles L. Proudfit, "Landor's Hobbyhorse: A Study in Romantic Orthography," *Studies in Romanticism*, VII (Summer 1968), 207–217.

LANDOR CHRONOLOGY

1775	Birth of Walter Savage Landor at Warwick, January 30.
1779–1782	School at Knowle.
1783	Enters Rugby School in January.
1791	Removed from Rugby in December.
1792	Studies under Rev. William Langley, rector of Fenny Bentley, near Ashbourne, Derbyshire; matriculates at Trinity College, Oxford, November 13.
1793	Takes up residence at Oxford in January.
1794	Rusticated from Oxford in June.
1795	*The Poems of Walter Savage Landor* and *Moral Epistle, Respectfully Dedicated to Earl Stanhope*; Landor aged 20.
1796	Meets Rose Aylmer at Swansea.
1797	*To the Burgesses of Warwick*.
1798	*Gebir* published in July; Landor aged 23.
1800	*Poems from the Arabic and Persian*.
1802	*Poetry, by the Author of Gebir*; deeply in love with Jane Sophia Swift (Ianthe); visits Paris, after the Peace of Amiens.
1803	New edition of *Gebir* and *Gebirus*, Latin version of *Gebir*.
1806	*Simonidea*.
1808	Meets Robert Southey at Bristol in April; purchases Llanthony Abbey in the summer; serves as a volunteer in the Spanish revolt against Napoleon in the autumn.
1809	*Three Letters, Written in Spain, to D. Francisco Riguelme*; resides at Bath in the spring.
1811	Meets Julia Thuillier at Bath in January and marries her on May 24; Landor aged 36.
1812	*Count Julian*; *Commentary on Memoirs of Mr. Fox* suppressed in March.
1813	Leaves Llanthony for Swansea in October.
1814	*Letters Addressed to Lord Liverpool*; leaves Julia after a violent quarrel and sails for France on September 2.

1815	Meets Francis Hare at Tours; Julia rejoins Walter at Tours in the spring; *Idyllia Nova Quinque*; leaves Tours in October and settles in Como, Italy.
1818	Birth of his first child, Arnold, on March 5, at Como; leaves Como in September following an altercation with the authorities; resides at Albaro, near Genoa, in October; moves to Pisa in November.
1820	Birth of daughter, Julia, on March 6, at Pisa; *Idyllia Heroica Decem*; Southey informs Landor in a letter dated August 14 that he is engaged in writing dialogues.
1821	Writing *Imaginary Conversations*; leaves Pisa for Palazzo Lozzi, Florence, in the summer.
1822	Informs Southey in March of the completion of fifteen new Conversations; sends first *Imaginary Conversations* to Longmans in early April; Julius Hare seeks a publisher for the *Conversations* during the summer; birth of a second son, Walter, on November 13, at Florence.
1823	John Taylor undertakes the publication of the *Imaginary Conversations* in the spring; the Conversation between Southey and Porson (containing a discussion of Wordsworth's poetry) appears in the *London Magazine* in July.
1824	First two volumes of *Imaginary Conversations* published in March; Landor aged 49.
1825	William Hazlitt visits Landor at Florence in February; publication of third volume of *Imaginary Conversations* suspended after a quarrel with Taylor; birth of third son, Charles, on August 5, at Florence; Jefferson Hogg visits Landor at Florence in November.
1826	Henry Colburn publishes the second edition of *Imaginary Conversations* in May.
1827	Meets Count D'Orsay and the Blessingtons.
1828	Colburn publishes third volume of *Imaginary Conversations* in May.
1829	James Duncan publishes volumes four and five of *Imaginary Conversations* in May; leaves Florence for Fiesole, and the villa Gherardesca, in the summer.

1830	Meets Crabb Robinson at Florence in August.
1831	*Gebir, Count Julian, and Other Poems.*
1832	Returns to England in May; renews friendship with Southey and meets Wordsworth in June; visits Charles Lamb and Samuel Taylor Coleridge in September; returns to Fiesole in November.
1833	Ralph Waldo Emerson visits Fiesole in May; Richard Monckton Milnes at Fiesole in the summer.
1834	*Citation and Examination of William Shakespeare.*
1835	Leaves Fiesole and his family in July; returns to England in the fall; Landor aged 60.
1836	*Pericles and Aspasia* in two volumes; *Letters of a Conservative*; meets John Forster, Mary Shelley, Elizabeth Barrett, and Robert Browning in May; *Terry Hogan; A Satire on Satirists, and Admonition to Detractors.*
1837	*High and Low Life in Italy* appears in Leigh Hunt's *Monthly Repository* from August to April 1838; takes lodgings at 35 St. James's Square, Bath, in November; *The Pentameron and Pentalogia.*
1838	Informs Lady Blessington on January 13 of his intention to publish a revised edition of the *Imaginary Conversations.*
1839	*Andrea of Hungary, and Giovanna of Naples.*
1840	Meets Alfred Tennyson and begins to see much of Charles Dickens early in the year; *Fra Rupert.*
1842	Contributes to *Foreign Quarterly Review* and *Blackwood's Edinburgh Magazine*; Dickens and Longfellow at Bath in October.
1843	Death of Southey on March 21.
1844	Assigns copyright of all the Conversations, published or unpublished, to Forster on January 24; celebrates his birthday with Dickens (and presumably Forster) at Bath; signs a revised copyright on July 26 that gives Forster permission to publish all of Landor's writings in the new edition.
1845	Verses to Browning appear in the *Morning Chronicle* (November 22).

1846 *The Works of Walter Savage Landor* in two volumes published by Edward Moxon in June; Landor aged 71.

1847 *Poemata et Inscriptiones*, a collection of Latin writings in prose and verse, published by Moxon in July; *The Hellenics of Walter Savage Landor*.

1848 *The Italics of Walter Savage Landor; Imaginary Conversation of King Carlo-Alberto and The Duchess Belgioioso.*

1849 Death of Lady Blessington on June 4.

1851 *Five Scenes* of Beatrice Cenci appear in *Fraser's Magazine* (January); *Popery: British and Foreign*; death of Ianthe on July 31; *Tyrannicide* published in December.

1853 *Imaginary Conversations of Greeks and Romans; The Last Fruit Off an Old Tree*; Landor aged 78.

1854 *Letters of an American, mainly on Russia and Revolution.*

1855 Death of Julius Hare on January 23; begins sending political letters and poems to the *Atlas* in March.

1856 *Antony and Octavius. Scenes for the Study*; death of his dog Pomero in February; "Alfieri and Metastasio" and "Menander and Epicurus" appear in *Fraser's Magazine* (April); becomes socially intimate with Geraldine Hooper and the Yescombes during the summer; *Letter from W. S. Landor to R. W. Emerson* appears in the fall.

1857 *Walter Savage Landor and the Honorable Mrs. Yescombe* published in early June following a domestic quarrel; *Mr. Landor Threatened* appears in late June in response to a visit from the Yescombes' lawyer; Forster intervenes on July 27 and averts a libel suit by having Landor sign a retractation; on August 4, the Yescombes begin to receive insulting letters and poems in Landor's handwriting.

1858 *Dry Sticks, Fagoted by Walter Savage Landor*; Yescombes issue writ for libel in June; unwisely counseled to flee the country by his lawyer, Landor arrives at Forster's London chambers on July 12; at Boulogne, France, on July 16; convicted of libel at Bristol Assizes on August 23; arrives at his villa at Fiesole on August 27; Landor aged 83.

1859	*Mr. Landor's Remarks on a Suit Preferred Against Him* issued in May; leaves his villa and is sheltered by Browning in July; moves to 2671 Via Nunziatina, Florence, in November; a new edition of *Hellenics* published and Landor ceases communication with Forster in December.
1861	Death of Mrs. Browning on June 29; Browning and Kate Field leave Italy in August.
1863	*Heroic Idyls, with Additional Poems*, published in the fall; resumes correspondence with Forster in December.
1864	Algernon Charles Swinburne visits Landor in March; last letter to Forster on September 9; death at Florence on September 17, aged 89; buried near Mrs. Browning in the Protestant Cemetery at Florence on September 19.

SELECTED BIBLIOGRAPHY

BECKER, GEORGE J. "The Political Idealism of Walter Savage Landor." Unpublished Ph.D. dissertation, University of Washington, 1937.
COLVIN, SIDNEY. *Landor.* ("English Men of Letters.") London, 1881.
DESELINCOURT, ERNEST. "Landor's Prose," *Wordsworthian and Other Studies.* Oxford: Clarendon Press, 1947.
ELWIN, MALCOLM. *Landor: A Replevin.* London: Macdonald, 1958.
———. *Savage Landor.* New York: Macmillan, 1941.
FLASDIECK, HERMANN M. "Walter Savage Landor und seine 'Imaginary Conversations,'" *Englische Studien,* LVIII (1924), 390–431.
FORSTER, JOHN. *Walter Savage Landor. A Biography.* 2 vols. London, 1869.
———. *The Works and Life of Walter Savage Landor.* 8 vols. London, 1876.
HAMILTON, G. ROSTREVOR. *Walter Savage Landor.* ("Writers and Their Work," No. 126.) London: Published for the British Council and the National Book League by Longmans, Green and Co., 1960.
LANDOR, WALTER SAVAGE. *Charles James Fox: A Commentary on His Life and Character,* ed. Stephen Wheeler. London: John Murray, 1907.
———. *The Complete Works of Walter Savage Landor,* ed. T. Earle Welby (Prose, Vols. I–XII) and Stephen Wheeler (Poems, Vols. XIII–XVI). 16 vols. London: Chapman and Hall, 1927–1936.
———. *Imaginary Conversations of Literary Men and Statesmen.* 2 vols. London, 1824.
———. *Imaginary Conversations of Literary Men and Statesmen.* 2 vols. 2d ed. rev. London, 1826.
———. *Imaginary Conversations of Literary Men and Statesmen.* London, 1828.
———. *Imaginary Conversations of Literary Men and Statesmen.* 2 vols. ("Second Series.") London, 1829.
———. *The Last Fruit Off an Old Tree.* London, 1853.
———. *Letters and Other Unpublished Writings of Walter Savage Landor,* ed. Stephen Wheeler. London, 1897.
———. *Letters of Walter Savage Landor, Private and Public,* ed. Stephen Wheeler. London, 1899.
———. *Poems by Walter Savage Landor,* ed. Geoffrey Grigson. London: Centaur Press, 1964.

LANDOR, WALTER SAVAGE. *The Poetical Works of Walter Savage Landor*, ed. Stephen Wheeler. 3 vols. Oxford: Clarendon Press, 1937.

———. *Selected Works of Walter Savage Landor*, ed. C. G. Crump. 10 vols. London, 1891–1893.

———. *Selections from the Writings of Walter Savage Landor*, ed. Sidney Colvin. ("The Golden Treasury Series.") London, 1882.

———. *The Works of Walter Savage Landor*, 2 vols. London, 1846.

MERCIER, VIVIAN. "The Future of Landor Criticism," *Some British Romantics: A Collection of Essays*, ed. James V. Logan, John E. Jordan, and Northrop Frye. Columbus: Ohio State University Press, 1966.

NICOLL, W. ROBERTSON, AND WISE, THOMAS JAMES. *Literary Anecdotes of the Nineteenth Century*. 2 vols. London, 1895–1896.

PETERSON, DORIS E. "Landor's Treatment of His Source Materials in the 'Imaginary Conversations Greek and Roman.'" Unpublished Ph.D. dissertation, University of Minnesota, 1942.

PRASHER, ALICE LAVONNE. "Walter Savage Landor's *Imaginary Conversations*: A Critical Edition of the First Eight Conversations in Volume One. [with] *Imaginary Conversations of Literary Men and Statesmen*. By Walter Savage Landor, Esq. The First Volume. 1824." Unpublished Ph.D. dissertation, Northwestern University, 1966.

PROUDFIT, CHARLES L. "Landor's Hobbyhorse: A Study in Romantic Orthography," *Studies in Romanticism*, VII (Summer 1968), 207–217.

———. "An Unrecorded Cancellans in the First Edition of Walter Savage Landor's *Imaginary Conversations of Literary Men and Statesmen*," *Notes and Queries*, CCXIII (September 1968), 345–346.

SUPER, R. H. "The Fire of Life," *Cambridge Review*, LXXXVI (January 16, 1965), 170–175.

———. *The Publication of Landor's Works*. London: Bibliographical Society, 1954. Supplement to the Bibliographical Society's *Transactions*, No. 18.

———. "Walter Savage Landor," *The English Romantic Poets and Essayists: A Review of Research and Criticism*, ed. C. W. Houtchens and L. H. Houtchens. 2d ed. rev. New York: Modern Language Association of America, 1966.

———. *Walter Savage Landor: A Biography*. New York: New York University Press, 1954.

VITOUX, PIERRE. *L'Œuvre de Walter Savage Landor*. Paris: Presses Universitaires de France, 1964.

WILLIAMS, STANLEY T. "Walter Savage Landor as a Critic of Literature," *PMLA*, XXXVIII (December 1923), 906–928.
WISE, THOMAS JAMES. *A Landor Library*. London: Printed for private circulation, 1928.
WISE, THOMAS JAMES, AND STEPHEN WHEELER. *A Bibliography of the Writings in Prose and Verse of Walter Savage Landor*. London: Bibliographical Society, 1919.

BOCCACCIO AND PETRARCA

Landor's knowledge and direct use of the writings of Giovanni Boccaccio (1313–1375) and Francesco Petrarch (1304–1374) create, in this Conversation, a believable, though imaginary, encounter which serves as a frame for the tale Boccaccio tells. Landor imbues his novella, the love story of Monna Tita Monalda and Amadeo degli Oricellari, with the tone, manner, and subject matter of Boccaccio. Several of the character types who people Boccaccio's stories appear here: a priest who meddles in the affairs of love, a young and virile monk who mediates a love affair, and a servant girl who finds herself in bed with the "distraught" lover of her mistress. Landor's lighthearted treatment of the affair and his unorthodox resolution of the lovers' problem—the surprising marriage between the lover, Amadeo, who seduced the mistress's maid, and the mistress, Monna Tita, who had planned to enter the convent—reflect the racy high spirits of Boccaccio's Decameron. *Petrarch's delightful interruptions of Boccaccio's tale, in which he expresses his moral gravity and deep understanding of human frailty, provide a sedate contrast to Boccaccio's roguishness.*

Landor admired both of the writers he engages in conversation here: Boccaccio, whom he calls "the most creative genius that the continent has produced since the *creation," and Petrarch, whom Landor considers "the defender of resuscitated Liberty, and the recoverer of ancient learning."*[1] *Landor's Florentine villa was near that of Boccaccio, and Landor delighted in the claim that it was on this estate that "Boccaccio led his women to bathe when they had left the first scene of their story-telling."*[2]

The devotion to historical accuracy in this Conversation indicates a thorough acquaintance with the works of the two Italian writers, for our knowledge of Petrarch's and Boccaccio's lives is derived almost entirely from their correspondence and their literary labors. Landor has the two poets meet at a time when the records indicate that a meeting did take place. According to Petrarch's correspondence, the poet made a pilgrimage to Rome in the fall of 1350, a year of jubilee. It was during this journey that he did actually meet Boccaccio outside of Florence for the first time.

Boccaccio. Remaining among us, I doubt not that you would soon receive the same distinctions in your native country as others have

---

[1] Landor to Miss Mary Boyle, September 12, 1842, quoted by James Russell Lowell in "Some Letters of Walter Savage Landor," *Century Magazine*, XXXV (February 1888), 520.

[2] John Forster, *Walter Savage Landor. A Biography* (2 vols.; London, 1869), II, 220. Hereafter referred to as Forster.

conferred upon you: indeed in confidence I may promise it. For greatly are the Florentines ashamed, that the most elegant of their writers and the most independent of their citizens lives in exile, by the injustice he had suffered in the detriment done to his property, through the intemperate administration of their laws.[3]

Petrarca. Let them recall me soon and honourably: then perhaps I may assist them to remove their ignominy, which I carry about with me wherever I go, and which is pointed out by my exotic laurel.[4]

Boccaccio. There is, and ever will be, in all countries and under all governments, an ostracism for their greatest men.

Petrarca. At present we will talk no more about it. To-morrow I pursue my journey toward Padua, where I am expected; where some few value and esteem me, honest and learned and ingenious men; although neither those Transpadane regions, nor whatever extends beyond them, have yet produced an equal to Boccaccio.[5]

Boccaccio. Then, in the name of friendship! do not go thither: form such rather from your fellow citizens. I love my equals heartily; and shall love them the better when I see them raised up here, from our own mother earth, by you.

Petrarca. Let us continue our walk.

Boccaccio. If you have been delighted (and you say you have been), at seeing again, after so long an absence, the house and garden wherein I have placed the relaters of my stories, as reported in the *Decameron*,[6] come a little way further up the ascent, and we will pass through the vineyard on the west of the villa. You will see presently another on the right, lying in its warm little garden close to the roadside, the scene lately of some-

---

[3] In October 1302, Petrarch's father, Ser Petracco, was banished from Florence for political reasons, and all his property in the city was confiscated. The property remained in the hands of Florentine officials for twenty-five years after Ser Petracco's death in 1326, thus forcing Petrarch and his brother Gherardo into economic exile, though both were free to return to Florence.

[4] On April 8, 1341, Petrarch was made poet laureate of Rome. One of the two governing Roman senators crowned Petrarch with laurel in the audience hall of the Senatorial Palace on the Capitoline.

[5] Among Petrarch's many Paduan friends were Francesco da Carrara, lord of Padua, Pietro Pileo, bishop of Padua, Giovanni Dondi, an eminent physician, and Bonaventura and Bonsembiante Badoer, both brothers and learned Augustinian monks. It was at Padua, probably near the end of March, 1351, that Petrarch received a letter of amnesty from the Florentines, personally delivered by Boccaccio.

[6] Petrarch did not read Boccaccio's *Decameron* until late in life, probably early in 1373; therefore, Boccaccio's comment upon Petrarch's delight in visiting once more (in 1350) "the house and garden wherein I have placed the relaters of my stories, as reported in the *Decameron*," is historically inaccurate, though dramatically appropriate.

what that would have looked well, as illustration, in the midst of your Latin reflections.[7] It shows us that people the most serious and determined may act at last contrariwise to the line of conduct they have laid down.

Petrarca. Relate it to me, Messer Giovanni; for you are able to give reality the merits and charms of fiction, just as easily as you give fiction the semblance, the stature, and the movement of reality.

Boccaccio. I must here forego such powers, if in good truth I possess them.

Petrarca. This long green alley, defended by box and cypresses, is very pleasant. The smell of box, although not sweet, is more agreeable to me than many that are; I can not say from what resuscitation of early and tender feeling. The cypress too seems to strengthen the nerves of the brain. Indeed, I delight in the odour of most trees and plants.[8]

Will not that dog hurt us? he comes closer.

Boccaccio. Dog! thou hast the colours of a magpie and the tongue of one: prythee be quiet: art thou not ashamed?

Petrarca. Verily he trots off, comforting his angry belly with his plenteous tail, flattened and bestrewn under it. He looks back, going on, and puffs out his upper lip without a bark.

Boccaccio. These creatures are more accessible to temperate and just rebuke than the creatures of our species, usually angry with less reason, and from no sense, as dogs are, of duty.[9] Look into that white arcade!

---

[7] Petrarch *De Remediis Utriusque Fortunae.*

[8] Landor's fondness for such shrubs and trees as the box and the cypress is expressed in the Imaginary Conversation "Marchese Pallavicini and Walter Landor," *The Works of Walter Savage Landor* (2 vols.; London, 1846), I, 39-42.

[9] Both Petrarch and Landor enjoyed the companionship of dogs. In these lines from an *epistola metrica*, translated by Ernest Hatch Wilkins, Petrarch honors one of his many canine friends:

> Light is my evening meal, seasoned with hunger
> And with the toil and fasting of the day.
> Companions have I none, save only three:
> My faithful dog, my servants, and myself...

Ernest Hatch Wilkins, *Life of Petrarch* (Chicago: University of Chicago Press, 1961), p. 20.

Similarly, Landor turns to Latin verse in order to praise Pomero, a deceased companion:

> Oh urn! never may you be a torn-up garden:
> The heart within is faithful, for it is the heart of a dog.
> Farewell, little heart! and eternal farewell to Pomero.
> But, if it is given to you, remember me.
>   Tr. Constance Wright, in Forster, II, 490.

Surely it was white the other day: and now I perceive it is still so: the setting sun tinges it with yellow.

Petrarca. The house has nothing of either the rustic or the magnificent about it; nothing quite regular, nothing much varied. If there is anything at all affecting, as I fear there is, in the story you are about to tell me, I could wish the edifice itself bore externally some little of the interesting, that I might hereafter turn my mind toward it, looking out of the catastrophe, though not away from it. But I do not even find the peculiar and uncostly decoration of our Tuscan villas: the central turret,[10] round which the kite perpetually circles, in search of pigeons or smaller prey, borne onward, like the Flemish skaiter, by effortless will in motionless progression. The view of Fiesole must be lovely from that window; but I fancy to myself it loses the cascade under the single high arch of the Mugnone.[11]

Boccaccio. I think so. In this villa . . come rather further off: the inhabitants of it may hear us, if they should happen to be in the arbour, as most people are at the present hour of day . . in this villa, Messer Francesco, lives Monna Tita Monalda, who tenderly loved Amadeo degli Oricellari. She however was reserved and coy; and father Pietro de' Pucci, an enemy to the family of Amadeo, told her never more to think of him; for that just before he knew her, he had thrown his arm round the neck of Nunciata Righi, his mother's maid, calling her most immodestly a sweet creature, and of a whiteness that marble would split with envy at.

Monna Tita trembled and turned pale, "Father, is the girl really so very fair?" said she anxiously.

"Madonna," replied the father, "after confession she is not much amiss: white she is, with a certain tint of pink, not belonging to her, but coming over her, as through the wing of an angel pleased at the holy function: and her breath is such, the very ear smells it: poor innocent sinful soul! Hei! The wretch, Amadeo, would have endangered her salvation."

"She must be a wicked girl to let him," said Monna Tita. "A young man of good parentage and education would not dare to do such a thing,

---

[10] Landor's Fiesolan villa, formerly belonging to the Count Gherardesca, was decorated with a central turret. In a letter to his sisters in England, written early in 1831, Landor mentioned the turret in a general description of the house: "In the centre of the house is a high turret, a dovecote. The house is 60 ft. high on the terrace-side, and 50 on the other; the turret is 18 ft. above the 60" (Forster, II, 231).

[11] The Mugnone, a tributary of the Arno, flows near Boccaccio's villa. It figures in two tales of the *Decameron*: The Third Story of The Eighth Day and The Fifth Story of The Ninth Day.

of his own accord. I will see him no more however. But it was before he knew me: and it may not be true. I can not think any young woman would let a young man do so, even in the last hour before Lent. Now in what month was it supposed to be?"

"Supposed to be!" cried the father indignantly: "in June; I say in June."

"O! that now is quite impossible: for on the second of July, forty-one days from this, and at this very hour of it, he swore to me eternal love and constancy. I will inquire of him whether it is true: I will charge him with it."

She did. Amadeo confessed his fault, and, thinking it a venial one, would have taken and kissed her hand as he asked forgiveness.

Petrarca. Children! children! I will go into the house, and if their relatives, as I suppose, have approved of the marriage, I will endeavour to persuade the young lady that a fault like this, on the repentance of her lover, is not unpardonable. But first, is Amadeo a young man of loose habits?

Boccaccio. Less than our others: in fact, I never heard of any deviation, excepting this.

Petrarca. Come then with me.

Boccaccio. Wait a little.

Petrarca. I hope the modest Tita, after a trial, will not be too severe with him.

Boccaccio. Severity is far from her nature; but, such is her purity and innocence, she shed many and bitter tears at his confession, and declared her unalterable determination of taking the veil among the nuns of Fiesole. Amadeo fell at her feet, and wept upon them. She pushed him from her gently, and told him she would still love him, if he would follow her example, leave the world, and become a friar of San Marco. Amadeo was speechless; and, if he had not been so, he never would have made a promise he intended to violate. She retired from him: after a time he arose, less wounded than benumbed by the sharp uncovered stones in the garden walk: and, as a man who fears to fall from a precipice goes farther from it than is necessary, so did Amadeo shun the quarter where the gate is, and, oppressed by his agony and despair, throw his arms across the sun-dial and rest his brow upon it, hot as it must have been on a cloudless day in August. When the evening was about to close, he was aroused by the cries of rooks over-head: they flew toward Florence, and beyond: he too went back into the city.

Tita fell sick from her inquietude. Every morning ere sunrise did Amadeo return, but could hear only from the labourers in the field that Monna Tita was ill, because she had promised to take the veil and had not taken it, knowing, as she must do, that the heavenly bridegroom is a bridegroom never to be trifled with, let the spouse be young and beautiful as she may be. Amadeo had often conversed with the peasant of the farm, who much pitied so worthy and loving a gentleman, and finding him one evening fixing some thick and high stakes in the ground, offered to help him. After due thanks, "It is time," said the peasant, "to rebuild the hovel and watch the grapes."

He went into the stable, collected the old pillars of his autumnal observatory, drove them into the ground, and threw the matting over them.

"This is my house," cried he. "Could I never, in my stupidity, think about rebuilding it before? Bring me another mat or two: I will sleep here to-night, to-morrow night, every night, all autumn, all winter."

He slept there, and was consoled at last by hearing that Monna Tita was out of danger, and recovering from her illness by spiritual means. His heart grew lighter day after day. Every evening did he observe the rooks, in the same order, pass along the same track in the heavens, just over San Marco: and it now occurred to him, after three weeks indeed, that Monna Tita had perhaps some strange idea, in choosing his monastery, not unconnected with the passage of these birds. He grew calmer upon it, until he asked himself whether he might hope. In the midst of this half-meditation, half-dream, his whole frame was shaken by the voices, however low and gentle, of two monks, coming from the villa and approaching him. He would have concealed himself under this bank whereon we are standing; but they saw him and called him by name. He now perceived that the younger of them was Guiberto Oddi, with whom he had been at school about six or seven years ago, and who admired him for his courage and frankness when he was almost a child.

"Do not let us mortify poor Amadeo," said Guiberto to his companion. "Return to the road: I will speak a few words to him, and engage him (I trust) to comply with reason and yield to necessity." The elder monk, who saw he should have to climb the hill again, assented to the proposal, and went into the road. After the first embraces and few words, "Amadeo! Amadeo!" said Guiberto, "it was love that made me a friar; let anything else make you one."

"Kind heart!" replied Amadeo. "If death or religion, or hatred of me, deprives me of Tita Monalda, I will die, where she commanded me, in the cowl. It is you who prepare her then to throw away her life and mine!"

"Hold! Amadeo!" said Guiberto, "I officiate together with good father Fontesecco, who invariably falls asleep amid our holy function."

Now, Messer Francesco, I must inform you that father Fontesecco has the heart of a flower. It feels nothing, it wants nothing; it is pure and simple, and full of its own little light. Innocent as a child, as an angel, nothing ever troubled him, but how to devise what he should confess. A confession costs him more trouble to invent than any Giornata in my *Decameron* cost me. He was once overheard to say on this occasion, "God forgive me in his infinite mercy, for making it appear that I am a little worse than he has chosen I should be!" He is temperate; for he never drinks more than exactly half the wine and water set before him. In fact, he drinks the wine and leaves the water, saying, "We have the same water up at San Domenico: we send it hither: it would be uncivil to take back our own gift, and still more to leave a suspicion that we thought other people's wine poor beverage." Being afflicted by the gravel,[12] the physician of his convent advised him, as he never was fond of wine, to leave it off entirely: on which he said, "I know few things; but this I know well: in water there is often gravel, in wine never. It hath pleased God to afflict me, and even to go a little out of his way in order to do it, for the greater warning to other sinners. I will drink wine, brother Anselmini, and help his work."

I have led you away from the younger monk.

"While father Fontesecco is in the first stage of beatitude, chanting through his nose the benedicite, I will attempt," said Guiberto, "to comfort Monna Tita."

"Good blessed Guiberto!" exclaimed Amadeo in a transport of gratitude, at which Guiberto smiled with his usual grace and suavity. "O Guiberto! Guiberto! my heart is breaking. Why should she want you to comfort her .. but .. comfort her then!" and he covered his face within his hands.

"Remember," said Guiberto placidly, "her uncle is bedridden: her aunt never leaves him: the servants are old and sullen, and will stir for nobody. Finding her resolved, as they believe, to become a nun, they are little assiduous in their services. Humour her, if none else does, Amadeo;

[12] Kidney stones.

let her fancy that you intend to be a friar; and, for the present, walk not on these grounds."

"Are you true, or are you traitorous?" cried Amadeo, grasping his friend's hand most fiercely.

"Follow your own counsel, if you think mine insincere," said the young friar, not withdrawing his hand, but placing the other on Amadeo's. "Let me however advise you to conceal yourself; and I will direct Silvestrina to bring you such accounts of her mistress as may at least make you easy in regard to her health. Adieu."

Amadeo was now rather tranquil; more than he had ever been, not only since the displeasure of Monna Tita, but since the first sight of her. Profuse at all times in his gratitude to Silvestrina, whenever she brought him good news, news better than usual, he pressed her to his bosom. Silvestrina Pioppi is about fifteen; slender, fresh, intelligent, lively, good-humoured, sensitive; and anyone but Amadeo might call her very pretty.

Petrarca. Ah Giovanni! here I find your heart obtaining the mastery over your vivid and volatile imagination. Well have you said, the maiden being really pretty, anyone but Amadeo might think her so. On the banks of the Sorga there are beautiful maids: the woods and the rocks have a thousand times repeated it: I heard but one echo: I heard but one name: I would have fled from them for ever at another.[13]

Boccaccio. Francesco, do not beat your breast just now: wait a little. Monna Tita would take the veil. The fatal certainty was announced to Amadeo by his true Guiberto, who had earnestly and repeatedly prayed her to consider the thing a few months longer.

"I will see her first! By all the saints of heaven I will see her!" cried the desperate Amadeo, and ran into the house, toward the still apartment of his beloved. Fortunately Guiberto was neither less active nor less strong than he, and overtaking him at the moment, drew him into the room opposite. "If you will be quiet and reasonable, there is yet a possibility left you," said Guiberto in his ear, although perhaps he did not think it. "But if you utter a voice or are seen by anyone, you ruin the fame of her you love, and obstruct your own prospects for ever. It being known that you have not slept in Florence these several nights, it will be suspected by the malicious that you have slept in the villa with the connivance of Monna Tita. Compose yourself: answer nothing: rest where you are: do not add a worse imprudence to a very bad one: I promise you my assistance, my

---

[13] The river is the Sorgue in Southern France, the place is Vaucluse, and the person is Petrarch's Laura. Landor gives the Italian spelling of the French river.

speedy return and best counsel: you shall be released at daybreak." He ordered Silvestrina to supply the unfortunate youth with the cordials usually administered to the uncle, or with the rich old wine they were made of; and she performed the order with such promptitude and attention, that he was soon in some sort refreshed.

Petrarca. I pity him from my soul, poor young man! Alas, we are none of us, by original sin, free from infirmities or from vices.

Boccaccio. If we could find a man exempt by nature from vices and infirmities, we should find one not worth knowing: he would also be void of tenderness and compassion. What allowances then could his best friends expect from him in their frailties? What help, consolation, and assistance, in their misfortunes? We are in the midst of a workshop well stored with sharp instruments: we may do ill with many, unless we take heed; and good with all, if we will but learn how to employ them.

Petrarca. There is somewhat of reason in this. You strengthen me to proceed with you: I can bear the rest.

Boccaccio. Guiberto had taken leave of his friend, and had advanced a quarter of a mile, which (as you perceive) is nearly the whole way, on his return to the monastery, when he was overtaken by some peasants, who were hastening homeward from Florence. The information he collected from them made him determine to retrace his steps. He entered the room again, and, from the intelligence he had just acquired, gave Amadeo the assurance that Monna Tita must delay her entrance into the convent; for that the abbess had that moment gone down the hill on her way toward Siena, to venerate some holy relics, carrying with her three candles, each five feet long, to burn before them; which candles contained many particles of the myrrh presented at the nativity of our Saviour by the wise men of the East. Amadeo breathed freely, and was persuaded by Guiberto to take another cup of old wine, and to eat with him some cold roast kid, which had been offered him for *merenda*.[14] After the agitation of his mind a heavy sleep fell upon the lover, coming almost before Guiberto departed; so heavy indeed that Silvestrina was alarmed. It was her apartment; and she performed the honours of it as well as any lady in Florence could have done.

Petrarca. I easily believe it: the poor are more attentive than the rich, and the young are more compassionate than the old.

Boccaccio. Oh Francesco! what inconsistent creatures are we!

[14] *Merenda* is luncheon, *meridiana*, eaten by the wealthier at the hour when the peasants dine. [*Landor's note*.]

Petrarca. True, indeed! I now foresee the end. He might have done worse.

Boccaccio. I think so.

Petrarca. He almost deserved it.

Boccaccio. I think that too.

Petrarca. Wretched mortals! our passions for ever lead us into this, or worse.

Boccaccio. Ay, truly; much worse generally.

Petrarca. The very twig on which the flowers grew lately, scourges us to the bone in its maturity.

Boccaccio. Incredible will it be to you, and, by my faith! to me it was hardly credible. Certain however is it, that Guiberto on his return by sunrise found Amadeo in the arms of sleep.

Petrarca. Not at all, not at all incredible: the truest lover would have done the same, exhausted by suffering.

Boccaccio. He was truly in the arms of sleep; but, Francesco, there was another pair of arms about him, worth twenty such, divinity as he is. A loud burst of laughter from Guiberto did not arouse either of the parties: but Monna Tita heard it, and rushed into the room, tearing her hair, and invoking the saints of heaven against the perfidy of man. She seized Silvestrina by that arm which appeared the most offending: the girl opened her eyes, turned on her face, rolled out of bed, and threw herself at the feet of her mistress, shedding tears, and wiping them away with the only piece of linen about her. Monna Tita too shed tears. Amadeo still slept profoundly; a flush, almost of crimson, overspreading his cheeks. Monna Tita led away, after some pause, poor Silvestrina, and made her confess the whole. She then wept more and more, and made the girl confess it again, and explain her confession. "I cannot believe such wickedness," she cried: "he could not be so hardened. O sinful Silvestrina! how will you ever tell Father Doni one half! one quarter! He never can absolve you."

Petrarca. Giovanni! I am glad I did not enter the house; you were prudent in restraining me. I have no pity for the youth at all: never did one so deserve to lose a mistress.

Boccaccio. Say, rather, to gain a wife.

Petrarca. Absurdity! impossibility!

Boccaccio. He won her fairly; strangely, and on a strange table, as he played his game. Listen! that guitar is Monna Tita's. Listen! what a fine voice (do not you think it?) is Amadeo's.

Amadeo (*Singing*).

    Oh! I have err'd!
  I laid my hand upon the nest
  (Tita, I sigh to sing the rest)
    Of the wrong bird.

Petrarca. She laughs too at it! Ah! Monna Tita was made by nature to live on this side of Fiesole.

LUCULLUS AND CÆSAR

Lucullus [*Lucius Licinius Lucullus*, ca. *117–56* B.C.], *from his youth up, was devoted to the genial and so-called "liberal" culture then in vogue, wherein the Beautiful was sought. And when he came to be well on in years, he suffered his mind to find complete leisure and repose, as it were after many struggles, in philosophy, encouraging the contemplative side of his nature, and giving timely halt and check, after his difference with Pompey, to the play of his ambition.*[1]

Landor chooses to represent this attractive side of Lucullus' character, as described in Plutarch's life of Lucullus, in this Conversation, omitting such unpleasant traits as affectation, lavishness, gluttony, ambition, and pride, which are also recorded by Plutarch. This simplification of character according to Landor's artistic and personal likes and desires is also seen in his portrayal of Caesar (ca. *102–44* B.C.). Although endowing Caesar with the necessary ambition and pride (the real motives for his visit to Lucullus), Landor carefully excludes Caesar's despotic and promiscuous ways which are clearly described in both Plutarch's and Suetonius' accounts of Caesar's life. Landor's Romans are creatures of his own desire, and in no way are they meant to be accurate, historical representations. Indeed, the author often endows his historical characters with his own preferences. Thus Lucullus is portrayed as preferring to dine quietly and unhurriedly in the company of two at the most, viewing with disdain the words and writings of most philosophers, and having an appetite for strawberries and milk.

Historically, Caesar's visit to Lucullus' Apennine villa during the summer of *58* B.C. could not have occurred, since the mutual suspicion and jealousy between Caesar and Pompey (Caesar's apparent motive for visiting Lucullus) had not developed at so early a date. Even if possible, such a meeting would have been highly improbable because of the political and temperamental differences between Lucullus and Caesar. Landor attempts to compensate for this by having Caesar say: "Betrayed and abandoned by those we had confided in, our next friendship, if ever our hearts receive any, or if any will venture in those places of desolation, flies forward instinctively to what is most contrary and dissimilar. Caesar is hence the visitant of Lucullus." As historical background Landor attempts to recreate the period immediately preceding the Roman Civil War between Caesar and his legions and Pompey and the forces of the Senate. Landor's interest in creating an air of historical exactness is that of the dramatic artist rather than the scholarly historian, for he makes little attempt to present an accurate chronology.

[1] Plutarch *Lucullus* 1. 4–5, in *Plutarch's Lives*, tr. Bernadotte Perrin ("The Loeb Classical Library"; Cambridge: Harvard University Press; London: W. Heinemann, 1959), Vol. II. Hereafter referred to as Plutarch *Lucullus*.

18   LUCULLUS AND CÆSAR

In this Conversation, the ennobling and idealizing process which the historical Lucullus and Caesar undergo helps to create an almost idyllic scene in which two Landorian characters discuss topics dear to the author's heart. The meeting of two men of such diverse temperaments has dramatic potential which Landor chooses not to exploit. Although Lucullus is aware that ambition motivates Caesar's visit to him, he greets Caesar's long initial speech about the unhappy state of political affairs with sincere concern for his guest's personal welfare, thereby preventing the development of conflict between the ambitious Caesar and the retired and scholarly Lucullus.

Cæsar. Lucius Lucullus, I come to you privately and unattended, for reasons which you will know; confiding, I dare not say in your friendship, since no service of mine toward you has deserved it, but in your generous and disinterested love of peace. Hear me on. Cneius Pompeius,[2] according to the report of my connexions in the city, had, on the instant of my leaving it for the province,[3] begun to solicit his dependants to strip me ignominiously of authority. Neither vows nor affinities can bind him.[4] He would degrade the father of his wife; he would humiliate his own children, the unoffending, the unborn; he would poison his own ardent love, at the suggestion of Ambition. Matters are now brought so far, that either he or I must submit to a reverse of fortune; since no concession can assuage his malice, divert his envy, or gratify his cupidity. No sooner could I raise myself up, from the consternation and stupefaction into which the certainty of these reports had thrown me, than I began to consider in what manner my own private afflictions might become the least noxious to the republic. Into whose arms then could I throw myself

[2] Gnaeus Pompeius (106–48 B.C.), called Magnus after 81 B.C., was an able politician and brilliant general who achieved his greatest military glory during the Third Mithridatic War. See n. 18 below.

[3] On March 1, 59 B.C., Caesar, one of the two Roman consuls for that year, had himself elected to the proconsulship of the province of Cisalpine Gaul and Illyricum, with a garrison of three legions under his command, for a term of five years. He left Rome for Gaul in 58 B.C. with an additional legion, and with Transalpine Gaul added to his proconsulship.

[4] In order to assure his election to the consulate for the year 59 B.C., Caesar formed a secret coalition (the First Triumvirate) with Pompey and Crassus in 60 B.C. At the close of Caesar's consulship, the three vowed to continue their coalition, which Caesar, before leaving for Gaul, attempted to strengthen by giving his daughter Julia in marriage to Pompey (59 B.C.) while himself marrying the daughter of Piso, one of the consuls-elect.

more naturally and more securely, to whose bosom could I commit and consign more sacredly the hopes and destinies of our beloved country, than his who laid down power in the midst of its enjoyments, in the vigour of youth, in the pride of triumph: when Dignity solicited, when Friendship urged, entreated, supplicated, and when Liberty herself invited and beckoned to him, from the senatorial order and from the curule chair?[5] Betrayed and abandoned by those we had confided in, our next friendship, if ever our hearts receive any, or if any will venture in those places of desolation, flies forward instinctively to what is most contrary and dissimilar. Cæsar is hence the visitant of Lucullus.

Lucullus. I had always thought Pompeius more moderate and more reserved than you represent him, Caius Julius! and yet I am considered in general, and surely you also will consider me, but little liable to be prepossessed by him.

Cæsar. Unless he may have ingratiated himself with you recently, by the administration of that worthy whom last winter his partisans dragged before the senate, and forced to assert publicly that you and Cato had instigated a party to circumvent and murder him; and whose carcase, a few days afterward, when it had been announced that he had died by a natural death, was found covered with bruises, stabs, and dislocations.[6]

---

[5] Lucullus was about fifty-one when his command of the war with Mithridates VI was wrested from him by Pompey (*Lex Manilia*, 66 B.C.) and about fifty-four when he celebrated a belated triumph in Rome (63 B.C.) under the shadow of his humiliation. By implying that Lucullus voluntarily withdrew from public life, Landor is in part following Plutarch, who states: "The Senate had conceived wondrous hopes that in him it would find an opposer of the tyranny of Pompey and a champion of the aristocracy, with all the advantage of great glory and influence; but he quitted and abandoned public affairs, either because he saw that they were already beyond proper control and diseased, or, as some say, because he had his fill of glory, and felt that the unfortunate issue of his many struggles and toils entitled him to fall back upon a life of ease and luxury" (*Lucullus* 38. 2). Yet both Plutarch (*Lucullus* 42. 4–43. 1) and Suetonius (*Julius* 20. 4) mention incidents which show Lucullus playing politics before he was forced into "voluntary" retirement. Landor here selects those historical details which contribute to the creation of a Lucullus who contrasts dramatically with the ambitious Caesar.

[6] This is a reference to the "Vettius affair" (59 B.C.). According to Plutarch: "As these proceedings [Pompey's use of armed force to overcome the opposition of the partisans of Cato and Lucullus to Pompey's political ambitions] were resented by the nobles, the partisans of Pompey produced a certain Vettius, whom, as they declared, they had caught plotting against the life of Pompey. So the man was examined in the Senate, where he accused sundry other persons, but before the people he named Lucullus as the man who had engaged him to kill Pompey. However, no one believed his story, nay, it was at once clear that the fellow had been put forward by the partisans of Pompey to make false and malicious charges, and the fraud was made all the plainer

Lucullus. You bring much to my memory which had quite slipped out of it, and I wonder that it could make such an impression on yours. A proof to me that the interest you take in my behalf began earlier than your delicacy will permit you to acknowledge. You are fatigued, which I ought to have perceived before.

Cæsar. Not at all: the fresh air has given me life and alertness: I feel it upon my cheek even in the room.

Lucullus. After our dinner and sleep, we will spend the remainder of the day on the subject of your visit.

Cæsar. Those Ethiopian slaves of yours shiver with cold upon the mountain here; and truly I myself was not insensible to the change of climate, in the way from Mutina.[7]

What white bread! I never found such even at Naples or Capua.[8] This Formian wine (which I prefer to the Chian) how exquisite![9]

Lucullus. Such is the urbanity of Cæsar, even while he bites his lip with displeasure. How! surely it bleeds! Permit me to examine the cup.

Cæsar. I believe a jewel has fallen out of the rim in the carriage: the gold is rough there.[10]

Lucullus. Marcipor![11] let me never see that cup again. No answer, I

---

when, a few days afterwards, his dead body was cast out of the prison. It was said, indeed, that he had died a natural death, but he bore the marks of throttling and violence, and the opinion was that he had been taken off by the very men who had engaged his services" (*Lucullus* 42. 7–8). Although Landor follows Plutarch in making Pompey responsible for the "Vettius affair," Suetonius places the blame upon Caesar (*Julius* 20. 5). By following Plutarch's account, Landor enables Caesar to imply his freedom from involvement in the affair.

[7] Mutina (modern Modena) was a Roman town in Cisalpine Gaul which controlled important roads and passes. Mutina acquired fame for its successful resistance to Pompey in 78 B.C. and to Antony in 43 B.C. during the Civil Wars.

[8] At the time of this imaginary meeting, Naples, or Neapolis, was a flourishing city, a former Greek colony, visited by wealthy Romans and famous for its Greek culture, luxurious living, and soft climate. Capua, the ancient capital of Campania, Italy, rivaled Carthage and Rome as a wealthy trading center in 218 B.C., and became noted for its luxuriousness and pride. By saying that he never found such white bread at either Naples or Capua, Caesar lavishes the highest possible praise upon his host.

[9] Formian wine is produced at Formia, called Formiae in Roman times, a town of Campania, Italy. Located on the Bay of Gaeta, Formiae lay on the Via Appia and was a resort area for wealthy Romans. Chian wine is made on the Greek island of Chios, located near the west coast of Asia Minor. Chios was a "free and allied state" under the Romans, and its *vinum Arvisium* was popular throughout the Roman Empire.

[10] In his account of Lucullus' ostentatious daily repasts, Plutarch mentions Lucullus' "dyed coverlets, and beakers set with precious stones" (*Lucullus* 40. 1).

[11] Marcipor, Lucullus' servant, is an imaginary character.

desire. My guest pardons heavier faults. Mind that dinner be prepared for us shortly.

Cæsar. In the meantime, Lucullus, if your health permits it, shall we walk a few paces round the villa? for I have not seen anything of the kind before.[12]

Lucullus. The walls are double: the space between them two feet: the materials for the most-part earth and stubble. Two hundred slaves, and about as many mules and oxen, brought the beams and rafters up the mountain: my architects fixed them at once in their places: every part was ready, even the wooden nails. The roof is thatched, you see.

Cæsar. Is there no danger that so light a material should be carried off by the winds, on such an eminence?

Lucullus. None resists them equally well.

Cæsar. On this immensely high mountain I should be apprehensive of the lightning, which the poets, and I think the philosophers too, have told us, strikes the highest.

Lucullus. The poets are right; for whatever is received as truth, is truth in poetry; and a fable may illustrate like a fact. But the philosophers are wrong; as they generally are, even in the commonest things; because they seldom look beyond their own tenets, unless through captiousness; and because they argue more than they meditate, and display more than they examine.[13] Archimedes[14] and Euclid[15] are, in my opinion, the worthiest

---

[12] Landor has drawn upon Plutarch (*Lucullus* 34–42. 3) for the pictures of Lucullus' splendid villa and his elegant way of life. The architectural arrangements of the villa and the detail of the rooms are not found in Plutarch, and appear to be the creations of Landor's imagination. There is an important difference between Landor's picture and its source: whereas Plutarch gives the impression of an oriental extravagance and luxuriousness exceeding Roman "good taste" (*Lucullus* 39–41), Landor presents Lucullus as living quite simply and frugally in the midst of this luxury.

[13] Lucullus did not have such adverse feelings toward philosophers and their systems: "He was fond of all philosophy, and well-disposed and friendly towards every school, but from the first he cherished a particular and zealous love for the Academy, not the New Academy, so-called, although that school at the time had a vigorous representative of the doctrines of Carneades in Philo, but the Old Academy, which at that time was headed by a persuasive man and powerful speaker in the person of Antiochus of Ascalon" (Plutarch *Lucullus* 42. 2–3). The "Old Academy" refers to the Academy begun by Plato about 385 B.C. At first the Academy was noted for important work done in science and mathematics, but during the third and second centuries B.C. emphasis was placed upon "skeptical studies." In the first century Antiochus of Ascalon turned from this "skepticism" and re-emphasized science and mathematics.

[14] Archimedes (*ca.* 287–212 B.C.) was the greatest mathematician of classical times.

[15] Euclid of Alexandria, famed mathematician (*fl. ca.* 300 B.C.).

of the name; they alone having kept apart to the demonstrable, the practical, and the useful. Many of the rest are good writers and good disputants; but unfaithful suitors of simple Science; boasters of their acquaintance with gods and goddesses, plagiaries and impostors. I had forgotten my roof, although it is composed of much the same materials as the philosophers. Let the lightning fall: one handful of silver, or less, repairs the damage.

Cæsar. Impossible! nor indeed one thousand; nor twenty, if those tapestries[16] and pictures are consumed.

Lucullus. True; but only the thatch would burn. For before the baths were tessellated, I filled the area with alum and water, and soaked the timbers and laths for many months, and covered them afterward with alum in powder, by means of liquid glue.[17] Mithridates taught me this.[18] Having in vain attacked with combustibles a wooden tower, I took it by

---

[16] Cæsar would regard such things attentively. "In *expeditionibus* tessellata et sectilia pavimenta circumtulisse; signa, tabulas, operis antiqui, semper animosissime comparâsse," says Suetonius. [*Landor's note.*] "He moved tessellated and mosaic floors around with him on his expeditions; he collected statues and pictures by artists of old sparing no expense" (Suetonius *Julius* 46–47).

[17] Landor is indebted to Aulus Gellius for this early account of fireproofing: "'In that book [the nineteenth book of the *Annals* of Quintus Claudius Quadrigarius] then I [Antonius Julianus] found it recorded, that when Lucius Sulla [138–78 B.C., commander of the Roman forces in the First Mithridatic War] attacked the Piraeus in the land of Attica, and Archelaus, praefect of king Mithridates, was defending it against him, Sulla was unable to burn a wooden tower constructed for purposes of defence, although it had been surrounded with fire on every side, because Archelaus had smeared it with alum.'

"The words of Quadrigarius in that book are as follows: 'When Sulla had exerted himself for a long time, he led out his troops in order to set fire to a single wooden tower which Archelaus had interposed. He came, he drew near, he put wood under it, he beat off the Greeks, he applied fire; though they tried for a considerable time, they were never able to set it on fire, so thoroughly had Archelaus covered all the wood with alum. Sulla and his soldiers were amazed at this, and failing in his attempt, the general led back his troops'" (*The Attic Nights of Aulus Gellius* xv. 1. 6–7, tr. John C. Rolfe [rev. ed.; "The Loeb Classical Library"; Cambridge: Harvard University Press; London: W. Heinemann, 1961], Vol. III).

[18] Mithridates VI, Eupator Dionysus (*ca.* 132–63 B.C.), was king of Pontus (in northeastern Asia Minor) and Rome's most able Oriental foe. During the Third Mithridatic War (74–66 B.C.), Lucullus drove Mithridates from Pontus in 72 B.C., but a mutiny of the Roman army enabled Mithridates to reclaim much of his empire in 67 B.C. Pompey assumed Lucullus' command in 66 B.C. and in the same year defeated the weakened forces of Mithridates at Nicopolis in Pontus. Mithridates fled and committed suicide in 63 B.C. Landor has apparently confused Lucullus with Sulla. See n. 17 above.

stratagem, and found within it a mass of alum, which, if a great hurry had not been observed by us among the enemy in the attempt to conceal it, would have escaped our notice. I never scrupled to extort the truth from my prisoners: but my instruments were purple robes and plate, and the only wheel in my armoury, destined to such purposes, was the wheel of Fortune.[19]

Cæsar. I wish, in my campaigns, I could have equalled your clemency and humanity: but the Gauls are more uncertain, fierce, and perfidious, than the wildest tribes of Caucasus;[20] and our policy can not be carried with us; it must be formed upon the spot. They love you, not for abstaining from hurting them, but for ceasing; and they embrace you only at two seasons; when stripes are fresh or when stripes are imminent. Elsewhere I hope to become the rival of Lucullus in this admirable part of virtue.

I shall never build villas, because . . but what are your proportions? Surely the edifice is extremely low.

Lucullus. There is only one floor: the heighth of the apartments is twenty feet to the cornice, five above it; the breadth is twenty-five; the length forty. The building, as you perceive, is quadrangular: three sides contain four rooms each: the other has many partitions and two stories, for domestics and offices. Here is my salt-bath.[21]

Cæsar. A bath indeed for all the Nereids named by Hesiod,[22] with room enough for the Tritons and their herds and horses.

Lucullus. Next to it, where yonder boys are carrying the myrrhine vases, is a tepid one of fresh water, ready for your reception.

Cæsar. I resign the higher pleasure for the inferior, as we all are apt to do; and I will return to the enjoyment of your conversation when I have indulged a quarter of an hour in this refreshment.

Lucullus. Meanwhile I will take refuge with some less elegant philosopher, whose society I shall quit again with less regret. (*Cæsar returning*). It is useless, O Caius Julius, to inquire if there has been any negligence or any omission in the service of the bath: for these are secrets which you never impart to the most favoured of your friends.

Cæsar. I have often enjoyed the luxury much longer, but never more

---

[19] See Plutarch *Lucullus* 14. 2, 19, 20; 23. 1–3, 29. 2–8; 32. 3–5.
[20] These warlike peoples lived in the Caucasus, a well-wooded mountain barrier between the Caspian and the Black Seas. Not much was known about the wild tribes who followed Mithridates VI until Pompey subdued the Iberi in 65 B.C.
[21] For Lucullus' love of costly baths, see Plutarch *Lucullus* 39. 2.
[22] Hesiod *Theogony* 233 ff.

24   LUCULLUS AND CÆSAR

highly. Pardon my impatience to see the remainder of your Apennine villa.

Lucullus. Here stand my two cows. Their milk is brought to me with its warmth and froth; for it loses its salubrity both by repose and by motion. Pardon me, Cæsar: I shall appear to you to have forgotten that I am not conducting Marcus Varro.[23]

Cæsar. You would convert him into Cacus:[24] he would drive them off. What beautiful beasts! how sleek and white and cleanly! I never saw any like them, excepting when we sacrifice to Jupiter[25] the stately leader from the pastures of the Clitumnus.[26]

Lucullus. Often do I make a visit to these quiet creatures, and with no less pleasure than in former days to my horses. Nor indeed can I much wonder that whole nations have been consentaneous in treating them as objects of devotion: the only thing wonderful is, that gratitude seems to have acted as powerfully and extensively as fear; indeed more extensively; for no object of worship whatever has attracted so many worshippers. Where Jupiter has one, the cow has ten: she was venerated before he was born, and will be when even the carvers have forgotten him.

Cæsar. Unwillingly should I see it; for the character of our gods has formed the character of our nation.[27] Serapis and Isis have stolen in among them within our memory,[28] and others will follow, until at last

---

[23] This is an allusion to Book II (on livestock) of the *De Re Rustica*, a three-volume treatise on farming written by Marcus Terentius Varro (116–27 B.C.). Poet, satirist, scientist, jurist, geographer, grammarian, and antiquarian, Varro was considered by many of his contemporaries to be the most learned Roman of the time.

[24] According to Roman legend, Cacus, a monster who lived in a cave on the Aventine (one of the hills of Rome), stole some cattle from Hercules and hid them in his cave. The lowing of Hercules' remaining oxen was answered by those in the cave, and Hercules, perceiving the theft, killed Cacus and recovered the cattle.

[25] Jupiter is chief among the Roman gods.

[26] The Clitumnus (the modern Clitunno) is a river in Umbria, Italy, which flows into the Tinia, a tributary of the Tiber. Its source, an abundant spring, is described by Pliny in *Epistulae* viii. 8.

[27] In 63 B.C., Julius Caesar was elected Pontifex Maximus (high priest of Roman religion), a position of great dignity and political importance. (Plutarch *Caesar* 7. 1–3; Suetonius *Julius* 13.)

[28] Following Caesar's intervention (48–47 B.C.) in the Egyptian dynastic struggle between Cleopatra VII and her brother-consort Ptolemy XIV, the Egyptian deities Serapis and Isis were introduced into Rome, primarily by means of Caesar's returning legions. Serapis, the Egyptian god Osiris endowed with characteristics taken from Zeus, Hades, and Asclepius, was viewed as ruler of the universe and was introduced into Egypt by Ptolemy I (*ca.* 367–*ca.* 283 B.C.) in an attempt to unite Greeks and Egyptians in a common religion. Isis, sister and wife of Osiris, ruled the underworld

Saturn will not be the only one emasculated by his successor.[29] What can be more august than our rites? The first dignitaries of the republic are emulous to administer them: nothing of low or venal has any place in them, nothing pusillanimous, nothing unsocial and austere. I speak of them as they were; before Superstition woke up again from her slumber, and caught to her bosom with maternal love the alluvial monsters of the Nile. Philosophy, never fit for the people, had entered the best houses, and the image of Epicurus[30] had taken the place of the Lemures.[31] But men can not bear to be deprived long together of anything they are used to; not even of their fears; and, by a reaction of the mind appertaining to our nature, new stimulants were looked for, not on the side of pleasure, where nothing new could be expected or imagined, but on the opposite. Irreligion is followed by fanaticism, and fanaticism by irreligion, alternately and perpetually.

Lucullus. The religion of our country, as you observe, is well adapted to its inhabitants. Our progenitor Mars hath Venus recumbent on his breast, and looking up to him, teaching us that pleasure is to be sought in the bosom of valour and by the means of war.[32] No great alteration, I think, will ever be made in our rites and ceremonies; the best and most imposing that could be collected from all nations, and uniting them to us by our complaisance in adopting them. The gods themselves may change names, to flatter new power: and indeed, as we degenerate, Religion will accommodate herself to our propensities and desires. Our heaven is now

---

with him and was, in addition, symbolic of the female reproductive force in nature. In this latter capacity her symbol was the cow.

[29] Saturn, an ancient Italian god of agriculture, came to be identified by the Romans with the Greek god Cronus. Caesar's allusion is to Zeus's deposition of his father Cronus and the other Titans.

[30] Epicurus (342/341–271/270 B.C.), famed Athenian philosopher, enjoyed the adoration of his disciples in death as well as in life. According to Diogenes Laertius, Epicurus, in his will, requested his followers to continue the practice of honoring his birthday with a celebration. See *Lives* 10. 18. That this practice was continued long after Epicurus' death is proved by Cicero in *De Finibus* ii. 101.

[31] In Roman religion, lemures, or larvae, were harmful spirits of the dead who were supposed to visit the houses of the living during the festival of the Lemuria (May 9, 11, and 13). According to Ovid they were exorcised by having black beans thrown at them to the accompaniment of the words: "Ghosts of my fathers, go forth!" (*Fasti*, v. 419–445, tr. Sir James George Frazer ["The Loeb Classical Library"; New York: G. P. Putnam's Sons; London: W. Heinemann, 1931]).

[32] Mars, god of war, and Venus, goddess of love, were identified by the Romans with their Greek counterparts, Ares and Aphrodite, who often appeared together as lovers.

popular: it will become monarchal: not without a crowded court, as befits it, of apparitors, and satellites and minions of both sexes, paid and caressed for carrying to their stern dark-bearded master prayers and supplications. Altars must be strown with broken minds, and incense rise amid abject aspirations. Gods will be found unfit for their places; and it is not impossible that, in the ruin imminent from our contentions for power, and in the necessary extinction both of ancient families and of generous sentiments, our consular fasces[33] may become the water-sprinklers of some upstart priesthood,[34] and that my son may apply for lustration to the son of my groom. The interest of such men requires that the spirit of arms and of arts be extinguished. They will predicate peace, that the people may be tractable to them: but a religion altogether pacific is the fomenter of wars and the nurse of crimes, alluring Sloth from within and Violence from afar. If ever it should prevail among the Romans, it must prevail alone: for nations more vigorous and energetic will invade them, close upon them, trample them under foot; and the name of Roman, which is now the most glorious, will become the most opprobrious upon earth.

Cæsar. The time I hope may be distant; for next to my own name I hold my country's.

Lucullus. Mine, not coming from Troy or Ida,[35] is lower in my estimation: I place my country's first.

You are surveying the little lake beside us.[36] It contains no fish: birds never alight on it: the water is extremely pure and cold: the walk round is pleasant; not only because there is always a gentle breeze from it, but because the turf is fine, and the surface of the mountain on this summit is perfectly on a level, to a great extent in length; not a trifling advantage to me, who walk often, and am weak. I have no alley, no garden, no inclosure: the park is in the vale below, where a brook supplies the ponds, and where my servants are lodged; for here I have only twelve in attendance.

---

[33] Fasces, bundles of wooden rods bound together and encircling an ax, were regarded as a symbol of authority in ancient Rome. In processions the Roman consul was preceded by twelve fasces carried by attendants called lictors.

[34] Lucullus' allusions to the rise of Christianity in this passage are anachronistic, since this imaginary meeting supposedly occurs in the summer of 58 B.C.

[35] See Suetonius *Julius* 6. 1.

[36] "'As for his [Lucullus'] works on the seashore and in the vicinity of Neapolis, where he suspended hills over vast tunnels, girdled his residences with zones of sea and with streams for the breeding of fish, and built dwellings in the sea,—when Tubero the Stoic saw them, he called him Xerxes in a toga'" (Plutarch *Lucullus* 39. 2–3).

Cæsar. What is that so white, toward the Adriatic?

Lucullus. The Adriatic itself. Turn round, and you may descry the Tuscan Sea. Our situation is reported to be among the highest of the Apennines[37] ... Marcipor has made the sign to me that dinner is ready. Pass this way.

Cæsar. What a library is here![38] Ah Marcus Tullius! I salute thy image. Why frownest thou upon me? collecting the consular robe and uplifting the right-arm, as when Rome stood firm again, and Catiline fled before thee.[39]

Lucullus. Just so; such was the action the statuary chose, as adding a new endearment to the memory of my absent friend.[40]

Cæsar. Sylla,[41] who honoured you above all men, is not here.

Lucullus. I have his *Commentaries*: he inscribed them, as you know, to me. Something even of our benefactors may be forgotten, and gratitude be unreproved.

Cæsar. The impression on that couch, and the two fresh honeysuckles in the leaves of those two books, would show, even to a stranger, that this room is peculiarly the master's. Are they sacred?

[37] Lucullus is reported to have had several country residences near Tusculum (see Plutarch *Lucullus* 39. 3–4), a famous resort town for wealthy Romans located about ten miles southeast of Rome in the Alban Hills. These volcanic hills are part of the great Apennine mountain range which traverses the entire peninsula of Italy.

[38] "But what he [Lucullus] did in the establishment of a library deserves warm praise. He got together many books, and they were well written, and his use of them was more honourable to him than his acquisition of them. His libraries were thrown open to all, and the cloisters surrounding them, and the study-rooms, were accessible without restriction to the Greeks, who constantly repaired thither as to an hostelry of the Muses, and spent the day with one another, in glad escape from their other occupations. Lucullus himself also often spent his leisure hours there with them, walking about in the cloisters with their scholars, and he would assist their statesmen in whatever they desired" (Plutarch *Lucullus* 42. 1–2).

[39] According to Plutarch, Lucullus spent large sums on paintings and statues (*Lucullus* 39. 2). Caesar's historical allusion is to Cicero's exposure of the anarchist Catiline's plan to overthrow the Republic during Cicero's consulship (63 B.C.).

[40] Cicero was banished from Rome in 58 B.C. for having put Romans to death without right of appeal, that is, for his execution of the Catilinarians. Caesar was the prime, though reluctant, cause of Cicero's exile, since he had tried unsuccessfully to win Cicero's political allegiance.

[41] Lucius Cornelius Sulla (138–78 B.C.), a great general and leader of the aristocratic party at Rome, recognized Lucullus' "constancy and mildness" as well as his "courage and understanding" during the Marsic War (90–89 B.C.) and "attached him to himself and employed him from first to last on business of the highest importance" (Plutarch *Lucullus* 2. 1). Sulla honored Lucullus by dedicating his *Commentaries* (twenty-two books written between 79 and 78 B.C.) to him (Plutarch *Lucullus* 1. 3).

28   LUCULLUS AND CÆSAR

Lucullus. To me and Cæsar.

Cæsar. I would have asked permission ..

Lucullus. Caius Julius, you have nothing to ask of Polybius and Thucydides; nor of Xenophon,[42] the next to them on the table.

Cæsar. Thucydides! the most generous, the most unprejudiced, the most sagacious, of historians. Now, Lucullus, you whose judgment in style is more accurate than any other Roman's,[43] do tell me whether a commander, desirous of writing his *Commentaries*, could take to himself a more perfect model than Thucydides.

Lucullus. Nothing is more perfect, nor ever will be: the scholar of Pericles,[44] the master of Demosthenes![45] the equal of the one in military science, and of the other not the inferior in civil and forensic; the calm dispassionate judge of the general by whom he was defeated;[46] his defender, his encomiast. To talk of such men is conducive not only to virtue but to health.

Cæsar. We have no writer who could keep up long together his severity and strength. I would follow him; but I shall be contented with my

---

[42] Polybius (*ca.* 203–*ca.* 120 B.C.) wrote a *Universal History* which describes the rapid rise of Roman supremacy in the Mediterranean from the First Punic War (264–241 B.C.) to the destruction of Carthage and Corinth (146 B.C.); Thucydides (*ca.* 455–*ca.* 400 B.C.) wrote a *History of the Peloponnesian War* which traces the war from its beginning in 431 B.C. until 411 B.C., where the work breaks off (the war ended in 404 B.C.); and Xenophon (*ca.* 430–*ca.* 354 B.C.) wrote the *Anabasis* (a history of the expedition of the younger Cyrus, son of Darius II, against his brother Artaxerxes II, king of Persia, in 401 B.C.) and the *Hellenica* (a history of Greece from 411 to 362 B.C.).

[43] "Lucullus was trained to speak fluently both Latin and Greek, so that Sulla, in writing his own memoirs, dedicated them to him, as a man who would set in order and duly arrange the history of the times better than himself. For the style of Lucullus was not only businesslike and ready; the same was true of many another man's in the Forum. There, 'Like smitten tunny, through the billowy sea it dashed,' although outside of the Forum it was 'Withered, inelegant, and dead.' But Lucullus, from his youth up, was devoted to the genial and so-called 'liberal' culture then in vogue, wherein the Beautiful was sought" (Plutarch *Lucullus* i. 3–4).

[44] Pericles (*ca.* 495–429 B.C.), Athenian statesman, was a brilliant orator, a military genius, and a man of incorruptible character. Thucydides, an ardent follower of Pericles, faithfully recorded the major political events from 433 to 429 B.C. and summarized Pericles' political strategy and character in his *History* (see i. 24–ii. 65).

[45] Demosthenes (384–322 B.C.), the famous orator, carefully studied the writings of Thucydides, Plato, and Isocrates as part of his rigorous oratorical training.

[46] During the winter of 424 B.C., Brasidas, a Spartan general, forced the Athenian colony of Amphipolis to surrender before Thucydides could arrive with help from Thasos, a Parian colony about a half day's sail away. Thucydides was disgraced and sent into an exile which lasted twenty years. (Thucydides *History of the Peloponnesian War* iv. 102–108.)

genius, if (Thucydides in sight) I come many paces behind, and attain by study and attention the graceful and secure mediocrity of Xenophon.[47]

Lucullus. You will avoid, I think, Cæsar, one of his peculiarities; his tendency to superstition.[48]

Cæsar. I dare promise this; and even to write nothing so flat and idle as his introduction to the *Cyropædia*.[49] The first sentence that follows it, I perceive, repeats the same word, with its substantive, four times. This is a trifle: but great writers and great painters do miracles or mischief by a single touch. Our authors are so addicted of late to imitate the Grecian, that a bad introduction is more classical than a good one. Not to mention any friend of yours, Crispus Sallustius,[50] who is mine, brought me one recently of this description; together with some detached pieces of a history, which nothing in our prose or poetry hath surpassed in animation.

Lucullus. We ought to talk of these things by ourselves; not before the vulgar; by which expression I mean the unlearned and irreverent, in forum and in senate. Our Cicero has indeed avoided such inelegance as that of Xenophon: one perhaps less pardonable may be found repeatedly in his works: I would say an inelegance not arising from neglect, or obtusity of ear, but coming forth in the absence of reflection. He often says, "*mirari soleo.*"[51] Now surely a wise man soon ceases to wonder at

[47] Caesar wrote "Commentaries" on the Gallic War (probably composed during the winter of 52–51 B.C.) and on the Civil War (unfinished).

[48] Xenophon's piety, which Landor considers superstition, is nowhere more evident than in the *Anabasis* (see n. 42 above). At the battle of Cunaxa (401 B.C.), Cyrus the Younger was defeated and killed, and Xenophon had to lead the remnants of the army to safety. During their retreat, Xenophon made no important decisions without first sacrificing to the gods and then following the omens. Landor attacks Xenophon's credulity in three Conversations—"Xenophon and Cyrus the Younger," "Alcibiades and Xenophon," and "Diogenes and Plato." See pp. 167, 168 nn. 34 and 35.

[49] Xenophon *Cyropaedia* i. 1–2. 1.

[50] Gaius Sallustius Crispus (86–*ca.* 34 B.C.), a partisan of Caesar, was reappointed quaestor by Caesar in 49 B.C., commanded one of Caesar's legions in 48–47 B.C., aided Caesar in Africa while praetor (46 B.C.), and was appointed proconsular governor of Numidia shortly thereafter. Sallust devoted his later years to writing historical monographs, the *Bellum Catilinae* (43? B.C.), the *Bellum Iugurthinum* (41? B.C.), and the *Historiae* (39–34? B.C.). His model was Thucydides.

[51] In these lines Landor has Lucullus criticize a stylistic habit of Cicero: Cicero's tendency to select words of a superlative nature when the context apparently does not call for them. For instance, Cicero writes: "While on many grounds, Brutus, I regard with a constant wonder the genius and virtues of our countrymen, I do so above all in those studies which at quite a late period became the object of their aspiration and were transferred to this State from Greece" (*Tusculan Disputations* iv. 1. 1, tr. J. E. King [rev. ed.; "The Loeb Classical Library"; Cambridge: Harvard University Press;

anything, and, instead of indulging in the habitude of wonder at one object, brings it closer to him, makes it familiar, discusses, and dismisses it. He told me in his last letter of an incredible love and affection for me.[52] Pardon me, Cæsar! pardon me, Genius of Rome! and Mercury! I exclaimed, "*the clown!*" laughing heartily. He would not that I should really have thought his regard *incredible*; on the contrary, that I should believe it and confide in it to its full extent, and that I should flatter myself it was not only possible but reasonable. In vain will any one remark to me, "*such phrases are common.*" In our ordinary language there are many beauties, more or less visible according to their place and season, which a judicious writer and forcible orator will subject to his arbitration and service: there are also many things which, if used at all, must be used cautiously. I may be much at my ease, without being in tatters, and without treading on the feet of those I come forward to salute. I arrogate to myself no superiority, in detecting a peculiar and latent mark upon that exalted luminary: his own effulgence showed me it. From Cicero down to me the distance is as great, as between the prince of the senate and the lowest voter. I influenced the friends of order; he fulminated and exterminated the enemies. I have served my country; he hath saved it.

This other is my dining-room. You expect the dishes.

Cæsar. I misunderstood . . I fancied . .

Lucullus. Repose yourself, and touch with the ebony wand, beside you, the sphynx on either of those obelisks, right or left.

Cæsar. Let me look at them first.

Lucullus. The contrivance was intended for one person, or two at most, desirous of privacy and quiet. The blocks of jasper in my pair, and of porphyry in yours, easily yield in their grooves, each forming one partition. There are four, containing four platforms. The lower holds four dishes, such as sucking forest-boars, venison, hares, tunnies, sturgeons, which you will find within; the upper three, eight each, but diminutive. The confectionary is brought separately; for the steam would spoil it,

---

London: W. Heinemann, 1966]). Landor believes that "a wise man soon ceases to wonder at anything"; thus, for Landor, Cicero's "constant wonder" (Landor's "*mirari soleo*") at "the genius and virtues of our countrymen" is an exaggeration which constitutes a stylistic flaw. Landor continues his criticism in Lucullus' comment upon Cicero's use of the word "incredible."

[52] No letter from Cicero to Lucullus exists. The Latin phrase *soleo mirari*, however, occurs twice in Cicero's correspondence: *Ad Atticum* x. 11. 2. 5, and *Ad Familiares* vii. 7. 1. 3.

if any should escape. The melons are in the snow thirty feet under us: they came early this morning from a place in the vicinity of Luni,[53] so that I hope they may be crisp, independently of their coolness.

Cæsar. I wonder not at anything of refined elegance in Lucullus: but really here Antiochia and Alexandria seem to have cooked for us,[54] and magicians to be our attendants.

Lucullus. The absence of slaves from our repast is the luxury: for Marcipor alone enters, and he only when I press a spring with my foot or wand. When you desire his appearance, touch that chalcedony, just before you.

Cæsar. I eat quick, and rather plentifully: yet the valetudinarian (excuse my rusticity, for I rejoice at seeing it) appears to equal the traveller in appetite, and to be contented with one dish.[55]

Lucullus. It is milk: such, with strawberries,[56] which ripen on the Apennines many months in continuance, and some other berries of sharp and grateful flavour, has been my only diet since my first residence here. The state of my health requires it; and the habitude of nearly three months renders this food not only more commodious to my studies and more conducive to my sleep, but also more agreeable to my palate, than any other.

Cæsar. Returning to Rome or Baiæ,[57] you must domesticate and tame

[53] Luna (modern Luni) was an ancient city of Etruria, Italy.

[54] At the time of this Conversation between Lucullus and Caesar, Alexandria, Egypt, and Antiocheia, Syria, were centers of luxurious Roman living. By suggesting that these two cities might have catered for their meal, Caesar once again lavishes praise upon his host.

[55] This portrait of Lucullus as an abstemious individual is of Landor's own invention and is contradicted by Plutarch (*Lucullus* 39–41).

[56] Lucullus' dish of milk and strawberries is an example of Landor's habit of endowing his favorite characters with his own tastes. In a letter to Lady Blessington, Landor says: "I am not indifferent to grace, to wit, to friendship, more than formerly—but I tremble at literary men. I am inclined to believe that I can have the best of them to myself for as little as a plate of strawberries at this season, and can avoid the dust of the little skirmishes in which they are perpetually engaged" (W. Robertson Nicoll and Thomas James Wise, *Literary Anecdotes of the Nineteenth Century* [2 vols.; London, 1895–1896], I, 191–192; hereafter referred to as Nicoll and Wise, *Literary Anecdotes*). In a letter to Mrs. Graves-Sawle, he wrote: "I began with the intention of saying how I had been occupied. First in eating strawberries and cream, with an interlude of ices, all day long" (*Letters of Walter Savage Landor, Private and Public*, ed. Stephen Wheeler [London, 1899], p. 158; hereafter referred to as *Letters, Private and Public*, ed. Wheeler).

[57] Baiae (modern Baia) was an ancient city of Campania, Italy, famous principally for its warm sulphur springs, its mild climate, and its luxuriant vegetation. Many wealthy Romans, including Caesar and Nero, built villas in this resort town.

them. The cherries you introduced from Pontus are now growing in Cisalpine and Transalpine Gaul, and the largest and best in the world perhaps are upon the more sterile side of Lake Larius.[58]

Lucullus. There are some fruits, and some virtues, which require a harsh soil and bleak exposure for their perfection.

Cæsar. In such a profusion of viands, and so savoury, I perceive no odour.

Lucullus. A flue conducts heat through the compartments of the obelisks; and if you look up, you may observe that those gilt roses, between the astragals in the cornice, are prominent from it half a span. Here is an aperture in the wall, between which and the outer is a perpetual current of air. We are now in the dog-days; and I have never felt in the whole summer more heat than at Rome in many days of March.

Cæsar. Usually you are attended by troops of domestics and of dinner-friends, not to mention the learned and scientific, nor your own family, your attachment to which, from youth upward, is one of the higher graces in your character. Your brother was seldom absent from you.

Lucullus. Marcus[59] was coming: but the vehement heats along the Arno, in which valley he has a property he never saw before, inflamed his blood; and he now is resting for a few days at Fæsulæ,[60] a little town

---

[58] According to Pliny: "Before the victory of Lucius Lucullus in the war against Mithridates, that is down to 74 B.C., there were no cherry-trees in Italy. Lucullus first imported them from Pontus, and in 120 years they have crossed the ocean and got as far as Britain" (*Natural History* xv. 30, 102, tr. H. Rackham ["The Loeb Classical Library"; Cambridge: Harvard University Press; London: W. Heinemann, 1960], Vol. IV). Lake Larius, now known as Lake Como, is located in northern Italy.

[59] Marcus Licinius Lucullus (d. *ca.* 55–50 B.C.), younger brother of Lucius Licinius Lucullus, was adopted by Marcus Terentius Varro, and was hence known as Marcus Terentius Varro Lucullus. Like his brother, Marcus belonged to the aristocratic party at Rome, served under Sulla during his military campaigns (Plutarch *Sulla* 27. 7–8), and was active in politics. According to Plutarch: "Of his [Lucius Licinius Lucullus'] affection for his brother Marcus there are many proofs, but the Romans dwell most upon the first. Although, namely, he was older than his brother, he was unwilling to hold office alone, but waited until his brother was of the proper age, and thus gained the favour of the people to such an extent that, although in absence from the city, he was elected aedile along with his brother" (*Lucullus* 1. 6). Plutarch concludes his *Lucullus* with these words: "Nor did he himself [Marcus] long survive Lucullus, but, as in age and reputation he came a little behind him, so did he also in the time of his death, having been a most affectionate brother" (43. 3).

[60] "According to Florus (iii. 18. 11), Faesulae was taken and ravaged with fire and sword during the Social War (B.C. 90–89): but it seems more probable that this did not take place till the great devastation of Etruria by Sulla, a few years later" (E. H. Bunbury in *Dictionary of Greek and Roman Geography*, ed. William Smith [2 vols.;

destroyed by Sylla within our memory, who left it only air and water, the best in Tuscany. The health of Marcus, like mine, has been declining for several months: we are running our last race against each other: and never was I, in youth along the Tiber, so anxious of first reaching the goal. I would not outlive him: I should reflect too painfully on earlier days, and look forward too despondently on future. As for friends, lampreys and turbots[61] beget them, and they spawn not amid the solitude of the Apennines. To dine in company with more than two, is a Gaulish and German thing.[62] I can hardly bring myself to believe that I have eaten in concert with twenty; so barbarous and herdlike a practice does it now appear to me; such an incentive to drink much and talk loosely; not to add, such a necessity to speak loud; which is clownish and odious in the extreme. On this mountain-summit I hear no noises, no voices, not even

---

London, 1873], I, *s.v.* "*Faesulae*"). Landor lived in the environs of Fiesole (ancient Faesulae), Italy, for many years.

[61] Lampreys are eellike, carnivorous fish that fasten themselves to their victims by means of a circular suctorial mouth. Turbots are large flatfish highly valued as food.

[62] Lucullus' preference for dining either alone or in the presence of two at the most is contradicted by Plutarch: "And it is true that in the life of Lucullus, as in an ancient comedy, one reads in the first part of political measures and military commands, and in the latter part of drinking bouts, and banquets, and what might pass for revel-routs, and torch-races, and all manner of frivolity" (*Lucullus* 39. 1–2). Landor is endowing Lucullus with his own preference. In a letter to Lady Blessington, he writes: "Beside, I am out of spirits at dinner if there are more than five or six people. To confess the truth, I like best dining quite alone, taking my glass of water, my coffee, and my siesta—uniting as much of the Christian as I remember with as much of the Turk as I can. There may be something wolfish in this solitariness—I cannot help it—I acknowledge that when I look at myself I seem rather too like little Red-Ridinghood's grandmama. Cleverness, learning, eloquence, are capital things. When they are brought round to me, I take my spoonful, but I do not desire the fumes of them at table" (Nicoll and Wise, *Literary Anecdotes*, I, 192). Richard Monckton Milnes (Lord Houghton), who visited the Landors' villa near Florence in the spring of 1833, observed and recorded that "his repugnance to common relations with mankind showed itself in a peculiar way with respect to the pleasures of the table, in which he took an unreserved enjoyment; his highest luxury was dining alone, and with little light, and he would often resort to Florence for that purpose. He said 'a spider was a gentleman—he eat his fly in secret.' But this dislike to conviviality did not at all prevent him from performing agreeably the duties of host, and the repast was ever seasoned with valuable talk" (*Monographs, Personal and Social* [2d ed.; London, 1873], p. 133). And Kate Field, Landor's young friend from America, recalls the following: "Landor often berated the custom of dinner-parties. 'I dislike large dinners exceedingly. This herding together of men and women for the purpose of eating, this clatter of knives and forks, barbarous. What can be more horrible than to see and hear a person talking with his mouth full?'" ("Last Days of Walter Savage Landor," *Atlantic Monthly*, XVII [June 1866], 696).

of salutation: we have no flies about us, and scarcely an insect or reptile.

Cæsar. Your amiable son is probably with his uncle:[63] is he well?

Lucullus. Perfectly: he was indeed with my brother in his intended visit to me: but Marcus, unable to accompany him hither, or superintend his studies in the present state of his health, sent him directly to his uncle Cato at Tusculum, a man fitter than either of us to direct his education, and preferable to any, excepting yourself and Marcus Tullius,[64] in eloquence and urbanity.

Cæsar. Cato is so great, that whoever is greater must be the happiest and first of men.

Lucullus. That any such be still existing, O Julius, ought to excite no groan from the breast of a Roman citizen. But perhaps I wrong you: perhaps your mind was forced reluctantly back again, on your past animosities and contests in the senate.[65]

Cæsar. I revere him, but can not love him.

Lucullus. Then, Caius Julius, you groaned with reason; and I would pity rather than reprove you.

On the ceiling, at which you are looking, there is no gilding, and little painting . . a mere trellis of vines bearing grapes, and the heads, shoulders, and arms, rising from the cornice only, of boys and girls climbing up to

---

[63] L.? Licinius Lucullus (*ca.* 65–42 B.C.), son of Lucullus by his second wife, Servilia, half-sister of Marcus Porcius Cato Uticensis (95–46 B.C.), was entrusted, upon his father's death, to his maternal uncle. A great-grandson of Cato the Censor, Cato was a man of strong character and great integrity. As the chief antagonist of Caesar and the Triumvirate, he sided with Pompey against Caesar at the outbreak of the Civil War (49 B.C.). After Pompey's defeat at Pharsalus (48 B.C.), he fled with a small force to Utica in Africa. Defeated at the battle of Thapsus (46 B.C.), he took his own life. At the time of this Conversation, Cato had a villa at Tusculum, a city southeast of Rome.

[64] Marcus Tullius Cicero (106–43 B.C.), who appears to have joined with Cato in seeing to the young Lucullus' education (Cicero *De Finibus* iii. 2. 7–9; *Ad Atticum* xiii. 6), felt that the youth showed much promise (Cicero *Philippicae* 10. 4. 8).

[65] Suetonius says that during Caesar's consulship Caesar "freely granted everything else that anyone took it into his head to ask, either without opposition or by intimidating anyone who tried to object. Marcus Cato, who tried to delay proceedings, was dragged from the House by a lictor at Caesar's command and taken off to prison. When Lucius Lucullus was somewhat too outspoken in his opposition, he filled him with such fear of malicious prosecution [for Lucullus' conduct during the war with Mithridates VI], that Lucullus actually fell on his knees before him" (*The Lives of the Caesars* i. 20. 3–4, tr. John C. Rolfe [rev. ed.; "The Loeb Classical Library"; Cambridge: Harvard University Press; London: W. Heinemann, 1951], Vol. I; hereafter referred to as Suetonius *Julius*).

steal them, and scrambling for them: nothing over-head: no giants tumbling down,[66] no Jupiter thundering,[67] no Mars and Venus caught at mid-day,[68] no river-gods pouring out their urns upon us: for, as I think nothing so insipid as a flat ceiling, I think nothing so absurd as a storied one.[69] Before I was aware, and without my participation, the painter[70] had adorned that of my bedchamber with a golden shower, bursting from varied and irradiated clouds. On my expostulation, his excuse was, that he knew the Danaë of Scopas,[71] in a recumbent posture, was to occupy the centre of the room. The walls, behind the tapestry and pictures, are quite rough. In forty-three days the whole fabric was put together and habitable.

The wine has probably lost its freshness: will you try some other?

Cæsar. Its temperature is exact; its flavour exquisite. Latterly I have never sat long after dinner, and am curious to pass through the other apartments, if you will trust me.

Lucullus. I attend you.

Cæsar. Lucullus! who is here? what figure is that on the poop of the vessel? can it be . . . [72]

---

[66] See n. 29 above.
[67] See n. 25 above.
[68] See n. 32 above.
[69] Lucullus' criticism of baroque ceilings is anachronistic in that such painting was not a Roman form of decoration. His criticism is, however, consistent with the typical nineteenth-century point of view.
[70] Lucullus' painter, Antipho, is an imaginary character.
[71] According to Greek legend, Danaë, daughter of Acrisius, king of Argos, was confined by her father to either an underground apartment or a brazen tower in an attempt to thwart the prophecy of an oracle who had declared that she would give birth to a son who would murder his grandfather. Nevertheless, Danaë gave birth to Perseus, fathered, according to some accounts, by Proteus, Acrisius' twin brother, or in other accounts, by Zeus, who visited Danaë in the form of a shower of gold. Landor and Antipho, Lucullus' roguish painter, prefer the latter as a decorative theme for Lucullus' bedroom. Scopas was a Parian sculptor of the fourth century B.C.
[72] The subject of Lucullus' painting is the story of Caesar's capture by Cilician pirates. According to Plutarch's account: "To begin with, then, when the pirates demanded twenty talents for his ransom, he laughed at them for not knowing who their captive was, and of his own accord agreed to give them fifty. In the next place, after he had sent various followers to various cities to procure the money and was left with one friend and two attendants among Cilicians, most murderous of men, he held them in such disdain that whenever he lay down to sleep he would send and order them to stop talking. For eight and thirty days, as if the men were not his watchers, but his royal body-guard, he shared in their sports and exercises with great unconcern. He also wrote poems and sundry speeches which he read aloud to them, and those

Lucullus. The subject was dictated by myself; you gave it.

Cæsar. Oh how beautifully is the water painted! how vividly the sun strikes against the snows on Taurus!⁷³ the grey temples and pier-head of Tarsus catch it differently, and the monumental mound on the left is half in shade. In the countenance of those pirates I did not observe such diversity, nor that any boy pulled his father back: I did not indeed mark them or notice them at all.

Lucullus. The painter, in this fresco, the last work finished, had dissatisfied me in one particular. "That beautiful young face," said I, "appears not to threaten death."

"Lucius," he replied, "if one muscle were moved, it were not Cæsar's: beside, he said it jokingly, though resolved."

"I am contented with your apology, Antipho: but what are you doing now? for you never lay down or suspend your pencil, let who will talk and argue. The lines of that smaller face in the distance are the same."

"Not the same," replied he, "nor very different: it smiles; as surely the goddess must have done, at the first heroic act of her descendant."⁷⁴

Cæsar. In her exultation and impatience to press forward, she seems to forget that she is standing at the extremity of the shell, which rises up

---

who did not admire these he would call to their faces illiterate Barbarians, and often laughingly threatened to hang them all. The pirates were delighted at this, and attributed his boldness of speech to a certain simplicity and boyish mirth. But after his ransom had come from Miletus and he had paid it and was set free, he immediately manned vessels and put to sea from the harbour of Miletus against the robbers. He caught them, too, still lying at anchor off the island, and got most of them into his power. Their money he made his booty, but the men themselves he lodged in the prison at Pergamum, and then went in person to Junius, the governor of Asia, on the ground that it belonged to him, as praetor of the province, to punish the captives. But since the praetor cast longing eyes on their money, which was no small sum, and kept saying that he would consider the case of the captives at his leisure, Caesar left him to his own devices, went to Pergamum, took the robbers out of prison, and crucified them all, just as he had often warned them on the island that he would do, when they thought he was joking" (*Caesar* 2, in *Plutarch's Lives*, tr. Bernadotte Perrin ["The Loeb Classical Library"; Cambridge: Harvard University Press; London: W. Heinemann, 1967], Vol. VII; hereafter referred to as Plutarch *Caesar*). See also Suetonius *Julius* 4. 1-2, 74. 1.

⁷³ The Taurus is a lofty mountain range that begins abruptly near the site of Tarsus, the chief city of Cilicia, in present-day Turkey. One of the most important commercial cities and centers of learning in Asia Minor, Tarsus was situated about ten miles from the sea in a fertile plain on both sides of the river Cydnus, which emptied into a lagoon called Rhegma (Rhegmi). The lagoon was connected with the sea and thus formed a safe natural harbor for the city.

⁷⁴ This is a reference to Venus, the tutelary deity and ancestor of the Julian family.

behind out of the water; and she takes no notice of the terror on the countenance of this Cupid who would detain her, nor of this who is flying off and looking back. The reflection of the shell has given a warmer hue below the knee: a long streak of yellow light in the horizon is on the level of her bosom; some of her hair is almost lost in it: above her head on every side is the pure azure of the heavens.

Oh! and you would not have led me up to this? You, among whose primary studies is the most perfect satisfaction of your guests!

Lucullus. In the next apartment are seven or eight other pictures from our history.

There are no more: what do you look for?

Cæsar. I find not among the rest any descriptive of your own exploits. Ah Lucullus! there is no surer way of making them remembered.

This, I presume by the harps in the two corners, is the music-room.

Lucullus. No indeed; nor can I be said to have one here: for I love best the music of a single instrument, and listen to it willingly at all times, but most willingly while I am reading.[75] At such seasons a voice or even a whisper disturbs me: but music refreshes my brain when I have read long, and strengthens it from the beginning. I find also that if I write anything in poetry (a youthful propensity still remaining) it gives rapidity and variety and brightness to my ideas. On ceasing, I command a fresh measure and instrument, or another voice; which is to the mind like a change of posture or of air to the body. My health is benefited by the gentle play thus opened to the most delicate of the fibres.

Cæsar. Let me augur that a disorder so tractable may be soon removed. What is it thought to be?

---

[75] Whereas Plutarch makes no mention of music in his *Lucullus*, Landor's letters, Conversations, and the memoirs of his friends attest to his enjoyment of many forms of music, ranging from operas and concerts to the solitary human voice. In a letter to Miss Rose Paynter, Landor said: "In seven months I went but three times to the theatre and four or five to the opera—nowhere else" (*Letters, Private and Public*, ed. Wheeler, p. 75). In a letter to John Forster, he wrote: "Last evening I took him [his dog, Pomero] to hear Luisina de Sodre play and sing. . . . Pomero was deeply affected and lay close to the [piano] pedal on her gown, singing in a great variety of tones, not always in time" (John Forster, *Walter Savage Landor. A Biography* [2 vols.; London, 1869], II, 427–428). And in a letter to Mrs. Graves-Sawle (Rose Paynter) he said: "I shall retain in my inmost heart the grateful memory of your kindness and compassion. How is it possible that I could ever forget the comfort you gave me when circumstances made it impossible for me to remain in Italy. How often have I listened to a voice sweeter if possible in conversing with me than in singing at my request" (*Letters, Private and Public*, ed. Wheeler, pp. 219–220).

Lucullus. There are they who would surmise and signify, and my physician did not long attempt to persuade me of the contrary, that the ancient realms of Æetes[76] have supplied me with some other plants than the cherry, and such as I should be sorry to see domesticated here in Italy.[77]

Cæsar. The Gods forbid! Anticipate better things. The reason of Lucullus is stronger than the medicaments of Mithridates; but why not use them too? Let nothing be neglected. You may reasonably hope for many years of life: your mother still enjoys it.[78]

Lucullus. To stand upon one's guard against Death, exasperates her malice and protracts our sufferings.

Cæsar. Rightly and gravely said: but your country at this time can not do well without you.

Lucullus. The bowl of milk which to-day is presented to me, will shortly be presented to my Manes.[79]

Cæsar. Do you suspect the hand?

Lucullus. I will not suspect a Roman: let us converse no more about it.

Cæsar. It is the only subject on which I am resolved never to think, as relates to myself. Life may concern us, death not; for in death we neither can act nor reason, we neither can persuade nor command; and our statues are worth more than we are, let them be but wax. Lucius, I will not divine your thoughts: I will not penetrate into your suspicions, nor suggest mine. I am lost in admiration of your magnanimity and for-

[76] According to Greek legend, Aeëtes, the father of Medea, was king of Colchis, the region at the east end of the Euxine, or Black, Sea, just south of the Caucasus Mountains. Colchis was one of the first countries conquered by Mithridates VI.

[77] Lucullus implies that his poor health is due to poison. According to Plutarch: "But Cornelius Nepos says that Lucullus lost his mind not from old age, nor yet from disease, but that he was disabled by drugs administered to him by one of his freedmen, Callisthenes; that the drugs were given him by Callisthenes in order to win more of his love, in the belief that they had such a power, but they drove him from his senses and overwhelmed his reason, so that even while he was still alive, his brother managed his property" (*Lucullus* 43. 1–2). See also n. 58 above.

[78] Cicero relates that he went from his villa to attend her funeral a few years afterward. [*Landor's note.*] See Cicero *Ad Atticum* xv. 1a. However, Cicero did not attend the funeral of Lucullus' mother. Landor has confused Cn. (Licinius) Lucullus with Lucius Licinius Lucullus, both friends of Cicero.

[79] The Roman Manes originally were the collective disembodied and immortal spirits of the dead. Offerings of warm milk, water, wine, honey, oil, and the blood of sacrificial animals were made three times a year (in August, October, and November) to propitiate the dead. Later the word "Manes" (which has no singular) referred to the spirit of the individual dead person.

bearance; that your only dissimulation should be upon the guilt of your assassin; that you should leave him power, and create him virtues.

Lucullus. Caius Julius, if I can assist you in anything you meditate, needful or advantageous to our country, speak it unreservedly.

Cæsar. I really am ashamed of my association with Crassus and Pompeius: I would not have anything in common with them, not even power itself. Unworthy and ignominious must it appear to you, as it does to me, to compromise with an auctioneer and a rope-dancer; for the meanness and venality of Crassus, the levity and tergiversation of Pompeius, leave them no better names. The bestiality of the one, the infidelity of the other, urge and inflame me with an inextinguishable desire of uniting my authority to yours for the salvation of the republic.

Lucullus. I foretold to Cicero, in the words of Lucretius on the dissolution of the world,

> Tria talia texta
> Una dies dabit exitio.[80]

Cæsar. Assist me in accomplishing your prophecy: or rather, accept my assistance: for I would more willingly hear a proposal from you than offer one. Reflections must strike you, Lucullus, no less forcibly than me, and perhaps more justly; you are calmer. Consider all the late actions of Cneius, and tell me who has ever committed any so indecorous with so grave a face? He abstained in great measure from the follies of youth, only to reserve them accumulated for maturer age. Human life, if I may venture to speak fancifully in your presence, hath its equinoxes. In the vernal its flowers open under violent tempests: in the autumnal it is more exempt from gusts and storms, more regular, serene, and temperate, looks complacently on the fruits it has gathered, on the harvests it has reaped, and is not averse to the graces of order, to the avocations of literature, to the genial warmth of honest conviviality, and to the mild necessity of repose. Thrown out from the course of Nature, this man stood aside and solitary, and found everything around him unattractive. And now, in the decline of life, he has recourse to those associates, of whom the best that can be said is, that they would have less disgraced its outset. Repulsing you and Cicero and Cato,[81] the leaders of his party and the propagators

---

[80] "These three [Crassus, Pompey, and Caesar] woven together in such a fabric will one day yield destruction" (Lucretius *De Rerum Natura* v. 94–95).

[81] Pompey's estrangement from Lucullus, Cicero, and Cato was not concurrent, as Landor leads the reader to believe.

40   LUCULLUS AND CÆSAR

of his power. Pompeius the Great takes the arm of Clodius,[82] and walks publicly with him in the forum; who nevertheless the other day headed a chorus (I am informed) of the most profligate and opprobrious youths in Rome, and sang responsively worse than Fescennine songs[83] to his dishonour.[84] Where was he? Before them? in court? defending a client? He came indeed with that intention; but sat mortified, speechless, and despondent. The senate connived at the indignity. Even Gabinius,[85] his flatterer and dependent, shuns him. The other consul[86] is alienated from him totally, and favours me through Calpurnia, who watches over my

---

[82] Following a political defeat in the Roman Senate at the hands of Cato and Lucullus, "Pompey was forced to fly for refuge to popular tribunes and attach himself to young adventurers. Among these the boldest and vilest was Clodius [d. 52 B.C.], who took him up and threw him down under the feet of the people, and keeping him ignobly rolled about in the dust of the forum, and dragging him to and fro there, he used him for the confirmation of what was said and proposed to gratify and flatter the people. He even went so far as to ask a reward for his services from Pompey, as if he were helping him instead of disgracing him, and this reward he subsequently got in the betrayal of Cicero, who was Pompey's friend and had done him more political favours than any one else. For when Cicero was in danger of condemnation [for illegally putting to death Roman citizens who were followers of Catiline (63 B.C.)] and begged his aid, Pompey would not even see him, but shut his front door upon those who came in Cicero's behalf, and slipped away by another" (Plutarch *Pompey* 46. 4–5, in *Plutarch's Lives*, tr. Bernadotte Perrin ["The Loeb Classical Library"; Cambridge: Harvard University Press; London: W. Heinemann, 1961], Vol. V; hereafter referred to as Plutarch *Pompey*).

[83] Fescennine songs (*Versus Fescennini*) were coarse Roman wedding songs and dissolute verses sung by Roman soldiers at triumphs.

[84] This is a reference to Clodius' attempt to humiliate Pompey at the trial of Milo in 56 B.C. Plutarch relates: "And finally, when Pompey appeared at a public trial, Clodius, having at his beck and call a rabble of the lewdest and most arrogant ruffians, stationed himself in a conspicuous place and put to them such questions as these: 'Who is a licentious imperator?' 'What man seeks for a man?' 'Who scratches his head with one finger?' And they, like a chorus trained in responsive song, as he shook his toga, would answer each question by shouting out 'Pompey.'

"Of course this also was annoying to Pompey, who was not accustomed to vilification and was inexperienced in this sort of warfare; but he was more distressed when he perceived that the senate was delighted to see him insulted and paying a penalty for his betrayal of Cicero" (*Pompey* 48. 7–49. 1).

[85] Although Aulus Gabinius (d. 48–47 B.C.) was "the most extravagant of Pompey's flatterers" (Plutarch *Pompey* 48. 3) and a consul (58 B.C.), he could not have shunned Pompey, as Landor has Caesar say, since the trial of Milo occurred two years after Gabinius' consulship.

[86] Lucius Calpurnius Piso Caesoninus, the father of Caesar's wife, Calpurnia, was elected consul along with Aulus Gabinius for the year 58 B.C. (Plutarch *Pompey* 48). At that time there was no alienation between Piso and Pompey.

security and interests at home. Julia,[87] my daughter, was given in marriage to Pompeius for this purpose only: she fails to accomplish it: politically then and morally, the marriage loses its validity by losing its intent. I go into Gaul, commander for five years: Crassus is preparing for an expedition against the Parthians:[88] the senate and people bend before Pompeius, but reluctantly and indignantly. Everything would be more tolerable to me, if I could permit him to boast that he had duped me: but my glory requires that, letting him choose his own encampment, square the declivities, clear the ground about the eminence, foss and pale it, I should storm and keep it. Whatever he may boast of his eloquence and military skill, I fear nothing from the orator who tells us what he would have spoken, nor from the general who sees what he should have done. My first proposal for accommodation and concord shall be submitted to you (if indeed you will not frame it for me), and, should you deem it unfair, shall be suppressed. No successive step shall be made by me without your concurrence: in short, I am inclined to take up any line of conduct, in conjunction with you, for the settling of the commonwealth. Does the proposal seem to you so unimportant on the one hand, or so impracticable and unreasonable on the other, that you smile and shake your head?

Lucullus. Cæsar! Cæsar! you write upon language and analogy;[89] no man better. Tell me then whether mud is not said to be settled when it sinks to the bottom? and whether those who are about to sink a state, do not in like manner talk of settling it?

Cæsar. I wish I had time to converse with you on language, or skill to

[87] Julia, daughter of Caesar and Cornelia, was married to Pompey in April, 59 B.C. (Plutarch *Pompey* 47. 5–6). It is highly improbable that her marriage was in the state Caesar describes in these lines at the time of this Conversation. She died in childbirth in 55 B.C.

[88] Although Caesar's words appear to allude to his first appointment as proconsul of Gaul (59 B.C.), the mention of Crassus' preparation "for an expedition against the Parthians" (see Plutarch *Pompey* 52. 3) places the date at 55 B.C.

It is interesting to note that the events referred to in Caesar's historical allusions, although they appear in the Conversation to have occurred within a brief period of time, actually took place over an eleven-year period—from the *Lex Manilia* (66 B.C.) to Caesar's second appointment to the proconsulship of Gaul (55 B.C.).

[89] Suetonius mentions that Caesar "left besides a work in two volumes 'On Analogy,' the same number of 'Speeches criticising Cato,' in addition to a poem, entitled 'The Journey'" (*Julius* 56. 5). And Plutarch says: "In his [Caesar's] reply to Cicero's 'Cato,' he himself deprecated comparison between the diction of a soldier and the eloquence of an orator who was gifted by nature and had plenty of leisure to pursue his studies" (*Caesar* 3. 2).

parry your reproofs with equal wit; for serious you can not be. At present let us remove what is bad; which must always be done before good of any kind can spring up.

The designs of Cneius are suspected by many in the senate, and his pride is obnoxious to all. Your party would prevail against him; for he has enriched fewer adherents than you have;[90] and even his best friends are for the most part in a greater degree yours.

Lucullus. I have enriched no adherents, Caius Julius. Many of my officers, it is true, are easy in their circumstances: they however gained their wealth, not from the plunder of our confederates, not from those who should enjoy with security their municipal rights and paternal farms in Italy, but from the enemy's camps and cities.[91]

Cæsar. We two might appease the public mind, preparing the leaders of the senate for our labours, and intimidating the factious.

Lucullus. Hilarity never forsakes you, Cæsar! and you are the happiest man upon earth in the facility with which you communicate it. Hear me, and believe me. I am about to mount higher than triumviral tribunal or than triumphal car. They who are under me will turn their faces from me; such are the rites: but not a voice of reproach or of petulance shall be heard, when the trumpets tell our city that the funereal flames are surmounting the mortal spoils of Lucullus.[92]

---

[90] Contrary to Caesar's assertion, Pompey enriched many more adherents than did Lucullus. According to Plutarch (*Lucullus* 5-6), Lucullus used wealth only once for political ends, and that was in 74 B.C., when he ensured his command of the war against Mithridates VI. Both Pompey and Caesar, on the other hand, used wealth in the most blatant and crass ways to achieve their political ends; see Plutarch *Pompey* 44, 51-52, 58; *Caesar* 28-29; Suetonius *Julius* 20, 23, 26-29.

[91] Lucullus' officers enriched themselves only at the expense of the enemy (Plutarch *Lucullus* 36. 7, 37. 2-4). Lucullus' oblique reference to Roman officers who obtained their wealth by other means may be a contemptuous reference to the following actions of Pompey: his plundering the gifts which Lucullus had bestowed upon his followers during his command of the war with Mithridates VI (Plutarch *Pompey* 31, *Lucullus* 36. 1-6); and his rewarding his veterans with lands belonging to other Italians (Plutarch *Lucullus* 42. 5-6, *Pompey* 48. 1-3). As consul in 59 B.C., Caesar saw that Pompey's actions toward Lucullus in Asia were ratified by the people and that land would be available in Campania, Italy, for Pompey's soldiers (second agrian law).

[92] Plutarch describes the reaction of the Roman populace to Lucullus' death: "However, when he died, the people grieved just as much as if his death had come at the culmination of his military and political services, and flocked together, and tried to compel the young nobles who had carried the body into the forum to bury it in the Campus Martius, where Sulla also had been buried. But no one had expected this, and preparations for it were not easy, and so his brother, by prayers and supplications,

Cæsar. Mildest and most equitable of men! I have been much wronged; would you also wrong me? Lucius, you have forced from me a tear before the time. I weep at magnanimity; which no man does who wants it.

Lucullus. Why can not you enjoy the command of your province, and the glory of having quelled so many nations?

Cæsar. I can not bear the superiority of another.[93]

Lucullus. The weakest of women feel so: but even the weakest of them are ashamed to acknowledge it: who hath ever heard any one? Have *you*, who know them widely and well?[94] Poetasters and mimes, labouring under such infirmity, put the mask on. You pursue glory: the pursuit is just and rational: but reflect that statuaries and painters have represented heroes calm and quiescent, not straining and panting like pugilists and gladiators.

From being for ever in action, for ever in contention, and from excelling in them all other mortals, what advantage derive we? I would not ask what satisfaction? what glory? The insects have more activity than ourselves, the beasts more strength, even inert matter more firmness and stability; the gods alone more goodness. To the exercise of this every country lies open; and neither I eastward nor you westward have found any exhausted by contests for it.

Must we give men blows because they will not look at us? or chain them to make them hold the balance evener?

Do not expect to be acknowledged for what you are, much less for what you would be; since no one can well measure a great man but upon the bier. There was a time when the most ardent friend to Alexander of Macedon,[95] would have embraced the partisan for his enthusiasm, who should have compared him with Alexander of Pheræ.[96] It must have been

---

succeeded in persuading them to suffer the burial to take place on the estate at Tusculum, where preparations for it had been made" (*Lucullus* 43. 2–3).

[93] Plutarch mentions the following anecdote about Caesar: "We are told that, as he was crossing the Alps and passing by a barbarian village which had very few inhabitants and was a sorry sight, his companions asked with mirth and laughter, 'Can it be that here too there are ambitious strifes for office, struggles for primacy, and mutual jealousies of powerful men?' Whereupon Caesar said to them in all seriousness, 'I would rather be first here than second at Rome'" (*Caesar* 11. 2–3).

[94] According to Suetonius, Caesar did know women "widely and well" (*Julius* 50–52). With the exception of italicizing "you" in this sentence, Landor never alludes to the sensual aspect of Caesar's life which Suetonius depicts so graphically.

[95] Alexander the Great (356–323 B.C.) was probably the greatest general of antiquity.

[96] Alexander of Pherae, a petty tyrant (369–358 B.C.), was defeated by Pelopidas at the battle of Cynoscephalae (364 B.C.).

at a splendid feast, and late at it, when Scipio should have been raised to an equality with Romulus, or Cato with Curius.[97] It has been whispered in my ear, after a speech of Cicero, "If he goes on so, he will tread down the sandal of Marcus Antonius in the long run, and perhaps leave Hortensius behind."[98] Officers of mine, speaking about you, have exclaimed with admiration, "He fights like Cinna."[99] Think, Caius Julius! (for you have been instructed to think both as a poet and as a philosopher)[100] that among the hundred hands of Ambition, to whom we may attribute them more properly than to Briareus,[101] there is not one which holds anything firmly. In the precipitancy of her course, what appears great is small, and what appears small is great. Our estimate of men is apt to be as inaccurate and inexact as that of things, or more. Wishing to have all on our side, we often leave those we should keep by us, run after those we should avoid, and call importunately on others who sit quiet and will not come. We can

[97] Scipio Africanus Major (236–184 B.C.), consul in 205 and 194 B.C., defeated Hannibal at the battle of Zama in 202 B.C., thus bringing the Second Punic War (218–201 B.C.) to a close. Romulus is one of the legendary founders of Rome. Marcus Porcius Cato "Censorius" (234–149 B.C.), consul in 195 B.C., fought in the Second Punic War and was known for his legal ability, literary talent, and traditional morality. Manius Curius Dentatus was a third-century Roman who, because of his plain, simple, and honest ways, became the symbol of a certain type of ancient Roman virtue and frugality. Landor might be indebted to Cicero for these examples of Roman greatness, since all four appear in a list of great men cited by Cicero in his *Paradoxa Stoicorum* I. 11–12. See also Cicero *Tusculanae Disputationes* i. 46. 110.

[98] Marcus Antonius, 143–87 B.C., an older contemporary of Cicero, was one of the leading orators of his day. Quintus Hortensius Hortalus, 114–50 B.C., was Cicero's chief rival in the Roman law courts. By the time of this Conversation, Cicero had, in fact, surpassed Marcus Antonius and Hortensius (the latter at the trial of Verres in 70 B.C.) as orators and was the leading rhetorician of the time.

[99] Lucius Cornelius Cinna, consul from 87 to 84 B.C., entered Rome in 87 B.C. with Sertorius, the exiled Marius, and their followers and massacred the supporters of Sulla, who was fighting Mithridates VI in the East. Cinna was a bold, active, though rash general, and his failure to command the confidence of his troops resulted in the mutiny at Brundisium (84 B.C.) in which he was killed.

[100] In 74 B.C., Caesar went to Rhodes (at that time a center of higher education) to study under Apollonius Molon, a famous rhetor who lectured in that city. A former teacher of Cicero, Apollonius Molon wrote on rhetoric and attacked both philosophy and Judaism. Caesar must have been instructed in poetry as well as in oratory and philosophy, since Plutarch tells how Caesar, while the captive of pirates, wrote and recited poems to them (*Caesar* 2. 2) and Suetonius mentions a poem, "The Journey," written by Caesar (*Julius* 56. 5).

[101] In Greek mythology, Briareos and his brothers Gyges and Cottus are known as Uranids and are described by Hesiod as huge monsters with a hundred arms and fifty heads. (*Theogony* 149 ff.)

not at once catch the applauses of the vulgar and expect the approbation of the wise. What are parties? Do men really great ever enter into them? Are they not ball-courts, where ragged adventurers strip and strive, and where dissolute youths abuse one another, and challenge, and game, and wager? If you and I can not quite divest ourselves of infirmities and passions, let us think however that there is enough in us to be divided into two portions, and let us keep the upper undisturbed and pure. A part of Olympus itself lies in dreariness and in clouds, variable and stormy;[102] but it is not the highest: there the gods govern. Your soul is large enough to embrace your country: all other affection is for less objects, and less men are capable of it. Abandon, O Cæsar! such thoughts and wishes as now agitate and propel you: leave them to mere men of the marsh, to fat hearts and miry intellects. Fortunate may we call ourselves to have been born in an age so productive of eloquence, so rich in erudition. Neither of us would be excluded, or hooted at, on canvassing for these honours. He who can think dispassionately and deeply as I do, is great as I am; none other: but his opinions are at freedom to diverge from mine, as mine are from his; and indeed, on recollection, I never loved those most who thought with me, but those rather who deemed my sentiments worth discussion, and who corrected me with frankness and affability.

Cæsar. Lucullus! you perhaps have taken the wiser and better part, certainly the pleasanter. I can not argue with you: I would gladly hear one who could, but you again more gladly. I should think unworthily of you if I thought you capable of yielding or receding. I do not even ask you to keep our conversation long a secret; so greatly does it preponderate in your favour; so much more of gentleness, of eloquence, and of argument. I came hither with one soldier, avoiding the cities, and sleeping at the villa of a confidential friend. To-night I sleep in yours, and, if your dinner does not disturb me, shall sleep soundly. You go early to rest, I know.

Lucullus. Not however by daylight. Be assured, Caius Julius, that greatly as your discourse afflicts me, no part of it shall escape my lips. If you approach the city with arms, with arms I meet you; then your denouncer and enemy,[103] at present your host and confidant.

Cæsar. I shall conquer you.

Lucullus. That smile would cease upon it: you sigh already.

[102] Mount Olympus, the highest mountain in Greece, was regarded as the home of the gods.

[103] This meeting as enemies outside the city of Rome never occurred, since Lucullus was dead when Caesar crossed the Rubicon (49 B.C.).

Cæsar. Yes, Lucullus, if I am oppressed I shall overcome my oppressor: I know my army and myself. A sigh escaped me; and many more will follow: but one transport will rise amid them, when, vanquisher of my enemies and avenger of my dignity, I press again the hand of Lucullus, mindful of this day.

MR. PITT AND MR. CANNING

Landor's avid interest in the political leaders and events of his time is evident in this *Imaginary Conversation* between Mr. Pitt and Mr. Canning. However, although William Pitt (1759–1806), First Lord of the Treasury and Chancellor of the Exchequer, received many visitors while on his deathbed, his friend George Canning (1770–1827), Treasurer of the Navy, was not among them. This dialogue is both a virulent attack upon two English statesmen whom Landor thoroughly despised and an attempt to indicate some of the ways in which unscrupulous politicians rise to power and maintain themselves in it. In an extended political lampoon Landor presents Pitt and Canning as caricatures.

Landor was a staunch Whig and admirer of the French Revolution in his youth, and his antipathy toward Pitt turned to a fierce hatred when England and France went to war in 1793. Many of his charges against Pitt were also made by such loyal Whigs as Charles James Fox and Richard Brinsley Sheridan. Both Landor and Sheridan held Pitt responsible for increasing the national debt, entering into an ill-advised war with France, and bestowing titles of nobility for political purposes. In more personal matters, Pitt's acknowledged eloquence, lengthy oratory, enjoyment of wine, and lack of interest in amassing wealth, furnish the author with material for his characterization of the statesman. Landor strays from the facts, however, and indulges in intimate and often false accusations in the references to Pitt's impotence, disbelief in God, lack of literary knowledge, and perjury at Tooke's trial.

In the caricature of George Canning, the author emphasizes in a similar manner those aspects of Canning's character and activities which lend themselves to exaggeration. Landor presents the statesman as a subservient follower of Pitt, and he distorts Canning's personal pleasures and faults, especially his enjoyment of wine and his shortness of temper in parliamentary debate. Landor haughtily emphasizes Canning's humble birth and misrepresents the statesman by portraying him both as a scholar of little merit and as a writer of poor satiric verse.

The author's biased attitude toward Pitt and Canning often moved the author to intemperate language, to the amusement of his friends, and gave rise to anecdotes such as that which Landor's brother, Robert, related in a letter to John Forster:

Yet [Walter] Birch often checked Walter's extravagant language by his laughter; and once he asked me how it could have happened that my brother should have met accidentally so many ladies, in an evening's walk *or two with him and me, every one of whom was incomparably the most beautiful creature whom he had ever seen? how each of twenty fools could be by much the greatest fool upon earth? and, above all, how Mr. Pitt could be the greatest rascal living, if Mr. Canning surpassed Mr. Pitt, and Lord Castlereagh surpassed Mr. Canning, and all three were infinitely exceeded as brutes and fools by their gracious sovereign king George the Third?*[1]

Reviewers of Landor's writings, however, were not always so tolerant, as indicated by this excerpt from a review of the Imaginary Conversations *(1826–1829):*

We dissent also from his antipathies to Pitt and Canning, as extravagant and unjust; from his prejudices against Fox, and the Whig party of his time, as immoderate and not always intelligible. The faults committed by these party-leaders were less those of the individuals, than of the systems they found and followed. Clubs and family connexions were the cradles of the statesmen, the fingerposts of the administrations of the day. Whigs and Tories halved an oligarchical principle between them, and contended for the predominence [sic] *of their respective sections. Neither Pitt nor Fox could look over and beyond their age, like Chatham or their contemporary Burke: they could only direct its passions and embody its prejudices. But when Mr. Landor would have us take Pitt for a man unversed in literature, and even hostile to it,—when he draws him systematically profligate and low-minded,—when, overlooking Fox's oratorical powers, he points to his historical performances,—we lament that such nebulae should be found upon the broad and luminous disk of the "Imaginary Conversations."*[2]

Pitt. Dear Canning, my constitution is falling to pieces, as fast as your old friend Sheridan would tell you, the constitution of the country is, under my management.[3] Of all men living, you are the person I am most

---

[1] John Forster, *Walter Savage Landor. A Biography* (2 vols.; London, 1869), I, 186–187. Hereafter referred to as Forster.

[2] *British and Foreign Review*, V (July 1837), 44.

[3] At the age of eight, George Canning was taken into the London household of his wealthy uncle, Stratford Canning. There the young Canning met many of the powerful Whig politicians, among them Richard Brinsley Sheridan (1751–1816) and Charles James Fox (1749–1806). Later, when the excesses of the French Revolution caused

desirous to appoint my successor.⁴ My ambition is unsatisfied, while any doubt of my ability to accomplish it remains upon my mind. Nature has withholden from me the faculty of propagating my species:⁵ nor do I at all repine at it, as many would do: since every great man must have some imbecile one very near him, if not next to him, in descent.

Canning. I am much flattered, sir, by your choice of me, there being so many among your relatives who might expect it for themselves. However, this is only another instance of your great disinterestedness.⁶

Pitt. You may consider it in that light if you will: but you must remember that those who have exercised power long together and without

---

many Whigs, including Canning, to align themselves with William Pitt and his followers, Sheridan and Fox remained loyal to the Whig cause and formed the nexus of the opposition to Pitt's ministry.

In a speech in the House of Commons on May 14, 1802, Sheridan said: "Of that ex-minister [Pitt] I would just say, that no man admires his splendid talents more than I do. If ever there was a man formed and fitted by nature to benefit his country, and to give it lustre, he is such a man. He has no low, little, mean, petty vices. He has too much good sense, taste, and talent to set his mind upon ribands, stars, titles, and other appendages and idols of rank. He is of a nature not at all suited to be the creature or tool of any court. (*Mr. Pitt bowed repeatedly.*) But while I thus say of him no more than I think his character and great talents deserve, I must tell him how grossly he has misapplied them in the politics of this country; I must tell him again how he has augmented our national debt, and of the lives he lost in this war. I must tell him he has done more against the privileges of the people, increased more the power of the crown, and injured more the constitution of his country than any minister I can mention" (*Speeches of the Late Right Honourable Richard Brinsley Sheridan*, ed. by a Constitutional Friend [5 vols.; London, 1816], V, 202–203).

⁴ Canning was Treasurer of the Navy during Pitt's last administration (May 12, 1804–January 23, 1806). There is no reason to suppose that Pitt intended Canning to be his successor.

⁵ Pitt's unmarried status and his strict personal morality were often crudely satirized by writers such as John Wolcot (1738–1819), known by the pseudonym Peter Pindar. For instance, in "Epistle VII" of "Great Cry and Little Wool," a collection of verse epistles, Wolcot ridiculed Pitt thus:

> Of sweet Woman he courts not the smile,
> Of Venus ne'er seen in the school;
> An *animal* rare in our isle:
> Heaven grant that he mayn't be a *mule**!"

*I do not allude to the proverbial quality of that animal, but to his well known inability of perpetuating his species.

[John Wolcot], *The Works of Peter Pindar, Esq.* (2d ed. rev.; 5 vols.; London, 1812), V, 196.

⁶ Although Pitt distributed titles and wealth as political favors among loyal party members, he never enriched himself at the public's expense.

control, seldom care much about affinities.[7] The Mamelukes do not look out for brothers and cousins: they have favourite slaves who leap into their saddles when vacant.[8]

Canning. Among the rich families, or the ancient aristocracy of the kingdom . . .

Pitt. Hold your tongue! prythee hold your tongue! I hate and always hated these. I do not mean the rich: they served me. I mean the old houses: they overshadowed me. There is hardly one however that I have not disgraced or degraded; and I have filled them with smoke and sore eyes by raising a vassal's hut above them.[9]

I desire to be remembered as the founder of a new system in England: I desire to bequeath my office by will, a verbal one: and I intend that you, and those who come after you, shall do the same!

As you are rather more rash than I could wish, and allow your words to betray your intentions; and as sometimes you run counter to them in your hurry to escape from them, having thrown them out foolishly where there was no occasion nor room; I would advise you never to speak until you have thoroughly learnt your sentences. Do not imagine that, because I have the gift of extemporary eloquence, you have the same. No man ever possessed it in the same degree, excepting the two fanatics, Wesley and Whitfield.[10]

Canning. In the same degree certainly not; but many in some measure.

Pitt. Some measure is not enough.

Canning. Excuse me: Mr. Fox possessed it greatly, though not equally with you, and found it enough for his purpose.

Pitt. Fox foresaw, as any man of acuteness may do, the weaker parts of

---

[7] Pitt assumed leadership of the government on December 19, 1783, and retained political control until his resignation on March 14, 1801. His second administration, begun May 12, 1804, ended with his death on January 23, 1806, exactly twenty-five years after he first took his seat in Parliament.

[8] Mamelukes were slaves, mainly of Turkish and Circassian descent, who served as horsemen in the armies of Saladin (1138–1193) and his sons. About 1250 they revolted and established the Mameluke dynasties, usually known as the Bahri (1250–1382) and Burji (1382–1517) dynasties, in Egypt.

[9] According to Landor: "It is only an extremely small part of the English nobility itself that can be called the aristocracy. Pitt, who despised, or perhaps hated it, made it a complete miscellany of fugitive pieces" (Walter Savage Landor, *Charles James Fox: A Commentary on His Life and Character*, ed. Stephen Wheeler [London: John Murray, 1907], p. 45; hereafter referred to as Landor, *Commentary*).

[10] John Wesley (1703–1791), Anglican clergyman and founder of the Methodist Church, and George Whitefield (1714–1770), also an Anglican clergyman, were both eloquent and powerful evangelical preachers.

the argument that would be opposed to him, and he always learnt his replies: I had not time for it. I owe everything to the facility and fluency of my speech, excepting the name bequeathed me by my father:[11] and although I have failed in everything I undertook,[12] and have cast in solid gold the clay colossus of France,[13] people will consider me after my death as the most extraordinary man of my age.

Canning. Do you groan at this? or does the pain in your bowels grow worse?[14] Shall I lift up the cushion of your other chair yonder?

[11] William Pitt, first Earl of Chatham (1708–1778), often called "the Elder" and "the Great Commoner," was one of England's greatest statesmen. See n. 33 below.

[12] "Perhaps I [Landor] have spoken too much on the omissions of a negligent, disjointed ministry, and, some will think, too vehemently against the leader [Pitt]. It is true that almost every possible case of mismanagement has been stated. *The facts exist.* This is my answer. Those who cannot see them, those who overlook them in the public records, are not likely to discover what we lost of prosperity by their inattention, or of glory by their inactivity. We have equally to regret that they failed in every thing abroad, and did *not* fail in almost every thing at home. If any man will come forward and prove even this to be exaggerated, and surely nothing worse can be uttered or imagined of a ministry—statesmen would be an absurd expression—I will then acknowledge myself a very violent and very base calumniator, an implacable enemy of my native land, and—what pensioners and reversionists think infinitely more discreditable—a man without a stake in it" (Landor, *Commentary,* p. 66).

[13] "But I [Landor] should be more contented, I must acknowledge it, if I could discover in history where any people hath been so fortunate as to survive such delinquency in the higher officers of state [Landor has previously alluded to the corrupt courts of the Roman emperors Lucius Aelius Aurelius Commodus (emperor A.D. 180–192) and Elagabalus (emperor A.D. 218–222)]; if I could find that nation in existence twenty years after such politicians and such polity. This idea of degradation and ruin stands so closely and so awfully before me, I lose for a moment all view of that vast colossus [Napoleon Bonaparte] which overshadows the whole continent of Europe, and which will never be considered as the cause, however he may be the instrument, of our subjugation" (Landor, *Commentary,* p. 23).

[14] According to Earl Stanhope, one of Pitt's biographers: "It is no wonder if, after the tidings and the hopes of a victory in Moravia, which were conveyed to Mr. Pitt, the sudden shock of the contrary intelligence proved too much for his enfeebled frame. I shall here insert the statement on this point which was put in writing by my father, and which seems to have been derived from the domestics in immediate attendance upon Mr. Pitt at Bath. . . .

"'The immediate cause of his death was the battle of Austerlitz [on December 2, 1805, in which the forces of Napoleon defeated the Russian and Austrian armies, thus destroying the confederacy established by Pitt between England, Russia, Austria, and Sweden]. I dined with him the day before his departure for Bath, when I found him in his usual spirits; and on inquiring after his health, I learnt from those about him that he had some flying gout, which it was hoped might become a regular fit. Such was, indeed, the effect of the Bath waters; but after he received the dispatches containing

Pitt. Oh! oh!

Canning. I will make haste, and then soften by manipulation those two or three letters of condolence.

Pitt. Oh! oh! . . . next to that cursed fellow who foiled me with his broken weapon, and befooled me with his half-wit, Bonaparte.

Canning. Be calmer, sir! be calmer.

Pitt. The gout and stone be in him! Port wine and Cheltenham-water![15] An Austrian wife,[16] Italian jealousy, his country's ingratitude, and his own ambition, dwell with him everlastingly.

Canning. Amen! let us pray!

Pitt. Upon my soul, we have little else to do. I hardly know where we can turn ourselves.

Canning. Hard indeed! when we can not do that!

Be comforted, sir! The worse the condition of the country, the greater is the want of us; the more power we shall possess, the more places we shall occupy and distribute.

Pitt. Statesmanlike reflection.

Canning. Those who have brought us into danger can alone bring us out, has become a maxim of the English people.

Pitt. If they should ever be strong again, they would crush us.

Canning. We have lightened them;[17] and, having less ballast, they sail before the wind at the good pleasure of the pilot.

Pitt. A little while ago I would have made you chancellor or speaker, for

---

the account of that most disastrous battle, he desired a map to be brought to him and to be left alone. His reflections were so painful that the gout was repelled, and attacked some vital organ'" (Earl Stanhope, *Life of the Right Honourable William Pitt* [4 vols.; London, 1861-1862], IV, 363).

[15] Cheltenham, a municipal and parliamentary borough of Gloucestershire, England, is well known for its mineral springs.

[16] Napoleon Bonaparte married Marie Louise, an Austrian archduchess, by proxy in Vienna on March 11, 1810, and in person at Paris on April 1-2, 1810.

[17] On May 20, 1831, at the height of the agitation over the Reform Bill proposed in the English Parliament, Landor wrote to his sisters in England: "You are a little too melancholy in regard to the times. Whatever is happening and about to happen was foreseen by me in the period of Pitt's war against France. He squandered the nation's wealth with more imprudence than the most wanton youth ever squandered his new inheritance; and the facility he found in raising supplies from a venal parliament shows the necessity of changing the system. The misfortune is that the change had not taken place fifty-five years earlier. Then we should not have lost America, except as a colony and a dependant, and by no means as a confederate and friend. But above all we should have had a debt of about 40 instead of 800 millions" (Forster, II, 240).

composing and singing that capital song of the *Pilot*:[18] so I thought it: at present I never hear the word but it gives me the sea-sickness, as surely as would a fishing-boat in the Channel. It sounds like ridicule.

Canning. We have weathered the storm.

Pitt. I have not. I never believed in any future state;[19] but I have made a very damnable one of the present, both for myself and others. We never were in such danger from without or from within. Money-lenders and money-voters are satisfied:[20] the devil must be in them if they are not: but we have taken the younger children's fortunes from every private gentleman in Great Britain.

Canning. Never think about it.

Pitt. I have formerly been in their houses: I have relatives and connections among them: if you had, you would sympathise.[21] I feel as little as any man can feel for others, you excepted. And this utter indifference, this concentration, which inelegant men call selfishness, is among the reasons why I am disposed to appoint you my successor. You are aware that, should the people recover their senses, they would drive us in a dungcart to the scaffold: *me* they can not: I shall be gone.

Canning. We must prevent the possibility: we must go on weakening them. The viper that has bitten escapes: the viper that lies quiet in the road, is cut asunder.

Pitt. Why! Canning! I find in you both more reasoning and more poetry than I ever found before. Go on in this manner, and your glory as a poet will not rest on *pilots* and *pebbles*, nor on a ditch-side nettle or two of neglected satire.[22] If you exhibit too much reflection, I may change my mind. You will do for my successor: you must not more than do.

[18] On May 28, 1802, Pitt's friends held a great dinner in honor of his birthday. It was for this occasion that Canning composed his well-known verses, "The Pilot that Weathered the Storm." See *The Poetical Works of the Right Hon. George Canning* (London, 1823), pp. 36–37.

[19] Pitt is supposed to have thrown himself upon the mercy of the Christian God at the hour of his death. See John Gifford, *A History of the Political Life of the Right Honourable William Pitt* (6 vols.; London, 1809), VI, 806–807. Hereafter referred to as Gifford, *William Pitt*.

[20] See n. 17 above.

[21] Although not of ignoble birth, Canning did not belong to any of the leading English families. His father, also named George Canning, led a difficult life in London as a tradesman and a literary man, after having been disowned by his family following a quarrel. Canning's mother, Mary Anne Costello Canning, unsuccessfully turned to the stage after her husband died on their son's first birthday. See n. 26 below.

[22] On November 20, 1797, Canning and a few chosen friends published the first number of *The Anti-Jacobin*, a periodical devoted to making the English Revolutionary

Canning. On the contrary, sir, I feel in your presence my deep inferiority.

Pitt. That of course.

Canning. Condescend to give me some precepts, which, if your disease should continue, it might be painfuller to deliver at any other time. Do not, however, think that your life is at all in danger, or that the supreme power can remain long together in any hands but yours.

Pitt. Attempt not to flatter me, Canning, with the prospect of much longer life. The doctors of physic have hinted that it is time I should divert my attention from the affairs of Europe to my own: and the doctors of divinity drive oftener to the chancellor's door[23] than to mine. The flight of these sable birds portends a change of season and a fall of bones.

I have warned you against some imprudences of yours: now let me warn you against some of mine. You are soberer than I am:[24] but when you are rather warm over claret, you prattle childishly. For a successful minister three things are requisite on occasion; to speak like an honest man, to act

---

party appear ridiculous. Although the contributors were anonymous, Canning's brilliant wit was soon recognized by many of the readers. Such satiric pieces as "The Friend of Humanity and the Knife-Grinder," "New Morality," and "Inscription for the Door of the Cell in Newgate, Where Mrs. Brownrigg, the Prentice-Cide, Was Confined Previous to Her Execution" are almost exclusively the work of Canning. His contributions ceased after July 9, 1798.

[23] Lord Eldon (1751–1838) was Lord Chancellor of England during Pitt's final illness. In having Pitt comment sarcastically upon the politically minded clergy, Landor is able to express his own feelings: "Hatred of Religion is engendered in many hearts by the anti-Christian wealth and offices of its lordly functionaries. France, Germany, and Italy herself, have trimmed and curtailed her phylacteries; in England and Ireland the old pattern has only been disfigured, and the massive bullion carefully covered over. Thirty generals and thirty admirals, the saviours of our country, divide among them a smaller revenue than the Bishop of London has been enjoying for many years" (quoted in *Letters of Walter Savage Landor, Private and Public*, ed. Stephen Wheeler [London, 1899], p. 287, from an excerpt of a letter entitled "European Revolutions" published in *The Examiner*, November 18, 1848).

[24] In Landor's "Moral Epistle" (1795), the poet comments upon Pitt's known enjoyment of wine:

> But—honest Minister, or sound Divine—
> He lies who tells us there is truth in wine.
> For George's Premier, never known to reel,
> Drinks his two bottles, Bacchus! at a meal.

The Complete Works of Walter Savage Landor, ed. T. Earle Welby and Stephen Wheeler (16 vols.; London: Chapman and Hall Ltd., 1927–1936), XVI, 286. Hereafter referred to as *Complete Works*.

like a dishonest one, and to be indifferent which you are called. Talk of God as gravely as if you believed in him. Unless you do this, I will not say what our Church does, you will be damned; but, what indeed is a politician's true damnation, you will be dismissed. Most very good men are stout partisans of some religion, and nearly all very bad ones. The old women about the prince are as notorious for praying as for prostitution; and if you lose the old women, you lose him. He is their prophet, he is their champion, and they are his Houris.[25]

Canning. I shall experience no difficulty in observing this commandment. In our days, only men who have some unsoundness of conscience and some latent fear, reason against religion; and those only scoff at it who are pushed back and hurt by it.

Pitt. Canning! you must have brought this with you from Oxford:[26]

---

[25] This is a reference to the Prince Regent, later George IV, king of England, 1820–1830, whose sexual escapades were notorious. Houris are young, beautiful virgin nymphs who dwell in the Mohammedan paradise.

In the 1829 edition of the *Imaginary Conversations* this passage reads: "Besides, if you lose the old women, you lose the Heir apparent. He is their champion, and they are his Houris." Some copies of this edition, however, have a cancel: "Besides, * * * * * * * * * * * * *" (see Textual Notes, p. 229). Since George IV was living when this Conversation was first published, the allusion was libelous; and apparently when Landor's publisher, James Duncan, became aware of it, he had a cancel leaf inserted in the remaining unsold copies. Such interference by the publisher was certainly warranted, for in 1813 John and Leigh Hunt were fined and imprisoned for publishing in *The Examiner* similar remarks concerning the Prince Regent. This tendency of Landor to state his opinions about his contemporaries and their activities in his writings often required the intervention of both his publishers and his friends to protect him from libel suits. See R. H. Super, *The Publication of Landor's Works* (Supplement to the Bibliographical Society's *Transactions*, No. 18; London: Bibliographical Society, 1954). See also Charles L. Proudfit, "An Unrecorded Cancellans in the First Edition of Walter Savage Landor's *Imaginary Conversations of Literary Men and Statesmen*," *Notes and Queries*, CCXIII (September 1968), 345–346.

[26] Canning entered Christ Church, Oxford, in October, 1788. According to Robert Bell: "New friendships sprung up at Christ Church, of a class materially calculated to influence, if not to decide, the subsequent direction of his life. Among his more immediate associates were the Hon. Mr. Jenkinson, afterward Earl of Liverpool, Mr. Sturges Bourne, Lord Holland, Lord Carlisle, Lord Seaford, Lord Granville, and Lord Boringdon. Most of these gentlemen, especially Mr. Jenkinson, were educated with a specific view to a participation in the government of the country; and Mr. Canning, although he could reckon upon none of the advantages of patronage or hereditary position, was soon admitted to the freedom of their intercourse by virtue of claims more powerful and commanding. His wit, eloquence, and scholarship established an ascendency among them, never wholly free, to be sure, from the jealousies of rank, but always superior to its naked accidents. He was here, for the first time, placed upon a familiar footing with lords and statesmen in training; here he took his first

the sentiment is not yours even by adoption: it is too profound for you, and too well expressed. You are brilliant by the multitude of flaws, and not by the clearness or the quantity of light.

Canning. On second thoughts, I am not quite sure, not perfectly satisfied, that it is, as one may say, altogether mine.

Pitt. This avowal suggests another counsel.

Prevaricate as often as you can defend the prevarication, being close pressed: but, my dear Canning! never .. I would say ... come, come, let me speak it plainly: my dear fellow, never lie.

Canning. How, sir! what, sir! pardon me, sir! But, sir! do you imagine I ever lied in my lifetime?

Pitt. The certainty that you never did, makes me apprehensive that you would do it awkwardly, if the salvation of the country (the only case in question) should require it.

Canning. I ought to be satisfied: and yet my feelings ... If you profess that you believe me incapable ...

Pitt. What is my profession? what is my belief? If a man believes a thing of me, how can I prevent or alter his belief? or what right have I to be angry at it? Do not play the fool before me. I sent for you to give you good advice. If you apprehend any danger of being thought, what it is impossible any man alive should ever think you, I am ready to swear in

---

lesson in aristocracy; and he used its admonitions wisely" (Robert Bell, *The Life of the Rt. Hon. George Canning* [New York, 1846], p. 59).

Landor matriculated at Trinity College, Oxford, on November 13, 1792, although he did not take up residence in the College until January, 1793. According to John Forster: "Landor was close on Canning's heels at Oxford, had been in communication with him more than once, and had not been very tolerant of many passages in his public life; but he never denied his possession of rare and exquisite powers, and it was upon my calling his attention to what seemed an unfair application of some remarks on the Castlereagh quarrel that these letters were written.

"'Arrogant as he was in pretension while holding office, indifferent to veracity in assertion, and swayed by vanity or resentment from any principle to its opposite, he was delightful in private society, adapting his conversation to the temper and abilities of those with whom he happened to converse. There he was never in opposition, but always in power: there his humour was easy and graceful: there his arrows were placed with the points downward, attracting all, wounding none. But minds, like bodies, if they prematurely swell out, then suddenly cease to grow in height and compass, and become sickly and irritable; Mr. Canning's did; and his tongue betrayed his distemper. His petulance in parliament made it incredible that, in addition to his witticisms in poetry, he had formerly been the rival of the otherwise unrivalled Sydney Smith in the piquancy and aptness of his criticism'" (Forster, II, 329).

your favour as solemnly as I swore at Tooke's trial.²⁷ I am presuming that you will become prime minister; you will then have plenty of folks ready to lie for you; and it would be as ungentlemanly to lie yourself as to powder your own hair or tie your own shoe-string. I usually had Dundas²⁸ at my elbow, who never lied but upon his honour, or supported the lie but upon his God. As for the more delicate duty of prevarication, take up those letters of inquiry and condolence, whether you have rubbed the seals off or not in your promptitude to serve me, and lay them carefully by; and some years hence, when anyone exclaims, "What would Mr. Pitt have said!" bring out one from your pocket, and cry, "This is the last

²⁷ John Horne Tooke (1736–1812), English radical and philologist, was arrested May 16, 1794, and charged with high treason. His trial lasted six days (November 17–22, 1794), and the jury deliberated only eight minutes before acquitting him: "In the course of Mr. Tooke's trial, Mr. Pitt was examined, on the part of the prisoner, in order to prove, that the meeting at the Thatched House Tavern, in 1782, of which he was a Member, had the same objects in view, as the Seditious Societies of the present time. His evidence, however, totally failed to establish this laboured point.—Mr. Pitt recollected that Mr. Tooke had been present at one of those meetings, the sense of which was to use means to recommend a petition to Parliament, in order to procure a reform, but there was no such idea as a Convention of the people, or affiliated Societies; and he did not consider that as a meeting of persons authorized to act for any but themselves" (Gifford, *William Pitt*, IV, 225–226). See also *The Trial of John Horne Tooke on a Charge of High Treason* (London, 1794), pp. 248–251.

Landor believes Pitt committed perjury at Tooke's trial:

> But Bacchus! Bacchus!—round whose thyrsus twined
> Tendrils and ivy playing unconfined—
> How art thou alter'd! *I*? yes *thou*, by Jove,
> Thou second Wyndham; what I say I prove.
> Tooke was on trial: Pitt was cited: came:
> Discovered treason raging; towers on flame;
> Daggers and pikes enormous, and a dart
> To fly *self-acted* at the Monarch's heart:
> But, questioned on his *own* account, each jot
> Of all he once had written he forgot.
> That which is real we forget with ease,
> But feign what never happen'd, when we please."
> "Moral Epistle," *Complete Works*, XVI, 286.

²⁸ Henry Dundas, Viscount Melville (1742–1811), British statesman, became solicitor general for Scotland in 1766 and Lord Advocate in 1775. He held minor positions in Parliament under the Marquess of Lansdowne and William Pitt, and in 1791 he entered the cabinet as Home Secretary. He was Pitt's Secretary for War from 1794 until 1801, during which time the two became very close friends. In 1804 Pitt made him First Lord of the Admiralty. In 1806 Lord Melville was impeached for the

letter his hand, stricken by death, could trace." Another time you may open one from Burke,[29] some thirty years after the supposed receipt of it, and say modestly, "Never but on this momentous occasion did that great man write to me. He foretold, in the true spirit of prophecy, all our difficulties." But remember; do not quote him upon finance; else the House will laugh at you. For Burke was as unable to cast up a tailor's bill, as Sheridan is to pay it.[30]

I was about to give you another piece of advice, which on recollection I find to be superfluous. Surely my head sympathises very powerfully with my stomach, which the physicians tell me is always the case, though not so much with us in office as with the honourable gentleman out. I was on the point of advising you never to neglect the delivery of long speeches: the minister who makes short speeches enjoys short power. Now, although I have constantly been in the habit of saying a great deal

---

misappropriation of public money while Treasurer of the Navy (1782–1800). Although acquitted, he never held office again.

Landor attacks Lord Melville in his *Commentary*: "A nobleman of most acute judgment [Lord Melville], well versed in all the usages of his country, rich, powerful, commanding, with a sway more absolute and unresisted than any of its ancient monarchs, the whole kingdom in which he was a subject, with all its boroughs, and its shires, and its courts, and its universities, and, in addition, as merely a fief, the empire of all India; who possessed more lucrative patronage than all the crowned heads in Europe.

"Let this illustrious character, to whom so many men of rank looked up as their protector, and whom senators and statesmen acknowledged as their guide; let this distinguished member of the British parliament break suddenly through the law which he himself had brought into the House for the conservation of our property, without necessity, without urgency, without temptation—and behold the consequence. True, he is impeached, but all the evidence of his guilt he is permitted to withhold, by a special decision in his favour, and the answers he returns to those who are authorised to examine him are evasive and jocose. One honest man, Admiral Nichols, Controller of the Navy, scandalised at such scenes of iniquity, hopeless of reforming them, and disdaining to sanction by his name and presence the belief that a single act of fraud and peculation had been examined as it should be, threw up his office instantaneously and retired from such unworthy associates" (Landor, *Commentary*, pp. 34–36).

[29] Edmund Burke (1729–1797), born in Ireland, was a writer, orator, and statesman.

[30] Burke was paymaster of the forces during the second ministry of Lord Rockingham (March–July 1782) and during the "Coalition" ministry (April–December 1783) (see n. 53 below). Sheridan was plagued with financial problems during most of his lifetime. His Drury Lane theater, twice rebuilt (1791–1794, 1809), his desire to lead a fashionable life in London, and his political activities involved him in numerous debts. Failing to secure a seat at Stafford in the elections of 1812, Sheridan lost the parliamentary privilege of immunity from arrest for debt. From that time until his death in 1816 he was harassed by creditors and moneylenders.

more than was requisite to the elucidation of my subject,[31] for the same reason as hares, when pursued, run over more ground than would bring them into their thickets, I would have avoided it with you, principally to save my breath. You can no more stop when you are speaking, than a ball can stop on an inclined plane. You bounce at every impediment, and run on; often with the very thing in your mouth that the most malicious of your adversaries would cast against you; and showing what you would conceal, and concealing what you would show. This is of no ill consequence to a minister: it goes for sincerity and plain dealing. It would never have done at Christ-church or Eton:[32] for boys dare detect anything, and laugh with all their hearts. I think it was my father who told me (if it was not my father I forget who it was) that a minister must have two gifts: the gift of places and the gift of the gab. Perfectly well do I remember his defence of this last expression, which somebody at table, on another occasion, called a vulgarism. At the end of the debate on it, he asked the gentleman whether all things ought not to have names; whether there was any better for this; and whether the learning and ingenuity of the company could invent one. The importance of the faculty was admirably exhibited, he remarked, by the word *gift:* he then added, with a smile, "The alliteration itself has its merit: these short sayings are always the better for it: a popgun must have a pellet at both ends."

Ah, Canning! why have I not remembered my father as perfectly in better things? I have none of his wit, little of his wisdom: but all his experience, all his conduct, were before me and within my reach. I will not think about him now, when it would vex and plague me.

Canning. It is better to think of ourselves than of others; to consider the present as everything, the past and future as nothing.

Pitt. In fact, they are nothing: they do not exist: what does not exist, is nothing.

[31] "Mr. Pitt was eloquent, so was Mr. Fox: so were Anytus and Melitus [Socrates' accusers], and all the demagogues whose vociferations have preceded the downfall of a state. In England it is for eloquence alone that men are chosen to fill the offices of government. If they can speak three hours together, it is thought, with reason, that they can do great things. Nevertheless it has been the opinion of some that there is a latent flaw and unsoundness in this reasoning, and that its application ought not to be universal or unreserved. They have suspected it hence has happened that, with such resources as no nation ever possessed, we have done so extremely little against an enemy who, according to the minister himself [Pitt], had no resources at all" (Landor, *Commentary*, pp. 60–61).

[32] Canning entered Eton in 1782. An outstanding student, he excelled in debate, scholarship, and literary pursuits. See n. 26 above.

Canning. Supposing me to be prime minister ... I am delighted at finding that the very idea has given a fresh serenity to your countenance.

Pitt. Because it makes me feel my power more intensely than ever; or at least makes me fancy I feel it. By my means, by my authority, you are to become the successor of a Shelburne, of a Rockingham, and a Chatham.[33]

Canning. Sir, I request you to consider ...

Pitt. Whether I have the right of alluding to what all have the right of recollecting, and which right all will exercise. I wish you as well as if, by some miracle in my favour, I had been enabled to beget you: that which I hope to do is hardly less miraculous; and, if I did not bring to my mind what you are, I should not feel what I am. Do not you partake of the sentiment? Would it be any great marvel or great matter, if the descendant of some ancient family stepped up to the summit of power; even with clean boots on? You must take many steps, and some very indirect ones; all which will only raise you in your own esteem, if you think like a politician.

You are prone to be confident and overweening. Be cautious not to treat parliament as you may fancy it deserves, and not to believe that you have bought votes when you have paid the money for them.

Canning. Why, sir?

Pitt. Because it will be expected of you in addition to speak for a given space of time. The people must be made to believe that their representatives are *persuaded*: and a few plain words are never thought capable of effecting this. Your zeal and anxiety to leave no scruple on the mind of any reasonable man, must be demonstrated by protestations and explanations; and your hatred of those who obscure the glory of England, in their attempts to throw impediments in your way, must burst forth vehemently,

---

[33] William Petty, first Marquis of Lansdowne, better known as Lord Shelburne (1737–1805), became, upon the death of the elder William Pitt, May 11, 1778, the leader of the followers of Chatham in Parliament. He was First Lord of the Treasury from July, 1782, until February, 1783. Charles Watson-Wentworth, second Marquis of Rockingham (1730–1782), was the recognized head of a large party representing the Whig aristocracy. He twice held the office of First Lord of the Treasury: from July, 1765, to August, 1766, and from March, 1782, to July, 1782. William Pitt, first Earl of Chatham (1708–1778), one of England's most brilliant statesmen, served as secretary of state for the southern department during the ministry of the Duke of Devonshire (1756–1757) and during all but the last year of the ministry of the Duke of Newcastle (1757–1762). The "Great Commoner" successfully conducted the Seven Years' War from 1756 until his resignation in 1761. Although the war continued until 1763, Pitt's effective war policy resulted in the extension of England's empire.

and stalk abroad, and now and then put on a suit that smells of gunpowder.[34]

Canning. I have no objection to that.

Pitt. It saves many arguments, and stops more; and in short is the only comprehensible kind of *political economy*.

Whenever the liberty or restriction of the press is in debate, you will do wisely to sport a few touches of wit, or to draw out a few sentences of declamation on blasphemy and blasphemers. I have observed by the countenances of country gentlemen, that there is something horrifying in the sound of the word, something that commands silence.

Canning. I do not well understand the meaning of it.

Pitt. Why should you? Are you to understand the meaning of everything you talk about? If you do, you will not be thought deep. Be fluent, and your audience will be over head and ears in love with you. Never stop short, and you will never be doubted. To be out of breath is the only sign of weakness that is generally understood in a chancellor of the exchequer.[35] The bets, in that case, are instantly against him, and the sounder in wind carries off the king's plate.[36]

Canning. I am aware that to talk solemnly of blasphemy, gives a man great weight at the time, and leaves it with him. But if a dissenter or a lawyer should ask me for a definition of a blasphemer?

Pitt. Wish the lawyer more prudence, and the dissenter more grace. Appeal to our forefathers.

Canning. To which of them? The elder would call the younger so, and the younger the elder.

---

[34] Pitt and Canning both participated in duels. During a debate in Parliament on May 25, 1798, concerning the navy, Pitt accused George Tierney of impeding public business. Even though the accusation was ruled unparliamentary, Pitt refused to withdraw it. As a consequence, the two men met in a duel on Putney Heath two days later. Although each fired twice, neither was injured. George Canning's duel with Viscount Castlereagh, which resulted from a complex political quarrel, also took place on Putney Heath, on September 21, 1809. Both men missed the first time they fired, but on the second shot, Canning's bullet grazed Castlereagh's coat and Castlereagh's bullet wounded Canning in the thigh. Canning was able, however, to walk away from the duelling field.

[35] Pitt was Chancellor of the Exchequer and First Lord of the Treasury in 1806, the time Landor has chosen for this imaginary meeting.

[36] Landor's horse-racing metaphor is appropriate to the point being made in this passage, that both the politician and the horse with the strongest lungs stand the best chance of carrying off the prize. Horse racing was a popular sport in eighteenth-century England, and the stakes were frequently cups and plates.

Pitt. Idiots! but go on.

Canning. In our own days the Lutheran denounces the Unitarian for it: *he* retorts the denunciation. The Catholic comes between, to reconcile and reclaim them. At first he simmers; then he bubbles and boils; at last, inflamed with charity, he damns them both. "To you, adopted heir of the Devil and Perdition," says he to the believer in God's unity, "it would be folly and impiety to listen a moment longer. And you, idle hair-splitter, are ignorant, or pretend to be, that transubstantiation rests upon the same authority as trinitarianism. The one doctrine shocks the senses, the other shocks the reason: both require to be shocked, that faith may be settled."

"Very like your Saint Augustin," interposes the Unitarian: "he should have written this. When Faith enters the school-room, Reason must not whisper: if she might, she would say perhaps, the question is, whether the senses or arithmetic be the most liable to error."

"Sir! sir!" cries again the Catholic, "you have no right to bring any question into the house of God without his leave, nor to push your sharp stick against the bellies of his sheep, making them shove one another and break the fold."

Pitt. Do not run wild in this way, retailing the merriment of your Oxford doctors in their snug parties. Such, I am sure, it must be: for you have not had time to read anything since you left Eton: you think but little, and that little but upon yourself: nor has indeed the wing of your wit either such a strength of bone in it or such a vividness of plumage.

Canning. I don't know that. I must confess, however, I drew a good deal both of my wit and my divinity from our doctors, when they had risen twice or thrice from the bottle, and turned their backs on us from the corner of the room.[37]

Pitt. I hope you will be rather more retentive; and remember at what time you are to lament, as well as at what time you are to joke and banter. On these occasions, lower your voice, assume an air of disdain or pity, bless God that such is the peculiar happiness of our most favoured country, every man may enjoy his opinion in security and peace.

Canning. But some, I shall be reminded, have been forced to enjoy it in solitude and prison.

Pitt. Never push an argument or a remark too far: and take care to have a fellow behind you who knows when to cry *question! question!* As for

---

[37] This is an allusion to the use of chamber pots, which were frequently located in the corner of the room.

reminding, those only whom you forget, will remind you of anything. Others will give you full credit for the wisdom of all your plans, the aptness of all your replies, the vivacity of all your witticisms, and the rectitude of all your intentions.

Canning. Unless it should fatigue you, sir, will you open your views of domestic polity a little wider before me?

Pitt. Willingly. Never choose colleagues for friendship or wisdom. If friends, they will be importunate: if wise, they may be rivals. Choose them for two other things quite different; for tractability and connections. A few men of business, quite enough for you, may be picked up anywhere on the road-side. Be particular in selecting for all places and employments the handsomest young men, and those who have the handsomest wives, mothers, and sisters. Every one of these brings a large party with him; and it rarely happens that any such is formidable for mental prowess. The man who can bring you three votes, is preferable to him who can bring you thrice your own quantity of wisdom. For, although in private life we may profit much by the acquisition of so much more of it than we had ourselves, yet in public we know not what to do with it. Often it stands in our way; often it hides us; sometimes we are oppressed by it. Oppose in all elections the man, whatever may be his party or principles, who is superior to yourself in attainments, particularly in ratiocination and eloquence. Bring forward, when places are found for all the men of rank who present themselves, those who believe they resemble you; young declaimers, young poets, young critics, young satirists, young journalists, young magazine-men, and young lampooners and libellers: that is, those among them who have never been more than ducked and cudgelled. Every soul of them will hope to succeed you by adoption.

My father made this remark,[38] in his florid way. When an insect dips into the surface of a stream, it forms a circle round it, which catches a quick radiance from the sun or moon, while the stiller water on every side flows without any; in like manner a small politician may attract the notice of the king or people, by putting into motion the pliant element about him; while quieter men pass utterly away, leaving not even this weak impression, this momentary sparkle. On which principle Dundas used to say, "Keep shoving, keep shoving!" I do not know whether the injunction was taken by all his acquaintance in the manner and in the direction he intended.

---

[38] Pitt's father never made it: but it was necessary to attribute it to some other person than Pitt himself. [*Landor's note.*]

A great deal has been spoken, in the House and out of the House, on parliamentary reform.

Canning. I have repeatedly said that without it there is no salvation for the country: this is embarrassing.

Pitt. Not at all: oppose it: say you have changed your mind: let that serve for your reason; and do not stumble upon worse by running against an adversary. You will find the country going on just as it has gone on.

Canning. Bad enough; God knows!

Pitt. But only for the country. People will see that the fields and the cattle, the streets and the inhabitants, look as usual. The houses stand, the chimneys smoke, the pavements hold together: this will make them wonder at your genius in keeping them up, after all the prophecies they have heard about their going down. Men draw their ideas from sight and hearing. They do not know that the ruin of a nation is in its probity, its confidence, its comforts. While they see every day the magnificent equipages of contractors and brokers, read of sumptuous dinners given by cabinet-ministers and army agents, and are invited to golden speculations in the East and in the West, they fancy there is an abundance of prosperity and wealth; whereas, in fact, it is in these very places that wealth and prosperity are shut up, accumulated, and devoured.

I deferred from session to session a reform in parliament; because, having sworn to promote it by all the means in my power, I did not wish to seem perjured to the people.[39] In the affair of Maidstone nobody could

[39] Pitt was a firm advocate of parliamentary reform during the first part of his political career: On May 7, 1782, he spoke to the House about the close-borough system of representation (see n. 42 below) and made a motion (defeated by only twenty votes) that a committee be created to inquire into the matter; on May 17, 1782, he spoke for a bill, which was defeated, that would shorten the duration of parliaments; on June 19, 1782, he spoke in favor of a bill designed to prevent bribery at elections (the bill was rendered ineffectual in committee); on May 7, 1783, he proposed a motion, which failed, that would add one hundred country members and several members for metropolitan districts to the House, and prevent corrupt voting in the boroughs; and on April 18, 1785, he made a second unsuccessful attempt to enact legislation for parliamentary reform.

After the French Revolution Pitt viewed parliamentary reform, as advocated by the radicals, as a threat to the English political system. During a discussion in the House upon the proposed Union of England and Ireland, he said (April 21, 1800): "In stating this, Sir, I have not forgotten what I have myself formerly said, and sincerely felt, upon this subject; but I know that all opinions must necessarily be subservient to times and circumstances; and that man who talks of his consistency, merely because he holds the same opinion for ten or fifteen years, when the circumstances under which that opinion was originally formed are totally changed, is a slave to the most idle vanity.

prove me so: I only swore I had forgotten what nobody but myself could swear that I remembered.⁴⁰ It was evident to the whole world that I was a perjured man; it was equally that I was a powerful one: and the same nation which would have sent another to the pillory, sent me to the Privy Council.⁴¹ It is inconceivable to you what pleasure I felt in committing it, when I reflected on the difference it proved between me and people in general. But beware of fancying you resemble me. My father's crutch was my sceptre, and it will fall into the grave with me. There is no bequeathing or devising this part of the inheritance. I improved it not a little. My adherents at Maidstone thought my father would have hesitated to forget so bravely. Appearances were against me. The main object of my early life, what I had repeated every day, what brought me into credit and into power, was unlikely to escape my memory in an instant; and in the midst

---

Seeing all that I have seen since the period to which I allude; considering how little chance there is of that species of Reform to which alone I looked, and which is as different from the modern schemes of Reform, as the latter are from the constitution; seeing that where the greatest changes have taken place the most dreadful consequences have ensued, and which have not been confined to that country where the change took place, but have spread their malignant influence in every quarter of the globe, and shaken the fabric of every government; seeing that in this general shock the Constitution of Great Britain has alone remained pure and untouched in its vital principles; when I see that it has resisted all the efforts of Jacobinism, sheltering itself under the pretence of a love of liberty; when I see that it has supported itself against the open attacks of its enemies, and against the more dangerous reforms of its professed friends; that it has defeated the unwearied machinations of France, and the no less persevering efforts of Jacobins in England; and that, during the whole of the contest, it has uniformly maintained the confidence of the people of England; I say, Sir, when I consider all these circumstances, I should be ashamed of myself if any former opinions of mine could now induce me to think that the form of representation which, in such times as the present, has been found amply sufficient for the purpose of protecting the interests, and securing the happiness, of the people, should be idly and wantonly disturbed, from any love of experiment, or any predilection for theory. Upon this subject, Sir, I think it right to state the inmost thoughts of my mind; I think it right to declare my most decided opinion, that, even if the times were proper for experiments, any, even the slightest, change in such a constitution must be considered as an evil" (quoted in Gifford, *William Pitt*, VI, 254–256).

⁴⁰ Landor has apparently confused the trial of Arthur O'Connor with the trial of John Horne Tooke. See n. 27 above. Arthur O'Connor (1763–1852), an Irish rebel and member of the United Irishmen, was arrested while on a trip to England and charged with high treason. His trial was held at Maidstone, Kent, in May, 1798. Many notable Whig politicians, including Fox, Sheridan, Erskine, and the Duke of Norfolk, appeared at the trial and spoke in O'Connor's defense.

⁴¹ Pitt became a member of the Privy Council when he was first appointed Chancellor of the Exchequer, at the age of twenty-three.

of those who at that time had surrounded me, applauded me, and followed me. Yet bishops and chancellors will drink to me after my death, as the most honest man that ever lived.

Canning. What! even when they can get nothing and want nothing from you?

Pitt. They want from me more than you are aware of: they want my example to stand upon. They will take their aim against our country from behind my statue.

Canning. She has fleshier parts about her than the heel, and their old snags will stick tight in them till they rattle in the coffin.

Pitt. Do not disturb them. You may give over your dalliance with reform whenever you are tired of it. You did not begin as a states-*man* but as a states-*boy*: you were under me: and you can not act more wisely than by telling folks that I had seen my error in the latter part of my life.

Canning. Perhaps they will not believe me.

Pitt. Likely enough! but courtesy and interest will require their acquiescence, and they will act as if they did. The noisiest of the opposition are the lawyers; partly from rudeness, partly from rapacity. Lay it down as a rule for your conduct, that the most honest one in parliament is as indifferent about his party as about his brief: whoever offers him his fee has him. Of these there is hardly an individual who had any more of a qualification than you or I had: yet they assume it, as well as we. Is there in this no fallacy, no fraud? Some of them were so wretchedly poor, that a borrowed watch-key hung from a broken shoe-string at their tattered fob; and when they could obtain on credit a yard of damaged muslin for their noses, they begged a pinch of snuff at the next box they saw open, and sneezed that they might reasonably display their acquisition.

Canning. I wonder that these people should cry out so loudly for a fairer representation.

Pitt. Some have really the vanity to believe that they would be chosen, and might choose their colleagues; others follow orders; the greater part wish no such thing; and, if they thought it likely to succeed, would never call for it. The fact is this: the most honest and independent members of parliament are elected by the rotten boroughs.[42] They pay down their own

---

[42] Before the Reform Act of 1832, the franchise within the English borough varied, and frequently it was possible for a wealthy individual or a privileged corporation to send a member to Parliament who represented only a particular interest rather than the population as a whole. These boroughs came to be called "rotten boroughs," a term derived from Chatham's description of borough representation as the "rotten part of the constitution."

money, and give their own votes: they are not subservient to the aristocracy nor to the treasury. The same can not be said on any other description of members. I never ventured to make such a remark in parliament. The people would be alarmed and struck with horror, if you clearly showed that the very best part of their representation is founded on nothing sounder than on rank corruption. Perhaps I am imprudent in suggesting the fact to you, knowing your *diabetes* of mind,[43] and having found that your tongue is as easily set in motion, and as unconsciously, as the head of a mandarin on the chimney-piece at an inn.

Cease to be speculative.

Canning. We cease to be speculative when we touch the object.

Pitt. It is then unnecessary to remind you that you want only a numerical majority. Talents count for talents; respectability for respectability. The veriest fag that Dundas ever breeched for the South gives as efficient a vote as a Romilly or a Newport.[44]

In the beginning of my career as minister, I sometimes wished that I could have become so and have been consistent. I have since found that

---

[43] The Greek word *diabetes* literally means "a passer through, a siphon." Landor finds this word appropriate in describing Canning's mentality and his propensity to enter into petulant discussions in Parliament. See n. 26 above.

[44] In English public school phraseology, a "fag" is a junior who performs certain services for a senior. Sir Samuel Romilly (1757–1818), law reformer and politician, became solicitor general in February, 1806, to the ministry popularly known as "All the Talents." A member of the committee for the impeachment of Lord Melville (see n. 28 above), Sir Samuel summed up the evidence at the trial in Westminster Hall in a speech of great power and eloquence. Sir John Newport (1756–1843), a politician, was appointed Chancellor of the Irish Exchequer in February, 1806, upon the formation of the ministry of "All the Talents."

Both Romilly and Newport receive high praise from Landor. According to John Forster: "He never changed or faltered in this love and admiration for Romilly; and one of his letters to me written after his 80th year expressed the delight with which he had again been reading the memoir of him by his sons. 'Of all the public men in England at any time he was the honestest. He may be compared with Phocion'" (Forster, II, 330). See also the Imaginary Conversations "Romilly and Perceval" and "Romilly and Wilberforce."

Landor comments as follows upon Newport: "There is a man in whose whole political life, and, I have heard also, in whose private, no opponent has been able, however invidious and acute, to detect an unwise, or dishonourable, or disingenuous action. Would to God I could leave any doubt or uncertainty of the person to whom I allude, and that the description were as applicable to any other as to Sir John Newport.

"This is the man who is destined, if any is, to appease the discontents of Ireland; and to soften the fanaticism of a church, which, in the paroxysm of its intemperance, has assailed the peaceable tenets of another, and staggered in every direction from its own" (Landor, *Commentary*, pp. 207–208).

inconsistency is taken for a proof of greatness in a politician. "He knows how to manage men; he sees what the times require: his great mind bends majestically to the impulse of the world."[45] These things are said, or will be. Certain it is, when a robe is blown out by the wind, showing now the outer side, now the inner, then one colour, then another, it seems the more capacious, and the richer.

If at any time you are induced by policy, or impelled by nature, to commit an action more ungenerous or more dishonest than usual; if at anytime you shall have brought the country into worse disgrace or under more imminent danger; talk and look bravely: swear, threaten, bluster: be witty, be pious: sneer, scoff: look infirm, look gouty: appeal to immortal God that you desire to remain in office so long only as you can be beneficial to your king and country: that however, at such a time as the present, you should be reluctant to leave the most flourishing of nations a prey to the wild passions of insatiate demagogues: and that nothing but the commands of your venerable sovran, and the unequivocal voice of the people that recommended you to his notice, shall ever make you desert the station to which the hand of Providence conducted you. They have keen eyes who can see through all these words: I have never found any such, and have tried thousands. The man who possesses them may read Swedenborg and Kant while he is being tossed in a blanket.[46]

Above all things keep your friends and dependents in good humour and good condition. If they lose flesh, you lose people's confidence. My cook, two summers ago, led me to this reflection at Walmer.[47] Finding him in the court-yard, and observing that, however round and rosy, he looked melancholy, and struck his hips with his fist very frequently as he walked along, I called to him, and when he turned round, inquired of him what had happened to discompose him. He answered that Sam Spack the butcher had failed.

"Well, what then?" said I, "unless you mean that his creditors may come upon me for the last two years' bill." He shook his head, and told me

[45] See n. 39 above.

[46] Emanuel Swedenborg (1688–1722), Swedish scientist, theologian, and philosopher, and Immanuel Kant (1724–1804), German philosopher, wrote copious and abstruse treatises which could hardly be read, let alone understood, by one being "tossed in a blanket." Landor's humorous hyperbole is in keeping with his decided dislike of politicians and metaphysicians who use language as a cover either for shady practices or for a paucity of thought.

[47] In August, 1792, King George III appointed Pitt Lord Warden of the Cinque Ports, a lifelong position carrying a yearly salary of £3,000. Walmer Castle, originally a blockhouse built by King Henry VIII for coastal defense, was the official residence of the lords warden of the Cinque Ports and is located in Kent.

that he had lent Sam Spack all he was worth, a good five hundred pounds. "The greater fool you!" replied I. "Why, sir!" said he, opening his hand to show the clearness of his demonstration, "who would not have lent him anything? when he swore and ate like the devil, and drank as if he was in hell, and his dog was fatter than the best calf in Kent."

It occurs to me that I owe this unfortunate cook several years' wages. Write down his name, William Ruffhead. You must do something to help him: a diversion on the coast of France would be sufficient: order one for him: in six months he may fairly pocket his quiet twenty thousands, and have his paltry three guineas a day for life. Write above the name, "deputy commissary." Ruffhead is so honest a creature, he will only be a dogfish in a shoal of sharks.

Never consent to any reduction in the national expenditure. Consider what is voted by parliament for public services as your own property.[48] The largest estate in England would go but a little way in procuring you partisans and adherents: these loosely counted millions purchase them. I have smiled when people in the simplicity of their hearts applauded me for neglecting the aggrandisement of my fortune. Every rood of land in the British dominions has a mine beneath it, out of which, by a vote of parliament, I oblige the proprietor to extract as much as I want, as often as I will. From every tobacco-pipe in England a dependent of mine takes a whiff; from every salt-vase a spoonful. I have given more to my family than is possessed by those of Tamerlane and Aurungzebe;[49] and I distribute to the amount of fifty millions a-year in the manner I deem convenient. What is any man's private purse other than that into which he can put his hand at his option? Neither my pocket nor my house,

---

[48] According to Richard Monckton Milnes (Lord Houghton): "When questioned as to Mr. Pitt's oratory, he [Landor] would say, 'It was a wonderful thing to hear, but I have seen others more wonderful—a fire-eater, and a man who eat live rats.' Of his neglect of wealth, 'Few people have sixty millions a year to spend: he spent on himself just what he chose, and gave away what he chose.' Pitt's negotiations with the Irish for Emancipation he assumed to be a diabolical treachery,—the minister being assured of the Sovereign's determination not to cede the point in question. The French war he described as 'a plot to make England a waste, to drive the gentry by war-taxes to taverns, and hells, and clubs, and transfer their wealth and position to the mercantile interest'" (Richard Monckton Milnes, Lord Houghton, *Monographs, Personal and Social* [2d ed.; London, 1873], pp. 86-87).

[49] Timur i Leng (the lame Timūr), commonly known as Tamerlane (1336–1405), a renowned Oriental conqueror, amassed a huge fortune as a result of his extensive conquests. Aurangzeb (1618–1707), one of the great Mogul emperors of Hindustan, both enriched and enlarged his empire during a reign of forty-nine years.

neither the bank nor the treasury, neither London nor Westminster, neither England nor Europe, are capacious enough for mine: it swings between the Indies, and sweeps the whole ocean.

Canning. I am aware of it. You spend only what you have time and opportunity for spending. No man gives better dinners: few better wine ..

Pitt. Canning! Canning! Canning! always blundering into some coarse compliment!

Reminding me of wine, you remind me of my death, and the cause of it.[50] To spite the French and Bonaparte, I would not drink claret: Madeira was too heating: hock was too light and acid for me.

Canning. Seltzer water takes off this effect; the Dean of Christchurch tells me.[51]

Pitt. It might have made my speeches windier than was expedient; and I declined to bring into action a steam-engine of such power, with Mr. Speaker in front and the treasury-bench in rear of me. The detestable beverage of Oporto[52] is now burning my entrails.

Canning. Beverage fit for the condemned.

Pitt. If condemned for poisoning.

As you must return to London in the morning, and as I may not be disposed or able to talk much at another time, what remains to be said I will say now.

Never be persuaded to compose a mixed administration of whigs and tories:[53] for, as you can not please them equally, each will plot eternally to supplant you by some leader of its party.

Employ men of less knowledge and perspicacity than yourself, if you can find them. Do not let any stand too close or too much above; because in both positions they may look down into your shallows and see the weeds at the bottom. Authors may be engaged by you; but never pamper

---

[50] See n. 14.

[51] Cyril Jackson (1746–1819) was dean of Christ Church, Oxford, from 1783 until his resignation in 1809. George Canning, Sir Robert Peel, and Charles Wynn were among the many illustrious men who attended Christ Church during Jackson's administration.

[52] Oporto, a city of Portugal, is known chiefly for its famous port wine. The treaty of Methuen (1703), which admitted Portuguese wines into England on easier terms than French or German wines, is largely responsible for their great popularity in England during the eighteenth century.

[53] In April, 1783, a mixed ministry, composed of Whigs, led by Fox, and Tories, led by Lord North, was officially recognized (although privately lamented) by George III. This ministry came to be known as the "Coalition." It lasted only until the following December.

them; keep them in wind and tractability by hard work. Many of them are trusty while they are needy: enrich them only with promised lands, enjoying the most extensive prospect and most favourable exposure. For my part, I little respect any living author. The only one, ancient or modern, I ever read with attention, is Bolingbroke, who was recommended to me for a model.[54] His principles, his heart, his style, have formed mine exclusively:[55] everything sits easy upon him: mostly I like

[54] "How little advantage has been derived to Mr. Pitt and Mr. Fox from the experience of past ages! Mr. Pitt, indeed, had as profound a contempt for literature and literary men as ever was avowed or felt by Attila and Totila; but Mr. Fox was a man of extensive and not superficial reading, and, on many occasions, of serious and of deep reflections" (Landor, *Commentary*, p. 99).

The Reverend George Pretyman (who took the name Tomline in June, 1803, when willed a large estate by Marmaduke Tomline) was one of Pitt's tutors at Cambridge: "It was my general rule to read with Mr. Pitt alternately, classics and mathematics; occasionally intermixing other branches of learning. He proceeded with a rapidity which can scarcely be conceived; and his memory was retentive in a degree of which I have known but few examples, although it had not been strengthened by the practice of repetition, so properly in use at public schools, but often omitted in private education. A tutor is generally satisfied, if he can give his pupil some knowledge of an author, by selecting for his perusal certain parts of his works; but there was scarcely a Latin or a Greek classical writer of eminence, the whole of whose works Mr. Pitt and I did not read together. He was a nice observer of their different styles, and alive to all their various and characteristic excellencies. The quickness of his comprehension did not prevent close and minute application. When alone, he dwelt for hours upon striking passages of an orator or historian, in noticing their turn of expression, in marking their manner of arranging a narrative, or explaining the avowed or secret motives of action. A few pages sometimes occupied a whole morning.

. . . .

"Amidst these severer studies [mathematics, natural philosophy, civil law], the lighter species of literature were by no means omitted; and I ought in particular to mention his intimate acquaintance with the historical and political writers of his own country [footnote: 'Middleton's Life of Cicero, and the political and historical works of lord Bolingbroke, were favorite books with Mr. Pitt in point of style; as were also the works of Hume and Robertson. He was not an admirer of Johnson's style, and still less of Gibbon's. He read Barrow's Sermons, at the desire of lord Chatham, who thought them admirably calculated to furnish the copia verborum.'], and his elegant taste for the beauties of the English poets" (George Tomline, *Memoirs of the Life of the Right Honorable William Pitt* [2d ed.; 3 vols.; London, 1821], I, 8–13).

[55] Englishmen who believed that George III was intent upon destroying parliamentary government during the first twenty years of his reign also often accepted the popular misconception that Viscount Bolingbroke's *The Idea of a Patriot King* (1749) was primarily responsible for the actions of the King and his ministers. Although essentially a Whig tract of the seventeenth century, Bolingbroke's *Patriot King*, when read as an extreme Tory work, was usually viewed in much the same light as was Machiavelli's *The Prince*. See Henry St. John, Viscount Bolingbroke, *The Idea of a*

him because he supersedes inquiry: the thing best to do and to inculcate. We should have been exterminated long ago, if the House of Commons had not thought so, and had not voted us a Bill of Indemnity:[56] which I was certain I could obtain as often as I should find it necessary, be the occasion what it might. Neither free governments nor arbitrary have such security: ours is constituted for evasion. I hope nobody may ever call me the *Pilot of the Escape-boat*. In Turkey I should have been strangled; in Algiers I should have been impaled; in America I should have mounted the gallows in the market-place; in Sweden I should have been pistoled at a public dinner or court-ball: in England I am extolled above my father.

Ah Canning! how delighted, how exultant was I, when I first heard this acclamation! When I last heard it, how sorrowful! how depressed! He was always thwarted, and always succeeded: I was always seconded, and always failed. He left the country flourishing; I leave it impoverished, exhausted, ruined. He left many able statesmen; I leave *you*.

Excuse me: dying men are destined to feel and privileged to say unpleasant things.

Good night! I retire to rest.

Patriot King, ed. Sydney W. Jackman (Indianapolis: Bobbs-Merrill Company, Inc., 1965), pp. vii–xxiii.

[56] "On the 14th of June [1805], Mr. Whitbread brought forward a subject of complaint against Mr. Pitt, for having sanctioned the advance of £40,000, in the autumn of 1796, by Lord Melville, to the house of Boyd and Benfield, for the purpose of enabling them to make good their instalments on the loan for which they had contracted, and which had fallen so as to bear a discount of six percent. The resolutions stated, that sufficient security was given for the payment of the money so advanced; and that it was actually repaid; and it was not pretended that any public loss or injury whatever had been sustained by the transaction. But it was censured as irregular, and deprecated as a precedent. Mr. Pitt justified himself to the perfect satisfaction of the House, and proved that he had no other motive for his conduct, on the occasion, than a wish to support public credit. The resolutions of Mr. Whitbread were accordingly rejected without a division, and, on the motion of Mr. Lascelles, it was 'resolved, that the measure of advancing forty thousand pounds to Messrs. Boyd and Co. upon unquestionable securities, which have been regularly discharged, was adopted for the purpose of averting consequences which might have proved highly injurious to the financial and commercial interests of the country; and, although not conformable to law, appeared at the time to be called for by the peculiar exigencies of public affairs!' A bill of indemnity, for this transaction, was afterwards brought in by Mr. Lascelles, and passed into a law" (Gifford, *William Pitt*, VI, 763–765).

JOHN OF GAUNT AND
JOANNA OF KENT

In this Imaginary Conversation, Landor selects a historically dramatic situation as background for revealing the characters of his two dramatis personae, John of Gaunt (1340–1399), Duke of Lancaster, and Joanna of Kent (1328–1385). In 1377, King Edward III was near death, and many Englishmen believed the haughty and powerful Gaunt covetous of the crown, which was to succeed to his ten-year-old nephew, Richard, son of Edward the Black Prince (1330–1376) and Joanna of Kent. This belief appeared to be justified during the tumultuous beginning of the ecclesiastical trial of John Wycliffe (ca. 1330–1384), a zealous religious reformer who preached against the worldliness of the clergy. Cited to appear before the Bishops for his outspoken criticism, Wycliffe was escorted to his trial at St. Paul's Cathedral on February 19, 1377, by such powerful supporters as Gaunt and Lord Henry Percy. Before the trial could commence, however, an argument ensued between the two opposing factions during which Gaunt spoke some harsh words to William Courtenay, Bishop of London. This public reproach incited the Londoners, many of whom had sided with Wycliffe, to riot against Gaunt. Raphael Holinshed, Landor's source for this Conversation, vividly describes the event:

> The same day that Wiclife was conuented thus at London, before the bishops and other lords [*in the Lady-Chapel of St. Paul's*], thorough a word spoken in reproch by the duke of Lancaster vnto the bishop of London, streightwaies the Londoners getting them to armour [*the citizens did not take up arms until the next day*], meant to haue slaine the duke, & if the bishop had not staid them, they had suerlie set fire on the dukes house at the Sauoie : and with much adoo might the bishop quiet them. Among other reprochfull parts which in despite of the duke they committed, they caused his armes in the publike stréet to be reuersed as if he had béene a traitor, or some notorious offender. The duke and the lord Henrie Percie, whom the citizens sought in his owne house to haue slaine him, if he had béen found, hearing of this riotous stur and rebellious commotion, forsooke their dinner [*they were dining with Sir John d'Ypres, a wealthy London merchant, at Ypres Inn*] and fled to Kenington, where the lord Richard, sonne to the prince [*Edward the Black Prince*], togither with his mother [*Princess Joanna*] then remained, exhibiting before their presence, a grieuous complaint of the opprobrious iniuries doone vnto them, by the wilfull outrage of the Londoners.[1]

[1] *Holinshed's Chronicles of England, Scotland, and Ireland* (6 vols.; London, 1807–1808), II, 705–706. Hereafter referred to as *Holinshed's Chronicles*.

Although Landor follows Holinshed in presenting John of Gaunt as a proud, brave, and impetuous hero, Joanna of Kent is the author's creation. Her rescue of Gaunt, the declared enemy of her son Richard, from a hostile London mob enables Landor to present a maternal yet noble and heroic woman whose likeness is not found in the historical record. The idealized and sympathetic portrait of Joanna is characteristic of Landor's treatment of his heroines and reflects his especially dignified and courteous attitude toward women. This personal trait impressed many of his contemporaries, among them Lady Blessington, who praised his "more than ordinary politeness toward women."[2]

Joanna. How is this, my cousin,[3] that you are besieged in your own house, by the citizens of London? I thought you were their idol.[4]

Gaunt. If their idol, madam, I am one which they may tread on as they list when down; but which, by my soul and knighthood! the ten best battle-axes among them shall find it hard work to unshrine.

Pardon me . . I have no right perhaps to take or touch this hand . . yet, my sister, bricks and stones and arrows are not presents fit for you: let me conduct you some paces hence.

Joanna. I will speak to those below in the street: quit my hand: they shall obey me.

Gaunt. If you intend to order my death, madam, your guards who have

---

[2] The Countess of Blessington, *The Idler in Italy* (3 vols.; London, 1839), II, 507.

[3] Joanna, called the fair maid of Kent, was cousin of the Black Prince, whom she married [October 10, 1361]. John of Gaunt was suspected of aiming at the crown in the beginning of Richard's minority, which, increasing the hatred of the people against him for favouring the sect of Wicliffe, excited them to demolish his house and to demand his impeachment. [*Landor's note.*]

Sir Sydney Armitage-Smith, John of Gaunt's biographer, rejects the popular view that Gaunt had designs upon the English throne during Richard's minority (see *John of Gaunt* [Westminster: Archibald Constable & Co. Ltd., 1904], pp. 121–159, 184–195). The Savoy, Gaunt's stately London palace, was destroyed during the Peasants' Rising in 1381 (see *Holinshed's Chronicles*, II, 738). There is no mention of "impeachment proceedings" against Gaunt in Holinshed's account.

[4] John of Gaunt, unlike his elder brother Edward the Black Prince, never captured the imagination of the English populace. His military victories were few, and Englishmen neither forgot nor forgave his disastrous invasion of France in 1373 at the head of a well-equipped army of about fifteen thousand men of whom nearly seven thousand perished from exposure and starvation. His intervention in the affairs of Parliament (1376–1377) and his claim to the throne of Castile and Leon (see n. 5 below) led many to believe that Gaunt coveted the English crown.

entered my court, and whose spurs and halberts I hear upon the staircase, may overpower my domestics; and, seeing no such escape as becomes my dignity, I submit to you. Behold my sword at your feet! Some formalities, I trust, will be used in the proceedings against me. Entitle me, in my attainder, not John of Gaunt, not Duke of Lancaster, not King of Castile;[5] nor commemorate my father,[6] the most glorious of princes, the vanquisher and pardoner of the most powerful; nor style me, what those who loved or who flattered me did when I was happier, cousin to the Fair Maid of Kent. Joanna! those days are over! But no enemy, no law, no eternity can take away from me, or move further off, my affinity in blood to the conqueror in the field of Cressy, of Poictiers, and Najora.[7] Edward was my brother when he was but your cousin; and the edge of my shield has clinked on his in many a battle. Yes, we were ever near, if not in worth, in danger.

Joanna. Attainder! God avert it! Duke of Lancaster, what dark thought ... Alas! that the Regency should have known it![8] I came hither, sir, for no such purpose as to ensnare or incriminate or alarm you.

These weeds might surely have protected me from the fresh tears you have drawn forth.

Gaunt. Sister, be comforted! this visor too has felt them.

Joanna. O my Edward! my own so lately![9] Thy memory .. thy beloved image .. which never hath abandoned me .. makes me bold; I dare not say generous; for in saying it I should cease to be so .. and who could be called generous by the side of thee! I will rescue from perdition the enemy of my son.

[5] John of Gaunt, born at Ghent (later corrupted into "Gaunt"), was created Earl of Richmond on September 29, 1342, and on November 13, 1362, was advanced to the rank of Duke of Lancaster. Following his marriage, in September, 1371, to Constance, the eldest daughter of the deceased King Pedro the Cruel (1334–1369), Gaunt conferred upon himself the title King of Castile and Leon.

[6] Edward III (1312–1377), king of England, 1327–1377, died June 21, nearly four months *after* the London riot. See *Holinshed's Chronicles*, II, 706.

[7] Edward III commanded the English army at the battle of Crécy (August 26, 1346), where his son Edward, afterwards called the Black Prince, displayed great courage and valor. The Black Prince himself led the victorious English armies at Poictiers (September 19, 1356) and Nájera (April 3, 1367). In the latter victory, Gaunt fought beside his elder brother. See *Holinshed's Chronicles*, II, 683–684.

[8] On July 17, 1377, the day after Richard's coronation, the Great Council of magnates selected a council of twelve whose task was to advise the leaders of state. Since actual rule was supposed to reside in the king, this council of twelve cannot, strictly speaking, be considered a Council of Regency.

[9] Edward the Black Prince died June 8, 1376.

Cousin, you loved your brother: love then what was dearer to him than his life: protect what he, valiant as you have seen him, can not! The father, who foiled so many, hath left no enemies: the innocent child, who can injure no one, finds them!

Why have you unlaced and laid aside your visor? Do not expose your body to those missiles. Hold your shield before yourself, and step aside. I need it not. I am resolved ..

Gaunt. On what, my cousin? Speak, and by the Lord! it shall be done. This breast is your shield; this arm is mine.

Joanna. Heavens! who could have hurled those masses of stone from below! they stunned me. Did they descend all of them together? or did they split into fragments on hitting the pavement?

Gaunt. Truly I was not looking that way: they came, I must believe, while you were speaking.

Joanna. Aside! aside! further back! disregard *me!* Look! that last arrow sticks half its head deep in the wainscot. It shook so violently, I did not see the feather at first.

No, no, Lancaster! I will not permit it. Take your shield up again; and keep it all before you. Now step aside .. I am resolved to prove whether the people will hear me.

Gaunt. Then, madam, by your leave ...

Joanna. Hold! forbear! Come hither! hither .. not forward.

Gaunt. Villains! take back to your kitchens those spits and skewers that you forsooth would fain call swords and arrows; and keep your bricks and stones for your graves!

Joanna. Imprudent man! who can save you? I shall be frightened: I must speak at once.

O good kind people! ye who so greatly loved me, when I am sure I had done nothing to deserve it, have I (unhappy me!) no merit with you now, when I would assuage your anger, protect your fair fame, and send you home contented with yourselves and me! Who is he, worthy citizens, whom ye would drag to slaughter?

True indeed he did revile some one; neither I nor you can say whom; some feaster and rioter, it seems, who had little right (he thought) to carry sword or bow, and who, to show it, hath slunk away. And then another raised his anger; he was indignant that, under his roof, a woman should be exposed to stoning. Which of you would not be as choleric in a like affront? In the house of which among you, should I not be protected as resolutely?

No, no: I never can believe those angry cries. Let none ever tell me again he is the enemy of my son, of his king, your darling child Richard. Are your fears more lively than a poor weak female's? than a mother's? yours, whom he hath so often led to victory, and praised to his father, naming each . . He, John of Gaunt, the defender of the helpless, the comforter of the desolate, the rallying signal of the desperately brave!

Retire, Duke of Lancaster! This is no time . .

Gaunt. Madam, I obey: but not through terror of that puddle at the house-door, which my handful of dust would dry up. Deign to command me!

Joanna. In the name of my son then, retire!

Gaunt. Angelic goodness! I must fairly win it.

Joanna. I think I know his voice that crieth out, "Who will answer for him?" An honest and loyal man's, one who would counsel and save me in any difficulty and danger. With what pleasure and satisfaction, with what perfect joy and confidence, do I answer our right-trusty and well-judging friend!

"Let Lancaster bring his sureties," say you, "and we separate." A moment yet before we separate; if I might delay you so long, to receive your sanction of those sureties; for in such grave matters it would ill become us to be over-hasty. I could bring fifty, I could bring a hundred, not from among soldiers, not from among courtiers, but selected from yourselves, were it equitable and fair to show such partialities, or decorous in the parent and guardian of a king to offer any other than herself.

Raised by the hand of the Almighty from amidst you,[10] but still one of you, if the mother of a family is a part of it, here I stand, surety for John of Gaunt, Duke of Lancaster, for his loyalty and allegiance.

Gaunt (*running toward Joanna*). Are the rioters then bursting into the chamber through the windows?

Joanna. The windows and doors of this solid edifice rattled and shook at the people's acclamation. My word is given for you: this was theirs in return. Lancaster! what a voice have the people when they speak out! It shakes me with astonishment, almost with consternation, while it establishes the throne: what must it be when it is lifted up in vengeance!

Gaunt. Wind; vapour . .

Joanna. . . Which none can wield nor hold. Need I say this to my cousin of Lancaster?

---

[10] Joanna was the daughter of Edmund of Woodstock (1301–1329), Earl of Kent and sixth son of Edward I and Margaret Wake (d. 1349), Countess of Kent, whose father, John Wake (d. 1300), served in Parliament as a baron from 1295 to 1299.

Gaunt. Rather say, madam, that there is always one star above which can tranquillise and control them.

Joanna. Go, cousin! another time more sincerity!

Gaunt. You have this day saved my life from the people: for I now see my danger better, when it is no longer close before me. My Christ! if ever I forget ..

Joanna. Swear not: every man in England hath sworn what you would swear. But if you abandon my Richard, my brave and beautiful child,[11] may .. Oh! I could never curse, nor wish an evil: but, if you desert him in the hour of need, you will think of those who have not deserted you, and your own great heart will lie heavy on you, Lancaster!

Am I graver than I ought to be, that you look dejected? Come then, gentle cousin, lead me to my horse, and accompany me home. Richard will embrace us tenderly. Every one is dear to every other upon rising out fresh from peril: affectionately then will he look, sweet boy, upon his mother and his uncle! Never mind how many questions he may ask you, nor how strange ones. His only displeasure, if he has any, will be, that he stood not against the rioters; or among them.[12]

Gaunt. Older than he have been as fond of mischief, and as fickle in the choice of a party.[13]

I shall tell him that, coming to blows, the assailant is often in the right; that the assailed is always.

---

[11] "He [Richard II] was séemelie of shape and fauor, & of nature good inough, if the wickednesse & naughtie demeanor of such as were about him had not altered it" (*Holinshed's Chronicles*, II, 868).

[12] Richard II showed great courage and presence of mind when confronted with angry mobs during the Peasants' Rising of 1381. On June 13, the young King attempted to reason with the rebels, led by Wat Tyler, while standing in his barge on the river Thames outside London. See *Holinshed's Chronicles*, II, 737. On the following day he found himself facing a hostile London mob whose leader, Tyler, had just been struck down by some of the King's men: "When the commons beheld this, they cried out, 'Our capteine is traitorouslie slaine, let vs stand togither and die with him: let vs shoot and reuenge his death manfullie:' and so bending their bowes, made them readie to shoot. The king shewing both hardinesse and wisdome at that instant, more than his age required, set his spurs to his horsse, and rode to them, saieng: 'What is the matter my men, what meane you? Will you shoot at your king? Be not troubled nor offended at the death of a traitor and ribald; I will be your king, capteine and leader, follow me into the fields, and you shall haue all things that you can desire.' . . . They mooued with these the kings words, followed him and the knights that were with him, into the open fields, not yet resolued whether they should set vpon the king and slea him, or else be quiet, and returne home with the kings charter" (*Holinshed's Chronicles*, II, 741).

[13] The court intrigues to which Gaunt alludes in these lines occurred after Richard's coronation on July 16, 1377.

THE LADY LISLE
AND ELIZABETH GAUNT

Following the ascension of James II to the throne of England in 1685, the Duke of Monmouth (James Scott, 1649–1685), pretender to the throne, incited a rebellion against the King. The Pretender was defeated on July 6, 1685, at the battle of Sedgemoor and was executed soon after. This initiated a series of executions that were ordered by James II in retaliation against the participants in the rebellion and their supporters. Among those executed were the Lady Lisle (ca. 1614–1685) and Elizabeth Gaunt (d. 1685). Landor's setting for his Imaginary Conversation between these two Englishwomen is a prison where both are awaiting death after having been unjustly convicted of treason for aiding outlawed followers of the Pretender. Although both Lady Lisle and Elizabeth Gaunt were executed in 1685, historically the meeting could not have occurred under the circumstances in which Landor places the two women, for Lady Lisle was executed more than a month and a half before Elizabeth Gaunt was convicted. Lady Lisle was arrested on July 26, tried at Winchester on August 27, and sentenced to death on August 28. On September 2, 1685, she was beheaded in the market place at Winchester. Elizabeth Gaunt was indicted for high treason and tried at the Old Bailey on October 19. She was then held at Newgate until she was burned to death at Tyburn on October 23.

Landor is indebted to Bishop Burnet's History of His Own Time *for a historical account of the events surrounding the trials and executions of these two women:*

Two executions were of such an extraordinary nature, that they deserve a more particular recital. The king apprehended that many of the prisoners had got into London, and were concealed there. So he said, those who concealed them were the worst sort of traitors, who endeavoured to preserve such persons to a better time. He had likewise a great mind to find out any among the rich merchants, who might afford great compositions to save their lives: for though there was much blood shed, there was little booty got to reward those who had served. Upon this the king declared, he would sooner pardon the rebels than those who harboured them.

There was in London one Gaunt, a woman that was an anabaptist, who spent a great part of her life in acts of charity, visiting the gaols, and looking after the poor of what persuasion soever they were. One of the rebels found her out, and she harboured him in her house; and was looking for an occasion of sending him out of the kingdom. He went about in the night, and came to hear what the king had said. So he, by an unheard of baseness, went and delivered himself, and accused her that harboured him. She was seized on and tried. There was no witness to prove that she knew that the person she harboured was a rebel, but he himself: her maid witnessed only, that he was entertained at her house. But though the crime was her harbouring a traitor, and was proved only by this infamous witness, yet the judge charged the jury to bring her in guilty, pretending that the maid was a second witness, though she knew nothing of that which was the criminal part. She was condemned, and burnt, as the law directs in the case of women convict of treason. She died with a constancy, even to a cheerfulness, that struck all that saw it. She said, charity was a part of her religion, as well as faith: this at worst was the feeding an enemy: so she hoped, she had her reward with him, for whose sake she did this service, how unworthy soever the person was, that made so ill a return for it: she rejoiced, that God had honoured her to be the first that suffered by fire in this reign: and that her suffering was a martyrdom for that religion which was all love. Pen, the quaker, told me, he saw her die. She laid the straw about her for burning her speedily; and behaved herself in such a manner, that all the spectators melted in tears.

The other execution was of a woman of greater quality: the lady Lisle. Her husband had been a regicide, and was one of Cromwell's lords, and was called the lord Lisle. He went at the time of the restoration beyond sea, and lived at Lausanne. But three desperate Irishmen, hoping by such a service to make their fortunes, went thither, and killed him as he was going to church [August 11, 1664]; and being well mounted, and ill pursued, got into France. His lady was known to be much affected with the king's death, and not easily reconciled to her husband for the share he had in it. She was a woman of great piety and charity. The night after the action, Hicks, a violent preacher among the dissenters, and Nelthorp, came to her house. She knew Hicks, and treated him civilly, not asking from whence they came. But Hicks told what brought them thither; for they had been with the duke of Monmouth. Upon which she went out of the room immediately, and ordered her chief servant to send an information concerning them to the next justice of peace, and in the mean while to suffer them to make their escape. But, before this could be done, a party came about the house, and took both them and her for harbouring them. [The infamous Judge] Jefferies resolved to make a sacrifice of her; and obtained of the king a promise that he would not pardon her. Which the king owned to the earl of Feversham, when he, upon the offer of a 1000l. if he could obtain her pardon, went and begged it. So she was brought to her trial. No legal proof was brought, that she knew that they were rebels: the names of the persons found in her house were in no proclamation: so there was no notice given to beware of them. Jefferies affirmed to the jury upon his honour, that the persons had confessed that they had been with the duke of Monmouth. This was the turning a witness against her, after which he ought not to have judged in the matter. And, though it was insisted on, as a point of law, that till the persons found in her house were convicted, she could not be found guilty, yet Jefferies charged the jury in a most violent manner to bring her in guilty. All the audience was strangely affected with so unusual a behaviour in a judge. Only the person most concerned, the lady herself, who was then past seventy, was so little moved at it, that she fell asleep. The jury brought her in not guilty. But the judge in great fury sent them out again. Yet they brought her in a second time not guilty. Then he seemed as in a transport of rage. He upon that threatened them with an attaint of jury. And they, overcome with fear, brought her in the third time guilty. The king would shew no other favour, but that he changed the sentence from burning to beheading. She died with great constancy of mind; and expressed a joy, that she thus suffered for an act of charity and piety.[1]

Landor dispenses altogether with dramatic action in this dialogue and directs his attention toward creating two saintly and idealized women who reveal their goodness through their conversation. In three separate instances, Landor departs from Burnet's account in order to emphasize the charity of the two women. Although Burnet states that Lady Lisle was "not easily reconciled to her husband for the share he had" in the death of Charles I (1649), Landor exalts Lady Lisle's love for her dead husband: "Smile on me, approve my last action in this world, O virtuous husband! O saint and martyr! my brave, compassionate, and loving Lisle!" Burnet records that Lady Lisle intended to inform the proper authorities that two followers of the defeated Duke of Monmouth were in her home, while simultaneously allowing the men to escape. Landor ignores the common sense of the real Lady Lisle and chooses to emphasize her charity: "I received in my house a wanderer who had fought under the rash and giddy Monmouth. He was hungry and thirsty, and I took him in. My Saviour had commanded, my king had forbidden it." Historically, the fugitive harbored in Elizabeth Gaunt's house heard of the King's proclamation and traded the life of the woman who saved him for his own freedom. Landor's selfless Elizabeth gives

[1] Gilbert Burnet, *Bishop Burnet's History of His Own Time* (6 vols.; Oxford, 1823), III, 57-60.

the fugitive a choice: "*Soon came to my ears the declaration of the king, that his majesty would rather pardon a rebel than the concealer of a rebel. The hope was a faint one: but it was a hope; and I gave it him.... Poor creature! he consented ... to betray me; and I am condemned to be burnt alive.*" Landor's idealizing and sentimentalizing of Lady Lisle and Elizabeth Gaunt is in keeping with his general attitude toward women, whom he treated with great respect and decorum.

Lady Lisle. Madam, I am confident you will pardon me; for affliction teaches forgiveness.

Elizabeth Gaunt. From the cell of the condemned we are going, unless my hopes mislead me, where alone we can receive it.[2]

Tell me, I beseech you, lady! in what matter or manner do you think you can have offended a poor sinner such as I am. Surely we come into this dismal place for our offences; and it is not here that any can be given or taken.

Lady Lisle. Just now, when I entered the prison, I saw your countenance serene and cheerful; you looked upon me for a time with an unaltered eye: you turned away from me, as I fancied, only to utter some expressions of devotion; and again you looked upon me; and tears rolled down your face. Alas! that I should, by any circumstance, any action or recollection, make another unhappy. Alas! that I should deepen the gloom in the very shadow of death.

Elizabeth Gaunt. Be comforted: you have not done it. Grief softens and melts and flows away with tears.

I wept because another was greatly more wretched than I myself. I wept at that black attire; at that attire of modesty and of widowhood.

Lady Lisle. It covers a wounded, almost a broken heart: an unworthy offering to our blessed Redeemer.

Elizabeth Gaunt. In his name let us now rejoice! Let us offer our prayers and our thanks at once together! We may yield up our souls perhaps at the same hour.

Lady Lisle. Is mine so pure? Have I bemoaned, as I should have done, the faults I have committed? Have my sighs arisen for the unmerited

---

[2] Burnet relates from William Penn, who was present, that Elizabeth Gaunt placed the faggots round her body with her own hands. Lady Lisle was not burnt alive, though sentenced to it, but hanged and beheaded. [*Landor's note.*]

mercies of my God? and not rather for him, the beloved of my heart, the adviser and sustainer I have lost!

Open, O gates of Death!

Smile on me, approve my last action in this world, O virtuous husband! O saint and martyr! my brave, compassionate, and loving Lisle!

Elizabeth Gaunt. And can not you too smile, sweet lady? are not you with him even now? Doth body, doth clay, doth air, separate and estrange free spirits? Bethink you of his gladness, of his glory; and begin to partake them.

O! how could an Englishman, how could twelve, condemn to death, condemn to so great an evil as they thought it and may find it, this innocent and helpless widow!

Lady Lisle. Blame not *that* jury! blame not the jury which brought against me the verdict of guilty. I was so: I received in my house a wanderer who had fought under the rash and giddy Monmouth.[3] He was hungry and thirsty, and I took him in. My Saviour had commanded,[4] my king had forbidden it.

Yet the twelve would not have delivered me over to death, unless the judge had threatened them with an accusation of treason in default of it. Terror made them unanimous: they redeemed their properties and lives at the stated price.[5]

[3] According to Bishop Burnet's account, Lady Lisle knowingly harbored two followers of the Pretender. Yet at her trial she denied knowing that the two fugitives, John Hickes (or Hicks) (1633–1685), a Nonconformist minister, and Richard Nelthorpe (or Nelthorp) (d. 1685) a lawyer, were traitors: "And I do repeat it, my lord, as I hope to attain salvation, I never did know Nelthorp, nor never did see him before in my life, nor did I know of any body's coming, but Mr. Hicks, and him I did know to be a nonconformist minister; and there being, as is well known, warrants out to apprehend all nonconformist ministers, I was willing to give him shelter from these warrants. I was come down but that week into the country, when this man came to me from Mr. Hicks, to know if he might be received at my house; and I told him, if Mr. Hicks pleased, he might come upon Tuesday in the evening, and should be welcome; but withal I told him, I must go away the Monday following from that place, but while I staid I would entertain him. And I beseech your lordship to believe, I had no intention to harbour him but as a nonconformist, and that I knew was no treason: It cannot be imagined, that I would venture the hazard of my own life, and the ruin both of myself and children, to conceal one that I never knew in my life, as I did not know Mr. Nelthorp, but had heard of him in the proclamation" (*Cobbett's Complete Collection of State Trials*, comp. T. B. Howell and T. J. Howell [33 vols.; London, 1809–1826], XI, 360–361; hereafter referred to as *State Trials*).

[4] See Matthew 25:35–40.

[5] Whereas Landor's Lady Lisle does not blame the jury that finally found her guilty, the historical Lady Lisle incriminated though forgave all who had a part in

Elizabeth Gaunt. I hope at least the unfortunate man, whom you received in the hour of danger, may avoid his penalty.

Lady Lisle. Let us hope it.[6]

Elizabeth Gaunt. I too am imprisoned for the same offence;[7] and I have little expectation that he who was concealed by me hath any chance of happiness, although he hath escaped. Could I find the means of conveying to him a small pittance, I should leave the world the more comfortably.

Lady Lisle. Trust in God; not in one thing or another, but in all. Resign the care of this wanderer to *his* guidance.

Elizabeth Gaunt. He abandoned that guidance.

Lady Lisle. Unfortunate! how can money then avail him!

Elizabeth Gaunt. It might save him from distress and from despair, from the taunts of the hard-hearted and from the inclemency of the godly.

Lady Lisle. In godliness, O my friend! there can not be inclemency.

Elizabeth Gaunt. You are thinking of perfection, my dear lady; and I marvel not at it; for what else hath ever occupied your thoughts! But godliness, in almost the best of us, often is austere, often uncompliant and

---

falsely convicting her. In a paper delivered to the sheriff shortly before her execution, she said: "I did as little expect to come to this place on this occasion as any person in this nation; therefore let us learn not to be high-minded, but fear the Lord: The Lord is a Sovereign, and will take what way he sees best to glorify himself by his poor creatures; therefore do humbly desire to submit to his will, praying him, that in patience I may possess my soul.

"My crime was entertaining a nonconformist minister, who is since sworn to have been in the late duke of Monmouth's army. I am told, if I had not denied them, it would not have affected me. I have no excuse but surprise and fear; which I believe my jury must make use of to excuse their verdict to the world.

"I have been told, the court ought to be counsel for the prisoner, instead of which, there was evidence given from thence; which, though it were but hearsay, might possibly affect my jury. My defence was such as might be expected from a weak woman: but such as it was, I did not hear it repeated again to the jury. But I forgive all persons that have done me wrong, and I desire that God will do so likewise" (*State Trials*, XI, 380).

[6] John Hickes was hanged at Glastonbury on October 6, 1685. Richard Nelthorpe was executed before the gate of Gray's Inn on October 30, 1685.

[7] Although Bishop Burnet's account indicates that Elizabeth Gaunt was tried for harboring James Burton, one of the followers of the Pretender, after the battle of Sedgemoor (1685), the record of her trial states that she was accused of having aided him after the abortive Rye House Plot two years earlier (*State Trials*, XI, 409–410). The Rye House Plot (April, 1683) originated with a group of men led by Richard Rumbold, a former Parliamentary soldier, who had planned to sally forth from Rye House, near Hoddesdon in Hertfordshire, on the road between London and Newmarket, and assassinate Charles II and the Duke of York.

rigid, proner to reprove than to pardon, to drag back or thrust aside than to invite and help onward.[8]

Poor man! I never knew him before: I can not tell how he shall endure his self-reproach, or whether it will bring him to calmer thoughts hereafter.

Lady Lisle. I am not a busy idler in curiosity; nor, if I were, is there time enough left me for indulging in it; yet gladly would I learn the history of events, at the first appearance so resembling those in mine.

Elizabeth Gaunt. The person's name I never may disclose; which would be the worst thing I could betray of the trust he placed in me. He took refuge in my humble dwelling, imploring me in the name of Christ to harbour him for a season. Food and raiment were afforded him unsparingly; yet his fears made him shiver through them. Whatever I could urge of prayer and exhortation was not wanting: still, although he prayed, he was disquieted. Soon came to my ears the declaration of the king, that his majesty would rather pardon a rebel than the concealer of a rebel. The hope was a faint one: but it *was* a hope; and I gave it him. His thanksgivings were now more ardent, his prayers more humble, and oftener repeated. They did not strengthen his heart: it was unpurified and unprepared for them. Poor creature! he consented with it to betray me;

[8] On the day of Elizabeth Gaunt's execution, the condemned woman gave the authorities a paper containing her final remarks, part of which reads: "And now as concerning my fact, as it is called, alas! it is but a little one, and might well become a prince to forgive; but, He that sheweth no mercy shall find none: and I may say of it, in the language of Jonathan, I did but taste a little honey, and lo, I must die for it; I did but relieve a poor, unworthy and distressed family, and, lo, I must die for it. I desire in the Lamblike will, to forgive all that are concerned; and to say, Lord, lay it not to their charge. But I fear and believe, that when he comes to make inquisition for blood, mine will be found at the door of the furious Judge (Withins,) who, because I could not remember things, through my dauntedness at Burton's wife and daughter's witness, and my ignorance, took advantage thereat, and would not hear me, when I had called to mind that which I am sure would have invalidated their evidence; and though he granted some things of the same nature to another, yet he granted it not to me. My blood will be also found at the door of the unrighteous jury, who found me guilty upon the single oath of an outlawed man, for there was none but his oath about the money, who is no legal witness, though he be pardoned, his outlawry not being recalled; and also the law requires two witnesses in point of life. And then about my going with him to the place mentioned, it was, by his own words, before he could be outlawed, for it was two months after his absconding; and though in a proclamation, yet not high-treason, as I have heard: so that I am clearly murdered by you. And also bloody Mr. Atterbury, who so insatiately hunted after my life; and though it is no profit to him, yet through the ill-will he bore me, left no stone unturned, as I have ground to believe, until he brought me to this; and shewed favour to Burton, who ought to have died for his own fault, and not have bought his life with mine" (*State Trials*, XI, 453).

and I am condemned to be burnt alive. Can we believe, can we encourage the hope, that in his weary way through life he will find those only who will conceal from him the knowledge of this execution? Heavily, too heavily, must it weigh on so irresolute and infirm a breast.

Let it not move you to weeping.

Lady Lisle. It does not: oh! it does not.

Elizabeth Gaunt. What then?

Lady Lisle. Your saintly tenderness, your heavenly tranquillity.

Elizabeth Gaunt. No, no: abstain! abstain! It was I who grieved: it was I who doubted. Let us now be firmer: we have both the same rock to rest upon. See! I shed no tears.

I saved his life, an unprofitable and (I fear) a joyless one: he, by God's grace, has thrown open to me, and at an earlier hour than ever I ventured to expect it, the avenue to eternal bliss.

Lady Lisle. O my good angel! that bestrewest with fresh flowers a path already smooth and pleasant to me, may those timorous men who have betrayed, and those misguided ones who have prosecuted us, be conscious on their deathbeds that we have entered it! And they too will at last find rest.

CHAUCER, BOCCACCIO, AND PETRARCA

This imaginary meeting between Geoffrey Chaucer (ca. 1340–1400), Giovanni Boccaccio (1313–1375), and Francesco Petrarch (1304–1374) in Arezzo, Italy, Petrarch's birthplace, could never have occurred, since Boccaccio did not visit Petrarch during Chaucer's journey to Italy (December 1, 1372–May 23, 1373). It is possible, however, that Chaucer could have met Petrarch at that time, but there is no positive evidence of such a meeting.[1]

"Chaucer, Boccaccio, and Petrarca" is unlike "Boccaccio and Petrarca" in that each of the speakers in this Conversation tells a tale, yet Landor does use the dialogue between the characters in a similar manner to provide a frame for the telling of the tales. Although the stories related by Boccaccio and Petrarch resemble and reflect the tone, style, and subject matter of the two Italians, this is not true of the tale told by Chaucer. Landor's story of Sir Magnus Lucy has little in common with Chaucer's Canterbury Tales, *and is instead an elaboration of a private joke in which Landor amuses himself at the expense of his old neighbors in Warwickshire, the Lucy family.*[2] *The setting of Chaucer's tale is the English countryside known to Landor as a youth, and the tale itself is based upon such intimate detail that only those directly involved—Landor, his old schoolfellow Henry Arden, and Arden's brother Humphrey—are able to appreciate some of the humor derived both from the caricature of Sir Magnus Lucy and from several of the incidents. Sir Magnus is unbelievably stupid, selfish, and greedy. Several of the situations in which he finds himself, such as the "battle of the bulrush" and the encounter with the undersheriff, are labored and lacking in spontaneity; yet others, such as the scene at the inn in the town of Babel and Sir Magnus Lucy's encounter with "sea-bots" are good farce.*

Petrarca. You have kept your promise like an Englishman, Ser[3] Geoffreddo: welcome to Arezzo. This gentleman is Messer Giovanni Boccaccio, of whose unfinished *Decameron,* which I opened to you in manuscript, you expressed your admiration when we met at Florence in the spring.[4]

---

[1] See *Chaucer Life-Records,* ed. Martin M. Crow and Clair C. Olson (Austin: University of Texas Press, 1966), p. 40.

[2] See nn. 22 and 23 below.

[3] *Ser* is commonly used by Boccaccio and others for *Messer.* [*Landor's note.*]

[4] Petrarch saw the complete *Decameron* probably quite early in 1373. If Petrarch and Chaucer met about this time, it would have been in Arquà or Padua instead of Florence, Italy.

Boccaccio. I was then at Certaldo,[5] my native place, filling up my stories, and have only to regret that my acquaintance with one so friendly and partial to me has been formed so late.[6]

How did Rome answer your expectation, sir?

Chaucer. I had passed through Pisa; of which city the Campo Santo, now nearly finished, after half a century from its foundation,[7] and the noble street along the Arno,[8] are incomparably more beautiful than anything in Rome.[9]

Petrarca. That is true. I have heard, however, some of your countrymen declare that Oxford is equal to Pisa, in the solidity, extent, and costliness of its structures.

Chaucer. Oxford is the most beautiful of our cities: it would be a very fine one if there were no houses in it.

Petrarca. How is that?

Chaucer. The lath-and-plaster white-washed houses look despicably mean under the colleges.

Boccaccio. Few see anything in the same point of view. It would gratify me highly, if you would tell me with all the frankness of your character and your country, what struck you most in '*the capital of the world*,' as the vilest slaves in it call their great open cloaca.

---

[5] Boccaccio was apparently at Certaldo, Italy, during the spring and summer of 1373. See Ernest Hatch Wilkins, *The Making of the "Canzoniere" and Other Petrarchan Studies* (Rome, 1951), p. 310.

[6] Boccaccio's words are historically inaccurate, since the influence of Italian literature (particularly Boccaccio's) upon Chaucer's literary work did not begin until after the poet's first visit to Italy in 1372/1373.

[7] The rectangular Campo Santo, marble buildings in the Italian Gothic style built by Giovanni di Simone from 1278 onward, stands, according to tradition, upon fifty-three shiploads of earth brought to Pisa, Italy, from Calvary by Archbishop Ubaldo de Lanfranchi in 1203. Landor is incorrect in implying that the foundation of the Campo Santo was laid in 1323, half a century before Chaucer's first visit to Italy. Landor records his impression of the Campo Santo in a letter to Southey written in the winter of 1818/1819: "Here is a cloister round an old cemetery called the Campo Santo, by much the best building I have seen in Italy. It is a light but not too florid Gothic, and by miracle no architect has been permitted to corrupt it" (John Forster, *Walter Savage Landor. A Biography* [2 vols.; London, 1869], I, 445; hereafter referred to as Forster).

[8] [Lungarno.] The Corso in Rome is now much finer. P. Leopold dismantled the walls of Pisa, and demolished more than fifty towers and turrets. Every year castellated mansions are modernised in Italy. [*Landor's note.*]

[9] There is written evidence that Chaucer visited Genoa and Florence sometime between his departure from London on December 1, 1372, and his return to London on May 23, 1373. Except for references to these two Italian cities, we have no knowledge of Chaucer's travels while in Italy.

Chaucer. After the remains of antiquity, I know not whether anything struck me more forcibly than the superiority of our English churches and monasteries.

Boccaccio. I do not wonder that yours should be richer and better built, although I never heard before that they are: for the money that is collected in Rome or elsewhere, by the pontiffs, is employed for the most part in the aggrandisement of their families. Messer Francesco, although he wears the habit of a churchman,[10] speaks plainlier on these subjects than a simple secular, as I am, dares to do.

Petrarca. We may however I trust, prefer the beauty and variety of our scenery to that of most in the world. Tuscany is less diversified, and, excepting the mountains above Camaldoli and Laverna, less sublime, than many other parts of Italy; yet where does Nature smile with more contented gaiety than in the vicinity of Florence? Great part of our sea-coast along the Mediterranean is uninteresting; yet it is beautiful in its whole extent from France to Massa. Afterward there is not a single point of attraction till you arrive at Terracina. The greater part of the way round the peninsula, from Terracina to Pesaro, has its changes of charms: thenceforward all is flat again.

Boccaccio. We can not travel in the most picturesque and romantic regions of our Italy, from the deficiency of civilisation in the people.

Chaucer. Yet, Messer Giovanni, I never journeyed so far through so enchanting a scenery as there is almost the whole of the way from Arezzo to Rome, particularly round Terni and Narni and Perugia.

Our master Virgil speaks of dreams that swarm upon the branches of one solitary elm.[11] In this country more than dreams swarm upon every spray and leaf; and every murmur of wood or water comes from and brings with it inspiration. Never shall I forget the hour when my whole soul was carried away from me by the cataract of Terni, and when all things existing were lost to me in its stupendous waters. The majestic woods that bowed their heads before it; the sun that was veiling his glory in mild translucent clouds over the furthest course of the river; the moon, that suspended her orb in the very centre of it; seemed ministering Powers, themselves in undiminished admiration of the marvel they had been looking on through unnumbered ages. What are the works of man in comparison with this? What indeed, are the other works of Nature?

---

[10] Petrarch became a cleric in 1330. See Ernest Hatch Wilkins' article "Petrarch's Ecclesiastical Career," *Speculum*, XXVIII (October 1953), 754–775.

[11] Vergil *Aeneid* vi. 282–285.

Petrarca. Ser Geoffreddo! this, which appears too great even for Nature, was not too great for man. Our ancestors achieved it. Curius Dentatus, in his consulate, forbade the waters of the Velinus to inundate so beautiful a valley, and threw them down this precipice into the Nar.[12] When the traces of all their other victories, all their other labours, shall have disappeared, this work of the earlier and the better Romans shall continue to perform its office, shall produce its full effect, and shall astonish the beholder as it astonished him at its first completion.

Chaucer. I was not forgetful that we heard the story from our guide: but I thought him a boaster: and now for the first time I learn that any great power hath been exerted for any great good. Roads were levelled for aggression, and vast edifices were constructed either for pride or policy, to commemorate some victory, to reward the Gods for giving it, or to keep them in the same temper. There is nothing of which men appear to have been in such perpetual apprehension, as the inconstancy of the deities they worship.

Many thanks, Ser Francesco, for reminding me of what the guide asserted, and for teaching me the truth. I thought the fall of the Velinus not only the work of Nature, but the most beautiful she had ever made on earth. My prevention,[13] in regard to the country about Rome, was almost as great, and almost as unjust to Nature, from what I had heard of it both at home and abroad. In the approach to the eternal city, she seems to have surrendered much of her wildness, and to have assumed all her stateliness and sedateness, all her awfulness and severity. The vast plain toward the sea abases the soul together with it; while the hills on the left, chiefly those of Tusculum and of Tibur, overshadow and almost overwhelm it with obscure remembrances, some of them descending from the heroic ages, others from an age more miraculous than the heroic, the Herculean

---

[12] Manius Curius Dentatus, consul in 290, 284, 275, and 274 B.C., partially drained Lake Velinus about 289 B.C. by diverting the waters of the Velino River into the Nera River below. The picturesque 650-foot cataract of Terni (Cascata della Marmore) is found at that spot where the waters of the Velino empty into the Nera.

On March 9, 1826, Landor, then living in Florence, wrote to his sister Ellen at Warwick: "While I was at Rome I was so occupied, as you may imagine, with the antiquities and magnificence of that city as to defer the business of letter writing.

"In general the road by Siena is as uninteresting and ugly as any upon earth, excepting only the vicinity of the lake of Bolsena, but nothing under the sun is more lovely than the vicinity of Narni and Terni and indeed the whole road throughout the Roman territory is beautiful and romantic in the extreme" (unpublished letter, a copy of which is in the possession of Miss Diana Landor, of Rugeley, Staffordshire, England).

[13] Prevention: prepossession, bias, or prejudice.

IMAGINARY CONVERSATIONS 99

infancy of immortal Rome. Soracte comes boldly forward, and stands alone.[14] Round about, on every side, we behold an infinity of baronial castles, many moated and flanked with towers and bastions; many following the direction of the precipitous hills, of which they cover the whole summit. Tracts of land, where formerly stood entire nations, are now the property of some rude baron, descendant of a murderer too formidable for punishment, or of a robber too rich for it: and the ruins of cities, which had sunk in luxury when England was one wide forest, are carted off by a herd of slaves and buffaloes, to patch up the crevices of a fort or dungeon.

Boccaccio. Messer Francesco groans upon this, and wipes his brow.

Petrarca. Indeed I do.

Three years ago my fancy and hopes were inflamed by what I believed to be the proximity of regeneration. Cola Rienzi[15] might have established good and equitable laws: even the Papacy, from hatred of the barons, would have countenanced the enaction of them, hoping at some future time to pervert and subjugate the people as before.[16] The vanity of this tribune, who corresponded with kings and emperors, and found them pliable and ductile, was not only the ruin of himself and of the government he had founded, but threw down, beyond the chance of retrieving it, the Roman name.[17]

[14] Soracte is a mountain in the province of Rome. Due to its isolated position and size, it is a striking part of the landscape about Rome.

[15] Cola di Rienzi's spectacular overthrow of the ruling Roman nobility in Rome did not take place in 1370—three years previous to this imaginary meeting—but in May, 1347. For a thorough account of Cola di Rienzi's political rise and fall, see Ernest Hatch Wilkins, *Life of Petrarch* (Chicago: University of Chicago Press, 1961), pp. 63–73 (hereafter referred to as *Life of Petrarch*).

[16] Although Petrarch was highly critical of the corruption surrounding the Papal Court at Avignon, France, the Papal Seat, 1309–1377, he never viewed the Holy Office as an instrument of perversion and subjugation of the people. Landor comments upon the Holy Office in a letter to Southey (1827?): "Remove all [civil] distinctions between Roman-catholic and Protestant, and soon will the laity be weary of the clergy. At present they meet for mutual support and counsel; these being no longer necessary, the bond will loosen and rot away. Grant them everything; everything at once: and if they act against the laws, punish them by the laws. If the pope incites them to insurrection or disobedience, punish him as you would do any other prince for the same offence. But of this there is no danger. Calculations of gain and interest are the only movers in the pontifical court, as in all others" (Forster, II, 99–100).

[17] Ernest Hatch Wilkins, in *Life of Petrarch* (p. 35), describes Cola di Rienzi as "the most spectacular figure of the fourteenth century.... Of plebeian birth, Cola was a brilliant, eloquent, highly imaginative, and inordinately ambitious young notary, a studious enthusiast for ancient Rome and for Early Christian Rome, obsessed with visions of a new Rome possessed of its pristine power and glory." Within one fateful

Let us converse no more about it. I did my duty;[18] yet our failure afflicts me, and will afflict me until my death. Jubilees, and other such mummeries, are deemed abundant compensation for lost dignity, lost power and empire, lost freedom and independence.[19] We who had any hand in raising up our country from her abject state, are looked on with jealousy by those wretches to whom cowardice and flight alone give the titles and rewards of loyalty; with sneers and scorn by those who share among themselves the emoluments of office; and, lest consolation be altogether wanting, with somewhat of well-meaning compassion, as weak misguided visionaries, by quiet good creatures who would have beslavered and adored us if we had succeeded.

---

year—1347—Cola overthrew the ruling nobility of Rome and established a constitution (May 19 and 20); had himself elected Tribune a few days later; affected personal display throughout his brief reign; had himself knighted on August 1; had himself crowned on the Capitoline (August 15); usurped the electoral powers of the Roman Catholic Church in Italy; waged war against several powerful Roman families; found himself threatened with excommunication by the pope through his legate, Cardinal de Déaulx (middle of October); and placed himself in such an untenable position that he was forced to abdicate on December 15.

[18] Petrarch felt it his duty to help Cola di Rienzi restore Rome to its former power and glory. A man of letters and peace, Petrarch turned to his pen and supported, cautioned, and finally chastised Cola's actions with the following letters: *Epistolae variae* 48, 38, 40; *Sené nomine* 2, 3; and *Familiares* VII. 7.

[19] This is a reference to the jubilee of 1350. In 1342 the citizens of Rome requested the new pope, Clement VI, who resided in Avignon, to accept the position of senator for life (the supreme governing authority was traditionally offered to each new pope), to declare the year 1350 a year of jubilee, and to return to Rome. Clement granted the first two requests but not the third. Petrarch, who had written an *epistola metrica* (*Metricae* II. 5) supporting these requests, was deeply disappointed by Clement's refusal to return to Rome.

Petrarch would not have considered a jubilee a "mummery." A devout churchman, Petrarch attended the jubilee of 1350. He had no quarrel with the religious forms of his day, only with the abuses which surrounded those forms. This passage of indignation is more characteristic of Landor than of Petrarch. In a letter to Southey of September, 1820, Landor wrote: "The Roman Catholic superstition appears to me infinitely worse than any other species of idolatry, because it has every evil inherent in it which any one of those has, and in addition is more propense to intolerance and idleness. Everything can be done by proxy. Men in Catholic countries pray to God and get children by proxy, and by proxy are damned or saved. The priest even eats and drinks for you at supper, and helps you to a slice of meat by putting into his mouth a piece of bread. A cannibal eats you because he is hungry or because he hates you; a Catholic kills you upon a full stomach for your own good and to please God. How very few men are not barbarous! how very few are free from cruel actions, even towards those whom they would be the happier for loving!" (Forster, I, 461).

The nation that loses her liberty is not aware of her misfortune at the time, any more than the patient is who receives a paralytic stroke. He who first tells either of them what has happened, is repulsed as a simpleton or a churl.

Boccaccio. When Messer Francesco talks about liberty, he talks loud. Let us walk away from the green,[20] into the cathedral, which the congregation is leaving.

Petrarca. Come now, Giovanni, tell us some affecting story, suitable to the gloominess of the place.

Boccaccio. If Ser Geoffreddo felt in honest truth any pleasure at reading my *Decameron*, he owes me a tithe at least of the stories it contains: for I shall not be so courteous as to tell him that one of his invention is worth ten of mine, until I have had all his ten from him: if not now, another day.

Chaucer. Let life be spared to me, and I will carry the tithe in triumph through my country, much as may be shed of the heavier and riper grain by the conveyance and the handling of it. And I will attempt to show Englishmen what Italians are; how much deeper in thought, intenser in feeling, and richer in imagination, than ever formerly: and I will try whether we can not raise poetry under our fogs, and merriment among our marshes. We must at first throw some litter about it, which those who come after us may remove.

Petrarca. Do not threaten, Ser Geoffreddo! Englishmen act.

Boccaccio. Messer Francesco is grown melancholy at the spectre of the tribune. Relate to us some amusing tale, either of court or war.

Chaucer. It would ill become me, signors, to refuse what I can offer: and truly I am loth to be silent, when a fair occasion is before me of adverting to those of my countrymen who fought in the battle of Cressy,[21] as did one or two or more of the persons that are the subjects of my narrative.

Boccaccio. Enormous and horrible as was the slaughter of the French in that fight, and hateful as is war altogether to you and me, Francesco! I do

---

[20] The cathedral of Arezzo stands on a green, in which are pleasant walks commanding an extensive view. [*Landor's note.*]

[21] On August 26, 1346, an English army of about fourteen thousand men led by King Edward III engaged and defeated a much larger French force commanded by King Philip VI at Crécy, France, in the first major engagement of what has come to be known as the Hundred Years' War. The English archers, using their longbows, outshot Philip's Genoese crossbowmen, causing much slaughter in the French ranks. The French were finally routed, King John of Bohemia and others of the nobility were slain, and Philip himself was forced to flee.

expect from the countenance of Ser Geoffreddo, that he will rather make us merry than sad.

Chaucer. I hope I may, the story not wholly nor principally relating to the battle.

Sir Magnus Lucy is a knight of ample possessions, and of no obscure family, in the shire of Warwick, one of our inland provinces.[22] He was left in his childhood under the guardianship of a mother, who loved him more fondly than discreetly. Beside which disadvantage, there was always wanting in his family the nerve or fluid, or whatever else it may be, on which the intellectual powers are nourished and put in motion.[23] The good lady Joan[24] would never let him enter the lists at jousts and tournaments, to which indeed he showed small inclination, nor would she encourage him to practise or learn any martial exercise. He was excused from the wars under the plea that he was subject to epilepsy; somewhat of which fit or another had befallen him in his adolescence, from having eaten too freely of a cold swan, after dinner. To render him justice, he had given once an indication of courage. A farmer's son upon his estate, a few years younger than himself, had become a good player at quarter-staff,[25] and was

[22] Landor makes Chaucer's story of Sir Magnus Lucy's travels the vehicle for an extended private joke. Through Sir Magnus, a ridiculous caricature, Landor pokes fun at the haughty old Lucy family of Warwickshire, England—the same family whose ancestor, Sir Thomas Lucy (1532–1600), supposedly had some deer poached by the young William Shakespeare about 1585. See Landor's treatment of this event in *Citation and Examination of William Shakespeare* (1834). Another ancestor, Sir William Lucy (d. 1347), fought bravely at the battle of Crécy. The comical incidents leading to Sir Magnus Lucy's entrance into the battle of Crécy seem to be Landor's comment upon the pride of the Lucy family in their famous progenitor, Sir William Lucy.

[23] A contemporary of Landor, George Lucy of Charlecote, courted Landor's cousin Sophia Venour before her marriage to Mr. Shuckbury in 1788. In a letter to Lady Blessington (dated Clifton, October 30, 1836) Landor says of Lucy and Sophia: "He was a greater fool and more ridiculous in his figure than his great progenitor. She burst out laughing at him. 'Miss Sophia,' said he, 'I did entertain the most sanguinary hopes.' However, she could not let him put them into execution" (Alfred Morrison, *The Blessington Papers* [London, 1895], p. 122; quoted in R. H. Super, *Walter Savage Landor: A Biography* [New York: New York University Press, 1954], p. 559). These words seem to suggest that the portrait of Sir Magnus Lucy was partially drawn from the unfortunate George Lucy, who died a bachelor on December 1, 1786.

[24] Neither Sir William Lucy nor George Lucy had a mother named Joan.

[25] Quarter-staff was a popular sport in England during the Middle Ages. The staff itself was of wood, usually oak, about six and one-half feet in length, often with the ends covered with iron. According to Joseph Strutt, it was used in the following manner: "In action it was grasped by one hand in the middle, and by the other between the middle and the end. When attacking, the latter hand shifted from one quarter of the staff to the other, giving the weapon a rapid circular motion, which brought the ends

invited to Charlecote, the residence of the Lucys,[26] to exhibit his address in this useful and manly sport. The lad was then about sixteen years old, or rather more; and another of the same parish, and about the same standing, was appointed his antagonist. The sight animated Sir Magnus; who, seeing the game over and both combatants out of breath, called out to Peter Crosby the conqueror,[27] and declared his readiness to engage with him, on these conditions. First, that he should have a helmet on his head with a cushion over it, both of which he sent for ere he made the proposal, and both of which were already brought to him, the one from a buck's horn in the hall, the other from his mother's chair in the parlour: secondly, that his visor should be down: thirdly, that Peter should never aim at his body or arms: fourthly and lastly, for he would not be too particular, that, instead of a cudgel, he should use a bulrush, enwrapt in the under-coat he had taken off, lest anything venomous should be sticking to it, as his mother said there might be, from the spittle or spawn of toads, evets, water-snakes, and adders.

Peter scraped back his right foot, leaned forward, and laid his hooked fingers on his brow, not without scratching it . . the multiform signification of humble compliance in our country. John Crosby, the father of Peter, was a merry jocose old man, not a little propense to the mischievous. He had about him a powder of sternutatory quality, whether in preparation for some trick among his boon companions, or useful in the catching of chub and bream, as many suspected, is indifferent to my story. This powder he inserted in the head of the bulrush, which he pretended to soften and to cleanse by rubbing, while he instructed his lad in the use and application of it. Peter learned the lesson so well, and delivered it so skilfully, that at the very first blow the powder went into the aperture of the visor, and not only operated on the nostrils, but equally on the two spherical, horny, fish-like eyes above it. Sir Magnus wailed aloud, dropped

---

on the adversary at unexpected points. . . . Bouts at quarter-staff are of frequent occurrence in all ballad histories of Robin Hood" (*The Sports and Pastimes of the People of England*, ed. J. C. Cox [2d ed. rev.; London: Methuen & Co., 1903], p. 214).

[26] Walter, son of Thurstane de Charlecote, received the village of Charlecote, in Warwickshire, by grant from Henry de Montfort about 1190. It is believed Walter's wife was a member of the great baronical family of Lucy, because their son called himself Sir William de Lucy. Charlecote manor, including Charlecote Hall (modernized in 1558/1559 by Sir Thomas Lucy), was in the possession of the Lucy family during Landor's lifetime.

[27] The characters Peter Crosby, his father John, Ralph Roebuck, and Edward and William à Brocton are imaginary and without historical counterparts.

his cudgel, tore with great effort (for it was well fastened) the pillow from his helmet, and implored the attendants to unbrace him,[28] crying, "O Jesu! Jesu! I am in the agonies of death: receive my spirit!"[29] John Crosby kicked the ancle of the farmer who sat next to him on the turf, and whispered, "He must find it first."

The mischief was attributed to the light and downy particles of the bulrush, detached by the unlucky blow; and John, springing up when he had spoken the words, and seizing it from the hand of his son, laid it lustily about his shoulders, until it fell in dust on every side, crying, "Scape-grace! scape-grace! born to break thy father's heart in splinters! Is it thus thou beginnest thy service to so brave and generous a master? Out of my sight!"

Never was the trick divulged by the friends of Peter until after his death, which happened lately at the battle of Cressy. While Peter was fighting for his king and country, Sir Magnus resolved to display his wealth and splendour in his native land. He had heard of princes and other great men travelling in disguise, and under names not belonging to them. This is easy of imitation: he resolved to try it: although at first a qualm of conscience came over him on the part of the Christian name which his godfathers and godmothers had given him, but which however was so distinguishing, that he determined to lay it aside, first asking leave of three saints, paying three groats[30] into the alms-box, saying twelve paternosters within the hour, and making the priest of the parish drunk at supper. He now gave it out by sound of horn, that he should leave Charlecote, and travel *incognito* through several parts of England. For this purpose he locked up the liveries of his valets, and borrowed for them from his tenants the dress of yeomanry. Three grooms rode forward in buff habiliments, with three led horses well caparisoned. Before noon he reached a small town called Henley in Arden,[31] as his host at the inn-door told him, adding, when the

---

[28] The late Middle English verb "unbrace" refers to the act of loosening the bands and braces forming part of one's clothing or armor.

[29] Sir Magnus' cry parodies the words uttered by Christ: "Father, into thy hands I commend my spirit" (Luke 23:46).

[30] The English groat, a silver piece first coined in 1351, was valued at four pence. It was not issued for circulation after 1662. As early as 1513 the word "groat" came to signify a very small sum. Landor uses this meaning of the word (obsolete by the late eighteenth century) to convey the impression of Sir Magnus as a miser.

[31] The various villages, towns, chases, forests, rivers, roads, and churchyards which play a part in Sir Magnus Lucy's English journey are part of the English countryside and were familiar to Landor. All but the seaport town of Hastings, in Sussex, are located

knight dismounted, that there were scholars who had argued in his hearing, whether the name of Arden were derived from another forest so called in Germany, or from a puissant family which bore it, being earls of Warwick in the reign of Edward the Confessor.[32] "It is the opinion of the abbot of Tewkesbury, and likewise of my very good master, him of Evesham," said the host, "that the Saxon earls brought over the name with them from their own country, and gave it to the wilder part of their dominions in this of ours."

"No such family now," cried the knight. "We have driven them out, bag and baggage, long ago, being braver men than they were."

A thought however struck him, that the vacant name might cover and befit him in this expedition; and he ordered his servants to call him Sir Nigel de Arden.[33]

Continuing his march northward, he protested that nothing short of the Trent (if indeed that river were not a fabulous one) should stop him; nay, by the rood, not even the Trent itself, if there were any bridge over it strong enough to bear a horse caparisoned, or any ford which he could see a herd of oxen, or a score of sheep fit for the butcher, pass across. Early on the second morning he was nigh upon twenty miles from home, at a hamlet we call Bromwicham,[34] where be two or three furnaces, and sundry smiths, able to make a horse-shoe in time of need, allowing them drink and leisure. He commanded his steward to disburse unto the elder of them one penny of lawful coin, advising the cunning man to look well and soberly at his steed's hoofs, and at those of the other steeds in his company; which being done, and no repairs being necessary, Sir Magnus then proceeded to the vicinity of another hamlet called Sutton Colefield, in which country is a well-wooded and well-stocked chase, belonging to my dread master the duke of Lancaster,[35] who often taketh his sport therein. Here, unhappily for the knight, were the keepers of the said chase hunting the red and fallow deer. The horse of the worshipful knight, having a great affection for dogs, and inspirited by the prancing and neighing of his fellow-creatures about him, sprang forward, and relaxed not any great matter of his mettle before he reached the next forest of Cannock, where

---

in the counties of Warwick and Stafford, where Landor spent most of his boyhood.

[32] Edward the Confessor (*ca.* 1003–1066), king of the English 1042–1066.

[33] There is no Sir Nigel de Arden in the long history of that English family.

[34] Bromwicham: an early spelling of the name of Birmingham, a city of northwestern Warwickshire, England.

[35] John of Gaunt, Duke of Lancaster (1340–1399), was the patron of Chaucer.

the buck that was pursued pierced the thickets and escaped his enemies. In the village of Cannock was the knight, at his extremity, fain to look for other farriery than that which is exercised by the craft in Bromwicham, and upon other flesh than horseflesh, and about parts less horny than hoofs, however hardened be the same parts by untoward bumps and contusions. This farriery was applied by a skilful and discreet leech, while Sir Magnus opened his missal on his bed in the posture of devotion, and while a priest, who had been called in to comfort him, was looking for the penitential psalms of good king David, the only service (he assured Sir Magnus) that had any effect in the removal or alleviation of such sufferings.

When the host at Cannock heard the name of his guest, "'Sblood!" cried he to his son, "ride over, Emanuel, to Longcroft, and inform the worshipful youths, Humphrey and Henry,[36] that one of their kinsmen is come over from the other side of Warwickshire to visit them, and has lost his way in the forest through a love of sport."

On his road into Rugeley, Emanuel met them together, and told them his errand. They had heard the horn as they were riding out, had joined the hunt, and were now returning home. Indignant at first that anyone should take the name of their family, they went on asking more and more questions, and their anger abated as their curiosity increased. Having an abundance of good-humour and of joviality in their nature, they agreed to act courteously, and turn the adventure into glee and joyousness. So they went back with Emanuel to his father's at Cannock, and were received by the townspeople with much deference and respect. The attendants of Sir Magnus observed it, and were earnest to see in what manner the adventure would terminate.

"Go," said Humphrey, "and tell your master Sir Nigel that his kinsmen are come to pay their duty to him." The clergyman who had been reading the penitential psalms, and had afterward said mass, opened the chamber-door for them, and conducted them to Sir Magnus. They began their compliments by telling him that, although the house at Longcroft was unworthy of their kinsman's reception, in the absence of their father . . .

---

[36] Historically, there was a Henry de Arden who was born sometime after 1323 and who died about 1400. The first Humphrey de Arden does not appear in the family until shortly after 1588. Landor's half-sister, Maria, married a distant cousin, Humphrey Arden, of Sutton Coldfield, on December 18, 1788. Landor's circle of friends included the brothers Henry (a fellow Rugbeian) and Humphrey Arden. See Textual Notes, pp. 239–240.

when they were interrupted by the knight, who cried aloud in a clear quaver, "Young gentlemen! I have no relative in these parts: I come from the very end of Warwickshire. Reverend sir priest! I do protest and vow I have no cognisance of these two young gentlemen."

As he spoke the sweat hung upon his brow: the cause of which neither the brothers nor the priest could interpret; but it really was lest they should have come to dine with him, and perhaps have moreover some retinue in the yard. Disclaimed so unceremoniously, Humphrey de Arden opened a leathern purse, and carefully took out his father's letter. Whereat the alarm of Sir Magnus increased beyond measure, from the uncertainty of its contents, and from the certainty of being discovered as the usurper of a noble name. His terrors however were groundless: the letter was this.

"SON HUMPHREY, I grieve that the varlet who promised me those three strong geldings, and took monies thereupon, hath mortally disappointed me; for verily we have hard work here, being one against seven or eight;[37] and, if matters go on in this guise, I must e'en fight afoot ere it be long; they having killed among them my brave old Black Jack, who had often winnowed them with his broken wind, which was not broken till they broke it. The drunken fat rogue that now fails me, would rather hunt on Colefield or (if he dare come so near to you) on Cannock, than lead the three good steeds in a halter up Yoxall Lane. Whenever ye find him, stand within law with him, and use whit-leather rather than Needwood holly, which might provoke the judge; and take the three hale nags, coming hither with them yourselves, and paying him forthwith three angels,[38] due unto him on the feast of Saint Barnabas and that other (Saint Jude, as I am now reminded), if ye have so many; if not, mortgage a meadow. And let this serve as a warrant from your loving father.[39]   ††"

"What is that to me?" cried in agony Sir Magnus. The priest took the letter and shook his head. "Sir priest! you see how it stands with us;"

---

[37] Such soon afterward was the disproportion of numbers at the battle of Cressy. *Landor's note.*] See n. 21 above.

[38] The English angel, a gold coin first minted in 1465 by Edward IV, had a value of 6s. 8d.

[39] The mark of a knight, instead of his name, is not to be wondered at. Out of the thirty-six barons who subscribed the Magna Charta, three only signed with their names. [*Landor's note.*]

Given the contentions among historians concerning both the Magna Carta, or Great Charter, of 1215 and the events that are supposed to have occurred at Runnymede between King John and his barons, Landor would have been well advised to look for another source as proof of illiteracy in thirteenth-century England.

said the knight. "Do deliver me from the lion's den and from the young lions!"[40]

"Friend!" said the priest gravely and sternly, "I know the mark of Sir Humphrey: and the handwriting is my own brother's, who, taking with him in his saddle-bag a goose-pie and twelve strings of black pudding for Sir Humphrey, left his cure at Tamworth but four months ago, and joined the army in France, in order to shrive the wounded. It is my duty to make known unto the sheriff whatever is irregular in my parish." "O! for the love of Christ! say nothing to the sheriff! I will confess all," exclaimed the knight.

The attendants and many of the customers and countryfolks had listened at the door, which was indeed wide-open; and the priest being now confirmed in his suspicion by the knight's offer to "confess all," walked slowly through them, mounted his palfrey, and rode over to the sheriff at Penkridge. The two young gentlemen were delighted on seeing the consternation of Sir Magnus and his company, and encouraged by the familiarity of one among them, led him aside and said, "It will be well and happy for you if you persuade the others of your party to return home speedily. The sheriff is a shrewd severe man, and will surely send every soul of you into Picardy,[41] excepting such as he may gibbet on the common for an ensample."

"Masters!" replied the Warwickshire wag, "I will return among them and frighten them into the road: but you two brave lads shall have your horses, and your father his, together with such attendants as you little reckon on. Are ye for the wars?"

"We were going," said they gaily, "whenever we could raise enough monies from our father's tenantry; for he, much as he desires to have us with him, is very loth to be badly equipped; and would peradventure see us rather slain in battle, or (what he thinks worse) not in it at all, than villanously mounted."

"Will ye take me?" cried the gallant yeoman.

"Gladly," answered they both together.

Ralph Roebuck was the name of this brave youngster; and, without

---

[40] See Daniel 6. The words "young lions" are found scattered throughout various books of the Old Testament: Job 4:10, 38:39; Psalms 34:10, 58:6, 104:21; Isaiah 5:29; Jeremiah 2:15; Ezekiel 19:2, 38:13; Nahum 2:11, 13; and Zechariah 11:3.

[41] Picardy is a region of northern France. This is a reference to subscription through arrest. At the time of Sir Magnus Lucy's trouble with the law, King Edward III had invaded northern France with his army in July, 1346.

another word, he ran among his fellows, and putting his hand above his ear, as our hunters are wont, shouted aloud, "Who's for hanging this fine morning?" "Ralph!" chimed they together, somewhat languidly, "what dost mean?"

"I mean," whispered he slowly and distinctly to the nearest, "that the country will be up in half an hour; that the priest is gone for the sheriff; and that if he went for the devil he could fetch him. I never knew a priest at a fault, whatever he winded. Whosoe'er has a horse able to carry him is in luck. In my mind there will be some heels without a stirrup under them, before to-morrow, kick as they may to find it. I must not however be unfaithful to my master, for whom I have spoken a fair word, and worn a smiling face, in my perils and tribulations, with these stout young gallants. Each to his own bit and bridle: the three led chargers let no man touch, on his life. For the rest, I will be spokesman, in lack of a better. May we meet again in Charlecote, at least half the number we set out!"

Away they ran, saddled their horses, and rode off. Ralph, who had lately been put in the stocks by his master, for drinking a cup too much and for singing a song by no means dissuasive of incontinence, now for the first time began to think of it again, and expected a like repose after less baiting. Presently came up a swart, thin, fierce little man, with four others bearing arms. He, observing Ralph, ordered him to "stand," in the king's name. Ralph had been standing, and stood, with his arms before him, hanging as if they were broken.

"Varlet and villain!" cried the under-sheriff, for such was the little man, "who art thou?"

"May it please your honour," answered he submissively, "my name is a real one and my own, such as it is."

"And what may it be, sirrah!"

"Ralph Roebuck."

"Egad!" cried the little man, starting at it, "that too sounds like a feigned one. Ye are all rogues and vagrants. Where are thy fellows?"

"I can answer only for myself, may it please your worship!" said Ralph.

"Where is thy leader, vagabond!" cried the magistrate, more and more indignant.

"God knows," answered Ralph, dolorously.

"Has he fled with the rest of his gang?"

"God grant he may," ejaculated Roebuck, "rather than hang upon the cursed tree."

The under-sheriff then ordered his people to hold Ralph in custody, and went and saluted the two De Ardens, who requested that clemency might be shown to everyone implicated in an offence so slight.

"We must consider of that," answered the under-sheriff. "Edward à Brocton, the priest of Cannock here, has given me this letter, which he swears is written by his brother William, priest of Tamworth, and marked by your worshipful father." The young men bowed. "Who is the rogue that defrauded him," resumed the under-sheriff, "in the three horses, to our lord the king's great detriment and discomfort?"

It was not for them, they replied, to incriminate anyone; nor indeed would they knowingly bring any man's blood on their heads if they could help it.

"The impostor in the house shall be examined," cried the little man, drawing his forefinger along his lips, for they were foamy. He went into the room, and found the knight in a shower of tears.

"Call my varlets! call my rogues!" cried Sir Magnus, wringing his hands and turning away his face.

"Rogues!" said the under-sheriff. "They are gone off, and in another county, or near upon it; else would I hang them all speedily, as I will thee, by God's pleasure. How many horses hast thou in the stable?"

"Sir! good sir! gentle sir! patience a little! let me think awhile!" said the knight.

"Ay, ay, ay! let thee think forsooth!" scornfully and canorously in well-sustained tenor hymned the son of Themis.[42] "This paper hath told me."

"Worthy sir!" said the knight, "hear reason! Hear truth and righteousness and justification by faith! Hear a sinner in tribulation, in the shadow of death!"

"Faith! sirrah! thou art very near the substance, if there be any," interposed the under-sheriff.

"Nay, nay! hold! I beseech you! as I have a soul to be saved"...

"Pack it up then! pack it up! I will give it a lift when it is ready."

"O sir sheriff, sir sheriff! I am disposed to swear on the rood, I am not, and never was, Sir Nigel de Arden."

At these words the under-sheriff laughed bitterly, and said, "Nor I neither;" and, going out of the room, ordered a guard to stand at the door.

Henry then took him by the arm and said softly, "Gildart! do not be severe with the poor young man below. It is true he is in the secret, which he swears he will not betray if he dies for it; but he promises us the three

[42] Themis is the personification of justice in Greek mythology.

horses without trial or suit or trouble or delay, and hopes you will allow his master to leave the kingdom in peace and safety under his conduct, promising to serve the king, together with us, faithfully in his wars."

"We could not do better," answered the under-sheriff, "if we were certain the fellow and his gang would not waylay and murder you on the road."

"Never fear!" cried Henry. "As we shall have other attendants, and are neither less strong nor (I trust) less courageous than he, we will venture, with your leave and permission."

This was given in writing. The under-sheriff ordered his guards to bring down the culprit, who came limping and very slow.

"Pity he can not feign and counterfeit a little better on the spur of the occasion!" said the under-sheriff. "He well answers the description of fat and lazy: as for drunken, it shall not be to-day, on Cannock ale or Burton beer."[43]

When the knight had descended the stairs, and saw Ralph Roebuck, he shrieked aloud with surprise and gladness, "O thou good and faithful servant! enter into the joy of thy lord!"[44]

"God's blood!" cried Ralph. "I must enter then into a thing narrower than a weasel's or a wasp's hole. To what evil have you led us?"

"Now you can speak for me!" said the knight.

Ralph shook his head and sighed, "It will not do, master! I am resolved to keep my promise, which you commanded upon first setting out, though it may cost me limb or life. Master! one word in your ear."

"No whisperings! no connivances! no plans or projects of escape!" cried the guard. They helped Sir Magnus into his saddle with more than their hands and arms; which, instead of officiousness, he thought an indignity, though it might be the practice of those parts. The two De Ardens mounted

---

[43] The English town of Cannock, Staffordshire, is situated on high ground and gravelly soil, and until 1736, when a conduit was built to carry water into the town, suffered from severe water shortages during the summer. It is believed that this scarcity of water gave rise to a common saying that Cannock had more ale than water. Cannock is reputed to have had five inns and three beer houses in 1834 to provide refreshment for a population that numbered about 1,100 in the early nineteenth century. See *Staffordshire Towns and Villages*, comp. Alfred Williams and Walter Henry Mallett (Lichfield, 1899). Burton-Upon-Trent (Staffordshire) has been one of England's great brewing centers since the early eighteenth century.

[44] Sir Magnus' words parody those of Jesus in the parable of the talents: "His lord said unto him, Well done, thou good and faithful servant: thou hast been faithful over a few things, I will make thee ruler over many things: enter thou into the joy of thy lord" (Matthew 25:21).

two of the richly caparisoned steeds; the third was led by their servant, who went homeward with those also which they had ridden, for what was necessary, being ordered to rejoin them at Lichfield. Ralph Roebuck sat alert on his own sorrel palfrey, a quick and active one, with open transparent nostrils. He would, as became him, have kept behind his master, if the knight had not called him to his side, complaining that the length and roughness of the roads had shaken his saddle so as to make it uneven and uneasy. Many and pressing were the offers of Ralph to set it right: Sir Magnus shook his head and answered that "man is born to suffering as the sparks fly upward."[45]

"I could wish, sir," said Ralph, "if it did not interfere with higher dispensations" . . .

"The very word! Ralph! the very word! thou rememberest it! I could not bring it nicely to mind. Several Sundays have passed since we heard it. Well! what couldst thou wish?"

"That your worship had under you at this juncture the cushion of our late good lady Joan, which might serve you now somewhat better than it did at the battle of the bulrush. We all serve best in our places."

"By our lady! Ralph! I never saw a man so much improved by his travels as thou art. What shall we both be ere we reach home again?"

Ralph persuaded his master how much better it were that his worship did not return too speedily among the cravens and recreants who had deserted him, and who probably would be pursued; and then what a shame and scandal it would be, if such a powerful knight as Sir Magnus should see them dragged from his own hall, and from under his own eyes to prison. If by any means it could be contrived to prolong the journey a few days, it would be a blessing; and the De Ardens, it might be hoped, would say nothing of the matter to the sheriff. Sir Magnus felt that his importance would be lowered by the seizure of his servants, in his presence, and under his roof; and he had other reasons for wishing to ride leisurely, in which his more active companions little participated. On their urging him to push forward, he complained that his horse had been neglected, and had neither tasted oat nor bean, nor even sweet meadow-hay, at Cannock. His company expressed the utmost solicitude that this neglect should be promptly remedied, and grieving that the next stage was still several miles distant, offered, and at the same time exerted, their best services, in bringing the hungry and loitering steed to a trot. Sir Magnus now had his shrewd suspicions, he said, that the saddle had been ill

---

[45] "Yet man is born unto trouble, as the sparks fly upward" (Job 5:7).

looked to, and doubted whether a nail from behind might not somehow have dropped lower. When he would have cleared up his doubts by the agency of his hand, again the whip, applied to his flinching steed, disturbed the elucidation; and his knuckles, instead of solving the knotty point, only added to its nodosity. At last he cried, "Roebuck! Roebuck! gently, softly! If we go on at this rate, in another half-hour I shall be black and bloody, as ever rook was that dropped ill-fledged from the rookery."

"The Lord hath well speeded our flight," said Ralph relenting: "he hath delivered us from our enemies. What miles and miles have we travelled, to all appearance in a few hours!"

"Not many hours indeed," answered the knight, still pondering. "What is yon red spire?" added he.

"The tower of Babel,"[46] replied Ralph composedly.

"I can not well think it," muttered Sir Magnus in suspense. "They would never have dared to rebuild it, after God's anger thereupon."

It was the spire of Lichfield cathedral.[47]

When they entered the city they found there some hundreds of French prisoners, taken in the late skirmishes, who were chattering and laughing and boasting of their invincibility. Their sunburnt faces, their meagre bodies, their loud cries, and the violence our surly countrymen expressed at not being understood by them, although as natives of Lichfield they spoke such good English, removed in part the doubts of Sir Magnus, even before he heard our host cry, "By God! a very Babel!" Later in the evening came some Welshmen, having passed through Shropshire and Cheshire with mountain sheep, for the fair next morning. These too were unintelligible in their language, and different from the others. They quarrelled with the French for mocking them, as they thought. Sir Magnus expressed his wonder that an Englishman, which the host was, should be found in such a far country, among the heathen; albeit some of them spoke English, not being able for their hearts and souls to do otherwise, since all the languages in the world were spoken there as a judgment on the ungodly. He confessed he had always thought Babel was in another

---

[46] See Genesis 11:1–9.

[47] Chaucer was probably familiar with the central spire of the Lichfield cathedral in southeastern Staffordshire, since most art historians believe the spire to have been erected at some time between 1296 and 1380. The spire Landor knew was a 1670 reconstruction of the original, which was destroyed, along with most of the cathedral, by the Parliamentary Forces in 1646.

place, though he could not put his finger upon it exactly. Nothing, he added, so clearly proved the real fact, as that the sheep themselves were misbegotten and blackfaced, and several of them altogether tawny, like a Moor's head he had seen, he told them, in the chancel-window of Saint Mary's at Warwick. "Which reminds me," said the pious knight, "that the hour of Angelus must be at hand, and, beside the usual service, I have several forms of thanksgiving to run through before I break bread again."

It was allowed him to go alone upstairs for his devotions, in which, ye will have observed, he was very regular. Meanwhile the landlord and his two daughters, two buxom wenches, were admitted into the secret; and it was agreed that at supper all should speak a jargon, by degrees more and more confused, and that at last every imaginable mistake should be made, in executing the orders of the company. The girls entered heartily into the device, and the rosy-faced father gave them hints and directions while the supper was being cooked. Sir Magnus came down, after a time, covered with sweat. He protested that the heat of the climate in these countries was intolerable, particularly in his bedroom: that indeed he had felt it before, in the open air, but only on certain portions of the body, which certain stars have an influence upon, and not at all in the face.

The oven had been heated just under the knight's bed, in order to supply loaves for the farmers and drovers the following day.

Supper was now served: bread however was wanting. The knight desired one of the young women to give him some. She looked at him in astonishment, shrank back, blushed, and hid her face in her apron. The father came forward furiously, and said many words, or rather uttered many sounds, which Sir Magnus could not understand. He requested his attendant Ralph to explain. Ralph made a few attempts at English, and, failing in it, spoke very fluently another tongue. The father and his daughters stared one at another, and brought a bucket of hot water, with a square of soap; then a goose's wing; then a sack of grey peas; then a blackbird in a cage; then a mustard-pot; then a handful of brown paper; then a pair of white rabbits, hanging by the ears. Sir Magnus now addressed the other girl. She appeared more willing to comply, and, making a sign at her father, whose back was turned in his anxiety to find what was called for, as if she would be kinder still when he was out of the way, laid her arm across the neck of the knight, and withdrew it hesitatingly and timidly. At this instant a great dog entered, allured by the smell of the meat. The knight's lips quivered, and the first accents he uttered audibly and distinctly were . . "Seeking whom he may devour."[48] Then falling on his knees he cried aloud, "O Lord! thy mercies are manifold! I am a sinner."[49]

The girl trembled from head to foot, ready to burst with the laughter she was suppressing, and kissed her father, and appeared to implore his pardon. He pushed her back and cried, "Away! I saw thee! I saw thee with these very eyes!" clenching his fist and striking his brow franticly. "I saw thy shadow upon the wall. No wickedness is hidden."[50]

"The hand-writing! the hand-writing! that was upon the wall too! perhaps upon this very one,"[51] exclaimed the conscience-stricken and aghast Sir Magnus. He fell on his knees, and praised the Lord for allowing to the host again the use of his mother-tongue; for the salvation of him a sinner; if indeed it were not the Lord himself who spake by the lips of his servant in the words, "No wickedness is hidden." After a prayer, he protested that, although indeed his heart was corrupt, as all hearts were, the devil had failed to inflame him universally. Not one knew what he said. Humphrey laughed and nodded assent; Henry offered him baked apples; Ralph brushed his doublet-sleeve.

Before it was light in the morning, the horses were at the door: nobody appeared: no money had been paid or demanded: nevertheless it seemed an inn. They mounted; they mused; they feared to meet each other's eyes: at last Ralph addressed one of the De Ardens in a low voice, but so as to be heard by his master. The two brothers tried each a monosyllable: Ralph shook his head, and they looked despondently. Attempts were renewed at intervals for several miles; when suddenly a distant bell was heard, probably from the cathedral, and Humphrey cried, "Matins! matins!" At

---

[48] "Be sober, be vigilant; because your adversary the devil, as a roaring lion, walketh about, seeking whom he may devour" (I Peter 5:8).

[49] "Yet thou in thy manifold mercies forsookest them not in the wilderness: the pillar of the cloud departed not from them by day, to lead them in the way; neither the pillar of fire by night, to shew them light, and the way wherein they should go.

. . . .

"Therefore thou deliveredst them into the hand of their enemies, who vexed them: and in the time of their trouble, when they cried unto thee, thou heardest them from heaven; and according to thy manifold mercies thou gavest them saviours, who saved them out of the hand of their enemies" (Nehemiah 9:19, 27).

[50] See Ezekiel 23.

[51] This is an allusion to "Belshazzar's Feast": "In the same hour came forth fingers of a man's hand, and wrote over against the candlestick upon the plaster of the wall of the king's palace: and the king saw the part of the hand that wrote" (Daniel 5:5).

this moment all spoke English perfectly, and the knight uttered many fervent ejaculations. The others related their sufferings and visions; and when they had ended, Sir Magnus said, he seemed to hear throughout the night the roaring of a fiery furnace, for all the world like King Nebuchadnezzar's;[52] only that sinful bodies, and not righteous ones, were moved and shoved backward and forward in it, until their bones grated like iron, and until his own teeth chattered so in his head he could hear them no longer.

His conductor was careful to avoid the county of Warwick, lest any one should recognise the knight, little as was the chance of it; for he never had been further from home than at Warwick, and there but twice, the distance being five good miles. On his way toward the coast, he wondered to find the stars so very like those at Charlecote; and some of them seemed to know him and wink at him. He thought indeed here were a good many more of them awake and stirring; because he had been longer out of doors than he had ever been before, at night. Slowly as he would have travelled, if he had been allowed his own way, on the sixth morning from his adventure at Cannock he had come within sight of the coast. To his questions no other answer was returned, than that the times were unquiet; that the roads were infested with robbers; and that the orders of a sheriff were as a king's. In the afternoon, the travellers descended the narrow holloway that leads into the seaport town of Hastings. Ralph pointed at some sailors who were stepping into a boat, and cried, "Master! what do you think of these?"

"I think, Roebuck," answered he, after pondering some moments, "that they are like unto those who go down into the great waters."[53]

The De Ardens were conveying their stores and horses aboard, to lose no time, when Ralph whispered in the ear of the knight, "Sir Knight! do not, for the love of Christ! do not venture with those two dare-devils any further. Let us take only a small boat, just large enough to enter the Avon. There is a short cut hereabout, if we could find it. For six pieces of gold we may hire as many sailors to hazard their liberties and lives for us, and see us safe at home again."

"Six pieces of gold!" repeated Sir Magnus very slowly and distinctly: "six pieces of gold, in these hard times, go well-nigh to purchase an acre of pasture-land."

[52] See Daniel 3.
[53] "They that go down to the sea in ships, that do business in great waters" (Psalm 107:23).

"True," replied Roebuck, "with a hundred of sand and a thousand of sea thrown in, as hoof and shank to a buttock of beef."

"Indeed!" interjected Sir Magnus. "Why, then, would not it be better to look out for some such investment of said monies, and to get the indentures fairly engrossed forthwith?"

"Investment! indentures!" cried Ralph. "Master! it is well for those who can carry by land and sea such fine learned words about with 'em, which are enough to show a man's gentility all the world over."

It is uncertain whether Sir Magnus heard him, for he continued to utter and repeat the substance of his reflections.

"What a quantity of fishes there must be in a thousand acres of deep salt water, being well looked to! Rats and otters might sneeze their hearts out before they could catch a fin, with the brine and foam bobbing up everlastingly and buffeting their whiskers: and the poachers must buy lime-kilns, and forests, and mines of pure poison, if they would make the fish drunk at the bottom. Furthermore, there never could be a lack of sand at Charlecote these twenty years to come, for kitchen or scullery or walk before the hall-windows, or repairs of cow-house or dove-cote: and many a cart-load would be lying in store for sale."

"There is great foresight and cleverness in all this," said Ralph: "and if your worship had only six gold pieces in the world, no time ought to be lost in running with 'em seaward. But to my foolishness, three for life and three for liberty seem reasonable enough. Pirates, and even fair-fighting enemies, such as those gentlemen over the way, demand for a knight's ransom as many hundreds."

The knight drew back and hesitated.

"Well, Sir!" said Ralph, "the business is none of mine. I have been let go ere now for an old song when I had angered my man: here I have angered nobody: I am safe anywhere, and welcome in most places."

"I am fain to learn that old song of his," said the knight inaudibly.

Roebuck continued, "I have no hall with antlers in it; I would rather eat a sucking pig than a swan, and a griskin than a heron; and I can do either with good-will about noon any day in seven, bating Friday, and without mounting up three long steps that run across the room, or resting my feet on a dainty mat of rushes. A good blazing kitchen fire is enough for me. I care neither for bucks nor partridges. As for spiced ale at christenings and weddings, I may catch a draught of it when it passes. Sack I have heard of: poor tipple, I doubt, that wants sweetening. But a horn of home-brewed beer, frothing leisurely, and humming lowly its contented tune, is suitable to my taste and condition; and I envy not the great and glorious who have a goose with a capon in his belly on the table, or even a peacock, his head as good as alive, and the proudest of his feathers to crown him."

The knight answered, "Somehow I do not like to part with my gold; I never saw any in coinage till last Easter;[54] and it seems so fresh and sunshiny and pleasant, I would keep it to look at in damp weather. Pay the varlets in groats."

"Sir Knight!" replied Ralph, "do not let them see your store of groats, which are very handy, and sundry of these likewise are quite new."

"Nobody would pay away new groats that could help it," sighed Sir Magnus.

"The gold must go, and make room for more," said Roebuck. The knight answered nothing; but turning round, lest anybody should notice his capacious and well-stored scrip,[55] he drew forth the six pieces, and, after a doubt and a trial with his thumb and finger, whether by reason of their roughness two peradventure might not stick together and make seven, he placed them in the palm of Roebuck, who took them with equal silence and less uncertainty. Great contentment was manifested by the worshipful knight that the two De Ardens had left him; and he ate a good dinner, and drank a glass of Rhenish, which he said was "pure sour;" and presently was anxious to go aboard the boat, if it was ready. Ralph conducted him to it and helped him in. The rowers for some time played their parts lustily, and then hoisted sail. Roebuck asked the oldest of them whether the wind was fair. "Passably," said he; "but unless we look sharp we may be carried into the Low Countries."

"I do not see anywhere that short cut, nor that brook which runs into the Avon," said Sir Magnus. "As for the Low Countries, no fear of them: the water rises before us, and we mount higher and higher every moment, insomuch that I begin to feel as if I were going up in a swing, like that between the elms."

[54] The first gold coined in England came out rather more than a year before this time, that is in 1344; the quantity was small, and probably the circulation not rapid nor extensive. [*Landor's note.*] In 1257, Henry III issued a gold penny, which was first valued at twenty pence silver, but the coinage was soon withdrawn. In 1344, Edward III attempted and failed to introduce a gold coinage. In 1351 a gold coinage was finally established with the introduction of the noble, containing 120 grains of gold, and its subdivisions, the half- and quarter-noble.

[55] The Middle English word "scrip" refers to a small bag or wallet often carried by pilgrims, shepherds, and beggars.

Presently old Ocean exacted from him his tribute, which the powerfullest not of knights only and barons, but of princes and kings must pay him in his own dominions, bending their heads and stretching out their arms and acknowledging his supremacy with tears and groans. He now fancied he had been poisoned on shore; and was confirmed in his belief, when Roebuck hummed a tune without any words to it, prodigal and profuse as he was of them on ordinary occasions; and when neither he nor any of the sailors would bring him such a trifle as water-gruel sweetened with clary wine, or camomile flowers picked with the dew upon them and simmered in fair spring water and in an earthen pan, or viper-broth with a spoonful of Venice-treacle in it, stirred with the tusk of a wild boar in the first quarter of the moon: the only things he asked them for. Soon however his pains abated; yet he complained that his eyesight was so affected, he seemed to see nothing but greenish water, like leek-porridge, albeit by his reckoning they must now be near the brook.

"Methinks," said he, "we are running after that great white ship yonder."

"Methinks so too," answered Ralph; crying, "How is this?" with apparent anger, to the sailors.

"It cannot be otherwise," said one of them: "the boat is the brig's own daughter: what mortal can keep them asunder? You might as well hope to hold tight by your teeth a two months' calf from its dam."

"Why didst not thou see to that, Ralph?" cried the knight in the bitterness of his soul. "Always rash and imprudent!"

Roebuck attempted to console his master with the display of the honours that would be shown him aboard the brig, when his quality should be discovered. Then, taking advantage of a shoal of porpoises, that rolled and darted in every direction round the boat, he showed them to Sir Magnus, who turned pale at seeing them so near him. "Never be frightened at a parcel of bots!"[56] cried Roebuck.

"Bots! what, those vast creatures?"

"Ay, surely," said one of the sailors. "The sea-horses void them by millions in a moment: you may sometimes see a thousand of them sticking on a single hair of their tails."

"Do those horses come within sight then?" said Sir Magnus tremulously.

"Only when they are itchy," answered the mariner; "and then they contrive to slip between a boat and a brig, and crack a couple or three at a time of these troublesome little insects."

[56] Bots are parasitical worms or maggots found in horses and other animals.

Sir Magnus said something to himself about the wonders of the great deep,[57] and praised God for having kept hitherto such a breed of bots out of his stables. He began to see clearly how fitted everything is to the place it occupies; and how certainly these creatures were created to be killed between brigs and boats.

Meditations must have their end, though they reach to Heaven.

Great as had been the consternation of Sir Magnus at the sight of the porpoises, and at the probability that a hair of some stray marine horse, covered over with them, might lie between him and the river; greater still was it, if possible, at approaching the brig, and discerning the two De Ardens. "What can they want with me?" cried he. "I am resolved not to go home with them."

Roebuck raised his spirits, by swearing that nothing of the kind should happen, while he had a drop of blood in his veins. "Hark! Sir Knight!" said he. "Observe how the two young gentlemen are behaving."

Gaily indeed did they accost him, and imperiously cried they to the crew, "Make way for Sir Magnus Lucy."

"Behold, sir, your glorious name hath already manifested itself," said Ralph.

A rope-ladder was let down; and the brothers knelt, and inclined their bodies, and offered their hands to aid him in mounting. "Here are honours paid to my master!" said Roebuck exultingly. Sir Magnus himself was highly gratified with his reception, and resolved to defer his interrogatory on the course they seemed to be taking. He was startled at dinner-time when the captain with strange familiarity entitled him "Sir Mag." The following words were even more offensive; for when the ship rolled somewhat, though moderately, the trencher of Sir Magnus fell into his lap; and the captain cried, "Nay, nay, Sir Mag! as much into gullet as gullet will hold, but clap nothing below the girdle." He protested he had no design to secrete anything. The sailors played and punned, as low men are wont, on his family name: and on his asking what the fellows meant by their impudence, a scholar from Oxford, of whom he inquired it, one who liked the logic of princes better than that of pedants, told him they wished to express by their words and gestures that he was, in the phrase of Horace, *ad unguem factus*.[58]

[57] "These see the works of the lord, and his wonders in the deep" (Psalm 107:24).
[58] The Latin phrase "ad unguem factus homo" ("a man without flaw") "involves a metaphor from sculpture, for the artist would pass his finger-nail over the marble, to test the smoothness of its joints" (translator's note, Horace *Satires* i. 5. 32–33, in

"I do not approve of any phrases," answered he, somewhat proudly, "and pray, sir, tell them so."

"Sir!" said Roebuck in his ear, "although you may be somewhat disappointed in the measure of respect paid to you aboard, you will be compensated on landing."

Sir Magnus thought hereby that his tenants would surely bring him pullets and chines. As they approached the coast, "I told you, sir!" exclaimed he. "Look at the bonfire on the very edge of the sands! they could not make it nearer you." A fire was blazing, and there were loud *huzzas* as the ship entered the port.

"I would still be incog. if possible," said Sir Magnus, hollowing his cheeks and voice, and recovering to himself a great part of his own estimation. "Give the good men this money; and tell them in future not to burn a serviceable boat for me, in want of brushwood. I will send them a cart-load of it another time, on due application."

The people were caulking a fishing-smack: they took the money, hooted at Sir Magnus, and turned again to their labour.

After the service of the day, the king of England was always pleased to watch the ships coming over, to observe the soldiers debarking, and to learn the names of the knights and esquires who successively crossed the channel. He happened to be riding at no great distance; and ordered one of his attendants to go and bring him information of the ship and her passengers, particularly as he had seen some stout horses put ashore. This knight was an intimate friend of De Arden the father, and laughed heartily at the adventure, as related by Humphrey. He repeated it to the king, word for word, as nearly as he could. "Marry!" said the king. "Three fat horses, with a bean-field (I warrant) in each, are but an inadequate price for such a name. I doubt whether we have another among us that was in any degree noble before the Norman conquest. We ourselves might have afforded three decent ones, in recompense for the dominion and property of nearly one whole county, and that county the fairest in England. Let the boys make the knight show his prowess, as some of his family have done. I observe they ride well, and have the prudence to exercise their horses on their first debarking, lest they grow

---

Satires, Epistles, Ars Poetica, tr. H. Rushton Fairclough [rev. ed.; "The Loeb Classical Library"; Cambridge: Harvard University Press; London: W. Heinemann, 1936]). This Latin expression, as applied to Sir Magnus, is an example of Landor's tendency on occasion to indulge in punning in the *Imaginary Conversations*.

stiff and lose their appetite. Tell them I shall be glad to hear of them, and then to see them."

Sir Magnus, the moment he set foot on shore, was welcomed to land by Roebuck. "No, no! rogue Ralph!" said he, nodding. "I know the Avon when I see it. Here we are ... None of your mummery, good people," cried he, somewhat angrily, when several ragged French, men, women, and children, asked him for charity. "We will have no Babel here, by God's blessing."

Soon came forward two young knights, and told him it was the king's pleasure he should pitch his tent above *Eu*, on the right of this same river *Brete*.[59]

"Youngsters!" cried he arrogantly, "I shall pitch nothing; neither tent (whatever it may be) nor quoit nor bar.[60] Know ye, I am Sir Magnus Lucy of Charlecote."

The young knights, unceremoniously as he had treated them, bowed profoundly, and said they bore the king's command, leaving the execution of it to his discretion.

"The king's," repeated he. "What have I done? Has that skipping squirrel of an under-sheriff been at the king's ear about me?"

They could not understand him; and, telling him that it would be unbecoming in them to investigate his secrets, made again their obeisance, and left him. He then turned toward Ralph; the polar star in every ambiguity of his courses.

"Honoured master, Sir Magnus!" answered Ralph, "let no strife be between us, nor ill blood, that alway maketh ill counsels boil uppermost in the pot."

"Roebuck!" said the knight, surveying him with silent admiration, "now speakest thou soundly and calmly; for thou hast taken time in the delivery thereof, and communed with thyself, before thou didst trust the least trustworthy of thy members. But I do surmise from thy manner, and from the thing spoken, that thou hast somewhat within thee which thou wouldst utter yet."

"Worshipful sir!" subjoined Ralph, "although I do not boast of my services, as who would? yet, truth is truth; I have saved your noble neck from the gallows; forasmuch as you took a name, worshipful sir! which

---

[59] Eu is a town in northwestern France, in the *département* of Seine-Inférieure, on the river Bresle.

[60] A quoit is a flat disk of stone or metal which is thrown as a test of strength and skill. A bar is a thick rod of wood or iron which is used in a similar manner.

neither king nor father ever gave you, and which belongeth to others rightfully. Now if both the name and the horses had been found at once upon you, a miracle only could have saved you from that bloody-minded under-sheriff. Providential was it for you, sir knight, that those two young gentlemen, whether in mercy they counterfeited the letter" . . .

"No, no, no! the priest's own brother wrote it: the priest deposed to the handwriting."

"Then," said Ralph calmly, lifting up the palms of his hands toward Sir Magnus, "let us praise the Lord!"

"Hei-day? Ralph! why! art even thou grown devout? Verily this is a great mercy; a great deliverance. I doubt whether the best part of it (praised be the Lord nevertheless!) be not rather for thee, than for such a sinner as I am. For thou hast lost no horse; and yet art touched as if thou hadst lost a stud: thou hast not suffered in the flesh; and yet thy spirit is very contrite."

"Master!" said Ralph, "only one thing is quite plain to me; which is, that Almighty God decrees we should render our best services to our country. Your three horses followed you for idle pomp; vanity prompted you to appear what you are not."

"Very wrong, Ralph!"

"And yet, Sir Magnus, if you had not committed this action, which in your pious and reasonable humility you call very wrong, perhaps three gallant youths (for Sir Magnus Lucy by God's grace shall be the third) had remained at home in that sad idleness, which leads to an unprivileged and tongue-tied old-age. We are now in France" . .

"Ralph! Ralph!" said Sir Magnus, "be serious still. Faith! I can hardly tell when thou art and when thou art not, being so unsteady a creature."

"Sir Magnus, I repeat it, we are now in Normandy or Picardy, I know not rightly which, where the king also is, and where it would be unseemly if any English knight were not. The eyes of England and of France are fixed upon us. Here we must all obey, the lofty as well as the humble."

"Obey? ay, to be sure, Ralph! Thou wilt obey me: thou art not great enough to obey the king: therefore set not thy heart upon it."

Ralph smiled and replied, "I offered my service to the young De Ardens, which they graciously accepted. As however they have their own servants with 'em, if you, my honoured master, can trust me, who have more than once deceived you, but never to your injury, I will with their permission continue to serve you, and that right faithfully. Whatever is wanting to the dignity of your appearance is readily purchased in this country, from the many traffickers who follow the camp, and from the great abundance of Normandy. So numerous too are the servants who have lost their masters, you may find as many as your rank requires, or your fortune can maintain. There are handier men among them than I am; and I do not ask of you any place of trust above my betters. Such as I am, either take me, Sir Magnus, or leave me with the two brave lads."

"Ralph!" answered the knight, "I can not do without thee; since I am here; as it seems I am!" and he sighed. "About those servants that have lost their masters . . I wish thou couldst have held thy peace. I would not fain have such unlucky varlets. But some of these masters, let us hope, may be found. Thou dost not mean they are dead; that is, killed!"

"Missing," said Ralph, consolatorily.

"I thought so: I corrected thee at the time. Now my three horses, the king being here, if thou speakest truth, I can have them up by certiorari at his Bench."

"They would be apt to leap it, I trow," replied Ralph, "with such riders upon their backs. Master, be easy about them!"

"Ismael[61] is very powerful: he could carry me anywhere in reason," said Sir Magnus.

"Do not let the story get wind," answered his counsellor, "lest we never hear the end of it. I promise you, my worthy master, you shall have Ismael again after the wars."

"He will have longer teeth, and fewer marks in his mouth, before that time," said sorrowfully Sir Magnus.

"No bridle can hold him, when he is wilful," replied Ralph; "and although peradventure he might carry your Worship clean through the enemy, once or twice, yet Ismael is not the horse to be pricked and goaded by pikes and arrows, without rearing and plunging, and kicking off helmets by the dozen, nine ells from the ground.[62] Let those Staffordshire lads break him in and bring him home."

"Tell them so! tell them so!" said Sir Magnus, rubbing his hands. "And find me one very strong and fleet, and very tractable, and that will do anything rather than plunge and rear at being pricked; if such bloody times should ever come over again in the world: for, as I never yet gave any man cause to mock at me, I will do my utmost to make all reverent of me, now I am near the king." Thus he spoke, being at last well aware that

---

[61] See n. 64 below.
[62] The English ell equals 45 inches. Nine ells would be 405 inches, or 33.75 feet.

he was indeed in France; although he was yet perplexed in spirit in regard to his having been at Babel.

However, some time afterward he was likewise cured of this scepticism; as by degrees men will be on such points, if they seek the truth in humility of spirit. Conversing one day with Roebuck on past occurrences, he said, after a pause, "Ralph! I have confessed unto thee many things, as thou likewise hast confessed many unto me; the which manner of living and communing was very pleasant to the gentle saints Paul and Timothy. And now I do indeed own that I have seen men in these parts beyond sea, and doubt not that there be likewise such in others, who in sundry matters have more of worldly knowledge than I have . . knowledge I speak of, not of understanding. In the vanity of my heart, having at that time seen little, I did imagine and surmise that Babel lay wider of us; albeit I could not upon oath or upon honour say where or whereabout. It pleased the Lord to enlighten me by signs and tokens, and not to leave me for the scorn of the heathen and the derision of the ungodly. Had I minded his word somewhat more, when in my self-sufficiency I thought I had minded little else and knew it off-hand, I should have remembered that we pray every sabbath for the peace of Jerusalem, and of Sion, and of Israel; meaning thereby (as the priest admonishes the simpler of the congregation) our own country, albeit other names have been given in these latter days to divers parts thereof. By the same token I might have apprehended that Babel lay at no vast distance."

Roebuck listened demurely, smacking his lips at intervals like a carp out of pond, and looking grave and edified. Tired however with this geographical discursion, burred and briared and braked with homilies, he reminded his master that no time was to be lost in looking for a gallant steed, worthy to bear a knight of distinction. "My father," said he, "made a song for himself, in readiness at fair or market, when he had a sorry jade to dispose of:—

> 'Who sells a good nag
> On his legs may fag
>   Until his heart be weary.
> Who buys a good nag,
> And hath groats in his bag,
>   May ride the world over full cheery.'"

"Comfortable thoughts, both of 'em!" said Sir Magnus. "I never sold my nags: and I have groats enow . . if nobody do touch the same. Not knowing well the farms about this country, and the day being more windy than I could wish it, and proposing still to remain for a while incognito, and being somewhat soiled in my apparel by the accidents of the voyage, and furthermore my eyes having been strained thereby a slight matter, it would please me, Roebuck, if thou wentest in search of the charger: the troublesome part of looking at his quarters, and handling him, and disbursing the moneys, I myself may, by God's providence, bring unto good issue."

Ralph accepted the commission, and performed it faithfully and amply. He returned with two powerful chargers, magnificently caparisoned, and told his master that he would grieve to the day of his death if he let either of them slip through his fingers. Sir Magnus first asked the prices, and then the names of them. He was informed that one was called Rufus, and the other Beauclerc, after two great English kings.[63] Inquiring of Ralph the history of these English kings, and whether he had ever heard of them, and on the confession of Ralph in the negative, he was vexed and discontented, and told Ralph he knew nothing. The owner of the horses was very fluent in the history of the two princes; which nearly lost him his customer; for the knight shook his head, saying he should be sorry to mount a beast of such an unlucky name as Rufus: above all, in a country where arrows were so rife. As for Beauclerc, he was unexceptionable.

"A horse indeed!" cried Roebuck; "in my mind, sir! Ismael is not fit to hold a candle to him."

"I would not say so much as that," gravely and majestically replied the knight: "but this Beauclerc has his points, Roebuck." Sir Magnus purchased the two horses, and acquired into the bargain the two pages of history appertaining to their names; which, proud as he was of displaying them on all occasions, he managed less dexterously. Before long he heard on every side the most exalted praises of Humphrey and Henry; and,

---

[63] Rufus, William II (*ca.* 1056–1100), third and favorite son of William I (the Conqueror), became king of England in 1087. An extremely vicious and oppressive king, Rufus was killed (possibly murdered) on August 2, 1100, while hunting with his younger brother Henry, Walter Tirel, Lord of Poix in Ponthieu, and others. The arrow that struck Rufus supposedly was shot by Walter Tirel. Landor dramatized this event in one of the five blank-verse scenes of the "Pentalogia," entitled "Walter Tyrrel and William Rufus" (*Pentameron and Pentalogia*, 1837). On August 5, three days after Rufus' death, Henry (1068–1135), later called Beauclerc, became King Henry I of England. He was an able, well-educated ruler who achieved considerable military glory with the battle of Tinchebrai (September 28, 1106) and in subsequent conflicts with Norman rebels.

although he was by no means invidious, he attributed a large portion of the merit to Ismael, and appealed to Roebuck whether he did not once hear him say that Jacob too would show himself one day or other.[64] Stimulated by the glory his horses had acquired, horses bred upon his own land, and by the notice they had attracted from our invincible Edward, under two mere striplings of half his weight, he himself within a week or fortnight was changed in character. Sloth and inactivity were no longer endurable to him. He exercised his chargers and himself in every practice necessary to the military career; and at last being presented to the king, Edward said to him that, albeit not being at Westminster, nor having his chancellor at hand, he could not legally enforce the payment of the three angels, still due (he understood) as part of the purchase-money of sundry chargers, nevertheless he would oblige the gallant knight who bought them to present him on due occasion a pair of spurs for his acquittance.

The ceremony was not performed in the presence of the king, whose affairs required him elsewhere, but in the presence of his glorious son, after the battle of Cressy.[65] Here Sir Magnus was surrounded, and perhaps would have fallen, being still inexpert in the management of his arms, when suddenly a young soldier, covered with blood, rushed between him and his antagonist, whom he levelled with his battle-axe, and fell exhausted. Sir Magnus had received many bruises through his armour, and noticed but little the event; many similar ones, or nearly so, having occurred in the course of the engagement. Soon however that quarter of the field began to show its herbage again in larger spaces; and at the distant sound of the French trumpets, which was shrill, fitful, and tuneless, the broken ranks of the enemy near him, waved, like a tattered banner in the wind, and melted, and disappeared. Ralph had fought resolutely at his side, and, though wounded, was little hurt. The knight called him aloud: at his voice not only Ralph came forward, but the soldier, who had preserved his life, rolled round toward him. Disfigured as he was with blood and bruises, Ralph knew him again: it was Peter Crosby of the bulrush. Sir Magnus

[64] The biblical names of Sir Magnus' horses, Ismael and Jacob, are appropriate: The Ishmael of Genesis was a natural-born warrior. Before his birth an angel prophesied: "And he will be a wild man; his hand will be against every man, and every man's hand against him" (Genesis 16:12). Although the Old Testament Jacob was not a warrior, he twice used his patience and clever intelligence to outwit his elder warrior-brother Esau. In the phrase "one day or other" Landor is planning on Jacob's ability to bide his time.

[65] Edward the Black Prince (1330–1376). He was sixteen years old at the time of the battle of Crécy.

did not find immediately the words he wanted to accost him: and indeed though he had become much braver, he had not grown much more courteous, much more generous, or much more humane. He took him however by the hand, thanked him for having saved his life, and hoped to assist in doing him the same good turn.

Roebuck in the meantime washed the several wounds of his former friend and playmate, from a cow's horn containing wine; of which, as he had reserved it only against thirst in battle, few drops were left. Gashes opened from under the gore; which made him wish that he had left it untouched; and he drew in his breath, as if he felt all the pain he awakened.

"Well meant, Ralph! but prythee give over!" said Crosby patiently. "These singings in my head are no merry-makings."

"Master!... if you are there... I would liefer have lain in Hampton churchyard among the skittles,[66] or as near them as might be, so as not to spoil the sport: and methinks had it been a score or two of years later, it were none the worse. Howsoever, God's will be done! Greater folks have been eaten here by the dogs. Welladay, and what harm? Dogs at any time are better beasts than worms, and should be served first. They love us, and watch us, and help us while we are living: the others don't mind us while we are good for anything. There are chaps, too, and feeding in clover, who think much as they do upon that matter.

"Give me thy hand, Ralph! Tell my father I have done my best. If thou findest a slash or two athwart my back and loins, swear to him, as thou safely mayest do on all the Gospels, and on any bone of any martyr, that they closed upon me and gave them when I was cutting my way through ... aweary with what had been done already ... to lend my last service ... to our worthy master."

Now, Messer Francesco, I may call upon you, having seen you long since throw aside your gravity, and at last spring up alert, as though you would mount for Picardy.

Petrarca. A right indeed have you acquired to call upon me, Ser Geoffreddo; but you must accept from me the produce of our country. Brave men appear among us every age almost; yet all of them are apt to look to themselves; none will hazard his life for another; none will trust his best friend. Such is our breed; such it always was. In affairs of love alone have we as great a variety as you have, and perhaps a greater. I am by nature very forgetful of light occurrences, even of those which much amused me at the time; and if your greyhound, Messer Geoffreddo, had

[66] Ninepins.

not been laying his muzzle between my knees, urging my attention, shivering at the cold of this unmatted marble, and treading upon my foot in preference, I doubt whether you would ever have heard from me the story I shall now relate to you.

It occurred the year before I left Avignon;[67] the inhabitants of which city, Messer Giovanni will certify, are more beautiful than any others in France.

Boccaccio. I have learnt it from report, and believe it readily: so many Italians have resided there so long, and the very flower of Italy: amorous poets, stout abbots, indolent priests, high-fed cardinals, handsome pages, gigantic halberdiers, and crossbow-men for ever at the mark.

Petrarca. Pish! pish! let me find my way through 'em, and come to the couple I have before my eyes, and the spaniel that was the prime mover in the business.

Tenerin de Gisors knew few things in the world; and, if he had known all therein, he would have found nothing so valuable, in his own estimation, as himself. The ladies paid much court to him, and never seemed so happy as in his presence: this disquieted him.

Boccaccio. How the deuce! he must have been a saint then: which accords but little with his vanity.

Petrarca. You might mistake there, Giovanni! The observation does not hold good in all cases, I can assure you.

Boccaccio. Well, go on with him.

Petrarca. I do think, Giovanni, you tell a story a great deal more naturally; but I will say plainly what my own eyes have remarked, and will let the peculiarities of men appear as they strike me, whether they are in symmetry with our notions of character, or not.

Chaucer. The man of genius may do this: no other will attempt it. He will discover the symmetry, the relations, and the dependencies, of the whole: he will square the strange problematic circle of the human heart.

Pardon my interruption; and indulge us with the tale of Tenerin.

Petrarca. He was disquieted, I repeat, by the gaiety and familiarity of the young women, who, truly to speak, betray at Avignon no rusticity of reserve. Educated in a house where music and poetry were cultivated, he

---

[67] Petrarch had several residences in Avignon: May, 1326–summer, 1337; summer, 1337–February, 1341 (Vaucluse and Avignon); spring, 1342–September, 1343 (Vaucluse and Avignon); late 1345–November, 1347 (Vaucluse and Avignon); and summer, 1351–May, 1353 (Vaucluse and Avignon). Landor might have had any one of these in mind.

had been hearing from his earliest days the ditties of broken hearts and desperation: and never had he observed that these invariably were sung under leering eyes, with smiles that turned every word upside-down, and were followed by the clinking of glasses, a hearty supper, and *what not!* Beside, he was very handsome; men of this sort, although there are exceptions, are usually cold toward the women; and he was more displeased that they should share the admiration which he thought due to himself exclusively, than pleased at receiving the larger part of theirs.

At Avignon, as with us, certain houses entertain certain parties. It is thought unpolite and inconstant ever to go from one into another, I do not mean in the same evening, but in your lifetime; and only the religious can do it without reproach. As bees carry and deposit the fecundating dust of certain plants, so friars and priests the exhilarating tales of beauty, and the hardly less exhilarating of frailty, covering it deeply with pity, and praising the mercy of the Lord in permitting it for an admonition to others.

There are two sisters in our city (I forgot myself in calling Avignon so), of whom among friends I may speak freely, and may even name them; Cyrilla de la Haye, and Egidia. Cyrilla, the younger, is said to be extremely beautiful: I never saw her, and few beside the family have seen her lately. She is spoken of among her female friends as very lively, very modest, fond of reading and of music: added to which advantages, she is heiress to her uncle the Bishop of Carpentras, now invested with the purple. For her fortune, and for the care bestowed on her education, she is indebted to her sister, who, having deceived many respectable young men with hopes of marriage, was herself at last deceived in them, and bore about her an indication that deceived no one. During the three years that her father lived after this too domestic calamity, he confined her in a country-house, leaving her only the liberty of a garden, fenced with high walls. He died at Paris: and the mother, who fondly loved Egidia, went instantly and liberated her, permitting her to return to Avignon, while she herself hid her grief, it is said, with young Gasparin de l'Œuf, in the villa. Egidia was resolved to enjoy the first moments of freedom, and perhaps to show how little she cared for an unforgiving father. No one however at Avignon, beyond the family, had yet heard anything of his decease. The evening of her liberation she walked along the banks of the Durance,[68] with her favourite spaniel, which had become fat and unwieldy by his confinement, and by lying all day under the southern wall of the garden, and, having

[68] The Durance, one of the principal rivers flowing from the French slope of the Alps toward the Mediterranean, joins the Rhône a little below Avignon.

never been combed nor washed, exhibited every sign of dirtiness and decrepitude. To render him smarter, she adorned him again with his rich silver collar, now fitting him no longer, and hardly by any effort to be clasped about his voluminous neck. He escaped from her, dragging after him the scarlet ribbon, which she had formed into a chain, that it might appear the richer with its festoons about it, and that she might hold the last object of her love the faster. On the banks of the river he struggled with both paws to disengage the collar, and unhappily one of them passed through a link of the ribbon. Frightened and half-blind, he ran on his three legs he knew not whither, and tumbled through some low willows into the Durance. Egidia caught at the end of the ribbon; and, the bank giving way, she fell with him into deep water. She had, the moment before, looked in vain for assistance to catch her spaniel for her, and had cast a reproachful glance toward the bridge, about a hundred paces off, on which Tenerin de Gisors was leaning, with his arms folded upon the battlement.

"Now," said he to himself, "one woman at least would die for me. She implored my pity before she committed the rash act . . as such acts are called on other occasions."

Without stirring a foot or unfolding an arm, he added pathetically from Ovid,

> Sic, ubi fata vocant, udis abjectus in herbis,
> Ad vada Mæandri concinit albus olor.[69]

We will not inquire whether the verses are the more misplaced by the poet, or were the more misapplied by the reciter. Tenerin now stepped forward, both to preserve his conquest and add solemnity to his triumph. He lost however the opportunity of saving his mistress, and saw her carried to the other side of the river by two stout peasants, who had been purchasing some barrels in readiness for the vintage, and who placed her with her face downward, that the water might run out of her mouth. He gave them a *livre*, on condition that they should declare he alone had saved the lady: he then quietly walked up to his neck in the stream, turned back again, and assisted (or rather followed) the youths in conveying her to the monastery near the city-gate.

---

[69] "Thus, at the summons of fate, casting himself down amid the watery grasses by the shallows of Maeander, sings the white swan" (Ovid *Heroides* vii. 1–2, in *Heroides, Amores*, tr. Grant Showerman ["The Loeb Classical Library"; Cambridge: Harvard University Press; London: W. Heinemann, 1963]).

Here he learned, after many vain inquiries, that the lady was no other than the daughter of Philibert de la Haye. Perpetually had he heard in every conversation the praises of Cyrilla; of her beauty, her temper, her reserve, her accomplishments; and what a lucky thing for her was the false step of her sister, immured for life, and leaving her in sole expectation of a vast inheritance. Hastening homeward, he dressed himself in more gallant trim, and went forthwith to the Bishop of Carpentras, then at Avignon, to whom he did not find admittance, as his lordship had only that morning received intelligence of his brother-in-law's decease. He expressed by letter his gratitude to Divine Providence, for having enabled him to rescue the loveliest of her sex from the horrors of a watery grave: announced his rank, his fortune (not indeed to be mentioned or thought of in comparison with her merits), and entreated the honour of a union with her, if his lordship could sympathise with him in feeling that such purity ought never to have been enfolded (might he say it?) in the arms of any man who was not destined to be her husband.

"Ah!" said the bishop when he had perused the letter, "the young man too well knows what has happened: who does not? The holy Father himself hath shed paternal tears upon it. Providential this falling into the water! this endangering of a sinful life! May it awaken her remorse and repentance, as it hath awakened his pity and compassion! His proceeding is liberal and delicate: he could not speak more passionately and more guardedly. He was (now I find) one of her early admirers. No reference to others; no reproaches. True love wears well. I do not like this matter to grow too public. I will set out for Carpentras in another hour, first writing a few lines, directing M. Tenerin to meet me at the palace this evening, as soon as may be convenient. We must forgive the fault of Egidia now she has found a good match; and we may put on mourning for the father, my worthy brother-in-law, next week."

Such were the cogitations and plans of the bishop; and he carried them at once into execution; for, knowing what the frailty of human nature is, as if he knew it from inspiration, he had by no means unshaken faith in the waters of the Durance as restorative or conservative of chastity.

Tenerin has been since observed to whistle oftener than to sing; and when he begins to warble any of his amatory lays, which seldom happens, the words do not please him as they used to do, and he breaks off abruptly. A friend of his said to him in my presence, "Your ear, Tenerin, has grown fastidious, since you walked up to it in the water on the first of August."

Boccaccio. Francesco! the more I reflect on the story you have related to us, the more plainly do I perceive how natural it is, and this too in the very peculiarity that appeared to me at first as being the contrary. Unless we make a selection of subjects, unless we observe their heights and distances, unless we give them their angles and shades, we may as well paint with white-wash. We do not want strange events, so much as those by which we are admitted into the recesses, or carried on amid the operations, of the human mind. We are stimulated by its activity; but we are greatly more pleased at surveying it leisurely in its quiescent state, uncovered and unsuspicious. Few however are capable of describing, or even of remarking it; while strange and unexpected contingencies are the commonest pedlary of the markets, and the joint patrimony of the tapsters.

I have drawn so largely from my brain for the production of a hundred stories, many of which I confess are witless and worthless, and many just as Ser Geoffreddo saw them, incomplete,[70] that if my memory did not come to my assistance, I should be mistrustful of my imagination.

Chaucer. Ungrateful man! the world never found one like it.

Boccaccio. Are Englishmen so Asiatic in the profusion of compliments?

I know not, Francesco, whether you may deem this cathedral a befitting place for narratives of love.

Petrarca. No place is more befitting; since if the love be holy, no sentiment is essentially so divine; and if unholy, we may pray the more devoutly and effectually in such an audience for the souls of those who harboured it. Beside which, the coolness of the aisles and their silence, and their solitariness at the extremity of the city, would check within us any motive or tendency to lasciviousness and lightness, if the subject should lie that way, and if your spirits should incautiously follow it, my friend, Giovanni, as (pardon my sincerity!) they are somewhat too propense.

Boccaccio. My scruples are satisfied and removed.

The air of Naples is not so inclement as that of our Arezzo: and there are some who will tell us, if we listen to them, that few places in the world are more favourable and conducive to amorous inclinations. I often heard it while I resided there; and the pulpit gave an echo to the public voice. Strange then it may appear to you, that jealousy should find a place in the connubial state, and after a year or more of marriage: nevertheless, so it happened.

The Prince of Policastro was united to a lady of his own rank; and yet he could not be quite so happy as he should have been with her. She

[70] The *Decameron.* See n. 4 above.

brought him a magnificent dowry; and I never saw valets more covered with lace, fringes, knots, and everything else that ought to content the lordly heart, than I have seen behind the chairs of the Prince and Princess of Policastro. Alas! what are all the blessings of this sublunary world, to the lord whose lady has thin lips! The princess was very loving; as much after the first year as the prince was after the first night. Even this would not content him.

Time, Ser Geoffreddo, remembering that Love and he, in some other planet, flew together, and neither left the other behind, is angry to be outstript by him, and challenges him to a trial of speed every day. The tiresome dotard is always distanced, yet always calls hoarsely after him; as if he had ever seen Love turn back again, any more than Love had seen him. Well, let them settle the matter between themselves.

Would you believe it? the princess could not make her husband in the least the fonder of her by all her assiduities; not even by watching him while he was awake, more assiduously than the tenderest mother ever watched her sleeping infant. Although, to vary her fascinations and enchantments, she called him wretch and villain, he was afterward as wretched and villanous as if she never had taken half the pains about him.

She had brought in her train a certain Jacometta, whom she persuaded to espy his motions. He was soon aware of it, and calling her to him, said,

"Discreet and fair Jacometta, the princess, you know very well, thinks me inattentive to her, and being unable to fix on any other object of suspicion, she marks out you, and boasts among her friends that she has persuaded a foolish girl to follow and watch me, that she may at last, by the temptation she throws into our way, rid herself of a beauty who in future might give her great uneasiness. Certainly, if my heart could wander, its wanderings would be near home. I do not exactly say I should prefer you to every woman on earth, for reason and gratitude must guide my passion; and, unless where I might expect to find attachment, I shall ever remain indifferent to personal charms. You may relate to your mistress whatever you think proper of this conversation. If you believe a person of your own sex can be more attached and faithful to you than the most circumspect of ours, then repeat the whole. If on the contrary you imagine that I can be hereafter of any use to you, and that it is my interest to keep secret any confidence with which you may honour me, the princess has now enabled us to avoid being circumvented by her. It can not hurt me: you are young, unsettled, incautious, and unsuspicious."

Jacometta held down her head in confusion: the prince taking her by the hand, requested her not to think he was offended. He persuaded her to let him meet her privately, that he might give her warning if anything should occur, and that he might assist her to turn aside the machinations of their enemy. The first time they met, nothing had occurred: he pressed her hand, slipt a valuable ring on one of the fingers, and passed. The second time nothing material, nothing but what might be warded off: let the worst happen, the friend who gave him information of the designs laid against her, would receive her. The princess saw with wonder and admiration the earnestness with which Jacometta watched for her. The faithless man could hardly move hand or foot without a motion on the part of her attendant. She had observed him near the chamber-door of Jacometta, and laughed in her heart at the beguiled deceiver. "Do you know, Jacometta, I myself saw him within two paces of your bedroom!"

"I am quite confident it was he, madam!" answered Jacometta: "and I do believe in my conscience he comes every night. What he wants I can not imagine. He seems to stop before the tuberoses[71] and carnations on the balustrade, whether to smell at them a little, or to catch the fresh breezes from Sorrento. I fancied at first he might be restless and unhappy (pardon me, madonna!) at your differences."

"No, no," said the princess, with a smile, "I understand what he wants: never mind: make no inquiries: he is little aware how we are planning to catch him: he has seen you look after him: he fancies that you care about him, that you really like him, absolutely love him . . I could almost laugh . . that you would (foolish man! foolish man! genuine Policastro!) listen to him. Do you understand?"

Jacometta's two ears reddened into transparency; and, clapping a hand on each, she cried, after a long sigh, "Lord! can he think of me? is he mad? does he take a poor girl for a princess? Generally I sleep soundly; but once or twice he has awakened me, perhaps not well knowing the passage. But if indeed he is so very wicked as to design to ruin me, and, what is

[71] Landor expresses his liking for white flowers such as the tuberose in a letter to Henry Crabb Robinson (received October, 1831): "I like white flowers better than any others; they resemble fair women. Lily, tuberose, orange, and the truly English syringa, are my heart's delight. I do not mean to say that they supplant the rose and violet in my affections, for these are our first loves, before we grew too fond of considering, and too fond of displaying our acquaintance with, others of sounding titles" (*Diary, Reminiscences, and Correspondence of Henry Crabb Robinson*, ed. Thomas Sadler [2 vols.; Boston, 1869], II, 160).

worse, to deceive the best of ladies, might it not be advisable to fasten in the centre and in the sides of the corridor, five, or six, or seven sharp swords, with their points toward whoever. .''

"Jacometta! do nothing violently; nothing rashly; nothing without me."

There was only one thing that Jacometta wished to do without the princess; and certainly she was disposed to do nothing violently or rashly; for she was now completely in the interest (these holy walls forbid me to speak more explicitly) of Policastro.

"We will be a match for him," said the princess. "You must leave your room-door open to-night."

Jacometta fell on her knees, and declared she was honest though poor . . an exclamation which I dare say, Messer Geoffreddo, you have often heard in Italy: it being the preface to every act of roguery and lubricity, unless from a knight or knight's lady. The Princess of Policastro was ignorant of this, and so was Jacometta when she used it. The mistress insisted; the attendant deprecated.

"Simple child! no earthly mischief shall befall you. To-night you shall sleep in my bed, and I in yours, awaiting the false wretch miscalled my husband."

Satisfied with the ingenuity of her device, the princess was excessively courteous to the prince at dinner, and indeed throughout the whole day. He on his part was in transports, he said, at her affability and sweet amiable temper. Poor Jacometta really knew not what to do: scarcely for one moment could she speak to the prince, that he might be on his guard.

"Do it! do it!" said he, pressing her hand as she passed him. "We must submit."

At the proper time he went in his slippers to the bedroom of the princess, and entered the spacious bed; which, like the domains of the rich, is never quite spacious enough for them. Jacometta was persuaded to utter no exclamation in the beginning, and was allowed to employ whatever vehemence she pleased at a fitter moment. The princess tossed about in Jacometta's bed, inveighing most furiously against her faithless husband; her passionate voice was hardly in any degree suppressed. Jacometta too tossed about in the princess's bed, and her voice laboured under little less suppression. At last the principal cause of vexation, with the jealous wife, was the unreasonable time to which her husband protracted the commission of his infidelity. After two hours or thereabout, she began to question whether he really had ever been unfaithful at all, began to be of opinion that there are malicious people in the world, and returned to her own chamber. She fancied she heard voices within, and listening attentively, distinguished these outcries.

"No resistance, madam! An injured husband claims imperatively his promised bliss, denied him not through antipathy, not through hatred, not through any demerits on his part, but through unjust and barbarous jealousy. Resist! bite! beat me! 'Villain'.. 'ravisher'.. am I? am I? Excruciated as I am, wronged, robbed of my happiness, of my sacred conjugal rights, may the blessed Virgin never countenance me, never look on me or listen to me, if this is not the last time I ask them, or if ever I accept them though offered."

At which, he rushed indignantly from the bed, threw open the door, and pushing aside the princess, cried raving, "Vile treacherous girl! standing there, peeping! half-naked! At your infantine age dare you thus intrude upon the holy mysteries of the marriage-bed?"

Screaming out these words, he ran like one possessed by the devil into his own room, bolted the door with vehemence, locked it, cursed it, slipped between the sheets, and slept soundly.

The princess was astonished: she asked herself, why did not I do this? why did not I do that? the reason was, she had learned her own part, but not his. Scarcely had she entered her chamber, when Jacometta fell upon her neck, sobbing aloud, and declaring that nothing but her providential presence could have saved her. She had muffled herself up, she said, folding the bed-clothes about her double and triple, and was several times on the point of calling up the whole household in her extremity, strict as was her mistress's charge upon her to be silent. The princess threw a shower of odoriferous waters over her, and took every care to restore her spirits and to preserve her from a hysterical fit, after such exertion and exhaustion. When she was rather more recovered, she dropped on her knees before her lady, and entreated and implored that, on the renewal of her love in its pristine ardour for the prince, she never would tell him in any moment of tender confidence, that it was she who was in the bed.

The princess was slow to give the promise; for she was very conscientious. At last however she gave it, saying, "The prince my husband has taken a most awful oath, never to renew the moments you apprehend. Our Lady strengthen me to bear my heavy affliction! Her divine grace has cured my agonised breast of its inveterate jealousy."

She paused for some time; then, drying her tears, for she had shed several, she invited Jacometta to sit upon the bedside with her. Jacometta did so; and the princess, taking her hand, continued; "I hardly know what is passing in my mind, Jacometta! I found it difficult to bear an injury, though an empty and unreal one; let me try whether the efforts I make will enable me to endure a misfortune .. on the faith of a woman, my dear Jacometta, no unreal nor empty one. Policastro is young: it would be unreasonable in me to desire he should lead the life of an anchorite, and perhaps not quite reasonable in him to expect the miracle of my blood congealing."

After this narration, Messer Francesco walked toward the high altar and made his genuflexion: the same did Messer Giovanni, and, in the act of it, slapped Ser Geoffreddo on the shoulder, telling him he might dispense with the ceremony, by reason of his inflexible boots and the buck-skin paling about his loins. Ser Geoffreddo did it nevertheless, and with equal devotion. His two friends then took him between them to the house of Messer Francesco, where dinner had been some time waiting.

ALEXANDER AND
THE PRIEST OF HAMMON

Alexander the Great (*356–323* B.C.) visited the oracle of Ammon at the oasis of Siwa, Libya, during his occupation of Egypt (*332–331* B.C.). This incident is recorded in Plutarch's Alexander *and* Arrian's Anabasis Alexandri. *According to Plutarch:*

> When Alexander had passed through the desert and was come to the place of the oracle, the prophet of Ammon gave him salutation from the god as from a father; whereupon Alexander asked him whether any of the murderers of his father had escaped him. To this the prophet answered by bidding him be guarded in his speech, since his was not a mortal father. Alexander therefore changed the form of his question, and asked whether the murderers of Philip had all been punished; and then, regarding his own empire, he asked whether it was given to him to become lord and master of all mankind. The god gave answer that this was given to him, and that Philip was fully avenged. Then Alexander made splendid offerings to the god and gave his priests large gifts of money.[1]

Arrian's account is basically the same, although there are a few variations.[2]

Landor draws freely upon Plutarch and Arrian for historical detail in this Conversation, departing from his sources only in one crucial instance, Alexander's avowed reason for visiting the oracle at Ammon. It is upon this imaginative departure from the sources—Alexander's desire to be proclaimed a god—that both the drama of the Conversation and the development of the characters rest. As the Conversation opens, Alexander, a vain, unscrupulous tyrant who desires to be publically recognized as a son of Jupiter by the Priest of Hammon, boasts to the Priest of his religious devotion to the gods. The Priest, who can grant such recognition, knows that Alexander's claim is false and proceeds to amuse himself at Alexander's expense by telling him that he must marry his sister, a daughter of Jupiter, in order to seal the recognition. The climactic scene occurs when Alexander, locked up in a dungeon with his bride, "a vast panting snake," admits his deception, and is freed by the Priest, who, having unveiled Alexander's pretention, grants Alexander his false claim. The Conversation concludes with one hypocrite promising to help further the ambitions of another. The Priest is drawn wholly from Landor's imagination, and though he is a hypocrite and a fraud, responds to Alexander with a humorous honesty with which Landor sympathizes. Alexander's portrait,

---

[1] Plutarch *Alexander* 27. 3–4, in *Plutarch's Lives*, tr. Bernadotte Perrin ("The Loeb Classical Library"; Cambridge: Harvard University Press; London: W. Heinemann, 1967), Vol. VII. Hereafter referred to as Plutarch *Alexander*.

[2] See Arrian *Anabasis* iii. 3–4.

although based on a selection of known historical personality traits, is drawn according to Landor's dramatic needs, personal dislike of the youthful conqueror of the world, and general hatred for tyrants.

Alexander. Like my father, as ignorant men called King Philip,[3] I have at all times been the friend and defender of the gods.

Priest. Hitherto it was rather my belief that the gods may befriend and defend us mortals: but I am now instructed that a king of Macedon has taken them under his shield. Philip, if report be true, was less remarkable for his devotion.

Alexander. He was the most religious prince of the age.

Priest. On what, O Alexander, rests the support of such an exalted title?

Alexander. Not only did he swear more frequently and more awfully than any officer in the army, or any priest in the temples, but his sacrifices were more numerous and more costly.

Priest. More costly? It must be either to those whose ruin is consummated or to those whose ruin is commenced; in other words, either to the vanquished, or to those whose ill-fortune is of earlier date, the born subjects of the vanquisher.

Alexander. He exhibited the surest and most manifest proof of his piety when he defeated Œnomarchus, general of the Phocians, who had dared to plough a piece of ground belonging to Apollo.[4]

Priest. Apollo might have made it as hot work for the Phocians who were ploughing his ground, as he formerly did at Troy to those unruly Greeks who took away his priest's daughter.[5] He shot a good many mules, to show

[3] Philip II of Macedon, *ca.* 382–336 B.C.

[4] In the autumn of 355 B.C., the Council of the Amphictyonic League (a religious and political association entrusted with the care of the temple and oracle at Delphi, Greece) declared a sacred war on the citizens of Phocis, Greece, because the Phocians had cultivated part of the land consecrated to Apollo and had refused to pay a fine of many talents levied for the misdemeanor. Upon the death of the Phocian general Philomelus, another leading Phocian, Onomarchus, continued the struggle. Both men plundered the treasury of the temple at Delphi in order to pay their mercenary forces. After defeating the Locrians and the Boeotians in several battles, Onomarchus forced Philip out of Thessaly toward the end of 353 B.C. Early in the following year Philip invaded Thessaly, supposedly for religious reasons. His army engaged and defeated Onomarchus at the battle of the Crocus Field (352 B.C.), slaying six thousand Phocians. His forces also drowned three thousand prisoners on the pretext of impiety.

[5] This incident is recounted in Book One of Homer's *Iliad*: Apollo, angered by Agamemnon's refusal to return the daughter of Chryses, heard the old priest's prayer

he was in earnest, and would have gone on shooting both cattle and men until he came at last to the offender.

Alexander. He instructed kings by slaying their people before their eyes: surely he would never set so bad an example as striking at the kings themselves. Philip, to demonstrate in the presence of all Greece his regard for Apollo of Delphi, slew six thousand, and threw into the sea three thousand, enemies of religion.

Priest. Alexander! Alexander! the enemies of religion are the cruel, and not the sufferers by cruelty. Is it unpardonable in the ignorant to be in error about their gods when the wise are in doubt about their fathers?

Alexander. I am not: Philip is not mine.

Priest. Probable enough.

Alexander. Who then is, or ought to be, but Jupiter himself?[6]

Priest. The priests of Pella[7] are abler to return an oracle on that matter than we of the Oasis.

Alexander. We have no oracle at Pella.

Priest. If you had, it might be dumb for once.

Alexander. I am losing my patience.

Priest. I have given thee part of mine, seeing thee but scantily provided; yet, if thy gestures are any signification, it sits but awkwardly upon thy shoulders.

Alexander. This to me! the begotten of a god! the benefactor of all mankind.

Priest. Such as Philip was to the three thousand, when he devised so magnificent a bath for their recreation. Plenty of pumice! rather a lack of napkins!

---

for revenge, and "sate him down apart from the ships and let fly a shaft: terrible was the twang of the silver bow. The mules he assailed first and the swift dogs, but thereafter on the men themselves he let fly his stinging arrows, and smote; and ever did the pyres of the dead burn thick" (*Iliad* i. 35–52, tr. A. T. Murray ["The Loeb Classical Library"; Cambridge: Harvard University Press; London: W. Heinemann, 1937], Vol. I).

[6] Landor alters his original sources by having Alexander propose the idea of his divinity to the Priest of Hammon. According to Plutarch, the Priest greets Alexander as the son of a god (*Alexander* 27. 3–6) and in Arrian's account Alexander approaches the Priest with the hope of learning more about his divinity (*Anabasis* iii. 3. 2). The drama of the Conversation depends upon Landor's change in this circumstance; for it is when the Priest finally "assents" to Alexander's repeated assertions of his divinity and prepares him for marriage with his "divine sister," a serpent, that Alexander is exposed as a fraud and a cynic, the climactic scene in this little drama.

[7] Pella was the capital of ancient Macedonia during the reigns of Philip II and Alexander the Great, who was born there.

Alexander. No trifling! no false wit!

Priest. True wit, to every man, is that which falls on another.

Alexander. To come at once to the point; I am ready to prove that neither Jason nor Bacchus, in their memorable expeditions,[8] did greater service to mankind than I have done, and am about to do.

Priest. Jason gave them an example of falsehood and ingratitude: Bacchus made them drunk: thou appearest a proper successor to these worthies.

Alexander. Such insolence to crowned heads! such levity on heroes and gods!

Priest. Hark ye, Alexander! we priests are privileged.

Alexander. I too am privileged to speak of my own great actions; if not as liberator of Greece and consolidator of her disjointed and jarring interests, at least as the benefactor of Egypt and of Jupiter.

Priest. Here indeed it would be unseemly to laugh; for it is evident on thy royal word that Jupiter is much indebted to thee; and equally evident, from the same authority, that thou wantest nothing from him but his blessing . . . unless it be a public acknowledgment that he has been guilty of another act of bastardy, more becoming his black curls than his grey decrepitude.

Alexander. Amazement! to talk thus of Jupiter!

Priest. Only to those who are in his confidence: a mistress for instance, or a son, as thou sayest thou art.

Alexander. Yea, by my head and by my sceptre am I. Nothing is more certain.

Priest. We will discourse upon that presently.

Alexander. Discourse upon it this instant.

Priest. How is it possible that Jupiter should be thy father, when . .

Alexander. When what?

Priest. Couldst not thou hear me on?

Alexander. Thou askest a foolish question.

Priest. I did not ask whether I should be acknowledged the son of Jupiter.

---

[8] The first is an allusion to Jason's dangerous though successful voyage to obtain the Golden Fleece from King Aeëtes of Colchis. Jason's subsequent divorce of the King's daughter, Medea, who enabled him to steal the Golden Fleece, is, as the Priest points out, a classic "example of falsehood and ingratitude." The second is a reference to the travels of Dionysus (Bacchus) in many lands in an attempt to establish his divinity and worship throughout the world. Dionysus gave gifts of vines and wine to those peoples who welcomed him and accepted his religion.

Alexander. Thou indeed!

Priest. Yet, by the common consent of mankind, lands and tenements are assigned to us, and we are called "*divine*," as their children; and there are some who assert that the gods themselves have less influence and less property on earth than we.

Alexander. All this is well: only use your influence for your benefactors.

Priest. Before we proceed any farther, tell me in what manner thou art or wilt ever be the benefactor of Egypt.

Alexander. The same exposition will demonstrate that I shall be likewise the benefactor of Jupiter. It is my intention to build a city,[9] in a situation very advantageous for commerce: of course the frequenters of such a mart will continually make offerings to Jupiter.

Priest. For what?

Alexander. For prosperity.

Priest. Alas! Alexander, the prosperous make few offerings; and Hermes has the dexterity to intercept the greater part of them.[10] In Egypt there are cities enough already: I should say too many: for men prey upon one another when they are penned together close.

Alexander. There is then no glory in building a magnificent city?

Priest. Great may be the glory.

Alexander. Here at least thou art disposed to do me justice.

Priest. I never heard until this hour that among thy other attainments was architecture.

Alexander. Scornful and insolent man! dost thou take me for an architect?

Priest. I was about to do so; and certainly not in scorn, but to assuage the feeling of it.

Alexander. How?

Priest. He who devises the plan of a great city, of its streets, its squares, its palaces, its temples, must exercise much reflection and many kinds of knowledge: and yet those which strike most the vulgar, most even the scientific, require less care, less knowledge, less beneficence, than what are called the viler parts, and are the most obscure and unobserved; the construction of the sewers; the method of exempting the aqueducts from

---

[9] Alexandria, Egypt. Accounts of Alexander's establishing the city of Alexandria are found in both Plutarch (*Alexander* 26. 2–6) and Arrian (*Anabasis* iii. 1. 5–2. 2). According to Plutarch, Alexander visited the oracle of Ammon while work on the city was in progress.

[10] Hermes (Mercury) is the prince and god of thieves.

the incroachment of their impurities; the conduct of canals for fresh air in every part of the house, attempering the summer heats; the exclusion of reptiles; and even the protection from insects. The conveniences and comforts of life in these countries, depend on such matters.

Alexander. My architect, I doubt not, has considered them maturely.

Priest. Who is he?

Alexander. I will not tell thee: the whole glory is mine: I gave the orders, and first conceived the idea.

Priest. A hound upon a heap of dust may dream of a fine city, if he has ever seen one; and a madman in chains may dream of building it, and may even give directions about it.

Alexander. I will not bear this.

Priest. Were it false, thou couldst bear it; thou wouldst call the bearing of it magnanimity; and wiser men would do the same for centuries. As such wisdom and such greatness are not what I bend my back to measure, do favour me with what thou wert about to say when thou begannest "nothing is more certain;" since I presume it must appertain to geometry, of which I am fond.

Alexander. I did not come hither to make figures upon the sand.

Priest. Fortunate for thee, if the figure thou wilt leave behind thee could be as easily wiped out.

Alexander. What didst thou say?

Priest. I was musing.

Alexander. Even the building of cities is in thy sight neither glorious nor commendable.

Priest. Truly, to build them is not among the undertakings I the most applaud in the powerful; but to destroy them is the very foremost of the excesses I abhor. All the cities of the earth should rise up against the man who ruins one. Until this sentiment is predominant, the peaceful can have no protection, the virtuous no encouragement, the brave no countenance, the prosperous no security. We priests communicate one with another extensively; and even in these solitudes thy exploits against Thebes have reached and shocked us.[11] What hearts must lie in the bosoms of those

---

[11] Following the death of Philip II, the Greek city of Thebes revolted, and Alexander, fearing a general uprising of the peoples his father had conquered, hastened to the rebellious city and issued fair terms of surrender. The Thebans refused, called for a general uprising against Alexander, and prepared for war. Alexander quickly defeated them, plundered and razed the city, and sold those who had wanted to revolt into slavery. His harsh actions, which he later regretted, were intended to serve as a warning to the other subject peoples of Greece. See Plutarch *Alexander* 11–13 and Arrian *Anabasis* i. 7–9.

who applaud thee for preserving the mansion of a deceased poet in the general ruin,[12] while the relatives of the greatest patriot that ever drew breath under heaven, of the soldier at whose hospitable hearth thy father learned all that thou knowest and much more, of Epaminondas[13] (dost thou hear me?), were murdered or enslaved. Now begin the demonstration than which "nothing is more certain."

Alexander. Nothing is more certain, or what a greater number of witnesses are ready to attest, than that my mother Olympias, who hated Philip, was pregnant of me by a serpent.[14]

Priest. Of what race?

Alexander. Dragon.

Priest. Thy mother Olympias hated Philip,[15] a well-made man, young, courageous, libidinous, witty, prodigal of splendour, indifferent to wealth,

---

[12] According to Arrian, Alexander saved the house of Pindar (518-438 B.C.) from the general destruction visited upon Thebes out of a sense of reverence for the dead poet (*Anabasis* i. 9. 10).

[13] Epaminondas (d. 362 B.C.) was a famous Theban statesman and general who established Thebes as a land power and himself as the greatest and most original of Greek military leaders through daring innovations in the tactics of the heavy infantry. Both Philip II and Alexander the Great improved upon Epaminondas' new military strategy. As a youth, Philip II attended Epaminondas' military school in Thebes. Plutarch records the following in his life of Pelopidas: "This was the Philip who afterwards waged war to enslave the Greeks, but at this time he was a boy and lived in Thebes with Pammenes. [Philip remained in Thebes as a hostage, sent there by Pelopidas to maintain Theban influence in Macedonia, until 364 B.C.] Hence he was believed to have become a zealous follower of Epaminondas, perhaps because he comprehended his efficiency in wars and campaigns, which was only a small part of the man's high excellence; but in restraint, justice, magnanimity, and gentleness, wherein Epaminondas was truly great, Philip had no share, either naturally or as a result of imitation" (Plutarch *Pelopidas* 26. 3-5, in *Plutarch's Lives*, tr. Bernadotte Perrin ["The Loeb Classical Library"; Cambridge: Harvard University Press; London: W. Heinemann, 1961], Vol. V).

[14] Olympias, daughter of Neoptolemus of Epirus, married Philip in 357 B.C. She gave birth to two children, Alexander and Cleopatra. Landor is indebted to Plutarch for the story of Alexander's being fathered by a god in the form of a serpent: "Moreover, a serpent was once seen lying stretched out by the side of Olympias as she slept, and we are told that this, more than anything else, dulled the ardour of Philip's attentions to his wife, so that he no longer came often to sleep by her side, either because he feared that some spells and enchantments might be practised upon him by her, or because he shrank from her embraces in the conviction that she was the partner of a superior being" (*Alexander* 2. 4).

[15] Philip's polygamous ways and Olympias' jealous temper led to a growing estrangement which became complete when Philip married Cleopatra in 337 B.C. Alexander sided with his mother, and withdrew with her to Epirus, where they remained until Philip's assassination the next year.

the greatest captain, the most jovial companion, and the most potent monarch in Europe.

Alexander. My father Philip, I would have thee to know . . I mean my reputed father . . was also the greatest politician in the world.

Priest. This indeed I am well aware of; but I did not number it among his excellences in the eyes of a woman: it would have been almost the only reason why she should have preferred the serpent, the head of the family. We live here, O Alexander, in solitude; yet we are not the less curious, but on the contrary the more, to learn what passes in the world around.

Olympias then did really fall in love with a serpent? and she was induced . .

Alexander. Induced! do serpents induce people! They coil and climb and subdue them.

Priest. The serpent must have been dexterous . .

Alexander. No doubt he was.

Priest. But women have such an abhorrence of serpents, that Olympias would surely have rather run away.

Alexander. How could she?

Priest. Or called out.

Alexander. Women never do that, lest somebody should hear them.

Priest. All mortals seem to bear an innate antipathy to this reptile.

Alexander. Mind! mind what thou sayest! Do not call my father a reptile.

Priest. Even thou, with all thy fortitude, wouldst experience a shuddering at the sight of a serpent in thy bed-clothes.

Alexander. Not at all. Beside, I do not hesitate in my belief that on this occasion it was Jupiter himself. The priests in Macedon were unanimous upon it.

Priest. When it happened?

Alexander. When it happened no one mentioned it, for fear of Philip.

Priest. What would he have done?

Alexander. He was choleric.

Priest. Would he have made war upon Jupiter?

Alexander. By my soul! I know not; but I would have done it in his place. As a son, I am dutiful and compliant: as a husband and king, there is not a thunderbolt in heaven that should deter me from my rights.

Priest. Did any of the priesthood see the dragon, as he was entering or retreating from the chamber?

Alexander. Many saw a great light in it.

Priest. He would want one.

Alexander. This seems like irony: sacred things do not admit it. What thousands saw, nobody should doubt. The sky opened, lightnings flew athwart it, and strange voices were heard.

Priest. Juno's the loudest, I suspect.

Alexander. Being a king, and the conqueror of kings, let me remind thee, surely I may be treated here with as much deference and solemnity as one priest uses toward another.

Priest. Certainly with no less, O king! Since thou hast insisted that I should devise the best means of persuading the world of this awful verity, thou wilt excuse me, in thy clemency, if my remarks and interrogatories should appear prolix.

Alexander. Remark anything; but do not interrogate and press me: kings are unaccustomed to it. I will consign to thee every land from the centre to the extremities of Africa; the Fortunate Isles will I also give to thee, adding the Hyperborean:[16] I wish only the consent of the religious who officiate in this temple, and their testimony to the world in declaration of my parentage.

Priest. Many thanks! we have all we want.

Alexander. I can not think you are true priests then; and if your oath on the divinity of my descent were not my object, and therefore not to be abandoned, I should regret that I had offered so much in advance, and should be provoked to deduct one half of the Fortunate Isles, and the greater part of the Hyperborean.

Priest. Those are exactly the regions, O king, which our moderation would induce us to resign. Africa, we know, is worth little: yet we are as well contented with the almonds, the dates, the melons, the figs, the fresh butter, the stags, the antelopes, the kids, the tortoises, and the quails about us, as we should be if they were brought to us after fifty days' journey through the desert.

Alexander. Really now, is it possible that, in a matter so evident, your oracle can find any obstacle or difficulty in proclaiming me what I am?

Priest. The difficulty (slight it must be acknowledged) is this: our Jupiter is horned.

Alexander. So was my father.

[16] The Fortunate Isles are the mythical winterless home, located in the far West, of the happy dead. The Hyperborean is a mythical land of sunshine and peace in the far North, inhabited by a legendary race of Apollo-worshipers.

Priest. The children of Jupiter love one another: this we believe here in Lybia.

Alexander. And rightly: no affection was ever so strong as that of Castor and Pollux. I myself feel a genuine love for them, and greater still for Hercules.[17]

Priest. If thou hadst a brother or sister on earth, Jove-born, thou wouldst embrace the same most ardently.

Alexander. As becomes my birth and heart.

Priest. O Alexander! may thy godlike race never degenerate!

Alexander. Now indeed the Powers above do inspire thee.

Priest. Jupiter, I am commanded by him to declare, is verily thy father.

Alexander. He owns me then! he owns me! What sacrifice worthy of this indulgence can I offer to him?

Priest. An obedient mind, and a camel-load of nard and amomum for his altar.[18]

Alexander. I smell here the exquisite perfume of benzoin.[19]

Priest. It grows in our vicinity. The nostrils of Jupiter love changes: he is consistent in all parts, being Jupiter. He has other sons and daughters in the world, begotten by him under the same serpentine form, although unknown to common mortals.

Alexander. Indeed!

Priest. I declare it unto thee.

Alexander. I can not doubt it then.

Priest. Not all indeed of thy comeliness in form and features, but awful

---

[17] It is dramatically appropriate for Alexander to claim kinship with semidivine beings such as Castor, Pollux, and Hercules, all of whom had mortal mothers and the same immortal father—Jupiter. This dramatic touch was suggested to Landor by Arrian's account of Alexander's visit to the oracle at Ammon: "After this an overmastering desire came upon Alexander to pay a visit to Ammon in Libya; partly to consult the oracle, since the oracle of Ammon was reputed to be infallible, and Perseus and Heracles were both said to have consulted it.... Then, besides, Alexander felt a kind of rivalry with Perseus and Heracles, being descended from them both; nay, he also traced his descent in part from Ammon, just as the legends traced the descent of Heracles and Perseus from Zeus" (Arrian *Anabasis Alexandri* iii. 3. 1–2, tr. E. Iliff Robson ["The Loeb Classical Library"; New York: G. P. Putnam's Sons; London: W. Heinemann, 1929], Vol. I).

[18] Nard (spikenard) is an aromatic substance obtained from an Eastern plant, the *Nardostachys jatamansi*, found in northern India. It was used in ancient times in the preparation of a costly ointment or oil. The amomum of the ancients was an aromatic plant that has never been certainly identified.

[19] Benzoin is a balsamic resin obtained from *Styrax benzoin*, a large tree found in Southeast Asia, and from other species of *Styrax*. It is often used as incense.

and majestic. It is the will of Jupiter, that, like the Persian monarchs, whose sceptre he hath transferred to thee, thou marryest thy sister.

Alexander. Willingly. In what land upon earth liveth she, whom thou designest for me?

Priest. The Destinies and Jupiter himself have conducted thee, O Alexander, to the place where thy nuptials shall be celebrated.

Alexander. When did they so?

Priest. Now; at this very hour.

Alexander. Let me see the bride, if it be lawful to lift up her veil.

Priest. Follow me.

Alexander. The steps of this cavern are dark and slippery; but it terminates, no doubt, like the Eleusinian, in pure light and refreshing shades.[20]

Priest. Wait here an instant: it will grow lighter.

Alexander. What do I see yonder?

Priest. Where?

Alexander. Close under the wall, rising and lowering, regularly and slowly, like a long weed on a quiet river, when a fragment hath dropped into it from the bank above.

Priest. Thou descriest, O Alexander, the daughter of Jupiter, the watchful virgin, the preserver of our treasures. Without her they might be carried away by the wanderers of the desert; but they fear, as they should do, the daughter of Jupiter.

Alexander. Hell and Furies! what hast thou been saying? I heard little of it. Daughter of Jupiter!

Priest. Hast thou any fancy for the silent and shy maiden? I will leave you together . . .

Alexander. Orcus and Erebus![21]

---

[20] The famed Eleusinian Mysteries were performed annually in the great sanctuary of Demeter, located at Eleusis in Attica. Part of the ceremony involved the worshiper in "toilsome wanderings and dangerous passages through the gloom, but the end is not yet, and then before the end all kinds of terror, shivering and quaking, sweating and amazement, when suddenly a wondrous light flashes forth to the worshipper, and pure regions and meadows receive him" (Stobaeus *Florilegium* 120. 28, quoted by L. C. Purser in *A Dictionary of Greek and Roman Antiquities*, ed. William Smith, William Wayte, and G. E. Marindin [2 vols.; 3d ed. rev.; London, 1890–1891], I, *s.v.* "Eleusinia").

[21] In Greek mythology Orcus (*Horkos*, oath) is an infernal deity who punishes perjury. Erebus (*Erebos*, primeval darkness), according to Hesiod (*Theogony* 123), is the son of Chaos and father of Aether (upper air) and Hemera (day) by his sister Nyx (night). In Homer, Erebus is the gloomy lower region through which the departed spirits pass into Hades (*Iliad* viii. 368).

Priest. Be discreet! Restrain your raptures until the rites are celebrated.

Alexander. Rites! Infernal pest! O horror! abomination! A vast panting snake!

Priest. Say "*dragon*," O king! and beware how thou callest horrid and abominable, the truly begotten of our lord thy father.

Alexander. What means this? inhuman traitor! Open the door again: lead me back. Are my conquests to terminate in the jaws of a reptile?

Priest. Do the kings of Macedon call their sisters such names?

Alexander. Let me out, I say!

Priest. Inconstant man! I doubt even whether the marriage hath been consummated. Dost thou question her worthiness? prove her, prove her. We have certain signs and manifestations that Jupiter begat this powerful creature, thy elder sister. Her mother hid her shame and confusion in the desert, where she still wanders, and looks with an evil eye on everything in the form of man. The poorest, vilest, most abject of the sex, holdeth her head no lower than she.

Alexander. Impostor!

Priest. Do not the sympathies of thy heart inform thee that this solitary queen is of the same lineage as thine?

Alexander. What temerity! what impudence! what deceit!

Priest. Temerity! How so, Alexander! Surely man can not claim too near an affinity to his Creator, if he will but obey him, as I know thou certainly wilt in this tender alliance. Impudence and deceit were thy other accusations: how little merited! I only traced the collateral branches of the genealogical tree thou pointedst out to me.

Alexander. Draw back the bolt: let me pass: stand out of my way. Thy hand upon my shoulder! Were my sword beside me, this monster should lick thy blood.

Priest. Patience! O king! The iron portal is in my hand: if the hinges turn, thy godhead is extinct. No, Alexander, no! it must not be.

Alexander. Lead me then forth. I swear to silence.

Priest. As thou wilt.

Alexander. I swear to friendship; lead me but out again.

Priest. Come; although I am much interested in the happiness of his two children whom I serve . . .

Alexander. Persecute me no longer; in the name of Jupiter!

Priest. I can hardly give it up. To have been the maker of such a match! what felicity! what glory! Think once more upon it. There are many who could measure themselves with thee, head to head; let me see the man who will do it with your child at the end of the year, if thou embracest with good heart and desirable success this daughter of deity.

Alexander. Enough, my friend! I have deserved it; but we must deceive men, or they will either hate us or despise us.[22]

Priest. Now thou talkest reasonably. I here pronounce thy divorce. Moreover, thou shalt be the son of Hammon in Libya,[23] of Mithras in Persia,[24] of Philip in Macedon, of Olympian Jove in Greece:[25] but never for the future teach priests new creeds.

Alexander. How my father Philip would have laughed over his cups at such a story as this!

Priest. Alexander! let it prove to thee thy folly.

Alexander. If such is my folly, what is that of others? Thou wilt acknowledge and proclaim me the progeny of Jupiter.

Priest. Ay, ay.

Alexander. People must believe it.

Priest. The only doubt will be among the shrewder, whether, being so extremely old and having left off his pilgrimages so many years, he could have given our unworthy world so spirited an offspring as thou art.

Come and sacrifice.

Alexander. Priest! I see thou art a man of courage: henceforward we are in confidence. Take mine with my hand: give me thine. Confess to me, as the first proof of it, didst thou never shrink back from so voracious and intractable a monster as that accursed snake?

Priest. We caught her young, and fed her on goat's milk, as our Jupiter himself was fed in the caverns of Crete.[26]

Alexander. Your Jupiter! *that* was another.

[22] Landor's conception of Alexander as a clever politician who is willing to deceive others about his divinity while not deceiving himself is suggested in Plutarch: "It is clear that Alexander himself was not foolishly affected or puffed up by the belief in his divinity, but used it for the subjugation of others" (*Alexander* 28. 3).

[23] Ammon, a major Libyan divinity, was subsequently worshiped in Egypt, in Greece, and in Italy. He was called Amon by the Hebrews, Zeus Ammon by the Greeks, and Jupiter Ammon by the Romans. The god was usually represented either as a ram or as a human being with a ram's head. In some instances he appeared as a human being with only the horns of a ram.

[24] Mithras is the Persian sun god.

[25] Zeus ("Olympian Jove") is supreme ruler of the Greek gods who reside on Mount Olympus.

[26] In Greek mythology, Zeus (identified with the Roman Jupiter), infant son of Cronus, was hidden by his mother, Rhea, in a cave on Mount Dicte or Mount Ida in Crete in order to protect him from being swallowed by his father. In the cave Zeus was suckled by the goat Amalthea.

Priest. Some people say so: but the same cradle serves for the whole family, the same story will do for them all. As for fearing this young personage in the treasury-vault, we fear her no more, son Alexander, than the priests of Egypt do his holiness the crocodile-god. The gods and their pedagogues are manageable to the hand that feeds them.

Alexander. Canst thou talk thus?

Priest. Of false gods, not of the true one.

Alexander. One! are there not many? Some dozens? some hundreds?

Priest. Not in our vicinity; praised be Hammon! And plainly to speak, there is nowhere another, let who will have begotten him, whether on cloud or meadow, feather-bed or barn-floor, worth a salt locust or a last year's date-fruit.

These are our mysteries, if thou must needs know them; and those of other priesthoods are the like.

Alexander, my boy, do not stand there, with thy arms folded and thy head aside, pondering. Jupiter the Ram [27] for ever!

Alexander. Glory to Jupiter the Ram!

Priest. Thou stoppest on a sudden thy prayers and praises to father Jupiter. Son Alexander! art thou not satisfied? What ails thee, drawing the back of thy hand across thine eyes?

Alexander. A little dust flew into them as the door opened.

Priest. Of that dust are the sands of the desert and the kings of Macedon.

---

[27] See n. 23 above.

DIOGENES AND PLATO

We have Landor's own testimony that "Diogenes and Plato" was one of his favorite Conversations. In 1838 he wrote the Countess of Blessington, "I received more pleasure from my Lucullus, my Epicurus, and my Diogenes, than I could receive from not only extensive popularity, but from eternal fame. They satisfied my heart, which is larger than the World's, and nearer home."[1] The term "Conversation," however, is somewhat misleading when applied to "Diogenes and Plato," for it is less of a conversation and more of a concentrated attack upon both the person and the philosophy of Plato. Indeed, much of Landor's pleasure in writing "Diogenes and Plato" certainly derived from the opportunity it gave him to express, through Diogenes, his opinions of many of Plato's ideas, engaging the two philosophers, so unlike in temperament, in conversation.

This biased attitude toward Plato is limited neither to "Diogenes and Plato" nor to a specific period in the writer's life. In a letter addressed to the Reverend Walter Birch, postmarked December 16, 1823, Landor wrote:

> Several of the summer and autumnal months were devoted by me exclusively to the attentive perusal of Plato. I was much surprised to find him so many degrees below his usual estimate. . . . Remember in how short a time Cicero wrote his philosophical works, yet surely they are more philosophical than Plato's, whose whole life was occupied (if not in the composition) in the contemplation of such matters. The best of his works is the Defence of Socrates; yet the defence is a saucy one, and therefore a bad one. His attack on the sophists, as he calls many great men, is nauseous from its repetition and sameness. His political ideas in great part are puerile, with many true remarks, however, and striking sentences. After this part of his works, I read the πολιτικα of Aristoteles. What a loss that we have not the remainder! How striking a contrast to the whimsies of his master! The style is admirable, and, what I did not expect, the periods most harmonious and perfect.[2]

Twenty-seven years later, in a letter to Mrs. Andrew Crosse (1850), Landor's attitude toward the philosopher was much the same: "Talk of Plato! the fellow is what Carlyle would call a sham and humbug."[3] And in 1856,

---

[1] Letter from W. S. Landor to the Countess of Blessington (postmarked Bath, October 15, 1838), W. Robertson Nicoll and Thomas James Wise, *Literary Anecdotes of the Nineteenth Century* (2 vols.; London, 1895–1896), I, 204–205.

[2] E. H. R. Tatham, "Some Unpublished Letters of W. S. Landor," *Fortnightly Review*, XCIII (February 1910), 372.

[3] Mrs. Andrew Crosse, *Red-Letter Days of My Life* (2 vols.; London, 1892), I, 188.

Landor defended Carlyle's refusal to read Plato in a letter to Ralph Waldo Emerson:

> You tell us, "he [Carlyle] does not read Plato." Perhaps there may be a sufficient reason for it.
>
> Resolved to find out what there is in this remarkable philosopher, I went daily for several weeks into the Magliabechian library at Florence, and thus refreshing my neglected Greek, I continued the reading of his works in the original from beginning to end. The result of this reading may be found in several of the Imaginary Conversations. That one of them between Lord Chesterfield and Lord Chatham contains observations on the cacophony of some sentences; and many more could have been added quite as exceptionable. Even Attic honey hath its impurities.[4]

In "Diogenes and Plato" Landor chooses to direct his criticism primarily toward the Laws and Timaeus *of Plato, but some of that philosopher's thoughts and statements in* The Republic, the Symposium, *the* Menexenus, *the* Minos, *and the* Phaedrus *are also brought before Landor's harsh judgment. Through Diogenes, Landor rejects, in the* Laws, *whatever governmental regulation he considers either excessively restrictive of personal freedom or capable of inviting injustice or tyranny. He also expresses his dislike for Plato's metaphysical speculation, ideas about love, and conception of the world. Since Landor sometimes misreads Plato or considers the philosopher's statements out of context, his criticism of Plato is not always warranted. It was not Landor's habit to overlook faults where he found them,[5] and the pains he took to expose the faults and absurdities he found in Plato prove this Conversation to be no exception to his usual procedure.*

Landor's Diogenes is both idealized and endowed with many of the author's opinions, ideas, and traits, while Plato is, for the most part, made into little more than an unpleasant caricature. The vindictive attack upon Plato appears to be motivated, on the one hand, by Landor's dislike of metaphysicians, Plato being the scapegoat, and on the other, by a sense of rivalry with the philosopher in the matter of writing dialogues.[6] In marshaling his attack upon Plato,

---

[4] *The Complete Works of Walter Savage Landor*, ed. T. Earle Welby and Stephen Wheeler (16 vols.; London: Chapman and Hall Ltd., 1927–1936), XII, 197. Hereafter referred to as *Complete Works*. In addition to "Lord Chesterfield and Lord Chatham," and the present Conversation, Landor's critical views of Plato appear in "Demosthenes and Eubulides," "Aristoteles and Callisthenes," "Marcus Tullius and Quinctus Cicero," and "Diogenes and a Citizen."

[5] See n. 71 below.

[6] On May 31, 1823, Landor remarked in a letter to his friend Robert Southey: "Before I wrote this conversation ['Marcus Tullius and Quinctus Cicero'], I would on

IMAGINARY CONVERSATIONS 159

Landor draws upon the writings of both Athenaeus and Diogenes Laertius. It is indeed apparent in the characterization of Diogenes the Cynic and in many of the attacks against Plato which Landor places in Diogenes' mouth that Diogenes Laertius' Lives of Eminent Philosophers *is the writer's primary source. Although Diogenes Laertius records several meetings in Athens between Diogenes the Cynic (ca. 400-ca. 325* B.C.*) and Plato (ca. 429-347* B.C.*), Landor's lack of concern for historical chronology thwarts any attempt to place this imaginary meeting at a given point in time.*

Diogenes. Stop! stop! come hither! Why lookest thou so scornfully and askance upon me?

Plato. Let me go; loose me; I am resolved to pass.

Diogenes. Nay then, by Jupiter and this tub![7] thou leavest three good ells of Milesian cloth behind thee.[8] Whither wouldst thou amble?

Plato. I am not obliged in courtesy to tell you.

Diogenes. Upon whose errand? Answer me directly.

Plato. Upon my own.

Diogenes. O! then I will hold thee yet awhile. If it were upon another'_, it might be a hardship to a good citizen, though not to a good philosopher.

Plato. That can be no impediment to my release: you do not think me one.[9]

Diogenes. No, by my father Jove!

Plato. Your father!

---

no account open Plato. I have since read twice over his dialogue [?] of Socrates, and am not so discouraged as I might have been" (quoted in John Forster, *Walter Savage Landor. A Biography* [2 vols.; London, 1869], II, 113; hereafter referred to as Forster).

[7] Diogenes Laertius mentions the famous tub which served as the home of Diogenes the Cynic: "He had written to some one to try and procure a cottage for him. When this man was a long time about it, he took for his abode the tub in the Metroön [the temple of Rhea at Athens], as he himself explains in his letters. And in summer he used to roll in it over hot sand, while in winter he used to embrace statues covered with snow, using every means of inuring himself to hardship" (*Lives of Eminent Philosophers* vi. 23, tr. R. D. Hicks ["The Loeb Classical Library"; Cambridge: Harvard University Press; London: W. Heinemann, 1965], Vol. II; hereafter referred to as Diogenes Laertius *Lives*, II. See also *Lives* vi. 43.

[8] The Ionian city of Miletus was famous for the fine quality of its woolen cloth. In the Greek system of measurement, three ells would roughly approximate three yards.

[9] According to Diogenes Laertius: "He [Diogenes] was great at pouring scorn on his contemporaries. The school of Euclides he called bilious, and Plato's lectures waste of time, the performances at the Dionysia great peep-shows for fools, and the demagogues the mob's lacqueys" (vi. 24, in *Lives*, II). See also *Lives* vi. 26.

Diogenes. Why not? Thou shouldst be the last man to doubt it. Hast not thou declared it irrational to refuse our belief to those who assert that they are begotten by the gods, though the assertion (these are thy words) be unfounded on reason or probability?[10] In me there is a chance of it: whereas in the generation of such people as thou art fondest of frequenting, who claim it loudly, there are always too many competitors to leave it probable.

Plato. Those who speak against the great, do not usually speak from morality, but from envy.

Diogenes. Thou hast a glimpse of the truth in this place; but as thou hast already shown thy ignorance in attempting to prove to me what a *man* is,[11] ill can I expect to learn from thee what is a *great man*.

Plato. No doubt your experience and intercourse will afford me the information.

Diogenes. Attend, and take it. The great man is he who hath nothing to fear and nothing to hope from another. It is he who, while he demonstrates the iniquity of the laws, and is able to correct them, obeys them peaceably. It is he who looks on the ambitious both as weak and fraudulent. It is he who hath no disposition or occasion for any kind of deceit, no reason for being or for appearing different from what he is. It is he who can call together the most select company when it pleases him.

Plato. Excuse my interruption. In the beginning of your definition I fancied that you were designating your own person, as most people do in describing what is admirable; now I find that you have some other in contemplation.

Diogenes. I thank thee for allowing me what perhaps I *do* possess, but what I was not then thinking of; as is often the case with rich possessors: in fact, the latter part of the description suits me as well as any portion of the former.

Plato. You may call together the best company, by using your hands in the call, as you did with me; otherwise I am not sure that you would succeed in it.

Diogenes. My thoughts are my company: I can bring them together, select them, detain them, dismiss them. Imbecile and vicious men can not

---

[10] See Plato *Timaeus* 40d–e. Plato's words in this passage from the *Timaeus* are ironical and were not intended to be taken literally.

[11] "Plato had defined Man as an animal, biped and featherless, and was applauded. Diogenes plucked a fowl and brought it into the lecture-room with the words, 'Here is Plato's man.' In consequence of which there was added to the definition, 'having broad nails'" (Diogenes Laertius vi. 40, in *Lives*, II).

do any of these things. Their thoughts are scattered, vague, uncertain, cumbersome; and the worst stick to them the longest; many indeed by choice, the greater part by necessity, and accompanied, some by weak wishes, others by vain remorse.

Plato. Is there nothing of greatness, O Diogenes! in exhibiting how cities and communities may be governed best, how morals may be kept the purest, and power become the most stabile?

Diogenes. Something of greatness does not constitute the great man. Let me however see him who hath done what thou sayest. He must be the most universal and the most indefatigable traveller, he must also be the oldest creature upon earth.

Plato. How so?

Diogenes. Because he must know perfectly the climate, the soil, the situation, the peculiarities, of the races, of their allies, of their enemies: he must have sounded their harbours, he must have measured the quantity of their arable land and pasture, of their woods and mountains: he must have ascertained whether there are fisheries on their coasts, and even what winds are prevalent.[12] On these causes, with some others, depend the bodily strength, the numbers, the wealth, the wants, the capacities, of the people.

Plato. Such are low thoughts.

Diogenes. The bird of wisdom flies low, and seeks her food under hedges: the eagle himself would be starved if he always soared aloft and against the sun. The sweetest fruit grows near the ground, and the plants that bear it require ventilation and lopping. Were this not to be done in thy garden,[13] every walk and alley, every plot and border, would be covered with runners and roots, with boughs and suckers. We want no poets or logicians or metaphysicians to govern us: we want practical men,

---

[12] Parts of knowledge which are now general, but were formerly very rare, and united in none. [*Landor's note.*]

[13] Diogenes Laertius alludes to Plato's "garden": "Having returned to Athens, he lived in the Academy, which is a gymnasium outside the walls, in a grove named after a certain hero, Hecademus, as is stated by Eupolis in his play entitled *Shirkers*: 'In the shady walks of the divine Hecademus.' Moreover, there are verses of Timon [of Phlius] which refer to Plato: 'Amongst all of them Plato was the leader, a big fish, but a sweet-voiced speaker, musical in prose as the cicala who, perched on the trees of Hecademus, pours forth a strain as delicate as a lily.' Thus the original name of the place was Hecademy, spelt with *e*" [*Lives of Eminent Philosophers* iii. 7–8, tr. R. D. Hicks (rev. ed.; "The Loeb Classical Library"; Cambridge: Harvard University Press; London: W. Heinemann, 1966), Vol. I]. Hereafter referred to as Diogenes Laertius *Lives*, I. See also *Lives* iii. 20.

honest men, continent men, unambitious men, fearful to solicit a trust, slow to accept, and resolute never to betray one. Experimentalists may be the best philosophers; they are always the worst politicians. Teach people their duties, and they will know their interests. Change as little as possible, and correct as much.[14]

Philosophers are absurd from many causes, but principally from laying out unthriftily their distinctions. They set up four virtues: fortitude, prudence, temperance, and justice.[15] Now a man may be a very bad one, and yet possess three out of the four. Every cut-throat must, if he has been a cut-throat on many occasions, have more fortitude and more prudence than the greater part of those whom we consider as the best men. And what cruel wretches, both executioners and judges, have been strictly just! how little have they cared what gentleness, what generosity, what genius, their sentence hath removed from the earth! Temperance and beneficence contain all other virtues. Take them home, Plato, split them, expound them; do what thou wilt with them, if thou but use them.

Before I gave thee this lesson, which is a better than thou ever gavest anyone, and easier to remember, thou wert accusing me of invidiousness and malice against those whom thou callest the great, meaning to say the powerful. Thy imagination, I am well aware, had taken its flight toward Sicily, where thou seekest thy great man,[16] as earnestly and undoubtingly

[14] Diogenes expresses Landor's attitude toward change: "We have lately been told, by sensible and by liberal men, that we must abstain from all organick changes. For my part, I would abstain from all changes whatever, were it possible. But smaller, made in time, obviate the necessity of greater" ("The Letters of a Conservative" [1836], *Complete Works*, XII, 230). See also "Letter from W. S. Landor to R. W. Emerson" (1856), *Complete Works*, XII, 205-206.

[15] For Plato's discussion of the four cardinal virtues see *The Republic* iv. 427e and *passim*.

[16] According to Diogenes Laertius: "He [Plato] made three voyages to Sicily, the first time to see the island and the craters of Etna: on this occasion Dionysius, the son of Hermocrates [Dionysius I, 430-367 B.C., tyrant of Syracuse], being on the throne, forced him to become intimate with him. But when Plato held forth on tyranny and maintained that the interest of the ruler alone was not the best end, unless he were also pre-eminent in virtue, he offended Dionysius, who in his anger exclaimed, 'You talk like an old dotard.' 'And you like a tyrant,' rejoined Plato. At this the tyrant grew furious and at first was bent on putting him to death; then, when he had been dissuaded from this by Dion and Aristomenes, he did not indeed go so far but handed him over to Pollis the Lacedaemonian, who had just then arrived on an embassy, with orders to sell him into slavery.

. . . .

"The second time he visited the younger Dionysius [Dionysius II, the eldest son of Dionysius I, became tyrant of Syracuse in 367/366 B.C., when about thirty years of

as Ceres sought her Persephone.[17] Faith! honest Plato, I have no reason to envy thy worthy friend Dionysius. Look at my nose! A lad seven or eight years old threw an apple at me yesterday, while I was gazing at the clouds, and gave me nose enough for two moderate men.[18] Instead of such a godsend, what should I have thought of my fortune if, after living all my lifetime among golden vases,[19] rougher than my hand with their emeralds and rubies, their engravings and embossments, among Parian caryatides and porphyry sphinxes, among philosophers with rings upon their fingers and linen next their skin, and among singing-boys and dancing-girls, to whom alone thou speakest intelligibly . .[20] I ask thee again, what should I in reason have thought of my fortune, if, after these facilities and superfluities, I had at last been pelted out of my house, not by one young rogue, but by thousands of all ages, and not with an apple (I wish I could say a rotten one), but with pebbles and broken pots; and, to crown my deserts, had been compelled to become the teacher of so promising a generation. Great men, forsooth! thou knowest at last who they are.

Plato. There are great men of various kinds.

Diogenes. No, by my beard, are there not.

Plato. What! are there not great captains, great geometricians, great dialecticians?

---

age], requesting of him lands and settlers for the realization of his republic. Dionysius promised them but did not keep his word. Some say that Plato was also in great danger, being suspected of encouraging Dion and Theodotas in a scheme for liberating the whole island; on this occasion Archytas the Pythagorean wrote to Dionysius, procured his pardon, and got him conveyed safe to Athens.

. . . .

"The third time he came to reconcile Dion and Dionysius, but, failing to do so, returned to his own country without achieving anything" (iii. 18-23, in *Lives*, I).

[17] According to Greek legend, Persephone, the beautiful daughter of Zeus and Demeter, was abducted one day by Hades while she was picking flowers in the meadows of Enna, Sicily. Hades made her queen of the lower world. Demeter (identified by the Romans with Ceres, probably an ancient Italian deity representing the generative power of nature) sought her daughter all over the world, neglecting her duties and causing the earth to become barren.

[18] Diogenes Laertius mentions Diogenes' being bothered by boys: "When some boys clustered round him and said, 'Take care he doesn't bite us,' he answered, 'Never fear, boys, a dog does not eat beetroot'" (vi. 45, in *Lives*, II). See also *Lives* vi. 43.

[19] Plato's aristocratic birth and upbringing are recorded by Diogenes Laertius. See *Lives* iii. 1, 4-6.

[20] "That Plato acted as choregus [a civic-minded citizen who provided a chorus for a religious festival] at Athens, the cost being defrayed by Dion, is stated by Athenodorus in the eighth book of a work entitled *Walks*" (Diogenes Laertius iii. 3, in *Lives*, I).

Diogenes. Who denied it? A great man was the postulate. Try thy hand now at the powerful one.

Plato. On seeing the exercise of power, a child can not doubt who is powerful, more or less; for power is relative. All men are weak, not only if compared to the Demiurgos,[21] but if compared to the sea or the earth, or certain things upon each of them, such as elephants and whales. So placid and tranquil is the scene around us, we can hardly bring to mind the images of strength and force, the precipices, the abysses . . .

Diogenes. Prythee hold thy loose tongue, twinkling and glittering like a serpent's in the midst of luxuriance and rankness. Did never this reflection of thine warn thee that, in human life, the precipices and abysses would be much further from our admiration, if we were less inconsiderate, selfish, and vile?[22] I will not however stop thee long, for thou wert going on quite consistently. As thy great men are fighters and wranglers, so thy mighty things upon the earth and sea are troublesome and intractable incumbrances. Thou perceivedst not what was greater in the former case, neither art thou aware what is greater in this. Didst thou feel the gentle air that passed us?[23]

---

[21] In Platonic philosophy the Demiurgos is the creator or maker of the world. See Plato *Timaeus* 27c–30d and *Philebus* 23d ff.

[22] Landor had few illusions concerning human nature: "Religion must be contented to dwell with the better of our affections, and must accommodate herself in some measure to our habits and modes of life, and among these to our frailties and deficiencies. She may suggest improvements: but even she, with all her authority, cannot force them upon us. Whenever she attempts it, we look coldly upon her, and rather leave our home than retain her for an inmate. All this may be wrong, but it is in human nature, where many things are wrong.

. . . .

"The use of religion on earth is to inculcate the moral law; in other words, in the words of Jesus Christ, to love our neighbour as ourselves. This, in the more obvious sense, is incompatible with our nature: for nobody ever did love his neighbour quite so well as himself, and never will. But we may be taught, and if we cannot be taught we may be obliged, to treat our neighbour as kindly and justly as we expect or desire to be treated by him" ("The Letters of a Conservative" [1836], *Complete Works*, XII, 228–231). See also "Popery, British and Foreign" (1851), *Complete Works*, XII, 74.

[23] By attributing an interest in the power of the air to Diogenes the Cynic, Landor has apparently confused his Diogenes with an early Greek natural philosopher of the same name, Diogenes of Apollonia. According to Diogenes Laertius: "The doctrines of Diogenes [of Apollonia] were as follows. Air is the universal element. There are worlds unlimited in number, and unlimited empty space. Air by condensation and rarefaction generates the worlds. Nothing comes into being from what is not or passes away into what is not. The earth is spherical, firmly supported in the centre, having its construction determined by the revolution which comes from heat and by the congealment caused by cold" (ix. 57, in *Lives*, II).

Plato. I did not, just then.

Diogenes. That air, so gentle, so imperceptible to thee, is more powerful not only than all the creatures that breathe and live by it; not only than all the oaks of the forest, which it rears in an age and shatters in a moment; not only than all the monsters of the sea, but than the sea itself, which it tosses up into foam, and breaks against every rock in its vast circumference; for it carries in its bosom, with perfect calm and composure, the incontrollable ocean and the peopled earth, like an atom of a feather.

To the world's turmoils and pageantries is attracted, not only the admiration of the populace, but the zeal of the orator, the enthusiasm of the poet, the investigation of the historian, and the contemplation of the philosopher: yet how silent and invisible are they in the depths of air! Do I say in those depths and deserts? No; I say at the distance of a swallow's flight; at the distance she rises above us, ere a sentence brief as this could be uttered.

What are its mines and mountains? Fragments wielded up and dislocated by the expansion of water from below; the most-part reduced to mud, the rest to splinters. Afterward sprang up fire in many places, and again tore and mangled the mutilated carcase, and still growls over it.

What are its cities and ramparts and moles and monuments? segments of a fragment, which one man puts together and another throws down. Here we stumble upon thy great ones at their work. Show me now, if thou canst, in history, three great warriors, or three great statesmen, who have acted otherwise than spiteful children.

Plato. I will begin to look for them in history when I have discovered the same number in the philosophers or the poets. A prudent man searches in his own garden after the plant he wants, before he casts his eyes over the stalls in Kenkrea or Keramicos.[24]

Returning to your observation on the potency of the air, I am not ignorant or unmindful of it. May I venture to express my opinion to you, Diogenes! that the earlier discoverers and distributers of wisdom, (which wisdom lies among us in ruins and remnants, partly distorted and partly concealed by theological allegory) meant by Jupiter the air in its agitated state, by Juno the air in its quiescent. These are the great agents, and therefore called the king and queen of the gods. Jupiter is denominated

---

[24] Cenchreae (Kenkrea), located on the Saronic Gulf near Corinth, served Corinth as the center for commercial trade with Asia. The Inner Ceramicus (Keramicos), a region northwest of the Acropolis in Athens, contained within it the Agora, a place of assembly which was also used as a market.

by Homer *the compeller of clouds:*[25] Juno receives them, and remits them in showers to plants and animals.

I may trust you, I hope, O Diogenes!

Diogenes. Thou mayest lower the gods in my presence, as safely as men in the presence of Timon.[26]

Plato. I would not lower them: I would exalt them.

Diogenes. More foolish and presumptuous still!

Plato. Fair words, O Sinopean![27] I protest to you my aim is truth.[28]

Diogenes. I can not lead thee where of a certainty thou mayest always find it; but I will tell thee what it is. Truth is a point; the subtilest and finest; harder than adamant; never to be broken, worn away, or blunted. Its only bad quality is, that it is sure to hurt those who touch it; and likely to draw blood, perhaps the life-blood, of those who press earnestly upon it. Let us away from this narrow lane skirted with hemlock,[29] and pursue our road again through the wind and dust, toward the *great* man and the *powerful.* Him I would call the powerful one, who controls the storms of his mind, and turns to good account the worst accidents of his fortune. The great man, I was going on to demonstrate, is somewhat more. He must be able to do this, and he must have an intellect which puts into motion the intellect of others.

Plato. Socrates then was your great man.

Diogenes. He was indeed; nor can all thou hast attributed to him ever make me think the contrary.[30] I wish he could have kept a little more at home, and have thought it as well worth his while to converse with his own children as with others.[31]

[25] See Homer *Iliad* i. 511, 517, 560 ff., and *Odyssey* i. 63 ff.

[26] Timon of Athens, the famous misanthrope (*ca.* 500–429 B.C.).

[27] Diogenes was a native of Sinope, a city located on the south shore of the Euxine, or Black, Sea in Asia Minor.

[28] "He [Plato] also said that the truth is the pleasantest of sounds. Another version of this saying is that the pleasantest of all things is to speak the truth. Again, of truth he speaks thus in the *Laws* [663e]: 'Truth, O stranger, is a fair and durable thing. But it is a thing of which it is hard to persuade men'" (Diogenes Laertius iii. 40, in *Lives,* I).

[29] Diogenes is alluding to the death of Socrates (469–399 B.C.), whose search for truth brought upon him the charge of impiety and the sentence of death by drinking hemlock. See n. 53 below.

[30] "They say that, on hearing Plato read the *Lysis,* Socrates exclaimed, 'By Heracles, what a number of lies this young man is telling about me!' For he has included in the dialogue much that Socrates never said" (Diogenes Laertius iii. 35, in *Lives,* I). See also Athenaeus *The Deipnosophists* xi. 507c–d.

[31] After meeting Landor in Italy in May, 1833, Ralph Waldo Emerson wrote in one of his journals: "I think it was of Socrates that Landor dared to say, so far can a

Plato. He knew himself born for the benefit of the human race.

Diogenes. Those who are born for the benefit of the human race, go but little into it: those who are born for its curse, are crowded.

Plato. It was requisite to dispel the mists of ignorance and error.

Diogenes. Has he done it? What doubt has he elucidated, or what fact has he established? Although I was but twelve years old and resident in another city [32] when he died, I have taken some pains in my inquiries about him from persons of less vanity and less perverseness than his disciples.[33] He did not leave behind him any true philosopher among them; any who followed his mode of argumentation, his subjects of disquisition, or his course of life; any who would subdue the malignant passions or coerce the looser; any who would abstain from calumny or from cavil; any who would devote his days to the glory of his country, or, what is easier and perhaps wiser, to his own well-founded contentment and well-merited repose. Xenophon,[34] the best of them, offered up

---

humoursome man indulge a whim, 'he was a vulgar sophist & he [Landor] could not forgive vulgarity in any body; if he saw it in a wise man he regretted it the more'" (*The Journals and Miscellaneous Notebooks of Ralph Waldo Emerson*, ed. William H. Gilman et al. [6 vols.; Cambridge: Belknap Press of Harvard University Press, 1960–1966], IV, 73). Emerson's note took the following form in his *English Traits*, published twenty-three years later: "He [Landor] invited me to breakfast on Friday. On Friday I did not fail to go, and this time with Greenough [an American sculptor living at Florence]. He entertained us at once with reciting half a dozen hexameter lines of Julius Cæsar's!—from Donatus, he said. He glorified Lord Chesterfield more than was necessary, and undervalued Burke, and undervalued Socrates" (*English Traits* [Boston, 1856], p. 14; hereafter referred to as *English Traits*). After reading *English Traits*, Landor wrote a letter to Emerson (1856) in an attempt to correct the American's false impressions and to justify many of his remarks uttered twenty-three years before. In respect to Socrates, he wrote: "I do not 'undervalue Socrates.' Being the cleverest of the Sophists, he turned the fraternity into ridicule: he eluded the grasp of his antagonist by anointing with the oil of quibble all that was tangible and prominent. To compare his philosophy (if indeed you can catch it) with the philosophy of Epicurus and Epictetus, whose systems meet, is insanity" (*Complete Works*, XII, 201).

[32] Since Diogenes was born at Sinope about 400 B.C., he could not have been twelve years old at the time of Socrates' death (399 B.C.). See Diogenes Laertius *Lives* vi. 20–21.

[33] Although Diogenes criticized several of Socrates' disciples (Diogenes Laertius *Lives* vi. 24 ff.), his scorn was not directed at any one group, but rather toward anyone who seemed to deserve it.

[34] Xenophon (*ca.* 430–*ca.* 354 B.C.), according to Diogenes Laertius, was a pupil of Socrates (*Lives* ii. 48) and "a worthy man in general, particularly fond of horses and hunting, an able tactician as is clear from his writings, pious, fond of sacrificing, and an expert in augury from the victims; and he made Socrates his exact model" (ii. 56, in *Lives*, I). For an example of Xenophon's fear of omens see his *Anabasis* iii. 1. 11–13. See also p. 29, n. 48.

sacrifices, believed in oracles, consulted soothsayers, turned pale at a jay, and was dysenteric at a magpie.[35]

Plato. He had then no courage? I was the first to suspect it.

Diogenes. Which thou hadst never been if others had not praised him for it: but his courage was of so strange a quality, that he was ready, if jay or magpie did not cross him, to fight for Spartan or Persian.[36] Plato, whom thou esteemest much more, and knowest somewhat less, careth as little for portents and omens as doth Diogenes. What he would have done for a Persian I can not say: certain I am that he would have no more fought for a Spartan than he would for his own father: yet he mortally hates the man who hath a kinder muse or a better milliner, or a seat nearer the minion of a king.[37] So much for the two disciples of Socrates who have acquired the greatest celebrity!

Plato. Why do you attribute to me invidiousness and malignity, rather than to the young philosopher who is coming prematurely forward into public notice, and who hath lately been invited by the King of Macedon to educate his son?[38]

---

[35] The magpie is traditionally considered an evil omen. The jay and the magpie are members of the same genus, and so similar structurally that the one is frequently mistaken for the other. Since the jay does not share the magpie's accorded role of evil portent, Landor is able to play upon the confusing similarity of the two birds, humorously emphasizing Xenophon's belief in omens.

[36] Diogenes' allusions are to Xenophon's service, first with Persians, and then with Spartans. In 401 B.C., Xenophon joined the expedition of Cyrus the younger, son of Darius II, against his brother Artaxerxes II, king of Persia. (See Xenophon *Anabasis* and Diogenes Laertius *Lives* ii. 49–50.) In 399 B.C., Xenophon gave his Cyrenian troops to Thibron, the Spartan general. He served under Agesilaus, king of Sparta, from 396 to 394 B.C., and received an estate at Scillus, near Olympia, for his services to the Spartan government. (See Diogenes Laertius *Lives* ii. 51–53.)

[37] Athenaeus, in *The Deipnosophists*, has Pontianus of Nicomedia say: "Plato had the reputation of being jealous and having by no means a good name so far as his character was concerned. For he actually mocked at Aristippus for going to live at the court of Dionysius, although he himself had voyaged to Sicily three times: once to see the streams of lava, on which occasion he, in company with the elder Dionysius, risked his life, and twice to visit the younger Dionysius" (xi. 507b–c, in *The Deipnosophists*, tr. Charles Burton Gulick [rev. ed.; "The Loeb Classical Library"; Cambridge: Harvard University Press; London: W. Heinemann, 1963], Vol. V; hereafter referred to as Athenaeus *The Deipnosophists*, V).

[38] In 343–342 B.C., Aristotle (384–322 B.C.), son of Nicomachus, was invited by Philip of Macedon to come to Pella and tutor his son, Alexander. Since Plato died in 347 B.C., he could not have known (as does Landor's Plato) of his young scholar's appointment. See Diogenes Laertius *Lives* v. 1, 4–5, 9–10. In speaking of "the young philosopher who is coming prematurely forward into public notice," Landor's Plato is

Diogenes. These very words of thine demonstrate to me, calm and expostulatory as they appear in utterance, that thou enviest in this young man, if not his abilities, his appointment. And prythee now demonstrate to me as clearly, if thou canst, in what he is either a sycophant or a malignant.

Plato. Willingly.

Diogenes. I believe it. But easily too?

Plato. I think so. Knowing the arrogance of Philip, and the signs of ambition which his boy (I forget the name) hath exhibited so early, he says, in the fourth book of his *Ethics* (already in the hands of several here at Athens, although in its present state unfit for publication), that "he who deems himself worthy of less than his due, is a man of pusillanimous and abject mind."[39]

Diogenes. His canine tooth, friend Plato, did not enter thy hare's fur here.

Plato. No; he sneered at Phocion,[40] and flattered Philip. He adds, "whether that man's merits be great, or small, or middling." And he supports the position by sophistry.

Diogenes. How could he act more consistently? Such is the support it should rest on. If the man's merits were great, he could not be abject.

Plato. Yet the author was so contented with his observation, that he expresses it again a hundred lines below.

Diogenes. Then he was not contented with his observation; for, had he

---

enviously alluding to Aristotle's leaving the Academy while Plato was still in charge. See Diogenes Laertius *Lives*, v. 2.

[39] Aristotle *Nicomachean Ethics* iv. 3. 7. Aristotle composed the *Nicomachean Ethics* during his second residence at Athens (335–323 B.C.), twelve to twenty-five years after Plato's death. This work, like Aristotle's other extant writings, was never prepared for publication.

[40] Phocion (fourth century B.C.), Athenian general and statesman, was highly respected by both friend and foe. The Athenians elected him general forty-five times, and both Philip II and Alexander, Macedonian conquerors of Greece, admired and respected him. See Plutarch *Phocion* 17. 4–6.

Phocion was one of Landor's heroes. Emerson relates that in conversation Landor "designated as three of the greatest of men, Washington, Phocion, and Timoleon; much as our pomologists, in their lists, select the three or the six best pears 'for a small orchard;' and did not even omit to remark the similar termination of their names. 'A great man,' he said, 'should make great sacrifices, and kill his hundred oxen, without knowing whether they would be consumed by gods and heroes, or whether the flies would eat them'" (*English Traits*, p. 14). See p. 69, n. 44, and Landor's Conversation "Æschines and Phocion."

been contented, he would have said no more about it. But, having seen lately his treatise,[41] I remember that he varies the expression of the sentiment, and, after saying a very foolish thing, is resolved on saying one rather less inconsiderate: on the principle of the hunter on the snows of Pindus,[42] who, when his fingers are frost-bitten, does not hold them instantly to the fire, but dips them first into cold water. Aristoteles[43] says, in his second trial at the thesis, "*for* he who is of low and abject mind, strips himself of what is good about him, and is, to a certain degree, bad, because he thinks himself unworthy of the good."[44]

Modesty and diffidence make a man unfit for public affairs: they also make him unfit for brothels: but do they therefore make him bad? It is not often that your scholar is lost in this way, by following the echo of his own voice. His greatest fault is, that he so condenses his thoughts as to render it difficult to see through them: he inspissates his yellow to black. However, I see more and more in him the longer I look at him: in you I see less and less. Perhaps other men may have eyes of another construction, and filled with a subtiler and more ethereal fluid.

Plato. Acknowledge at least that it argues a poverty of thought to repeat the same sentiment.

Diogenes. It may or it may not. Whatever of ingenuity or invention be displayed in a remark, another may be added which surpasses it. If, after this and perhaps more, the author, in a different treatise, or in a different place of the same, throws upon it fresh materials, surely you must allow that he rather hath brought forward the evidence of plenteousness than of poverty. Much of invention may be exhibited in the variety of turns and aspects he makes his thesis assume. A poor friend may give me to-day a portion of yesterday's repast; but a rich man is likelier to send me what is preferable, forgetting that he had sent me as much a day or two before.

---

[41] Since Diogenes lived until about 325 B.C., he might have been familiar with Aristotle's *Nicomachean Ethics*. According to Diogenes Laertius, Aristotle and Diogenes were acquaintances (*Lives* v. 18).

[42] Pindus is the ancient name of a group of rugged mountains in northern Greece which separate Thessaly from Epirus.

[43] Landor had definite ideas about orthography. In the second Conversation between Southey and Landor, the two interlocutors discuss Landor's spelling of "Aristoteles":

Southey. I perceive you adhere to ... the termination of Aristo*teles*.

Landor. If we were to say Arist*otle*, why not Themis*tocle*, Empe*docle*, and Peri*cle*? (*The Works of Walter Savage Landor* [2 vols.; London, 1846], II, 161; hereafter referred to as *Works*). For a detailed study of Landor's orthographic practices, see Charles L. Proudfit, "Landor's Hobbyhorse: A Study in Romantic Orthography," *Studies in Romanticism*, VII (Summer 1968), 207–217.

[44] Aristotle *Nicomachean Ethics* iv. 3. 35.

They who give us all we want, and beyond what we expected, may be pardoned if they happen to overlook the extent of their liberality. In this matter thou hast spoken inconsiderately and unwisely: but whether the remark of Aristoteles was intended as a slur on Phocion is uncertain. The repetition of it makes me incline to think it was; for few writers repeat a kind sentiment, many an unkind one: and Aristoteles would have repeated a just observation rather than an unjust, unless he wished either to flatter or malign. The gods rarely let us take good aim on these occasions, but dazzle or overcloud us. The perfumed oil of flattery, and the caustic spirit of malignity, spread over an equally wide surface. Here both are thrown out of their jars by the same pair of hands at the same moment; the sweet (as usual) on the bad man, the unsweet (as universal) on the good. I never heard before that they had fallen on the hands of Phocion and of Philip. Thou hast furnished me with the suspicion, and I have furnished thee with the supports for it. Do not, however, hope to triumph over Aristoteles, because he hath said one thoughtless thing: rather attempt to triumph *with* him on saying many wise ones. For a philosopher I think him very little of an impostor. He mingles too frequently the acute and dull; and thou too frequently the sweet and vapid. Try to barter one with the other, amicably; and not to twitch and carp. You may each be the better for some exchanges; but neither for cheapening one another's wares. Do thou take my advice the first of the two; for thou hast the most to gain by it. Let me tell thee also that it does him no dishonour to have accepted the invitation of Philip as future preceptor of his newly-born child. I would rather rear a lion's whelp and tame him, than see him run untamed about the city, especially if any tenement and cattle were at its outskirts. Let us hope that a soul once Attic can never become Macedonian; but rather Macedonian than Sicilian.

Aristoteles, and all the rest of you, must have the wadding of straw and saw-dust shaken out, and then we shall know pretty nearly your real weight and magnitude.

Plato. A philosopher ought never to speak in such a manner of philosophers.

Diogenes. None other ought, excepting now and then the beadle. However, the gods have well protected thee, O Plato, against his worst violence. Was this raiment of thine the screen of an Egyptian temple?[45] or merely

---

[45] Although Diogenes had nothing but contempt for effeminacy and fine dress (see Diogenes Laertius *Lives* vi. 46, 54, 66), he never, according to Diogenes Laertius, attacked Plato on those grounds. Athenaeus, however, does comment upon the elaborate attire worn by Plato and his followers in *The Deipnosophists* xi. 509b–e.

the drapery of a thirty-cubit Isis?[46] or peradventure a holiday suit of Darius for a bevy of his younger concubines?[47] Prythee do tarry with me, or return another day, that I may catch a flight of quails with it as they cross over this part of Attica.

Plato. It hath always been the fate of the decorous to be calumniated for effeminacy by the sordid.

Diogenes. Effeminacy! By my beard! he who could carry all this Milesian bravery on his shoulders,[48] might, with the help of three more such able men, have tost Typhoëus[49] up to the teeth of Jupiter.

Plato. We may serve our country, I hope, with clean faces.

Diogenes. More serve her with clean faces than with clean hands: and some are extremely shy of her when they fancy she may want them.

Plato. Although on some occasions I have left Athens, I can not be accused of deserting her in the hour of danger.

Diogenes. Nor proved to have defended her: but better desert her on some occasions, or on all, than praise the tyrant Critias; the cruellest of the thirty who condemned thy master.[50] In one hour, in the hour when that

---

[46] In Egyptian religion Isis was the wife of Osiris, god of the Underworld, and the mother of Horus, the sun.

[47] "Philip of Macedon did not, to be sure, take women along with him on his campaigns, as did Darius, the one who was deposed by Alexander; for Darius, although engaged in a war in which his entire empire was at stake, took round with him three hundred and sixty concubines, according to the account given by Dicaearchus in the third book of his *History of Greece*" (Athenaeus *The Deipnosophists* xiii. 557b, tr. Charles Burton Gulick ["The Loeb Classical Library"; Cambridge: Harvard University Press; London: W. Heinemann, 1959], Vol. VI; hereafter referred to as Athenaeus *The Deipnosophists*, VI).

[48] Landor is punning when he speaks of "Milesian bravery," for the city of Miletus is known not only for its fine woolen cloth, but also for the bravery of its citizens who led the Ionian revolt against Darius in 500 B.C. (see Herodotus *History* vi. 19, 20) and who held out against Alexander the Great's invasion in 334 B.C. after all the other Ionian cities had fallen, being defeated only after a long siege. See Arrian *Anabasis* i. 19.

[49] Typhoeus, a monster with a hundred heads, fearful eyes, and terrible voices, fought Zeus for the mastery of mortals and immortals. After a fearful struggle, Typhoeus was subdued with a thunderbolt from Zeus. (Hesiod *Theogony* 819-869.)

[50] Although Plato honored the memory of his cousin Critias (*ca.* 460-403 B.C.), one of the leaders of the Thirty Tyrants at Athens (June, 404-January, 403 B.C.), in four of his dialogues (*Charmides, Protagoras, Timaeus,* and *Critias*), he did not approve of the rule of the Thirty. See Plato *Epistle* VII. 324b-325b.

Socrates' trial and condemnation were instigated by Anytus (fifth and fourth centuries B.C.), one of the restorers of Athenian democracy (June, 403 B.C.), and not by the Thirty as Diogenes would have us believe. In an earlier Conversation, "Aristoteles and Callisthenes," Landor has Aristotle say: "Now, Callisthenes! if Socrates and Anytos were in the same chamber, if the wicked had mixed poison for the virtuous, the

friend was dying, when young and old were weeping over him,⁵¹ where *then* wert thou?

Plato. Sick at home.⁵²

Diogenes. Sick! how long? of what malady? In such torments, or in such debility, that it would have cost thee thy life to have been carried to the prison? or hadst thou no litter; no slaves to bear it; no footboy to inquire the way to the public prison, to the cell of Socrates? The medicine he took could never have made thy heart colder, or thy legs more inactive and torpid in their movement toward a friend.⁵³ Shame upon thee! scorn! contempt! everlasting reprobation and abhorrence!

Plato. Little did I ever suppose that, in being accused of hard-heartedness, Diogenes would exercise the office of accuser.

Diogenes. Not to press the question, nor to avoid the recrimination, I will enter on the subject at large; and rather as an appeal than as a disquisition. I am called hard-hearted; Alcibiades⁵⁴ is called tender-hearted. Speak I truly or falsely?

Plato. Truly.

Diogenes. In both cases?

Plato. In both.

Diogenes. Pray, in what doth hardness of heart consist?

Plato. There are many constituents and indications of it: want of sympathy with our species is one.

Diogenes. I sympathise with the brave in their adversity and afflictions, because I feel in my own breast the flame that burns in theirs: and I do

---

active in evil for the active in good, and some Divinity had placed it in your power to present the cup to either, and, touching your head, should say, 'This head also is devoted to the Eumenides if the choice be wrong,' what would you resolve?" (*Works*, I, 232).

⁵¹ See Plato *Phaedo* 117b–e.

⁵² See Plato *Phaedo* 59b.

⁵³ "He [Socrates] walked about and, when he said his legs were heavy, lay down on his back, for such was the advice of the attendant. The man who had administered the poison [hemlock] laid his hands on him and after a while examined his feet and legs, then pinched his foot hard and asked if he felt it. He said 'No'; then after that, his thighs; and passing upwards in this way he showed us that he was growing cold and rigid. And again he touched him and said that when it reached his heart, he would be gone" (Plato *Phaedo* 117e–118, in *Euthyphro, Apology, Crito, Phaedo, Phaedrus*, tr. H. N. Fowler ["The Loeb Classical Library"; Cambridge: Harvard University Press; London: W. Heinemann, 1960]; hereafter referred to as Plato *Phaedo*).

⁵⁴ Alcibiades (*ca.* 450–404 B.C.) was a pupil and intimate friend of Socrates as well as a brilliant Athenian general and statesman. See Thucydides *History* v–viii; Xenophon *Hellenica* i; Plato *Alcibiades I* and *Symposium*; and Plutarch *Alcibiades*.

not sympathise with others, because with others my heart hath nothing of consanguinity. I no more sympathise with the generality of mankind than I do with fowls, fishes, and insects. We have indeed the same figure and the same flesh, but not the same soul and spirit. Yet, recall to thy memory, if thou canst, any action of mine bringing pain of body or mind to any rational creature. True indeed, no despot or conqueror should exercise his authority a single hour if my arm or my exhortations could prevail against him.[55] Nay more: none should depart from the earth without flagellations, nor without brands, nor without exposure, day after day, in the market-place of the city where he governed.[56] This is the only way I know of making men believe in the justice of their gods. And if they never were to believe in it at all, it is right that they should confide in the equity of their fellow-men. Even this were imperfect: for every despot and

[55] Landor's hatred of kings, princes, despots, and conquerors and his advocacy of tyrannicide find their way into many of his writings. In the Conversation "Landor, English Visiter, and Florentine Visiter," he says: "Far am I from the inclination of lighting up a fire to invite around it the idle, the malevolent, the seditious: I would however subscribe my name, to ensure the maintenance of those persons who shall have lost their country for having punished with death its oppressor, or for having attempted it and failed. Let it first be demonstrated that he hath annulled the constitutional laws, or retracted his admissal or violated his promise of them, or that he holds men not born his subjects, nor reduced to that condition by legitimate war, in servitude and thraldom, or hath assisted or countenanced another in such offences. No scorn, no contumely, no cruelty, no single, no multiplied, injustice, no destruction, is enough, excepting the destruction of that upon which all society is constituted, under which all security rests, and all hope lies at anchor, faith. Public wrongs may and ought to be punished by private vindication, where the tongue of Law is paralysed by the bane of Despotism; and the action which in civil life is the worst, becomes, where civism lies beneath power, the most illustrious that magnanimity can achieve. The calmest and wisest men that ever lived were unanimous in this sentence; it is sanctioned by the laws of Solon, and sustained by the authority of Cicero and Aristoteles. The latter, mild and moderate as he was, goes a great way farther than I have ventured. Teachers, the timid and secluded, point it out to youth among a thousand pages; colleges ring with it over chants and homilies; Piety closes her thumbed lesson and articulates less tremulously this response. The street cries *Caesar*, the study whispers *Brutus*. Degenerate men have never been so degenerate, the earth is not yet so effete, as not to rear up one imitator of one great deed" (*Works*, I, 333-334). See also, in *Complete Works*, XII, "Capital Punishment" (1849), p. 177; "What We Have and What We Owe" (1850), p. 175; and "Letter from W. S. Landor to R. W. Emerson" (1856), pp. 203-204.

[56] In the Conversation "The Abbé Delille and Walter Landor," Landor says: "How many of your most glorious [French] kings would, if they had been private men in any free country, or even in their own, have been condemned to the pillory and the galleys! ... he [Boileau] ought to have known that kings do not carry the burden of thrones, but that thrones carry theirs" (*Works*, I, 100).

conqueror inflicts much greater misery than any human body can suffer. Now then plainly thou seest the extent of what thou wouldst call my cruelty. We who have ragged beards are cruel by prescription and acclamation; while they who have pumiced faces and perfumed hair, are called cruel only in the moments of tenderness, and in the pauses of irritation. Thy friend Alcibiades [57] was extremely good-natured: yet, because the people of Melos, descendants from the Lacedæmonians, stood neutral in the Peloponesian war, and refused to fight against their fathers, the good-natured man, when he had vanquished and led them captive, induced the Athenians to slaughter all among them who were able to bear arms: and we know that the survivors were kept in irons until the victorious Spartans set them free.

Plato. I did not approve of this severity.

Diogenes. Nor didst thou at any time disapprove of it. Of what value are all thy philosophy and all thy eloquence, if they fail to humanise a bosom-friend, or fear to encounter a misguided populace?

Plato. I thought I heard Diogenes say he had no sympathy with the mass of mankind. What could excite it so suddenly in behalf of an enemy?

Diogenes. Whoever is wronged is thereby my fellow-creature, although he were never so before. Scorn, contumely, chains, unite us.

Plato. Take heed, O Diogenes! lest the people of Athens hear you.

Diogenes. Is Diogenes no greater than the people of Athens? Friend Plato! I take no heed about them. Somebody or something will demolish me sooner or later. An Athenian can but begin what an ant, or a beetle, or a worm will finish.[58] Any one of the three would have the best of it.

---

[57] According to Plutarch: "But all this statecraft and eloquence and lofty purpose and cleverness was attended with great luxuriousness of life, with wanton drunkenness and lewdness, with effeminacy in dress,—he [Alcibiades] would trail long purple robes through the market place,—and with prodigal expenditures.

. . . .

"And he picked out a woman from among the prisoners of Melos to be his mistress, and reared a son she bore him. This was an instance of what they called his kindness of heart, but the execution of all the grown men of Melos [in the summer of 416 B.C.; see Thucydides *History* v. 116. 2–4] was chiefly due to him, since he supported the decree therefor" (*Alcibiades* 16. 1, 5, in *Plutarch's Lives*, tr. Bernadotte Perrin ["The Loeb Classical Library"; Cambridge: Harvard University Press; London: W. Heinemann, 1959], Vol. IV).

[58] "Perdiccas having threatened to put him [Diogenes] to death unless he came to him, 'That's nothing wonderful,' quoth he, 'for a beetle or a tarantula would do the same.' Instead of that he would have expected the threat to be that Perdiccas would be quite happy to do without his company" (Diogenes Laertius vi. 44, in *Lives*, II).

While I retain the use of my tongue, I will exercise it at my leisure and my option.[59] I would not bite it off, even for the pleasure of spitting it in a tyrant's face, as that brave girl Egina did.[60] But I would recommend that, in his wisdom, he should deign to take thine preferably, which, having always honey upon it, must suit his taste better.

Plato. Diogenes! if you must argue or discourse with me, I will endure your asperity for the sake of your acuteness: but it appears to me a more philosophical thing to avoid what is insulting and vexatious, than to breast and brave it.

Diogenes. Thou hast spoken well.

Plato. It belongs to the vulgar, not to us, to fly from a man's opinions to his actions, and to stab him in his own house for having received no wound in the school. One merit you will allow me: I always keep my temper; which you seldom do.

Diogenes. Is mine a good or a bad one?

Plato. Now must I speak sincerely?

Diogenes. Dost thou, a philosopher, ask such a question of me, a philosopher? Ay, sincerely or not at all.

Plato. Sincerely as you could wish, I must declare then your temper is the worst in the world.

Diogenes. I am much in the right, therefore, not to keep it. Embrace me: I have spoken now in thy own manner. Because thou sayest the most malicious things the most placidly,[61] thou thinkest or pretendest thou art sincere.

Plato. Certainly those who are most the masters of their resentments, are likely to speak less erroneously than the passionate and morose.

Diogenes. If they would, they might: but the moderate are not usually the most sincere: for the same circumspection which makes them moderate, makes them likewise retentive of what could give offence: they are also

---

[59] According to Diogenes Laertius: "Being asked what was the most beautiful thing in the world, he [Diogenes] replied, 'Freedom of speech'" (vi. 69, in *Lives*, II).

[60] No Egina of this description is found in either classical literature or folklore.

[61] Athenaeus, in *The Deipnosophists*, has Pontianus of Nicomedia say: "Hegesander of Delphi, in his *Commentaries* discussing Plato's malice toward everyone, writes also these words: 'After the death of Socrates his intimate friends, gathered together on a certain occasion, were very despondent. Plato joined them, and taking up the cup he exhorted them not to be downcast, because he was competent to lead the School himself, and proposed a toast to Apollodorus. But he said: "I would rather have taken the cup of poison from Socrates than this toast of wine from you"'" (xi. 507a–b, in *The Deipnosophists*, V).

timid in regard to fortune and favour, and hazard little. There is no mass of sincerity in any place. What there is must be picked up patiently, a grain or two at a time; and the season for it is after a storm, after the over-flowing of banks, and bursting of mounds, and sweeping away of landmarks. Men will always hold something back: they must be shaken and loosened a little, to make them let go what is deepest in them, and weightiest and purest.

Plato. Shaking and loosening as much about you as was requisite for the occasion, it became you to demonstrate where, and in what manner, I had made Socrates appear less sagacious and less eloquent than he was: it became you likewise to consider the great difficulty of finding new thoughts and new expressions for those who had more of them than any other men, and to represent them in all the brilliancy of their wit and in all the majesty of their genius. I do not assert that I have done it; but if I have not, what man has? what man has come so nigh to it? He who could bring Socrates, or Solon,[62] or Diogenes, through a dialogue, without disparagement, is much nearer in his intellectual powers to them, than any other is near to him.

Diogenes. Let Diogenes alone, and Socrates, and Solon. None of the three ever occupied his hours in tinging and curling the tarnished plumes of prostitute Philosophy, or deemed anything worth his attention, care, or notice, that did not make men brave and independent. As thou callest on me to show thee where and in what manner thou hast misrepresented thy teacher, and as thou seemest to set an equal value on eloquence and on reasoning, I shall attend to thee awhile on each of these matters, first inquiring of thee whether the axiom is Socratic, that it is never becoming to get drunk, *unless* in the solemnities of Bacchus?[63]

Plato. This god was the discoverer of the vine and of its uses.

Diogenes. Is drunkenness one of its uses, or the discovery of a god? If Pallas or Jupiter hath given us reason, we should sacrifice our reason with

---

[62] Solon (*ca.* 635–*ca.* 561/560 B.C.) was a great Athenian statesman and lawgiver as well as a poet. Landor has an Imaginary Conversation "Solon and Pisistratus."

[63] "Drinking to excess is a practice that is nowhere seemly—save only at the feasts of the God, the Giver of wine,—nor yet safe" (Plato *Laws* vi. 775b, tr. R. G. Bury ["The Loeb Classical Library"; Cambridge: Harvard University Press; London: W. Heinemann, 1942], Vol. I; hereafter referred to as Plato *Laws*, I). Diogenes Laertius records Plato's sentiment: "To drink to excess was nowhere becoming, he used to say, save at the feasts of the god who was the giver of wine" (iii. 39, in *Lives*, I). Since the *Laws* is not one of the Socratic dialogues, it contains Plato's, and not Socrates', ideas.

more propriety to Jupiter or Pallas. To Bacchus is due a libation of wine; the same being his gift, as thou preachest.

Another and a graver question.

Did Socrates teach thee that "slaves are to be scourged, and by no means admonished as though they were the children of the master?"[64]

Plato. He did not argue upon government.

Diogenes. He argued upon humanity, whereon all government is founded:[65] whatever is beside it is usurpation.

Plato. Are slaves then never to be scourged, whatever be their transgressions and enormities?

Diogenes. Whatever they be, they are less than his who reduced them to their condition.

Plato. What! though they murder his whole family?

Diogenes. Ay, and poison the public fountain of the city. What am I saying? and to whom? Horrible as is this crime, and next in atrocity to parricide, thou deemest it a lighter one than stealing a fig or grape. The stealer of these is scourged by thee; the sentence on the poisoner is to cleanse out the receptacle.[66] There is however a kind of poisoning, which,

---

[64] "We ought to punish slaves justly, and not to make them conceited by merely admonishing them as we would free men" (Plato *Laws* vi. 777e, in *Laws*, I). According to Diogenes Laertius: "One day, when Xenocrates had come in, Plato asked him to chastise his slave, since he was unable to do it himself because he was in a passion. Further, it is alleged that he said to one of his slaves, 'I would have given you a flogging, had I not been in a passion'" (iii. 38–39, in *Lives*, I).

[65] In "What We Have and What We Owe" (1850), Landor writes: "Of what use is any form of Government which fails to protect the lives and properties of the people?" (*Complete Works*, XII, 174).

[66] "Water above all else in a garden is nourishing; but it is easy to spoil. For while soil and sun and wind, which jointly with water nourish growing plants, are not easy to spoil by means of sorcery or diverting or theft, all these things may happen to water; hence it requires the assistance of law. Let this, then, be the law concerning it:—if anyone wantonly spoil another man's water, whether in spring or in pond, by means of sorcery, digging, or theft, the injured party shall sue him before the city-stewards, recording the amount of the damage sustained; and whosoever is convicted of damaging by poisons shall, in addition to the fine, clean out the springs or the basin of the water, in whatever way the laws of the interpreters declare it right for the purification to be made on each occasion and for each plaintiff" (Plato *Laws* viii. 845d–e, tr. R. G. Bury ["The Loeb Classical Library"; Cambridge: Harvard University Press; London: W. Heinemann, 1942], Vol. II; hereafter referred to as Plato *Laws*, II). "And if a slave, without the consent of the master of the plots, touches any of such fruit, he shall be beaten with stripes as many as the grapes in the bunch or the figs on the fig tree" (Plato *Laws* viii. 845a, in *Laws*, II). Plato's remarks have to do with the laws of agriculture (*Laws* viii. 842e–846c) and thus should be read in their proper context.

to do thee justice, comes before thee with all its horrors, and which thou wouldst punish capitally, even in such a sacred personage as an aruspex or diviner: I mean the poisoning by incantation.[67] I, my whole family, my whole race, my whole city, may bite the dust in agony from a truss of henbane[68] in the well; and little harm done forsooth![69] Let an idle fool

---

[67] "A division in our treatment of poisoning cases is required by the fact that, following the nature of mankind, they are of two distinct types. The type that we have now expressly mentioned is that in which injury is done to bodies by bodies according to nature's laws. Distinct from this is the type which, by means of sorceries and incantations and spells (as they are called), not only convinces those who attempt to cause injury that they really can do so, but convinces also their victims that they certainly are being injured by those who possess the power of bewitchment. In respect of all such matters it is neither easy to perceive what is the real truth, nor, if one does perceive it, is it easy to convince others. And it is futile to approach the souls of men who view one another with dark suspicion if they happen to see images of moulded wax at doorways, or at points where three ways meet, or it may be at the tomb of some ancestor, to bid them make light of all such portents, when we ourselves hold no clear opinion concerning them. Consequently, we shall divide the law about poisoning under two heads, according to the modes in which the attempt is made; and, as a preliminary, we shall entreat, exhort, and advise that no one must attempt to commit such an act, or to frighten the mass of men, like children, with bogeys, and so compel the legislator and the judge to cure men of such fears, inasmuch as, first, the man who attempts poisoning knows not what he is doing either in regard to bodies (unless he be a medical expert) or in respect of sorceries (unless he be a prophet or diviner). So this statement shall stand as the law about poisoning:—Whosoever shall poison any person so as to cause an injury not fatal either to the person himself or to his employes, or so as to cause an injury fatal or not fatal to his flocks or to his hives,—if the agent be a doctor, and if he be convicted of poisoning, he shall be punished by death; but if he be a lay person, the court shall assess in his case what he shall suffer or pay. And if it be held that a man is acting like an injurer by the use of spells, incantations, or any such mode of poisoning, if he be a prophet or diviner, he shall be put to death; but if he be ignorant of the prophetic art, he shall be dealt with in the same way as a layman convicted of poisoning, —that is to say, the court shall assess in his case also what shall seem to them right for him to suffer or pay" (Plato *Laws* xi. 932e–933e, in *Laws*, II).

[68] Henbane is the popular name of a plant, found in many parts of the world, which yields a poisonous alkaloid that can be used either for medicinal purposes or as a deadly poison.

[69] In addition to misunderstanding the passage from Plato's *Laws* quoted in n. 66 above, Landor is apparently unaware of Plato's severe penalty for murder: "He that is convicted shall be punished by death, and he shall not be buried in the land of the victim, because of the shamelessness as well as impiety of his act. If the culprit flees and refuses to come up for judgment, he shall be exiled with an unending exile; and if any such person sets foot in the country of the murdered man, he of the dead man's relatives or of the citizens that first meets with him shall slay him with impunity, or else bind him and hand him over to those magistrates who have judged the case, to be slain" (*Laws* ix. 871d–e, in *Laws*, II).

set an image of me in wax before the fire, and whistle and caper to it, and purr and pray, and chant a hymn to Hecate [70] while it melts, intreating and imploring her that I may melt as easily; and thou wouldst, in thy equity and holiness, strangle him at the first stave of his psalmody.

Plato. If this is an absurdity, can you find another?

Diogenes. Truly, in reading thy book, I doubted at first, and for a long continuance, whether thou couldst have been serious; and whether it were not rather a satire on those busy-bodies who are incessantly intermeddling in other people's affairs. It was only on the protestation of thy intimate friends that I believed thee to have written it in earnest. As for thy question, it is idle to stoop and pick out absurdities from a mass of inconsistency and injustice: but another and another I could throw in, and another and another afterward, from any page in the volume.[71] Two bare staring falsehoods lift their beaks one upon the other, like spring frogs. Thou sayest that no punishment, decreed by the laws, tendeth to evil.[72] What! not if immoderate? not if partial? Why then repeal any penal statute while the subject of its animadversion exists? In prisons the less criminal are placed among the more criminal, the inexperienced in vice together with the hardened in it. This is part of the punishment, though it precedes the sentence: nay, it is often inflicted on those whom the judges acquit: the law, by allowing it, does it.

---

[70] Hecate is a goddess in Greek mythology who, among other things, presides over the art of sorcery and witchcraft.

[71] Landor defends faultfinding in literary criticism in the Imaginary Conversation "Southey and Landor":

> *Landor.* . . . Johnson asks, "What Englishman can take delight in transcribing passages, which, if they lessen the reputation of Milton, diminish, in some degree, the honour of our country!" I hope the honour of our country will always rest on truth and justice. It is not by concealing what is wrong that anything right can be accomplished. There is no pleasure in transcribing such passages, but there is great utility. Inferior writers exercise no interest, attract no notice, and serve no purpose. Johnson has himself done great good by exposing great faults in great authors. [*Works*, II, 74.]

Landor relates this amusing story in his letter to Emerson: "I was thought unfriendly to Scott for one of the friendliest things I ever did toward an author. Having noted all the faults of grammar and expression in two or three of his volumes, I calculated that the number of them, in all, must amount to above a thousand. Mr. Lockhart, who married his daughter, was indignant at this, and announced at the same time (to prove how very wrong I was) that they were corrected in the next edition" (*Complete Works*, XII, 198).

[72] "For no penalty that is legally imposed aims at evil, but it effects, as a rule, one or other of two results,—it makes the person who suffers it either better or less bad" (Plato *Laws* ix. 854e, in *Laws*, II).

The next is, that he who is punished by the laws is the better for it, or, however, the less depraved.⁷³ What! if anteriorly to the sentence he lives and converses with worse men, some of whom console him by deadening the sense of shame, others by removing the apprehension of punishment? Many laws as certainly make men bad, as bad men make many laws: yet under thy regimen they take us from the bosom of the nurse,⁷⁴ turn the meat about upon the platter,⁷⁵ pull the bed-clothes off, make us sleep when we would wake, and wake when we would sleep,⁷⁶ and never cease to rummage and twitch us, until they see us safe landed at the grave.⁷⁷

⁷³ See n. 72 above. According to Landor: "It has been said, and has been repeated over and over again with less and less hesitation and reflection, that the reforming of the defender is the main purport of his punishment. I deny it totally" ("Capital Punishment" [1849], *Complete Works*, XII, 176).
⁷⁴ "As soon as they have reached the age of three, all the children from three to six must meet together at the village temples, those belonging to each village assembling at the same place. Moreover, the nurses of these children must watch over their behaviour, whether it be orderly or disorderly; and over the nurses themselves and the whole band of children one of the twelve women already elected must be appointed annually to take charge of each band, the appointment resting with the Law-wardens.... After the age of six, each sex shall be kept separate, boys spending their time with boys, and likewise girls with girls; and when it is necessary for them to begin lessons, the boys must go to teachers of riding, archery, javelin-throwing and slinging, and the girls also, if they agree to it, must share in the lessons, and especially such as relate to the use of arms" (Plato *Laws* vii. 794a-d, in *Laws*, II). "And, of all wild creatures, the child is the most intractable; for in so far as it, above all others, possesses a fount of reason that is as yet uncurbed, it is a treacherous, sly and most insolent creature. Wherefore the child must be strapped up, as it were, with many bridles—first, when he leaves the care of nurse and mother, with tutors, to guide his childish ignorance, and after that with teachers of all sorts of subjects and lessons, treating him as becomes a freeborn child" (Plato *Laws* vii. 808d-e, in *Laws*, II).
⁷⁵ This appears to be a sarcastic remark directed in particular toward Plato's desire for a law which would bring men and women together for public meals (see *Laws* vi. 780a-781d) and in general toward Plato's desire to regulate both the public and the private aspects of a citizen's life (*Laws* vi. 780a).
⁷⁶ "So this being nature's law [providing the body with proper exercise and nourishment and the soul with learning and moral training], a programme must be framed for all the freeborn men, prescribing how they shall pass their time continuously, from dawn to dawn and sunrise on each successive day.... That any citizen, indeed, should spend the whole of any night in sleep, instead of setting an example to his household by being himself always the first to awaken and rise—such a practice must be counted by all a shameful one, unworthy of a free man, whether it be called a custom or a law" (Plato *Laws* vii. 807d-808a, in *Laws*, II).
⁷⁷ "Then finally, when he [the lawgiver] arrives at the completion of the whole constitution, he has to consider in what manner in each case the burial of the dead should be carried out, and what honours should be assigned to them" (Plato *Laws* i. 632c, in *Laws*, I).

We can do nothing (but be poisoned) with impunity. What is worst of all, we must marry certain relatives and connections,[78] be they distorted, blear-eyed, toothless, carbuncled, with hair (if any) eclipsing the reddest torch of Hymen,[79] and with a hide outrivalling in colour and plaits his trimmest saffron robe. At the mention of this indeed, friend Plato! even thou, although resolved to stand out of harm's way, beginnest to make a wry mouth, and findest it difficult to pucker and purse it up again, without an astringent store of moral sentences. Hymen is indeed no acquaintance of thine. We know the delicacies of love which thou wouldst reserve for the gluttony of heroes and the fastidiousness of philosophers.[80] Heroes, like gods, must have their own way; but against thee and thy confraternity of elders I would turn the closet-key, and your mouths might water over, but your tongues should never enter, those little pots of comfiture. Seriously, you who wear embroidered slippers ought to be very cautious of treading in the mire. Philosophers should not only live the simplest

---

[78] "Accordingly, the law that we shall enact, as the best in our power touching such matters, will be this:—If a man dies intestate and leaves daughters, that brother who is born of the same father or of the same mother and who is without a lot shall take the daughter [in marriage] and the lot of the deceased; failing a brother, if there be a brother's son, the procedure shall be the same, provided that the parties be of an age suited the one to the other; failing one of these, the same rule shall hold for a sister's son; then, fourthly, for a father's brother; and, fifthly, for his son; and, sixthly, for the son of a father's sister. In like manner, if a man leaves female children, the right of kinship shall proceed always by degrees of consanguinity, going up through brothers and brothers' children, first the males, and secondly the females in one line" (Plato *Laws* xi. 924e–925a, in *Laws*, II).

[79] Hymen (Hymenaeus), the god of marriage, is generally represented in works of art as a handsome youth carrying a bridal torch in his hand.

[80] Landor makes this comment in his essay "Francesco Petrarca" (1843): "Throughout life we have been accustomed to hear of the Platonic: absurd as it is everywhere, it is most so here. Nothing in the voluminous works of Plato authorizes us to affix this designation to simple friendship, to friendship exempt from passion. On the contrary, the philosopher leaves us no doubt whatever that his notion of love is sensual.* [Landor's note reads: 'A mysterious and indistinct idea, not dissipated by the closest view of the original, led the poetical mind of Shelley into the labyrinth that encompassed the garden of Academus. He has given us an accurate and graceful translation of the most eloquent of Plato's dialogues (*Symposium*). Consistently with modesty he found it impossible to present the whole to his readers; but as the subject is entirely on the nature of love, they will discover that nothing is more unlike Petrarca's. The trifles, the quibbles, the unseasonable jokes, of what is exhibited in very harmonious Greek, and in English nearly as harmonious, pass uncensured and unnoticed by the fascinated Shelley.'] He says expressly what species of it, and from what bestowers, should be the reward of sages and heroes [see *Symposium* 178c–179b, 179e–180b, 184a–185d]" (*Complete Works*, XII, 35–36).

lives, but should also use the plainest language. Poets, in employing magnificent and sonorous words, teach philosophy the better by thus disarming suspicion, that the finest poetry contains and conveys the finest philosophy. You will never let any man hold his right station: you would rank Solon with Homer for poetry.[81] This is absurd. The only resemblance is, in both being eminently wise. Pindar too makes even the cadences of his dithyrambics keep time to the flute of Reason. My tub, which holds fiftyfold thy wisdom, would crack at the reverberation of thy voice.

Plato. Farewell.

Diogenes. Not quite yet. I must physic thee a little with law again before we part; answer me one more question. In punishing a robbery, wouldst thou punish him who steals everything from one who wants everything, less severely than him who steals little from one who wants nothing?

Plato. No: in this place the iniquity is manifest: not a problem in geometry is plainer.

Diogenes. Thou liedst then . . in thy sleep perhaps . . but thou liedst. Differing in one page from what was laid down by thee in another,[82] thou

---

[81] "And one of our fellow-tribesmen—whether he really thought so at the time or whether he was paying a compliment to Critias—declared that in his opinion Solon was not only the wisest of men in all else, but in poetry also he was of all poets the noblest. Whereat the old man . . . was highly pleased and said with a smile: 'If only, Amynander, he had not taken up poetry as a by-play but had worked hard at it like others, and if he had completed the story he brought here from Egypt, instead of being forced to lay it aside owing to the seditions and all the other evils he found here on his return,—why then, I say, neither Hesiod nor Homer nor any other poet would ever have proved more famous than he'" (Plato *Timaeus* 21b–d, in *Timaeus, Critias, Cleitophon, Menexenus, Epistles*, tr. R. G. Bury ["The Loeb Classical Library"; Cambridge: Harvard University Press; London: W. Heinemann, 1942]; hereafter referred to as Plato *Timaeus*).

[82] "But if any citizen is ever convicted of such an act,—that is, of committing some great and infamous wrong against gods [such as robbing a temple], parents, or State—the judge shall regard him as already incurable, reckoning that, in spite of all the training and nurture he has had from infancy, he has not refrained from the worst iniquity. For him the penalty is death, the least of evils; and, moreover, by serving as an example, he will benefit others, when himself disgraced and removed from sight beyond the borders of the country" (Plato *Laws* ix. 854e–855a, in *Laws*, II). "For those who disobey, this shall be the law concerning impiety:—If anyone commits impiety either by word or deed, he that meets with him shall defend the law by informing the magistrates, and the first magistrates who hear of it shall bring the man up before the court appointed to decide such cases as the laws direct. . . . And if a man be convicted, the court shall assess one penalty for each separate act of impiety. Imprisonment shall be imposed in every case; . . . and since men are involved in impiety from the three causes which we have described [atheism; the belief that gods exist but have no concern for

wouldst punish what is called *sacrilege* with death. The magistrates ought to provide that the temples be watched so well, and guarded so effectually, as never to be liable to thefts. The gods, we must suppose, can not do it by themselves; for, to admit the contrary, we must admit their indifference to the possession of goods and chattels: an impiety so great, that sacrilege itself drops into atoms under it. He however who robs from the gods, be the amount what it may, robs from the rich; robs from those who can want nothing, although, like the other rich, they are mightily vindictive against petty plunderers.[83] But he who steals from a poor widow a loaf of bread, may deprive her of everything she has in the world; perhaps, if she be bedridden or paralytic, of life itself.

I am weary of this digression on the inequality of punishments;[84] let us come up to the object of them. It is not, O Plato! an absurdity of thine alone, but of all who write and of all who converse on them, to assert that they both are and ought to be inflicted publicly, for the sake of deterring from offence. The only effect of public punishment, is, to show the rabble how bravely it can be borne; and that everyone who hath lost a toenail hath suffered worse. The virtuous man, as a reward and a privilege, should be permitted to see how calm and satisfied a virtuous man departs. The criminal should be kept in the dark about the departure of his fellows, which is oftentimes as unreluctant: for to him, if indeed no reward or privilege, it would be a corroborative and a cordial. Such things ought to be taken from him, no less carefully than the instruments of destruction or evasion. Secrecy and mystery should be the attendants of punishment, and the sole persons present should be the injured, or two of his relatives, and a functionary delegated by each tribe, to witness and register the execution of justice.

---

men; the belief that gods can be won over by offerings and prayers], and from each such cause two forms of impiety result—consequently those who sin in respect of religion fall into six classes which require to be distinguished, as needing penalties that are neither equal nor similar" (Plato *Laws* x. 907d–908b, in *Laws*, II). This latter passage, it should be noted, is preceded by the following: "As to temple-robbing [854b ff.], whether done by open violence or secretly, it has been already stated summarily what the punishment should be; and in respect of all the outrages, whether of word or deed, which a man commits, either by tongue or hand, against the gods, we must state the punishment he should suffer, after we have first delivered the admonition" (Plato *Laws* x. 885b, in *Laws*, II).

[83] According to Diogenes Laertius: "Once he [Diogenes] saw the officials of a temple leading away some one who had stolen a bowl belonging to the treasurers, and said, 'The great thieves are leading away the little thief'" (vi. 45, in *Lives*, II). See also *Lives* vi. 73.

[84] See n. 82 above.

Trials, on the contrary, should be public in every case.⁸⁵ It being presumable that the sense of shame and honour is not hitherto quite extinguished in the defendant, this, if he be guilty, is the worst part of his punishment; if innocent, the best of his release. From the hour of trial until the hour of return to society (or the dust) there should be privacy, there should be solitude.

Plato. It occurs to me, O Diogenes! that you agree with Aristoteles on the doctrine of necessity.⁸⁶

Diogenes. I do.

Plato. How then can you punish, by any heavier chastisement than coercion, the heaviest offences? Everything being brought about, as you hold, by fate and predestination . .

Diogenes. Stay! Those terms are puerile, and imply a petition of a principle:⁸⁷ keep to the term *necessity*. Thou art silent. Here then, O Plato! will I acknowledge to thee, I wonder it should have escaped thy perspicacity that *free-will* itself is nothing else than a part and effluence of *necessity*. If everything proceeds from some other thing, every impulse from some other impulse, that which impels to choice or will must act among the rest.

Plato. Every impulse from some other (I must so take it) under God, or the first cause.⁸⁸

Diogenes. Be it so: I meddle not at present with infinity or eternity: when I can comprehend them I will talk about them.⁸⁹ You metaphysicians

---

⁸⁵ See Plato *Laws* ix. 855d.

⁸⁶ See Aristotle *Metaphysics* v. 5, vi. 3, xi. 8. 4-8.

⁸⁷ A *petitio principii* (petition of principle) is a logical fallacy in which a premise, which is either equivalent to or dependent upon the conclusion, is taken for granted.

⁸⁸ See Aristotle *Metaphysics* xii. 6-7. 9.

⁸⁹ Diogenes Laertius records the following: "He [Diogenes] used also to say that when he saw physicians, philosophers and pilots at their work, he deemed man the most intelligent of all animals; but when again he saw interpreters of dreams and diviners and those who attended to them, or those who were puffed up with conceit of wealth, he thought no animal more silly" (vi. 24, in *Lives*, II). "When some one was discoursing on celestial phenomena, 'How many days,' asked Diogenes, 'were you in coming from the sky?'" (Diogenes Laertius vi. 39, in *Lives*, II).

Landor, like Diogenes, has little sympathy toward metaphysics: "In the letters now edited by Mr. Warter, I find that in the *Whitehaven Journal* there was inserted a criticism, in which, on the strength of this poem [*Gebir*], I am compared and preferred to Goethe. I am not too much elated. Neither in my youthful days nor in any others have I thrown upon the world such trash as 'Werther' and 'Wilhelm Meister,' nor flavoured my poetry with the corrugated spicery of metaphysics" ("Letter from W. S. Landor to R. W. Emerson" (1856), *Complete Works*, XII, 200).

kill the flower-bearing and fruit-bearing glebe with delving and turning over and sifting, and never bring up any solid and malleable mass from the dark profundity in which you labour. The intellectual world, like the physical, is inapplicable to profit and incapable of cultivation a little way below the surface .. of which there is more to manage, and more to know, than any of you will undertake.

Plato. It happens that we do not see the stars at even-tide, sometimes because there are clouds intervening, but oftener because there are glimmerings of light: thus many truths escape us from the obscurity we stand in; and many more from that crepuscular state of mind, which induceth us to sit down satisfied with our imaginations and unsuspicious of our knowledge.

Diogenes. Keep always to the point, or with an eye upon it, and instead of saying things to make people stare and wonder, say what will withhold them hereafter from wondering and staring. This is philosophy; to make remote things tangible, common things extensively useful, useful things extensively common, and to leave the least necessary for the last. I have always a suspicion of sonorous sentences. The full shell sounds little, but shows by that little what is within. A bladder swells out more with wind than with oil.

Plato. I would not neglect politics nor morals, nor indeed even manners: these however are mutable and evanescent: the human understanding is immovable and for ever the same in its principles and its constitution, and no study is so important or so inviting.

Diogenes. Your sect hath done little in it. You are singularly fond of those disquisitions in which few can detect your failures and your fallacies, and in which, if you stumble or err, you may find some countenance in those who lost their way before you.

Is not this school-room of mine, which holdeth but one scholar, preferable to that out of which have proceeded so many impetuous in passion, refractory in discipline, unprincipled in adventure, and (worst of all) proud in slavery?[90] Poor creatures who run after a jaded mule or palfrey, to pick up what he drops along the road, may be certain of a cabbage the larger and the sooner for it; while those who are equally assiduous at the heel of kings and princes, hunger and thirst for more, and usually gather less. Their attendance is neither so certain of reward nor so honest; their patience is scantier, their industry weaker, their complaints louder. What shall we say of their philosophy? what of their virtue?

[90] See n. 33 above.

What shall we say of the greatness whereon their feeders plume themselves? not caring they indeed for the humbler character of virtue or philosophy. We never call children the greater or the better for wanting others to support them: why then do we call men so for it? I would be servant of any helpless man for hours together: but sooner shall a king be the slave of Diogenes than Diogenes a king's.

Plato. Companionship, O Sinopean, is not slavery.

Diogenes. Are the best of them worthy to be my companions? Have they ever made you wiser? have you ever made them so? Prythee, what is companionship where nothing that improves the intellect is communicated, and where the larger heart contracts itself to the model and dimension of the smaller? 'Tis a dire calamity to *have* a slave; 'tis an inexpiable curse to *be* one.[91] When it befalls a man through violence he must be pitied: but where is pity, where is pardon, for the wretch who solicits it, or bends his head under it through invitation? Thy hardness of heart toward slaves, O Plato, is just as unnatural as hardness of heart toward dogs would be in me.[92]

Plato. You would have none perhaps in that condition.

Diogenes. None should be made slaves, excepting those who have attempted to make others so,[93] or who spontaneously have become the instruments of unjust and unruly men. Even these ought not to be scourged every day perhaps: for their skin is the only sensitive part of them, and such castigation might shorten their lives.

Plato. Which, in your tenderness and mercy, you would not do.

Diogenes. Longevity is desirable in them; that they may be exposed in coops to the derision of the populace on holidays; and that few may serve the purpose.

Plato. We will pass over this wild and thorny theory, into the field of civilisation in which we live; and here I must remark the evil consequences that would ensue, if our domestics could listen to you about the hardships they are enduring.

---

[91] "When he [Diogenes] was advised to go in pursuit of his runaway slave, he replied, 'It would be absurd, if Manes can live without Diogenes, but Diogenes cannot get on without Manes'" (Diogenes Laertius vi. 55, in *Lives*, II).

[92] For Plato's "hardness of heart toward slaves," see n. 64 above. Diogenes' concern for dogs is mentioned by Diogenes Laertius: "Another version [of Diogenes' death] is that, while trying to divide an octopus amongst the dogs, he was so severely bitten on the sinew of the foot that it caused his death" (vi. 77, in *Lives*, II). See also *Lives* vi. 78–79.

[93] For Landor's feelings toward despots and tyrants, see n. 55 above.

Diogenes. And is it no evil that truth and beneficence should be shut out at once from so large a portion of mankind? Is it none when things are so perverted, that an act of beneficence might lead to a thousand acts of cruelty, and that one accent of truth should be more pernicious than all the falsehoods that have been accumulated, since the formation of language, since the gift of speech! I have taken thy view of the matter; take thou mine. Hercules was called just and glorious, and worshipped as a deity, because he redressed the grievances of others: is it unjust, is it inglorious, to redress one's own?[94] If that man rises high in the favour of the people, high in the estimation of the valiant and the wise, high before God, by the assertion and vindication of his holiest law, who punishes with death such as would reduce him or his fellow citizens to slavery,[95] how much higher rises he, who, being a slave, springs up indignantly from his low estate, and thrusts away the living load that intercepts from him, what even the reptiles and insects, what even the bushes and brambles of the roadside, enjoy!

Plato. We began with definitions: I rejoice, O Diogenes, that you are warmed into rhetoric, in which you will find me a most willing auditor: for I am curious to collect a specimen of your prowess, where you have not yet established any part of your celebrity.[96]

Diogenes. I am idle enough for it: but I have other things yet for thy curiosity, other things yet for thy castigation.

Thou wouldst separate the military from the citizens; from artisans and from agriculturists.[97] A small body of soldiers, who never could be anything else, would in a short time subdue and subjugate the industrious and

---

[94] "This was the gist of his [Diogenes'] conversation; and it was plain that he acted accordingly, adulterating currency in very truth [see n. 200 below], allowing convention no such authority as he allowed to natural right, and asserting that the manner of life he lived was the same as that of Heracles when he preferred liberty to everything" (Diogenes Laertius vi. 71, in *Lives*, II).

[95] For Landor's opinions upon tyrannicide, see n. 55 above.

[96] According to Diogenes Laertius: "The man [Diogenes] had in fact a wonderful gift of persuasion, so that he could easily vanquish anyone he liked in argument. At all events a certain Onesicritus of Aegina is said to have sent to Athens the one of his two sons named Androsthenes, and he having become a pupil of Diogenes stayed there; the father then sent the other also, the aforesaid Philiscus, who was the elder, in search of him; but Philiscus also was detained in the same way. When, thirdly, the father himself arrived, he was just as much attracted to the pursuit of philosophy as his sons and joined the circle—so magical was the spell which the discourses of Diogenes exerted." (vi. 75–76, in *Lives*, II).

[97] See Plato *The Republic* iii. 415c–417b.

the wealthy. They would begin by demanding an increase of pay; then they would insist on admission to magistracies; and presently their general would assume the sovereignty, and create new offices of trust and profit for the strength and security of his usurpation. Soldiers, in a free state, should be enrolled from those principally who are most interested in the conservation of order and property; chiefly the sons of tradesmen in towns: first, because there is the less detriment done to agriculture; the main thing to be considered in all countries: secondly, because such people are pronest to sedition, from the two opposite sides of enrichment and poverty: and lastly, because their families are always at hand, responsible for their fidelity, and where shame would befall them thickly in case of cowardice, or any misconduct. Those governments are the most flourishing and stabile, which have the fewest idle youths about the streets and theatres: it is only with the sword that they can cut the halter.

Thy faults arise from two causes principally: first, a fondness for playing tricks with argument and with fancy:[98] secondly, swallowing from others what thou hast not taken time enough nor exercise enough to digest.[99]

Plato. Lay before me the particular things you accuse me of drawing from others.

Diogenes. Thy opinions on numbers are distorted from those of the Chaldeans, Babylonians, and Syrians;[100] who believe that numbers, and letters too, have peculiar powers, independent of what is represented by them on the surface.

[98] "In spite of this he [Plato] too was ridiculed by the Comic poets. At any rate Theopompus in his *Hedychares* says: 'There is not anything that is truly one, even the number two is scarcely one, according to Plato'" (Diogenes Laertius iii. 26, in *Lives*, I).

[99] "Further, he [Plato] derived great assistance from Epicharmus the Comic poet, for he transcribed a great deal from him, as Alcimus says in the essays dedicated to Amyntas, of which there are four. In the first of them he writes thus.
. . . .

"These and like instances Alcimus notes through four books, pointing out the assistance derived by Plato from Epicharmus" (Diogenes Laertius iii. 9–17, in *Lives*, I). See also *Lives* iii. 37–38 and Athenaeus *The Deipnosophists* xi. 508c–d.

[100] "Vision, in my view, is the cause of the greatest benefit to us, inasmuch as none of the accounts now given concerning the Universe would ever have been given if men had not seen the stars or the sun or the heaven. But as it is, the vision of day and night and of months and circling years has created the art of number and has given us not only the notion of Time but also means of research into the nature of the Universe" (Plato *Timaeus* 47a–b). Diogenes Laertius states that Plato visited the mathematicians Euclides and Theodorus and the Pythagorean philosophers Philolaus and Eurytus after Socrates' death (*Lives* iii. 6). See n. 104 below.

Plato. I have said more, and often differently.

Diogenes. Thou hast indeed. Neither they nor Pythagoras ever taught, as thou hast done, that the basis of the earth is an equilateral triangle, and the basis of water a rectangular.[101] We are then informed by thy sagacity, that "the world has no need of eyes, because nothing is left to be looked at out of it; nor of ears, because nothing can be heard beyond it; nor of any parts for the reception, concoction, and voidance, of nutriment; because there can be no secretion nor accretion."[102]

This indeed is very providential. If things were otherwise, foul might befall your genii, who are always on active service: a world would not bespatter them so lightly as we mortals are bespattered by a swallow. Whatever is asserted on things tangible, should be asserted from experiment only. Thou shouldst have defended better that which thou hast stolen:[103] a thief should not only have impudence, but courage.

Plato. What do you mean?

Diogenes. I mean that every one of thy whimsies hath been picked up somewhere by thee in thy travels;[104] and each of them hath been rendered more weak and puny by its place of concealment in thy closet. What thou hast written on the immortality of the soul, goes rather to prove the immortality of the body; and applies as well to the body of a weasel or an eel as to the fairer one of Agathon or of Aster.[105] Why not at once intro-

---

[101] According to Plato: "To earth let us give the cubic form; for of the four Kinds earth is the most immobile and the most plastic body, and of necessity the body which has the most stable bases must be pre-eminently of this character. Now of the triangles we originally assumed, the basis formed by equal sides is of its nature more stable than that formed by unequal sides; and of the plane surfaces which are compounded of these several triangles, the equilateral quadrangle, both in its parts and as a whole, has a more stable base than the equilateral triangle. Wherefore, we are preserving the probable account when we assign this figure to earth" (*Timaeus* 55e–56a). "And the third solid [the icosahedron, or molecule of water] is composed of twice sixty of the elemental triangles conjoined, and of twelve solid angles, each contained by five plane equilateral triangles, and it has, by its production, twenty equilateral triangular bases" (*Timaeus* 55b).

[102] Plato *Timaeus* 33c.

[103] See n. 99 above.

[104] "Then at the age of twenty-eight, according to Hermodorus, he [Plato] withdrew to Megara to Euclides, with certain other disciples of Socrates. Next he proceeded to Cyrene on a visit to Theodorus the mathematician, thence to Italy to see the Pythagorean philosophers Philolaus and Eurytus, and thence to Egypt to see those who interpreted the will of the gods; and Euripides is said to have accompanied him thither" (Diogenes Laertius iii. 6, in *Lives*, I). See also n. 106 below.

[105] According to Diogenes Laertius: "Aristippus in his fourth book *On the Luxury of the Ancients* says that he [Plato] was attached to a youth named Aster, who joined him

duce a new religion?[106] since religions keep and are relished in proportion as they are salted with absurdity, inside and out; and all of them must have one great crystal of it for the centre; but Philosophy pines and dies unless she drinks limpid water. When Pherecydes and Pythagoras felt in themselves the majesty of contemplation, they spurned the idea that flesh and bones and arteries should confer it; and that what comprehends the past and the future, should sink in a moment and be annihilated for ever.[107] No, cried they, the power of thinking is no more in the brain than in the hair, although the brain may be the instrument on which it plays. It is not corporeal, it is not of this world; its existence is eternity, its residence is infinity. I forbear to discuss the rationality of their belief, and pass on straightway to thine; if indeed I am to consider as one, belief and doctrine.

Plato. As you will.

---

in the study of astronomy, as also to Dion who has been mentioned above, and, as some aver, to Phaedrus too. His passionate affection is revealed in the following epigrams which he is said to have written upon them: 'Star-gazing Aster, would I were the skies,/ To gaze upon thee with a thousand eyes.' And another: 'Among the living once the Morning Star,/Thou shin'st, now dead, like Hesper from afar.' . . . There is another upon Agathon: 'While kissing Agathon, my soul leapt to my lips, as if fain, alas! to pass over to him'" (iii. 29, 32, in *Lives*, I). Plato's *Symposium* represents a feast held at the home of Agathon, an Athenian tragic poet known for his personal beauty.

[106] He alludes to the various worships of Egypt, and to what Plato had learned there. [*Landor's note.*] See n. 104 above.

[107] Diogenes Laertius states that Pythagoras (*ca.* 582–500 B.C.), a pupil of Pherecydes (*fl. ca.* 540 B.C.), taught the following: "All things live which partake of heat—this is why plants are living things—but all have not soul, which is a detached part of aether, partly the hot and partly the cold, for it partakes of cold aether too. Soul is distinct from life; it is immortal, since that from which it is detached is immortal. Living creatures are reproduced from one another by germination; there is no such thing as spontaneous generation from earth. The germ is a clot of brain containing hot vapour within it; and this, when brought to the womb, throws out, from the brain, ichor, fluid and blood, whence are formed flesh, sinews, bones, hairs, and the whole of the body, while soul and sense come from the vapour within. . . . The soul of man, he says, is divided into three parts, intelligence, reason, and passion. Intelligence and passion are possessed by other animals as well, but reason by man alone. The seat of the soul extends from the heart to the brain; the part of it which is in the heart is passion, while the parts located in the brain are reason and intelligence. The senses are distillations from these. Reason is immortal, all else mortal. The soul draws nourishment from the blood; the faculties of the soul are winds, for they as well as the soul are invisible, just as the aether is invisible. The veins, arteries, and sinews are the bonds of the soul. But when it is strong and settled down into itself, reasonings and deeds become its bonds. When cast out upon the earth, it wanders in the air like the body" (viii. 28, 30–31, in *Lives*, II).

Diogenes. I should rather then regard these things as mere ornaments; just as many decorate their apartments with lyres and harps, which they themselves look at from the couch, supinely complacent, and leave for visitors to admire and play on.

Plato. I foresee not how you can disprove my argument on the immortality of the soul, which, being contained in the best of my dialogues,[108] and being often asked for among my friends, I carry with me.

Diogenes. At this time?

Plato. Even so.

Diogenes. Give me then a certain part of it for my perusal.

Plato. Willingly.

Diogenes. Hermes and Pallas! I wanted but a cubit of it, or at most a fathom, and thou art pulling it out by the plethron.[109]

Plato. This is the place in question.

Diogenes. Read it.

Plato (reads). "Sayest thou not that death is the opposite of life, and that they spring the one from the other?" "*Yes.*" "What springs then from the living?" "*The dead.*" "And what from the dead?" "*The living.*" "Then all things alive spring from the dead."

Diogenes. Why that repetition? but go on.

Plato (reads). "Souls therefore exist after death in the infernal regions."[110]

Diogenes. Where is the *therefore?* where is it even as to *existence?* As to the *infernal regions*, there is nothing that points toward a proof, or promises an indication. Death neither springs from life, nor life from death. Although death is the inevitable consequence of life, if the observation and experience of ages go for anything, yet nothing shows us, or ever hath signified, that life comes from death. Thou mightest as well say that a barley-corn dies before the germ of another barley-corn grows up from it: than which nothing is more untrue: for it is only the protecting part of the germ that perishes, when its protection is no longer necessary. The consequence, that souls exist after death, cannot be drawn from the corruption of the body, even if it were demonstrable that out of this

---

[108] Plato *Phaedo*.

[109] In the Greek system of measurement, a normal cubit represents the distance from the point of the elbow to the point of the middle finger (twenty-four finger breadths), a fathom the distance which a man can stretch with both arms (six feet), and a plethron one hundred Greek feet (the English foot is a little longer than the Greek).

[110] Plato *Phaedo* 71d-e.

corruption a live one could rise up.[111] Thou hast not said that the soul is among those dead things which living things must spring from: thou hast not said that a living soul produces a dead soul, or that a dead soul produces a living one.

Plato. No indeed.

Diogenes. On my conscience, thou hast said however things no less inconsiderate, no less inconsequent, no less unwise; and this very thing must be said and proved, to make thy argument of any value. Do dead men beget children?

Plato. I have not said it.

Diogenes. Thy argument implies it.

Plato. These are high mysteries, and to be approached with reverence.

Diogenes. Whatever we can not account for, is in the same predicament. We may be gainers by being ignorant, if we can be thought mysterious. It is better to shake our heads and to let nothing out of them, than to be plain and explicit in matters of difficulty. I do not mean in confessing our ignorance or our imperfect knowledge of them, but in clearing them up perspicuously: for, if we answer with ease, we may haply be thought good-natured, quick, communicative; never deep, never sagacious; not very defective possibly in our intellectual faculties, yet unequal and chinky, and liable to the probation of every clown's knuckle.

Plato. The brightest of stars appear the most unsteady and tremulous in their light; not from any quality inherent in themselves, but from the vapours that float below, and from the imperfection of vision in the surveyor.[112]

---

[111] Athenaeus, in *The Deipnosophists*, has Pontianus of Nicomedia say: "Now in regard to the statements in his [Plato's] dialogues, what *can* one say, really? The soul, for example, which he conceives as deathless, and which at the dissolution of the body is separated from it, is so spoken of by Homer first. For Homer has said that the soul of Patroclus 'went down to the house of Hades, bewailing its doom, leaving manhood and youth.' [*Iliad* xvi. 856.] Be that as it may, even if one could affirm that the doctrine is Plato's, I cannot see what help we have got from him. For even though one concedes that the souls of the dead change into other beings, and mount upward to the higher and purer region since they share in the quality of lightness, what good does that do us? For we have neither remembrance of where we once were, nor consciousness whether we ever existed at all, and so what gratification is derived from that kind of deathlessness?" (xi. 507e-f, in *The Deipnosophists*, V).

[112] "I believe that the earth is very large and that we who dwell between the pillars of Hercules and the river Phasis live in a small part of it about the sea, like ants or frogs about a pond, and that many other people live in many other such regions. For I believe there are in all directions on the earth many hollows of very various forms and

Diogenes. To the stars again! Draw thy robe round thee; let the folds fall gracefully, and look majestic. That sentence is an admirable one; but not for me. I want sense, not stars.[113] What then? Do no vapours float below the others? and is there no imperfection in the vision of those who look at *them*, if they are the same men, and look the next moment? We must move on: I shall follow the dead bodies, and the benighted driver of their fantastic bier, close and keen as any hyena.[114]

---

sizes, into which the water and mist and air have run together; but the earth itself is pure and is situated in the pure heaven in which the stars are, the heaven which those who discourse about such matters call the ether; the water, mist and air are the sediment of this and flow together into the hollows of the earth. Now we do not perceive that we live in the hollows, but think we live on the upper surface of the earth, just as if someone who lives in the depth of the ocean should think he lived on the surface of the sea, and, seeing the sun and the stars through the water, should think the sea was the sky, and should, by reason of sluggishness or feebleness, never have reached the surface of the sea, and should never have seen, by rising and lifting his head out of the sea into our upper world, and should never have heard from anyone who had seen, how much purer and fairer it is than the world he lived in. Now I believe this is just the case with us; for we dwell in a hollow of the earth and think we dwell on its upper surface; and the air we call the heaven, and think that is the heaven in which the stars move. But the fact is the same, that by reason of feebleness and sluggishness, we are unable to attain to the upper surface of the air; for if anyone should come to the top of the air or should get wings and fly up, he could lift his head above it and see, as fishes lift their heads out of the water and see the things in our world, so he would see things in that upper world; and, if his nature were strong enough to bear the sight, he would recognize that that is the real heaven and the real light and the real earth. For this earth of ours, and the stones and the whole region where we live, are injured and corroded, as in the sea things are injured by the brine, and nothing of any account grows in the sea, and there is, one might say, nothing perfect there, but caverns and sand and endless mud and mire, where there is earth also, and there is nothing at all worthy to be compared with the beautiful things of our world. But the things in that world above would be seen to be even more superior to those in this world of ours" (Plato *Phaedo* 109a–110b).

[113] See n. 89 above.

[114] Diogenes Laertius reports many anecdotes concerning Diogenes' "doggish" character: "He described himself as a hound of the sort which all men praise, but no one, he added, of his admirers dared go out hunting along with him" (vi. 33, in *Lives*, II). "When Plato styled him a dog, 'Quite true,' he said, 'for I come back again and again to those who have sold me'" (vi. 40, in *Lives*, II). "Alexander once came and stood opposite him and said, 'I am Alexander the great king.' 'And I,' said he, 'am Diogenes the Cynic [Hound].' Being asked what he had done to be called a hound, he said, 'I fawn on those who give me anything, I yelp at those who refuse, and I set my teeth in rascals'" (vi. 60, in *Lives*, II). See also *Lives* vi. 45, 46, 55, 61, 76.

Plato. Certainly, O Diogenes, you excell me in elucidations and similies: mine was less obvious. Lycaon[115] became against his will, what you become from pure humanity.

Diogenes. When Humanity is averse to Truth, a fig for her!

Plato. Many, who profess themselves her votaries, have made her a less costly offering.

Diogenes. Thou hast said well, and I will treat thee gently for it.

Plato. I may venture then in defence of my compositions, to argue that neither simple metaphysics nor strict logic would be endured long together in a dialogue.

Diogenes. Few people can endure them anywhere; but whatever is contradictory to either is intolerable. The business of a good writer is to make them pervade his works, without obstruction to his force or impediment to his facility; to divest them of their forms, and to mingle their potency in every particle. I must acknowledge that, in matters of love, thy knowledge is twice as extensive as mine is: yet nothing I ever heard is so whimsical and silly as thy description of its effects upon the soul, under the influence of beauty. The *wings* of the soul, thou tellest us, are *bedewed;* and certain *germs* of theirs expand from every part of it.[116]

The only thing I know about the soul is, that it makes the ground slippery under us when we discourse on it, by virtue (I presume) of this *bedewing;* and beauty does not assist us materially in rendering our steps the steadier.

[115] "But Lycaon brought a human baby to the altar of Lycaean Zeus, and sacrificed it, pouring out its blood upon the altar, and according to the legend immediately after the sacrifice he was changed from a man to a wolf (*lycos*)" (Pausanias *Description of Greece* viii. 2. 3, tr. W. H. S. Jones ["The Loeb Classical Library"; Cambridge: Harvard University Press; London: W. Heinemann, 1966], Vol. III). See also Ovid *Metamorphoses* i. 215–239.

[116] "But he who is newly initiated, who beheld many of those realities, when he sees a god-like face or form which is a good image of beauty, shudders at first. . . . And as he looks upon him, a reaction from his shuddering comes over him, with sweat and unwonted heat; for as the effluence of beauty enters him through the eyes, he is warmed; the effluence moistens the germ of the feathers, and as he grows warm, the parts from which the feathers grow, which were before hard and choked, and prevented the feathers from sprouting, become soft, and as the nourishment streams upon him, the quills of the feathers swell and begin to grow from the roots over all the form of the soul; for it was once all feathered" (Plato *Phaedrus* 251a–b, in *Euthyphro, Apology, Crito, Phaedo, Phaedrus,* tr. H. N. Fowler ["The Loeb Classical Library"; Cambridge: Harvard University Press; London: W. Heinemann, 1960]; hereafter referred to as Plato *Phaedrus*).

Plato. Diogenes! you are the only man that admires not the dignity and stateliness of my expressions.[117]

Diogenes. Thou hast many admirers; but either they never have read thee, or do not understand thee, or are fond of fallacies, or are incapable of detecting them. I would rather hear the murmur of insects in the grass than the clatter and trilling of cymbals and timbrels over-head. The tiny animals I watch with composure, and guess their business: the brass awakes me only to weary me: I wish it under ground again, and the parchment on the sheep's back.

Plato. My sentences, it is acknowledged by all good judges, are well constructed and harmonious.

Diogenes. I admit it: I have also heard it said that thou art eloquent.

Plato. If style, without elocution, can be.

Diogenes. Neither without nor with elocution is there eloquence, where there is no ardour, no impulse, no energy, no concentration. Eloquence raises the whole man: thou raisest our eyebrows only. We wonder, we applaud, we walk away, and we forget. Thy eggs are very prettily speckled; but those which men use for their sustenance are plain white ones. People do not every day put on their smartest dresses; they are not always in trim for dancing, nor are they practising their steps in all places. I profess to be no weaver of fine words, no dealer in the plumes of phraseology, yet every man and every woman I speak to understands me.

Plato. Which would not always be the case if the occulter operations of the human mind were the subject.

Diogenes. If what is occult must be occult for ever, why throw away words about it? Employ on every occasion the simplest and easiest, and range them in the most natural order. Thus they will serve thee faithfully, bringing thee many hearers and readers from the intellectual and uncorrupted. All popular orators, victorious commanders, crowned historians, and poets above crowning, have done it. Homer, for the glory of whose birthplace none but the greatest cities dared contend,[118] is alike

---

[117] Athenaeus, in *The Deipnosophists*, has Pontianus of Nicomedia say: "Hence Timon well said of him: 'What portentous platitudes Plato plaited purposely!'" (xi. 505e, in *The Deipnosophists*, V).

[118] Many cities have claimed to be the birthplace of Homer; indeed, "if we number all those that we find mentioned in different passages of ancient writers, we have seventeen or nineteen cities mentioned as the birth-places of Homer; but the claims of most of these are so suspicious and feeble, that they easily vanish before a closer examination" (William Ihne, in *A Dictionary of Greek and Roman Biography and Mythology*, ed. William Smith [3 vols; London, 1876], s.v. "Homerus"). This confusion

the highest and the easiest in poetry. Herodotus, who brought into Greece more knowledge of distant countries than any or indeed than all before him, is the plainest and gracefulest in prose. Aristoteles, thy scholar, is possessor of a long and lofty treasury, with many windings and many vaults at the sides of them, abstruse and dark. He is unambitious of displaying his wealth; and few are strong-wristed enough to turn the key of his iron chests. Whenever he presents to his reader one full-blown thought, there are several buds about it which are to open in the cool of the study; and he makes you learn more than he teaches.

Plato. I can never say that I admire his language.

Diogenes. Thou wilt never say it; but thou dost. His language, where he wishes it to be harmonious, is highly so: and there are many figures of speech exquisitely beautiful, but simple and unobtrusive. You see what a fine head of hair he might have if he would not cut it so short.[119] Is there as much true poetry in all thy works, prose and verse, as in that *Scolion* of his on Virtue?[120]

Plato. I am less invidious than he is.

Diogenes. He may indeed have caught the infection of malignity, which all who live in the crowd, whether of a court or a school, are liable to contract. We had dismissed that question: we had buried the mortal and corruptible part of him, and were looking into the litter which contains

---

arose in part because many poems whose real author was forgotten were attributed to Homer and the citizens of the communities in which these poems originated claimed their city to be Homer's birthplace, and in part because Homer's real history was lost and the question of his birthplace arose after his works were famous. Of all the cities, Chios and Smyrna in Asia Minor have the best claims.

[119] "Aristotle was Plato's most genuine disciple; he spoke with a lisp, as we learn from Timotheus the Athenian in his book *On Lives*; further, his calves were slender (so they say), his eyes small, and he was conspicuous by his attire, his rings, and the cut of his hair" (Diogenes Laertius v. 1, in *Lives*, I).

[120] According to Diogenes Laertius, Aristotle composed the following scolion (an early type of Greek drinking song) while at the court of Hermias of Atarneus (Asia Minor): "O virtue, toilsome for the generation of mortals to achieve, the fairest prize that life can win, for thy beauty, O virgin, it were a doom glorious in Hellas even to die and to endure fierce, untiring labours. Such courage dost thou implant in the mind, imperishable, better than gold, dearer than parents or soft-eyed sleep. For thy sake Heracles, son of Zeus, and the sons of Leda endured much in the tasks whereby they pursued thy might. And yearning after thee came Achilles and Ajax to the house of Hades, and for the sake of thy dear form the nursling of Atarneus too was bereft of the light of the sun. Therefore shall his deeds be sung, and the Muses, the daughters of Memory, shall make him immortal, exalting the majesty of Zeus, guardian of strangers, and the grace of lasting friendship" (v. 7-8, in *Lives*, I).

his true and everlasting effigy: and this effigy the strongest and noblest minds will carry by relays to interminable generations. We were speaking of his thoughts and what conveys them. His language then, in good truth, differs as much from that which we find in thy dialogues, as wine in the goblet differs from wine spilt upon the table. With thy leave, I would rather drink than lap.

Plato. Methinks such preference is contrary to your nature.

Diogenes. Ah, Plato! I ought to be jealous of thee, finding that two in this audience can smile at thy wit, and not one at mine.

Plato. I would rather be serious, but that my seriousness is provocative of your moroseness. Detract from me as much as can be detracted by the most hostile to my philosophy, still it is beyond the power of any man to suppress or to conceal from the admiration of the world the amplitude and grandeur of my language.

Diogenes. Thou remindest me of a cavern I once entered.[121] The mouth was spacious; and many dangling weeds and rampant briers caught me by the hair above, and by the beard below, and flapped my face on each side. I found it in some places flat and sandy; in some rather miry; in others I bruised my shins against little pointed pinnacles, or larger and smoother round stones. Many were the windings, and deep the darkness. Several men came forward with long poles and lighted torches on them, promising to show innumerable gems, on the roof and along the sides, to some ingenuous youths whom they conducted. I thought I was lucky, and went on among them. Most of the gems turned out to be drops of water; but some were a little more solid. These, however, in general, gave way and crumbled under the touch: and most of the remainder lost all their brightness by the smoke of the torches underneath. The farther I went in, the fouler grew the air and the dimmer the torchlight. Leaving it, and the youths, and the guides, and the long poles, I stood a moment in wonder at the vast number of names and verses graven at the opening, and forbore to insert the ignoble one of Diogenes.

The vulgar indeed and the fashionable do call such language as thine the noblest and most magnificent: the scholastic bend over it in paleness, and with the right hand upon the breast, at its unfathomable depth: but what would a man of plain simple sound understanding say upon it? what would a metaphysician? what would a logician? what would Pericles? Truly, he had taken thee by the arm, and kissed that broad well-perfumed

---

[121] Diogenes derides "the amplitude and grandeur" of Plato's language by relating an anecdote that parodies Plato's famed allegory of the cave in *The Republic* (vii. 514a–518b).

forehead, for filling up with light (as thou wouldst say) the dimple in the cheek of Aspasia,[122] and for throwing such a gadfly in the current of her conversation. She was of a different sect from thee both in religion and in love, and both her language and her dress were plainer.

Plato. She, like yourself, worshipped no deity in public: and probably both she and Aristoteles find the more favour with you from the laxity of their opinions in regard to the Powers above.[123] The indifference of Aristoteles to religion may perhaps be the reason why king Philip bespoke him so early for the tuition of his successor;[124] on whom, destined as he is to pursue the conquests of the father, moral and religious obligations might be incommodious.

Diogenes. Kings who kiss the toes of the most gods, and the most zealously, never find any such incommodiousness. In courts, religious ceremonies cover with their embroidery moral obligations; and the most dishonest and the most libidinous and the most sanguinary kings (to say nothing of private men) have usually been the most punctual worshippers.

Plato. There may be truth in these words. We however know your contempt for religious acts and ceremonies, which, if you do not comply with them, you should at least respect, by way of an example.[125]

---

[122] Pericles (*ca.* 495–429 B.C.), Athenian statesman and orator, formed a lasting union (following an unhappy marriage) with the celebrated courtesan Aspasia of Miletus about 450 or 445 B.C. According to Diogenes Laertius: "Others affirm that he got the name Plato from the breadth of his style, or from the breadth of his forehead, as suggested by Neanthes" (iii. 4, in *Lives*, I).

[123] "About this time also [*ca.* 431 B.C.] Aspasia was put on trial for impiety, Hermippus the comic poet being her prosecutor, who alleged further against her that she received free-born women into a place of assignation for Pericles. And Diopeithes brought in a bill providing for the public impeachment of such as did not believe in gods, or who taught doctrines regarding the heavens, directing suspicion against Pericles by means of Anaxagoras [*ca.* 500–*ca.* 428 B.C., philosopher, teacher, and friend of Pericles]" (Plutarch *Pericles* 32. 1–2, in *Plutarch's Lives*, tr. Bernadotte Perrin ["The Loeb Classical Library"; Cambridge: Harvard University Press; London: W. Heinemann, 1958], Vol. III). Athenaeus, in *The Deipnosophists*, has Myrtilus of Thessaly say: "Antisthenes the Socratic says that when in love with Aspasia he [Pericles] would go in and out of her house twice a day to greet the wench, and once, when she was prosecuted on a charge of impiety he, while pleading in her behalf, wept more tears than when his life and property were endangered" (xiii. 589e, in *The Deipnosophists*, VI).

[124] See n. 38 above.

[125] Diogenes Laertius records: "One day he [Diogenes] saw a woman kneeling before the gods in an ungraceful attitude, and wishing to free her of superstition, according to Zoïlus of Perga, he came forward and said, 'Are you not afraid, my good woman, that a god may be standing behind you?—for all things are full of his presence —and you may be put to shame?'" (vi. 37–38, in *Lives*, II). See also *Lives* vi. 39, 42–43.

Diogenes. What! if a man lies to me, should I respect the lie for the sake of an example! Should I be guilty of duplicity, for the sake of an example! Did I ever omit to attend the Thesmophoria? the only religious rite worthy of a wise man's attendance. It displays the union of industry and law.[126] Here is no fraud, no fallacy, no filching: the gods are worshipped for their best gifts, and do not stand with open palms for ours. I neither laugh nor wonder at anyone's folly.[127] To laugh at it, is childish or inhuman, according to its nature; and to wonder at it, would be a greater folly than itself, whatever it may be.

Must I go on with incoherencies and inconsistencies?

Plato. I am not urgent with you.

Diogenes. Then I will reward thee the rather.

Thou makest poor Socrates tell us that a beautiful vase is inferior to a beautiful horse; and as a beautiful horse is inferior to a beautiful maiden, in like manner a beautiful maiden is inferior in beauty to the immortal gods.[128]

Plato. No doubt, O Diogenes!

Diogenes. Thou hast whimsical ideas of beauty: but, understanding the word as all Athenians and all inhabitants of Hellas understand it, there is no analogy between a horse and a vase. Understanding it as thou perhaps mayest choose to do on the occasion, understanding it as applicable to the service and utility of man and gods, the vase may be applied to more frequent and more noble purposes than the horse. It may delight men in health; it may administer to them in sickness; it may pour out before the

---

[126] The Thesmophoria, a women's festival, was celebrated throughout Greece at the time of seed planting (October and November). It was held in honor of the goddess Demeter Thesmophoros, who presided over agriculture and all the settled laws and customs of the people.

According to Diogenes Laertius, Diogenes' thoughts upon law are: "Again as to law: that it is impossible for society to exist without law; for without a city no benefit can be derived from that which is civilized. But the city is civilized, and there is no advantage in law without a city; therefore law is something civilized" (vi. 72, in *Lives*, II).

[127] The historical Diogenes did wonder at the folly of men: "He would say that men strive in digging [the competitive digging of trenches formed part of the athletes' preparation at Olympia] and kicking to outdo one another, but no one strives to become a good man and true. And he would wonder that the grammarians should investigate the ills of Odysseus, while they were ignorant of their own. Or that the musicians should tune the strings of the lyre, while leaving the dispositions of their own souls discordant; that the mathematicians should gaze at the sun and the moon, but overlook matters close at hand; that the orators should make a fuss about justice in their speeches, but never practise it; or that the avaricious should cry out against money, while inordinately fond of it" (Diogenes Laertius vi. 27-28, in *Lives*, II).

[128] Plato *Greater Hippias* 288e-289b.

protectors of families and of cities the wine of sacrifice. But if it is the quality and essence of beauty to gratify the sight, there are certainly more persons who can receive gratification from the appearance of a beautiful vase than a beautiful horse. Xerxes brought into Hellas with him thousands of beautiful horses and many beautiful vases.[129] Supposing now that all the horses which were beautiful seemed so to all good judges of their symmetry, it is probable that scarcely one man in fifty would fix his eyes attentively on one horse in fifty; but undoubtedly there were vases in the tents of Xerxes which would have attracted all the eyes in the army and have filled them with admiration. I say nothing of the women, who in Asiatic armies are as numerous as the men,[130] and who would every one admire the vases, while few admired the horses. Yet women are as good judges of what is beautiful as thou art, and for the most part on the same principles. But, repeating that there is no analogy between the two objects, I must insist that there can be no just comparison: and I trust I have clearly demonstrated that the postulate is not to be conceded. We will nevertheless carry on the argument and examination, for "the beautiful virgin is inferior in beauty to the immortal gods."[131] Is not Vulcan an immortal god? are not the Furies and Discord immortal goddesses? Ay, by my troth are they; and there never was any city and scarcely any family on earth to which they were long invisible. Wouldst thou prefer them to a golden cup, or even to a cup from the potter's? Would it require one with a dance of Bacchanals[132] under the pouting rim? would it require one foretasted by Agathon?[133] Let us descend from the deities to the horses. Thy dress is as well adapted to horsemanship as thy words are in general to discourse.

[129] Xerxes I, son of Darius and Atossa, and king of Persia 485–465 B.C., invaded the Greek states in the spring of 480 B.C. with a huge army of Persians and men sent by Persia's allies. According to Herodotus, in Xerxes' forces "the number of the horsemen was shown to be eighty thousand, besides the camels and the chariots" (*History* vii. 84–87, tr. A. D. Godley ["The Loeb Classical Library"; Cambridge: Harvard University Press; London: W. Heinemann, 1938], Vol. III; hereafter referred to as Herodotus *History*, III).

[130] Herodotus records: "The number of those whom Xerxes son of Darius led as far as the Sepiad headland and Thermopylae was five millions, two hundred and eighty-three thousand, two hundred and twenty.

"That is the number of Xerxes' whole armament: but none can say what was the exact sum of cooking women, and concubines, and eunuchs; nor of the beasts of draught and burden, and the Indian dogs that were with the host, could any one tell the number, so many they were" (vii. 186–187, in *History*, III).

[131] See n. 128 above.

[132] Bacchanals: drunken, frenzied votaries of Bacchus (Dionysus), the god of wine. See n. 63 above.

[133] See n. 105 above.

Such as thou art, would run out of the horse's way; and such as know thee best, would put the vase out of thine.

Plato. So then, I am a thief, it appears, not only of men's notions, but of their vases!

Diogenes. Nay, nay, my good Plato! Thou hast however the frailty of concupiscence for things tangible and intangible, and thou likest well-turned vases no less than well-turned sentences: therefore they who know thee would leave no temptation in thy way, to the disturbance and detriment of thy soul. Away with the horse and vase! we will come together to the quarters of the virgin. Faith! my friend, if we find her only just as beautiful as some of the goddesses we were naming, her virginity will be as immortal as their divinity.

Plato. I have given a reason for my supposition.

Diogenes. What is it?

Plato. Because there is a beauty incorruptible, and for ever the same.[134]

Diogenes. Visible beauty? beauty cognizable in the same sense as of vases and of horses? beauty that in degree and in quality can be compared with theirs? Is there any positive proof that the gods possess it? and all of them? and all equally? Are there any points of resemblance between Jupiter and the daughter of Acrisius?[135] any between Hatè and Hebe?[136]

---

[134] In the *Symposium* Plato has Socrates quote Diotima as saying, "When a man has been thus far tutored in the lore of love, passing from view to view of beautiful things, in the right and regular ascent, suddenly he will have revealed to him, as he draws to the close of his dealings in love, a wondrous vision, beautiful in its nature; and this, Socrates, is the final object of all those previous toils. First of all, it is ever-existent and neither comes to be nor perishes, neither waxes nor wanes; next, it is not beautiful in part and in part ugly, nor is it such at such a time and other at another, nor in one respect beautiful and in another ugly, nor so affected by position as to seem beautiful to some and ugly to others. Nor again will our initiate find the beautiful presented to him in the guise of a face or of hands or any other portion of the body, nor as a particular description or piece of knowledge, nor as existing somewhere in another substance, such as an animal or the earth or sky or any other thing; but existing ever in singularity of form independent by itself, while all the multitude of beautiful things partake of it in such wise that, though all of them are coming to be and perishing, it grows neither greater nor less, and is affected by nothing" (Plato *Symposium* 210e–211b, in *Lysis, Symposium, Gorgias* tr. W. R. M. Lamb ["The Loeb Classical Library"; Cambridge: Harvard University Press; London: W. Heinemann, 1961]).

[135] See p. 35, n. 71.

[136] According to Hesiod, Ate, or Ruin, was the daughter of Discord (*Theogony* 225–230), and Hebe, the daughter of Zeus and Hera (*Theogony* 921–923). Ate led both gods and men to commit rash actions which inevitably brought about suffering and unhappiness (see Homer *Iliad* xix. 126 ff.), whereas Hebe, the personification of youth, was the fair cupbearer of the immortal gods. See Homer *Iliad* iv. 2.

whose sex being the same brings them somewhat nearer. In like manner thou confoundest the harmony of music with symmetry in what is visible and tangible:[137] and thou teachest the stars how to dance to their own compositions, enlivened by fugues and variations from thy master-hand.[138] This, in the opinion of thy boy scholars, is sublimity! Truly it is the sublimity which he attains who is hurled into the air from a ballista.[139] Changing my ground, and perhaps to thy advantage, in the name of Socrates I come forth against thee; not for using him as a wide-mouthed mask, stuffed with gibes and quibbles; not for making him the most sophistical of sophists, or (as thou hast done frequently) the most improvident of statesmen and the worst of citizens; my accusation and indictment is, for representing him, who had distinguished himself on the field of battle above the bravest and most experienced of the Athenian leaders (particularly at Delion and Potidea), as more ignorant of warfare than the worst-fledged crane that fought against the Pygmies.[140]

[137] "Thus it was that in the midst between fire and earth God set water and air, and having bestowed upon them so far as possible a like ratio one towards another—air being to water as fire to air, and water being to earth as air to water,—he joined together and constructed a Heaven visible and tangible. For these reasons and out of these materials, such in kind and four in number, the body of the Cosmos was harmonized by proportion and brought into existence" (Plato *Timaeus* 32b-c).

[138] "But the choric dances of these same stars and their crossings one of another, and the relative reversals and progressions of their orbits, and which of the gods meet in their conjunctions, and how many are in opposition, and behind which and at what times they severally pass before one another and are hidden from our view, and again re-appearing send upon men unable to calculate alarming portents of the things which shall come to pass hereafter,—to describe all this without an inspection of models [such as a celestial globe] of these movements would be labour in vain" (Plato *Timaeus* 40c-d).

[139] *Ballista* is the Latin term for an early artillery piece capable of discharging large stones and arrows.

[140] Diogenes feels that Plato erred in having Socrates, a seasoned soldier, apparently accept as truth the fantastic tale he tells of the Persians marching hand in hand through the territory of Eretria. See n. 143 below. Diogenes Laertius comments upon Socrates' bravery in battle: "He served on the expedition to Amphipolis [422 B.C.]; and when in the Battle of Delium [424 B.C.] Xenophon had fallen from his horse, he stepped in and saved his life. For in the general flight of the Athenians he personally retired at his ease, quietly turning round from time to time and ready to defend himself in case he were attacked. Again, he served at Potidaea [431–430 B.C.], whither he had gone by sea, as land communications were interrupted by the war; and while there he is said to have remained a whole night without changing his position, and to have won the prize of valour" (ii. 22–23, in *Lives*, I).

Homer alludes to the legendary warfare between the Pygmies (who lived in Africa, India, or Scythia) and the cranes: "Now when they were marshalled, the several

Plato. I am not conscious of having done it.

Diogenes. I believe thee: but done it thou hast. The language of Socrates was Attic and simple: he hated the verbosity and refinement of wranglers and rhetoricians; and never would he have attributed to Aspasia, who thought and spoke like Pericles, and whose elegance and judgment thou thyself hast commended,[141] the chaff and litter thou hast tossed about with so much wind and wantonness, in thy dialogue of *Menexenus*.[142]

---

companies with their captains, the Trojans came on with clamour and with a cry like birds, even as the clamour of cranes ariseth before the face of heaven, when they flee from wintry storms and measureless rain, and with clamour fly toward the streams of Ocean, bearing slaughter and death to Pigmy men, and in the early dawn they offer evil battle" (*Iliad* iii. 1–7, tr. A. T. Murray ["The Loeb Classical Library"; Cambridge: Harvard University Press; London: W. Heinemann, 1937], Vol. I).

[141] "I suppose, my friend, Pericles is the most perfect orator in existence.... All great arts demand discussion and high speculation about nature; for this loftiness of mind and effectiveness in all directions seem somehow to come from such pursuits. This was in Pericles added to his great natural abilities; for it was, I think, his falling in with Anaxagoras, who was just such a man, that filled him with high thoughts and taught him the nature of mind and of lack of mind, subjects about which Anaxagoras used chiefly to discourse, and from these speculations he drew and applied to the art of speaking what is of use to it" (Plato *Phaedrus* 269e–270a).

[142] After Socrates satirizes orators and their art in Plato's *Menexenus* (234c–235d), he repeats a funeral oration for the Athenian dead which he claims he heard Aspasia composing. See *Menexenus* 236a–249d. C. G. Crump suggests that Socrates' oration in the *Menexenus* "is possibly a parody on the funeral oration ascribed to Pericles in the 2nd book of Thucydides" ("Diogenes and Plato," *Imaginary Conversations: By Walter Savage Landor*, ed. C. G. Crump [6 vols.; London, 1891], I, 100 n.).

A. E. Taylor notes that "probably,... the real purpose of the discourse [funeral oration] is to imitate and at the same time, by adroit touches of concealed malice, to satirize popular 'patriotic oratory'" (*Plato: The Man and His Work* [7th ed.; London: Methuen & Co. Ltd., 1960], p. 43). Taylor believes that since Socrates' discourse "treats first of the glorious inheritance and traditions of the community into which the future warriors were born and in which they were brought up, then of their own achievements, by which they have approved themselves worthy of such an origin, and finally of the considerations which should moderate the grief of their surviving friends and relatives ... it exhibits a close parallel with the discourse of Pericles in Thucydides, the 'funeral speech'" (p. 42). According to Taylor, many readers of this discourse, like Landor, have regarded it seriously: "The satire of the actual 'Funeral Discourse' is so subtly mixed with sympathetic appreciation that it would be easy to mistake the whole speech for a serious encomium—a mistake which has actually been made by a good many interpreters of Plato" (p. 44).

Taylor also comments on the role Socrates attributes to Aspasia in the *Menexenus*: "And we still have to explain why Socrates should pretend that Aspasia too is still a well-known figure at Athens, and that he has learned his discourse from her. Again, we cannot account for this use of Aspasia by appealing to the passage (*Menexenus*, 236b) where Socrates is made to credit her with the authorship of the famous 'funeral

Now, to omit the other fooleries in it, Aspasia would have laughed to scorn the most ignorant of her tire-women, who should have related to her the story thou tellest in her name, about the march of the Persians round the territory of Eretria.[143] This narrative seems to thee so happy an attempt at history, that thou betrayest no small fear lest the reader should take thee at thy word, and lest Aspasia should in reality rob thee or Socrates of the glory due for it.

Plato. Where lies the fault?

Diogenes. If the Persians had marched, as thou describest them, forming a circle, and from sea to sea, with their hands joined together; fourscore shepherds with their dogs, their rams, and their bell-wethers, might have killed them all, coming against them from points well-chosen. As however great part of the Persians were horsemen, which thou appearest to have quite forgotten, how could they go in single line with their hands joined, unless they lay flat upon their backs along the backs of their horses, and

---

speech,' delivered by Pericles in the first year of the Archidamian war, and reported by Thucydides [*History* ii. 35–46]. Plato's object is not to ridicule oratory of this kind by the insinuation that its tone is what might be expected from a woman and an *hetaera*. The remains of the *Aspasia* of Aeschines of Sphettus, make it clear that the view, which underlies the proposals of *Republic* v., that 'the goodness of a woman and that of a man are the same,' was a genuine doctrine of Socrates, and that he quite seriously believed in the 'political capacity' of Aspasia. His profession of owing his own 'Funeral Discourse' to her is, no doubt, only half-serious, but it is quite in keeping with what we know to have been his real conviction" (p. 42).

[143] "Then Darius, accusing us and the Eretrians of having plotted against Sardis, dispatched fifty myriads of men in transports and warships, together with three hundred ships of war, and Datis as their commander; and him the king ordered to bring back the Eretrians and Athenians in captivity, if he wished to keep his own head. He then sailed to Eretria [490 B.C.] against men who were amongst the most famous warriors in Greece at that time, and by no means few in number; them he overpowered within three days, and lest any should escape he made a thorough search of the whole of their country; and his method was this. His soldiers marched to the limits of Eretria and posted themselves at intervals from sea to sea; then they joined hands and passed through the whole of the country, in order that they might be able to report to the king that not a man had escaped out of their hands" (Plato *Menexenus* 240a–c, in *Timaeus, Critias, Cleitophon, Menexenus, Epistles*, tr. R. G. Bury ["The Loeb Classical Library"; Cambridge: Harvard University Press; London: W. Heinemann, 1942]).

In the *Laws* Plato states: "So within a very short time Datis, with his many myriads, captured by force the whole of the Eretrians; and to Athens he sent on an alarming account of how not a man of the Eretrians had escaped him: the soldiers of Datis had joined hands and swept the whole of Eretria clean as with a draw-net. This account— whether true, or whatever its origin—struck terror into the Greeks generally, and especially the Athenians" (iii. 698c–d, in *Laws*, I).

unless the horses themselves went tail to tail, one pulling on the other? Even then the line would be interrupted, and only two could join hands. A pretty piece of net-work is here! and the only defect I can find in it is, that it would help the fish to catch the fisherman.

Plato. This is an abuse of wit, if there be any wit in it.

Diogenes. I doubt whether there is any; for the only man that hears it does not smile. We will be serious then. Such nonsense, delivered in a school of philosophy, might be the less derided; but it is given us as an oration, held before an Athenian army, to the honour of those who fell in battle. The beginning of the speech is cold and languid: the remainder is worse; it is learned and scholastic.

Plato. Is learning worse in oratory than languor?

Diogenes. Incomparably, in the praises of the dead who died bravely, played off before those who had just been fighting in the same ranks.[144] What we most want in this business is sincerity; what we want least are things remote from the action. Men may be cold by nature, and languid from exhaustion, from grief itself, from watchfulness, from pity; but they cannot be idling and wandering about other times and nations, when their brothers and sons and bosom-friends are brought lifeless into the city, and the least inquisitive, the least sensitive, are hanging immovably over their recent wounds. Then burst forth their names from the full heart; their fathers' names come next, hallowed with lauds and benedictions that flow over upon their whole tribe; then are lifted their helmets and turned round to the spectators; for the grass is fastened to them by their blood, and it is befitting to show the people how they must have struggled to rise up, and to fight afresh for their country. Without the virtues of courage and patriotism, the seeds of such morality as is fruitful and substantial spring up thinly, languidly, and ineffectually. The images of great men should be stationed throughout the works of great historians.

Plato. According to your numeration, the great men are scanty: and pray, O Diogenes! are they always at hand?

Diogenes. Prominent men always are. Catch them and hold them fast, when thou canst find none better. Whoever hath influenced the downfall or decline of a commonwealth, whoever hath altered in any degree its social state, should be brought before the high tribunal of history.

[144] See Plato *Menexenus* 237b–249d. In Aspasia's funeral oration more emphasis is placed on the exploits of the ancestors of the Athenian dead (237b–244c) than upon the brave deeds of the newly dead themselves.

Plato. Very mean intellects have accomplished these things. Not only battering-rams have loosened the walls of cities, but foxes and rabbits have done the same. Vulgar and vile men have been elevated to power by circumstances: would you introduce the vulgar and vile into the pages you expect to be immortal?

Diogenes. They never can blow out immortality. Criminals do not deform by their presence the strong and stately edifices in which they are incarcerated. I look above them and see the image of Justice: I rest my arm against the plinth where the protectress of cities raises her spear by the judgment-seat. Thou art not silent on the vile; but delightest in bringing them out before us, and in reducing their betters to the same condition.

Plato. I am no writer of history.

Diogenes. Every great writer is a writer of history, let him treat on almost what subject he may. He carries with him for thousands of years a portion of his times: and indeed if only his own effigy were there, it would be greatly more than a fragment of his country.

In all thy writings I can discover no mention of Epaminondas,[145] who vanquished thy enslavers the Lacedæmonians; nor of Thrasybulus,[146] who expelled the murderers of thy preceptor. Whenever thou again displayest a specimen of thy historical researches, do not utterly overlook the fact that these excellent men were living in thy days; that they fought against thy enemies; that they rescued thee from slavery; that thou art indebted to them for the whole estate of this interminable robe, with its valleys and hills and wastes; for these perfumes that overpower all mine; and moreover for thy house, thy grove, thy auditors, thy admirers, and thy admired.

Plato. Thrasybulus, with many noble qualities, had great faults.

Diogenes. Great men too often have greater faults than little men can find room for.

---

[145] Epaminondas (d. 362 B.C.), a Theban statesman and general, defeated the Spartans, victors of the Peloponnesian War (431–404 B.C.), at the battle of Leuctra in 371 B.C. Following this victory, Epaminondas repeatedly invaded the Peloponnese, dealt Sparta a fatal blow by freeing Messenia (370–369 B.C.), and defeated the Spartans at the battle of Mantinea (362 B.C.), where he died of wounds.

[146] Thrasybulus (d. 388 B.C.), an Athenian naval commander and leader of the democratic party in Athens, was banished by the Thirty Tyrants in 404 B.C. At Thebes he formed a band of seventy exiles, organized an army, defeated the troops of the Thirty (403 B.C.), and re-established democracy at Athens. See n. 50 above.

Plato. Epaminondas was undoubtedly a momentous man, and formidable to Lacedæmon, but Pelopidas [147] shared his glory.

Diogenes. How ready we all are with our praises when a cake is to be divided; if it is not ours!

Plato. I acknowledge his magnanimity, his integrity, his political skill, his military services, and, above all, his philosophical turn of mind: but, since his countrymen, who knew him best, have until recently been silent on the transcendency of his merits, I think I may escape from obloquy in leaving them unnoticed. His glorious death appears to have excited more enthusiastic acclamation than his patriotic heroism.[148]

Diogenes. The sun colours the sky most deeply and most diffusely when he hath sunk below the horizon; and they who never said "How beneficently he shines!" say at last, "How brightly he set!" They who believe that their praise gives immortality, and who know that it gives celebrity and distinction, are iniquitous and flagitious in withdrawing it from such exemplary men, such self-devoted citizens, as Epaminondas and Thrasybulus.

Great writers are gifted with that golden wand which neither ages can corrode nor violence rend asunder, and are commanded to point with it toward the head (be it lofty or low) which nations are to contemplate and to revere.

Plato. I should rather have conceived from you that the wand ought to designate those who merit the hatred of their species.

Diogenes. This too is another of its offices, no less obligatory and sacred.

Plato. Not only have I particularized such faults as I could investigate and detect, but in that historical fragment, which I acknowledge to be mine (although I left it in abeyance between Socrates and Aspasia),[149] I have lauded the courage and conduct of our people.[150]

Diogenes. Thou recountest the glorious deeds of the Athenians by sea and land, staidly and circumstantially, as if the Athenians themselves, or any nation of the universe, could doubt them. Let orators do this when some other shall have rivalled them; which, as it never hath happened in

---

[147] Pelopidas (*ca.* 410–364 B.C.), a Theban statesman and general, acquired renown for his leadership of the Sacred Band, a picked corps of three hundred Thebans, especially in the battles of Tegyra (375 B.C.) and Leuctra (371 B.C.). He was killed in action while defeating Alexander of Pherae at Cynoscephalae (364 B.C.). Pelopidas was the equal of Epaminondas in nearly all respects save originality. See p. 147, n. 13.

[148] For accounts of Epaminondas' personal traits, deeds, and heroic death, see Cornelius Nepos *Epaminondas* and Plutarch *Pelopidas*.

[149] See Plato *Menexenus* 236a–249d for Socrates' funeral oration.

[150] See n. 142 above.

the myriads of generations that have passed away, is never likely to happen in the myriads that will follow. From Asia, from Africa, fifty nations came forward in a body, and assailed the citizens of one scanty city: fifty nations fled from before them. All the wealth and power of the world, all the civilisation, all the barbarism, were leagued against Athens; the ocean was covered with their pride and spoils; the earth trembled; mountains were severed, distant coasts united: Athens gave to Nature her own again; and equal laws were the unalienable dowry brought by Liberty to the only men capable of her defence or her enjoyment. Did Pericles, did Aspasia, did Socrates foresee, that the descendents of those, whose heroes and gods were at best but like them, should enter into the service of Persian satraps, and become the parasites of Sicilian kings?[151]

Plato. Pythagoras, the most temperate[152] and retired of mortals, entered the courts of princes.

Diogenes. True; he entered them and cleansed them: his breath was lustration; his touch purified. He persuaded the princes of Italy to renounce their self-constituted and unlawful authority:[153] in effecting which purpose, thou must acknowledge, O Plato! that either he was more

---

[151] See n. 16 above.

[152] "Above all, he [Pythagoras] forbade as food red mullet and blacktail, and he enjoined abstinence from the hearts of animals and from beans, and sometimes, according to Aristotle, even from paunch and gurnard. Some say that he contented himself with just some honey or a honeycomb or bread, never touching wine in the daytime, and with green beans boiled or raw for dainties, and fish but rarely. His robe was white and spotless, his quilts of white wool, for linen had not yet reached those parts. He was never known to over-eat, to behave loosely, or to be drunk. He would avoid laughter and all pandering to tastes such as insulting jests and vulgar tales. He would punish neither slave nor free man in anger" (Diogenes Laertius viii. 19–20, in *Lives*, II).

[153] "After that [Pythagoras' visit to the Egyptian sanctuaries] he returned to Samos to find his country under the tyranny of Polycrates; so he sailed away to Croton in Italy, and there he laid down a constitution for the Italian Greeks, and he and his followers were held in great estimation; for, being nearly three hundred in number, so well did they govern the state that its constitution was in effect a true aristocracy (government by the best)" (Diogenes Laertius viii. 3, in *Lives*, II). Landor contradicts this view of Pythagoras as a wise counselor of princes in *Pericles and Aspasia* (1836): "It is false that Pythagoras, on returning from his voyage in Egypt, was indignant at finding a tyrant in his native city. Polycrates was in possession of the supreme power when the philosopher left the island, and used it with clemency and discretion. The traveller might have gone and might have returned with discontent, but indignation is adverse to favours, and these he was by no means reluctant to accept. Finding he could not be the principal man among his fellow-citizens, he resolved to attain that rank where the supremacy was yet unoccupied. ... Love of supremacy was the motive in all his injunctions and in all his actions. He avoided the trouble of office and the danger of responsibility: he excluded the commons [of Croton], and called to him the nobles, who alone were deemed worthy of serving him" (*Works*, II, 427).

eloquent than thou art, or that he was juster. If, being in the confidence of a usurper,[154] which in itself is among the most heinous of crimes, since they virtually are outlaws, thou never gavest him such counsel at thy ease and leisure, as Pythagoras gave at the peril of his life, thou in this likewise wert wanting to thy duty as an Athenian, a republican, a philosopher. If thou offeredst it, and it was rejected, and after the rejection thou yet tarriedst with him, then wert thou, friend Plato! an importunate sycophant and self-bound slave.

Plato. I never heard that you blamed Euripides in this manner for frequenting the court of Archeläus.[155]

Diogenes. I have heard thee blame him for it; and this brings down on thee my indignation. Poets, by the constitution of their minds, are neither acute reasoners nor firmly minded. Their vocation was allied to sycophancy from the beginning: they sang at the tables of the rich: and he who could not make a hero could not make a dinner. Those who are possessed of enthusiasm are fond of everything that excites it: hence poets are fond of festivals, of wine, of beauty, and of glory. They can not always make their selection; and generally they are little disposed to make it, from indolence of character. Theirs partakes less than others of the philosophical and the heroic. What wonder if Euripides hated those who deprived him of his right, in adjudging the prize of tragedy to his competitors? From hating the arbitrators who committed the injustice, he proceeded to hate the people who countenanced it.[156] The whole frame of government is bad to those who have suffered under any part. Archeläus praised Euripides' poetry:[157] he therefore liked Archeläus: the Athenians

---

[154] For Plato's visits to the court of Dionysius, see n. 16 above.

[155] "When Euripides [*ca.* 485–406 B.C.] was in Macedonia at the court of Archelaus [*ca.* 407 B.C.], and had become an intimate friend of the king, returning home one night from a dinner with the monarch he was torn by dogs, which were set upon him by a rival of his, and death resulted from his wounds" (*The Attic Nights of Aulus Gellius* xv. 20. 9, tr. John C. Rolfe [rev. ed.; "The Loeb Classical Library"; Cambridge: Harvard University Press; London: W. Heinemann, 1961], Vol. III; hereafter referred to as *The Attic Nights of Aulus Gellius*).

[156] Aulus Gellius mentions the following: "In contests in comedy Menander was often defeated by Philemon, a writer by no means his equal, owing to intrigue, favour, and partisanship. When Menander once happened to meet his rival, he said: 'Pray pardon me, Philemon, but really, don't you blush when you defeat me?'

"Marcus Varro says that Euripides also, although he wrote seventy-five tragedies, was victor with only five, and was often vanquished by some very poor poets" [*The Attic Nights of Aulus Gellius* xvii. 4. 1–3).

[157] According to Solinus, Archelaus thought highly of Euripides: "Archelaus was a lover of literature to so marvellous a degree that he granted the tragic poet Euripides

bantered his poetry:[158] therefore he disliked the Athenians. Beside, he could not love those who killed his friend and teacher:[159] if thou canst, I hope thy love may be for ever without a rival.

Plato. He might surely have found, in some republic of Greece, the friend who would have sympathized with him.

Diogenes. He might: nor have I any more inclination to commend his choice than thou hast right to condemn it. Terpander and Thales and Pherecydes were at Sparta with Lycurgus:[160] and thou too, Plato, mightst have found in Greece a wealthy wise man ready to receive thee, or (where words are more acceptable) an unwise wealthy one. Why dost thou redden and bite thy lip? Wouldst thou rather give instruction, or not give it?

Plato. I would rather give it, where I could.

Diogenes. Wouldst thou rather give it to those who have it already, and do not need it, or to those who have it not, and do need it?

---

supremacy in wise counsel: not satisfied with contributing to the expenses of his [Euripides'] funeral, he had his hair shorn and so proclaimed by his countenance the terrors he had conceived in his heart" (*Collectanea Rerum Memorabilium* 9. 14).

[158] See Aristophanes *The Acharnians* 394–490; *The Knights* 18–20; *The Clouds* 1371–1377; *The Wasps* 61, 1414; *The Peace* 146–150; *The Frogs* 53–82, 96–105; and *The Lysistrata* 283–285, 368–369.

[159] Since Socrates' death occurred eight years after Euripides went to the court of Archelaus (407 B.C.), it could not have been one of the reasons for his leaving Athens. According to Diogenes Laertius, Socrates and Euripides were friends (*Lives* ii. 18, 22, 45). Aulus Gellius says: "Later, turning from attention to bodily exercise to the desire of training his [Euripides'] mind, he was a pupil of the natural philosopher Anaxagoras and the rhetorician Prodicus, and, in moral philosophy, of Socrates" (*The Attic Nights of Aulus Gellius* xv. 20. 4).

[160] "But Agis replied that he was not astonished to find Leonidas, who had been reared in foreign lands and had children by an oriental marriage, ignorant that Lycurgus [see Plutarch *Lycurgus* for an account of the traditional founder of the Spartan constitution and military system] had banished from the state debts and loans along with coined money, and that foreigners in the cities were held by him in less displeasure than men to whom the Spartan practices and ways of living were not congenial; these, indeed, he sought to drive away, not because he was hostile to their persons, but because he feared lest their lives and manners should contaminate the citizens, and breed in them a love of luxury, effeminacy, and greed; for certainly Terpander [*fl. ca.* 647 B.C., the famous musician of Lesbos who founded the Spartan school of music] and Thales [*fl. ca.* 680 B.C., a musician from Gortyn, Crete, who composed songs which exhorted obedience to the law] and Pherecydes [*fl. ca.* 550 B.C., a mythologist and cosmologist from Syros] were foreigners, and yet, because the teachings of their songs and philosophy always accorded with those of Lycurgus, they were held in surpassing honour at Sparta" (Plutarch *Agis and Cleomenes* 10. 2–4, in *Plutarch's Lives*, tr. Bernadotte Perrin ["The Loeb Classical Library"; Cambridge: Harvard University Press; London: W. Heinemann, 1959], Vol. X).

Plato. To these latter.

Diogenes. Impart it then to the unwise; and to those who are wealthy in preference to the rest, as they require it most, and can do most good with it.

Plato. Is not this a contradiction to your own precepts, O Diogenes! Have you not been censuring me, I need not say how severely, for my intercourse with Dionysius?[161] and yet surely he was wealthy, surely he required the advice of a philosopher, surely he could have done much good with it.

Diogenes. An Athenian is more degraded by becoming the counseller of a king, than a king is degraded by becoming the schoolmaster of paupers in a free city. Such people as Dionysius are to be approached by the brave and honest from two motives only: to convince them of their inutility, or to slay them for their iniquity.[162] Our fathers and ourselves have witnessed in more than one country the curses of kingly power. All nations, all cities, all communities, should enter into one great hunt, like that of the Scythians[163] at the approach of winter, and should follow it up unrelentingly to its perdition. The diadem should designate the victim: all who wear it, all who offer it, all who bow to it, should perish. The smallest, the poorest, the least accessible village, whose cottages are indistinguishable from the rocks around, should offer a reward for the heads of these monsters, as for the wolf's, the kite's, and the viper's.

Thou tellest us, in thy fourth book on *Polity*, that it matters but little whether a state be governed by many or one, if the one is obedient to the laws.[164] Why hast not thou likewise told us, that it little matters whether the sun bring us heat or cold, if he ripens the fruits of the earth by cold as perfectly as by heat? Demonstrate that he does it, and I subscribe to the proposition. Demonstrate that kings, by their nature and education, are obedient to the laws; bear them patiently; deem them no impediment to their wishes, designs, lusts, violences; that a whole series of monarchs hath been of this character and condition, wherever a whole series hath been permitted to continue; that under them independence of spirit, dignity of mind, rectitude of conduct, energy of character, truth of expression, and even lower and lighter things, eloquence, poetry, sculpture,

---

[161] See n. 16 above.

[162] See n. 55 above. Compare Diogenes' words on tyrannicide in this passage with Landor's poem "Tyrannicide" (1851), *Complete Works*, XV, 61–62.

[163] The Scythians were a nomadic people of Indo-European speech who lived for the most part in what is now southern Russia. Their armies, composed of mounted archers, were feared by both friend and foe.

[164] Plato *Laws* iv. 709a–715d.

painting, have flourished more exuberantly than among the free. On the contrary, some of the best princes have rescinded the laws they themselves introduced and sanctioned. Impatient of restraint and order are even the quiet and inert of the species.

Plato. There is a restlessness in inactivity: we must find occupation for kings.

Diogenes. Open the fold to them and they will find it themselves: there will be plenty of heads and shanks on the morrow. I do not see why those who, directly or indirectly, would promote a kingly government, should escape the penalty of death, whenever it can be inflicted,[165] any more than those who decoy men into slave-ships.

Plato. Supposing me to have done it, I have used no deception.

Diogenes. What! is it no deception to call people out of their homes, to offer them a good supper and good beds if they will go along with thee; to take the key out of the house-door, that they may not have the trouble of bearing the weight of it; to show them plainly through the window the hot supper and comfortable bed, to which indeed the cook and chamberlain do beckon and invite them, but inform them however on entering, it is only on condition that they never stir a foot beyond the supper-room and bed-room; to be conscious, as thou must be, when they desire to have rather their own key again, eat their own lentils, sleep on their own pallet, that thy friends the cook and chamberlain have forged the title-deeds, mortgaged the house and homestead, given the lentils to the groom, made a horse-cloth of the coverlet and a manger of the pallet; that, on the first complaint against such an apparent injury (for at present they think and call it one), the said cook and chamberlain seize them by the hair, strip, scourge, imprison, and gag them, showing them through the grating what capital dishes are on the table for the more deserving, what an appetite the fumes stir up, and how sensible men fold their arms upon the breast contentedly, and slumber soundly after the carousal.

Plato. People may exercise their judgment.

Diogenes. People may spend their money. All people have not much money; all people have not much judgment. It is cruel to prey or impose on those who have little of either. There is nothing so absurd that the ignorant have not believed: they have believed, and will believe for ever, what thou wouldst teach: namely, that others who never saw them, never are likely to see them, will care more about them than they should care about themselves. This pernicious fraud begins with perverting the intellect, and proceeds with seducing and corrupting the affections, which

[165] See n. 55 above.

it transfers from the nearest to the most remote, from the dearest to the most indifferent. It enthrals the freedom both of mind and body; it annihilates not only political and moral, but, what nothing else however monstrous can do, even arithmetical proportions, making a unit more than a million. Odious is it in a parent to murder or sell a child, even in time of famine: but to sell him in the midst of plenty, to lay his throat at the mercy of a wild and riotous despot, to whet and kiss and present the knife that immolates him, and to ask the same favour of being immolated for the whole family in perpetuity, is not this an abomination ten thousand times more execrable?

Let Falsehood be eternally the enemy of Truth, but not eternally her mistress: let Power be eternally the despiser of Weakness, but not eternally her oppressor: let Genius be eternally in the train or in the trammels of Wealth, but not eternally his sycophant and his pander.

Plato. What a land is Attica! in which the kings themselves were the mildest and best citizens, and resigned the sceptre; deeming none other worthy of supremacy than the wisest and most warlike of the immortal Gods.[166] In Attica the olive and corn were first cultivated.[167]

[166] "*Fr.* 1. The Athenians originally had a royal government. It was when Ion came to dwell with them that they were first called Ionians. [For when he came to dwell in Attica, as Aristotle says, the Athenians came to be called Ionians, and Apollo was named their ancestral god....] ... *Fr.* 3. And these sections were continually quarrelling; but Theseus made a proclamation and brought them together on an equal and like footing.... *Fr.* 4. [And that Theseus first leant towards the mob, as Aristotle says, and relinquished monarchical government, even Homer seems to testify, when he applies the term 'people' (see *Iliad*, ii. 547) in the Catalogue of Ships to the Athenians only]" (Aristotle *The Athenian Constitution*, frr. 1–4, in *Athenian Constitution, Eudemian Ethics, Virtues and Vices*, tr. H. Rackham [rev. ed.; "The Loeb Classical Library"; Cambridge: Harvard University Press; London: W. Heinemann, 1961]). The passages in brackets are parts of *The Athenian Constitution* quoted by later Greek writers, collected by scholars, and included in the manuscripts discovered in Egypt in 1880.

[167] According to Pausanias: "About the olive they [the Athenians] have nothing to say except that it was testimony the goddess [Athena] produced when she contended [with Poseidon, who created the horse] for their land. Legend also says that when the Persians fired Athens the olive was burnt down, but on the very day it was burnt it grew again to the height of two cubits" (*Description of Greece* i. 27. 2, tr. W. H. S. Jones, ["The Loeb Classical Library"; Cambridge: Harvard University Press; London: W. Heinemann, 1964], Vol. I; hereafter referred to as Pausanias *Description of Greece*, I). "But the Athenians and those who with them ... know that Triptolemus, son of Celeus, was the first to sow seed for cultivation" (Pausanias i. 14. 2, in *Description of Greece*, I). "They [the Athenians] say that the plain called Rharium was the first to be sown and the first to grow crops, and for this reason it is the custom to use sacrificial barley and to make cakes for the sacrifices from its produce. Here there is shown a threshing-floor called that of Triptolemus and an altar" (Pausanias i. 38. 6, in *Description of Greece*, I).

Diogenes. Like other Athenians, thou art idly fond of dwelling on the antiquity of the people, and wouldst fain persuade thyself, not only that the first corn and olive, but even that the first man, sprang from Attica. I rather think that what historians call the emigration of the Pelasgians under Danaüs,[168] was the emigration of those *'shepherds,'*[169] as they continued to be denominated, who, having long kept possession of Egypt, were besieged in the city of Aoudris, by Thoutmosis, and retired by capitulation. These probably were of Chaldaic origin. Danaüs, like every wise legislator, introduced such religious rites as were adapted to the country in which he settled.[170] The ancient being once relaxed, admission

[168] Herodotus mentions Danaus' emigration from Egypt to Greece (*History* ii. 91). See also Apollodorus *The Library* ii. 1. 4 and Pausanias *Description of Greece* ii. 16. 1. The Pelasgi apparently were a North Aegean people who were widely dispersed by Bronze Age migrations.

[169] The Hyksos, or "Shepherd Kings," were the earliest invaders of Egypt. According to the Jewish historian Flavius Josephus: "The kings of the so-called shepherds, enumerated above, and their descendants, remained masters of Egypt, according to Manetho [an Egyptian priest, *ca.* 323–*ca.* 246 B.C., who wrote a history of Egypt in Greek], for five hundred and eleven years.

"'Then the kings of the Thebaid and of the rest of Egypt rose in revolt against the shepherds, and a great war broke out, which was of long duration. Under a king named Misphragmouthosis, the shepherds, he [Manetho] says, were defeated, driven out of all the rest of Egypt, and confined in a place called Auaris, containing ten thousand *arourae.* The shepherds, according to Manetho, enclosed the whole of this area with a great strong wall, in order to secure all their possessions and spoils. Thoummosis, the son of Misphragmouthosis (he continues), invested the walls with an army of 480,000 men, and endeavoured to reduce them to submission by siege. Despairing of achieving his object, he concluded a treaty, under which they were all to evacuate Egypt and go whither they would unmolested. Upon these terms no fewer than two hundred and forty thousand, entire households with their possessions, left Egypt and traversed the desert to Syria'" (*Against Apion* i. 84–90, in *The Life, Against Apion,* tr. H. St. J. Thackeray ["The Loeb Classical Library"; New York: G. P. Putnam's Sons; London: W. Heinemann, 1926]).

[170] Pausanias records: "The most famous building in the city of Argos is the sanctuary of Apollo Lycius (*Wolf-god*). The modern image was made by the Athenian Attalus, but the original temple and wooden image were the offering of Danaus. I am of opinion that in those days all images, especially Egyptian images, were made of wood. The reason why Danaus founded a sanctuary of Apollo Lycius was this. On coming to Argos he claimed the kingdom against Gelanor, the son of Sthenelas. Many plausible arguments were brought forward by both parties, and those of Sthenelas were considered as fair as those of his opponent; so the people, who were sitting in judgment, put off, they say, the decision to the following day. At dawn a wolf fell upon a herd of oxen that was pasturing before the wall, and attacked and fought with the bull that was the leader of the herd. It occurred to the Argives that Gelanor was like the bull and Danaus like the wolf; for as the wolf will not live with men, so Danaus up to that time had not lived with them. It was because the wolf overcame the bull that Danaus won the

was made gradually for honouring the brave and beneficent, who in successive generations extended the boundary of the colonists, and defended them against the resentment and reprisal of the native chieftains.

Plato. This may be; but evidence is wanting.

Diogenes. Indeed it is not quite so strong and satisfactory as in that piece of history, where thou maintainest that '*each of us is the half of a man.*'[171] By Neptune! a vile man too, or the computation were overcharged.

Plato. We copy these things from old traditions.[172]

Diogenes. Copy rather the manners of antiquity than the fables; or copy those fables only which convey the manners. That one man was cut off another, is a tradition little meriting preservation. Any old woman who drinks and dozes, could recite to us more interesting dreams, and worthier of the Divinity.

Surely thy effrontery is of the calmest and most philosophical kind, that thou remarkest to me a want of historic evidence, when I offered a suggestion; and when thou thyself hast attributed to Solon the most improbable falsehoods on the antiquity and the exploits of your ancestors, telling us that time had '*obliterated*' these '*memorable*' annals. What is obliterated at home, Solon picks up fresh and vivid in Egypt. An Egyptian priest, the oldest and wisest of the body, informs him that Athens was built a thousand years before Sais, by the goddess Neithes, as they call her, but as we, Athenè, who received the *seed* of the city from the Earth and Vulcan. The records of Athens are lost, and those of Sais mount up no higher than eight thousand years.[173] Enough to make her talk like an old woman.

---

kingdom. Accordingly, believing that Apollo had brought the wolf on the herd, he founded a sanctuary of Apollo Lycius" (ii. 19. 3–4, in *Description of Greece*, I).

[171] In the *Banquet* [*Symposium* 191d]. No two qualities are more dissimilar than the imagination of Plato and the imagination of Shakspeare. The *Androgyne* was probably of higher antiquity than Grecian fable. Whencesoever it originated, we can not but wonder how Shakspeare met with it. In his *King John*, the citizen of Angers says of the Lady Blanche and of the Dauphin, "He is the half-part of a blessed man,/ Left to be finished by such a *she*;/ And *she* a fair divided excellence/ Whose fulness of perfection lies in him" [II, i, 437–440].

What is beautiful in poetry may be infantine in philosophy, and monstrous in physics. [*Landor's note.*]

In this note Landor fails to acknowledge the imaginative nature of Aristophanes' mythological account of the origin of love and the dramatic framework in which it is presented.

[172] See Plato *Symposium* 189d–191d.
[173] See Plato *Timaeus* 20d–25d.

I have, in other places and on other occasions, remarked to those about me many, if not equal and similar, yet gross absurdities in thy writings.

Plato. Gently! I know it. Several of these, supposing them to be what you denominate them, are originally from others, and from the gravest men.

Diogenes. Gross absurdities are usually of that parentage: the idle and weak produce but petty ones, and such as gambol at theatres and fairs. Thine are good for nothing: men are too old, and children too young, to laugh at them. There is no room for excuse or apology in the adoption of another's foolery. Imagination may heat a writer to such a degree, that he feels not what drops from him or clings to him of his own: another's is taken up deliberately, and trimmed at leisure. I will now proceed with thee. I have heard it affirmed (but, as philosophers are the affirmers, the assertion may be questioned), that there is not a notion or idea, in the wide compass of thy works, originally thy own.

Plato. I have made them all mine by my manner of treating them.

Diogenes. If I throw my cloak over a fugitive slave to steal him, it is so short and strait, so threadbare and chinky, that he would be recognised by the idlest observer who had seen him seven years ago in the market-place: but if thou hadst enveloped him in thy versicoloured and cloudlike vestiary, puffed and effuse, rustling and rolling, nobody could guess well what animal was under it, much less what man. And such a tissue would conceal a gang of them, as easily as it would a parsley-bed, or the study yonder of young Demosthenes.[174] Therefore, I no more wonder that thou art tempted to run in chase of butterflies, and catchest many, than I am at discovering that thou breakest their wings and legs by the weight of the web thou throwest over them; and that we find the head of one indented into the body of another, and never an individual retaining the colour or character of any species. Thou hast indeed, I am inclined to believe, some ideas of thy own: for instance, when thou tellest us that a well-governed city ought to let her walls go to sleep along the ground.[175] Pallas forbid that

---

[174] See p. 28, n. 45.

[175] "As to walls, Megillus, I would agree with your Sparta in letting the walls lie sleeping in the ground, and not wake them up, and that for the following reasons" (Plato *Laws* vi. 778d, in *Laws*, I). The idea of having a city without walls (except for the defenders who become the "walls") is, of course, not original with Plato. Plutarch says: "And when they [the citizens of Sparta] asked about fortifying their city, he [Lycurgus] answered: 'A city will be well fortified which is surrounded by brave men and not by bricks'" (*Lycurgus* 19. 4, in *Plutarch's Lives*, tr. Bernadotte Perrin ["The Loeb Classical Library"; Cambridge: Harvard University Press; London: W. Heinemann, 1959], Vol. I).

any city should do it where thou art! for thou wouldst surely deflower her, before the soldiers of the enemy could break in on the same errand. The poets are bad enough: they every now and then want a check upon them: but there must be an eternal vigilance against philosophers. Yet I would not drive you all out of the city-gates, because I fain would keep the country parts from pollution.[176]

Plato. Certainly, O Diogenes, I can not retort on you the accusation of employing any language or any sentiments but your own, unquestionably the purest and most genuine Sinopèan.[177]

Diogenes. Welcome to another draught of it, my courteous guest! By thy own confession, or rather thy own boast, thou stolest every idea thy voluminous books convey; and therefore thou wouldst persuade us that all other ideas must have an archetype; and that God himself, the Demiurgos, would blunder and botch without one.[178] Now can not God, by thy good leave, gentle Plato! quite as easily form a thing as conceive it? and execute it as readily at once as at twice? Or hath he rather, in some slight degree, less of plastic power than of mental? Seriously, if thou hast received these fooleries from the Egyptian priests,[179] prythee, for want of

[176] Diogenes mocks Plato's banishment of certain kinds of poets from his city (see *The Republic* viii. 568b, x. 595a, 607a) by permitting philosophers to remain within the city walls where they can be constantly observed.

[177] See n. 27 above.

[178] According to Plato: "Now first of all we must, in my judgment, make the following distinction. What is that which is Existent always and has no Becoming? And what is that which is Becoming always and never is Existent? Now the one of these is apprehensible by thought with the aid of reasoning, since it is ever uniformly existent; whereas the other is an object of opinion with the aid of unreasoning sensation, since it becomes and perishes and is never really existent. Again, everything which becomes must of necessity become owing to some Cause; for without a cause it is impossible for anything to attain becoming. But when the artificer of any object, in forming its shape and quality, keeps his gaze fixed on that which is uniform, using a model of this kind, that object, executed in this way, must of necessity be beautiful; but whenever he gazes at that which has come into existence and uses a created model, the object thus executed is not beautiful. . . . However, let us return and inquire further concerning the Cosmos, —after which of the Models did its Architect construct it? . . . Now if so be that this Cosmos is beautiful and its Constructor good, it is plain that he fixed his gaze on the Eternal; but if otherwise (which is an impious supposition), his gaze was on that which has come into existence. But it is clear to everyone that his gaze was on the Eternal; for the Cosmos is the fairest of all that has come into existence, and He the best of all the Causes" (*Timaeus* 27d–29a). See also n. 21 above.

Landor expresses his disdain for Plato's archetypes in the second Conversation between Southey and Landor: "Aristoteles *knew*, as others do, that Plato entertained the whimsy of God working from an archetype; but he himself was too sound and solid for the admission of such a notion" (*Works*, II, 172).

[179] See n. 104 above.

articles more valuable to bring among us, take them back on thy next voyage, and change them against the husk of a pistachio dropt from the pouch of a sacred ape.

Thy God is like thyself, as most men's Gods are: he throws together a vast quantity of stuff, and leaves his workpeople to cut it out and tack it together, after their own fashion and fancy. These demons or genii are mischievous and fantastical imps: it would have been better if they had always sitten with their hands before them, or played and toyed with one another, like the young folks in the garden of Academus.[180] As thou hast modified the ideas of those who went before thee, so those who follow thee will modify thine. The wiser of them will believe, and reasonably enough, that it is time for the Demiurgos to lay his head upon his pillow, after heating his brains with so many false conceptions, and to let the world go on its own way, without any anxiety or concern.

Beside, would not thy dialogues be much better and more interesting, if thou hadst given more variety to the characters, and hadst introduced them conversing on a greater variety of topics?[181] Thyself and

[180] See n. 13 above.

[181] Diogenes serves as Landor's mouthpiece in this discussion of the writing of dialogues. Landor aspired to write dialogues which simulate actual conversation with its digressions and subtle psychological interplay of character rather than a more rigid and set literary form where the dialogue serves as a conventional tool for philosophical inquiry. He notes his intentions in his Conversation between the two Ciceros in a letter to his friend Robert Southey, May 31, 1823: "Before I wrote this conversation, I would on no account open Plato. I have since read twice over his dialogue [?] of Socrates, and am not so discouraged as I might have been. I have given Cicero his variety, and his rambling from topic to topic, ever pardonable in a conversation between two; but the few touches of paternal tenderness I now give were wanting, and I should have passed many sleepless nights at the faultiness of my work if I had omitted them. For I have attempted in every conversation to give not only one opinion of the speakers, but enough to show their character" (Forster, II, 113).

In "Southey and Landor," the writer both asserts that digression belongs in his dialogues, since digressions are frequent in actual conversation, and draws a rather literal distinction between a dialogue and a disquisition, a distinction he employs in this discussion in attacking Plato's use of the dialogue:

Landor. ... I shall seize upon this conjecture of yours, and say everything that comes into my head on the subject. Beside which, if any collateral thoughts should spring up, I may throw them in also; as you perceive I have frequently done in my *Imaginary Conversations*, and as we always do in real ones.

Southey. When we adhere to one point, whatever the form, it should rather be called a disquisition than a conversation. Most writers of dialogue take but a single stride into questions the most abstruse, and collect a heap of arguments to be blown away by the bloated whiffs of some rhetorical charlatan, tricked out in a multiplicity of ribbons for the occasion. [*Works*, II, 58–59.]

Prodicus,[182] if thou wouldst not disdain to meet him, might illustrate the nature of allegory, might explain to your audience where it can enter gracefully, and where it must be excluded: we should learn from you, perhaps, under whose guidance it first came into Greece: whether anyone has mentioned the existence of it in the poems of Orpheus and Musæus [183] (now so lost that we possess no traces of them), or whether it was introduced by Homer, and derived from the tales and mythology of the East. Certainly he has given us for deities such personages as were never worshipped in our country;[184] some he found, I suspect, in the chrysalis state of metaphors, and hatched them by the warmth of his genius into allegories, giving them a strength of wing by which they were carried to the summit of Olympus. Euripides and Aristophanes might discourse upon comedy and tragedy,[185] and upon that species of poetry which, though the earliest and most universal, was cultivated in Attica with little success until the time of Sophocles.

Plato. You mean the Ode.[186]

---

[182] Prodicus of Ceōs (fifth century B.C.) was a Sophist and contemporary of Socrates. Plato represents his teacher as being friendly toward the Sophist, although Socrates always mingles irony with his praise of Prodicus' teaching. See *The Apology* 19e, *Phaedrus* 267b, *Theaetetus* 151a–b, *Laches* 197d, *Protagoras* 315d–e, *Meno* 96d, *Euthydemus* 305c, *Cratylus* 384b, *Greater Hippias* 282c–d, *Charmides* 163d, *Theages* 127e–128a, *The Republic* x. 4.

[183] Orpheus, thought to be either a Thracian or a mythological figure, was the center of the religion of Orphism founded during the archaic age of Greece, its doctrines laid down in poems no longer extant. Musaeus, a legendary Thracian poet, was supposed to have been a pupil of Orpheus.

[184] "But whence each of the gods came into being, or whether they had all for ever existed, and what outward forms they had, the Greeks knew not till (so to say) a very little while ago; for I suppose that the time of Hesiod and Homer was not more than four hundred years before my own; and these are they who taught the Greeks of the descent of the gods, and gave to all their several names, and honours, and arts, and declared their outward forms" (Herodotus *History* ii. 53, tr. A. D. Godley [rev. ed.; "The Loeb Classical Library"; Cambridge: Harvard University Press; London: W. Heinemann, 1966], Vol. I).

[185] Euripides (*ca.* 485–406 B.C.), famed Greek tragedian (see nn. 155, 156, 157, and 159 above), and Aristophanes (*ca.* 450–*ca.* 385 B.C.), Athenian writer of Old Comedy (see n. 158 above), were contemporaries.

[186] The ode is "a form of stately and elaborate lyrical verse.... The original signification of an ode was a chant, a poem arranged to be sung to an instrumental accompaniment. There were two great divisions of the Greek *melos* or song; the one the personal utterance of the poet, the other, as Professor G. G. Murray says, 'the choric song of his band of trained dancers.' Each of these culminated in what have been called odes, but the former, in the hands of Alcaeus, Anacreon and Sappho, came closer to what modern criticism knows as lyric, pure and simple. On the other hand, the choir-song, in which the poet spoke for himself, but always supported, or interpreted, by a chorus,

Diogenes. I do. There was hardly a corner of Greece, hardly an islet, where the children of Pallas were not called to school and challenged by choristers.

Plato. These disquisitions entered into no portion of my plan.

Diogenes. Rather say, ill-suited thy genius; having laid down no plan whatever for a series of dialogues. School-exercises, or, if thou pleasest to call them so, *disquisitions*, require no such form as thou hast given to them, and they block up the inlets and outlets of conversation, which, to seem natural, should not adhere too closely to one subject. The most delightful parts both of philosophy and of fiction might have opened and expanded before us, if thou hadst selected some fifty or sixty of the wisest, most eloquent, and most facetious, and hadst made them exert their abilities on what was most at their command.

Plato. I am not certain that I could have given to Aristophanes all his gaiety and humour.

Diogenes. Art thou certain thou hast given to Socrates all his irony and perspicacity, or even all his virtue?

Plato. His virtue I think I have given him fully.

Diogenes. Few can comprehend the whole of it, or see where it is separated from wisdom. Being a philosopher, he must have known that marriage would render him less contemplative and less happy,[187] though

---

led up to what is now known as ode proper.... It is probable that the Greek odes gradually lost their musical character; they were accompanied on the flute, and then declaimed without any music at all. The ode, as it was practised by the Romans, returned to the personally lyrical form of the Lesbian lyrists" (Edmund Gosse in the *Encyclopaedia Britannica*, ed. Hugh Chisholm [11th ed.; Cambridge: University Press, 1911], Vol. XX., *s.v.* "ode").

[187] "Some one asked him [Socrates] whether he should marry or not, and received the reply, 'Whichever you do you will repent it'" (Diogenes Laertius ii. 33, in *Lives*, I). According to Diogenes Laertius, Diogenes said some rather harsh things about marriage and bringing children into the world: "He would praise those who were about to marry and refrained, those who intending to go on a voyage never set sail, those who thinking to engage in politics do no such thing, those also who purposing to rear a family do not do so, and those who make ready to live with potentates, yet never come near them after all" (vi. 29, in *Lives*, II). "Some one lately wed had set up on his door the notice: 'The son of Zeus, victorious Heracles,/ Dwells here; let nothing evil enter in.'/ To which Diogenes added 'After war, alliance'" (vi. 50, in *Lives*, II). "Being asked what was the right time to marry, Diogenes replied, 'For a young man not yet: for an old man never at all'" (vi. 54, in *Lives*, II). Landor's own unhappy marriage prompted this remark: "How few are aware of the right moment, men or women! Generally the choice is made too soon, and then the repentance is necessarily the longer, and usually the more poignant" (letter to Miss Rose Paynter, May 26, 1841), *Letters of Walter Savage Landor, Private and Public*, ed. Stephen Wheeler [London, 1899], p. 77).

he had chosen the most beautiful, the most quiet, the most obedient, and most affectionate woman in the world;[188] yet he preferred what he considered his duty as a citizen to his peace of mind.

Plato. He might hope to beget children in sagacity like himself.

Diogenes. He can never have hoped it at all, or thought about it as became him. He must have observed that the sons of meditative men are usually dull and stupid; and he might foresee that those philosophers or magistrates whom their father had excelled would be, openly or covertly, their enemies.

Plato. Here then is no proof of his prudence or his virtue. True indeed is your remark on the children of the contemplative; and we have usually found them rejected from the higher offices, to punish them for the celebrity of their fathers.

Diogenes. Why didst not thou introduce thy preceptor arguing fairly and fully on some of these topics? Wert thou afraid of disclosing his inconsistencies? A man to be quite consistent must live quite alone. I know not whether Socrates would have succeeded in the attempt; I only know I have failed.

Plato. I hope, most excellent Diogenes, I shall not be accused of obstructing much longer so desirable an experiment.

Diogenes. I will bear with thee some time yet. The earth is an obstruction to the growth of seed; but the seed can not grow well without it. When I have done with thee, I will dismiss thee with my usual courtesy.

---

[188] Diogenes' praise of Socrates' wife, Xanthippe, is seen to be ironical when we read several of Diogenes Laertius' descriptions of her treatment of Socrates: "When Xanthippe first scolded him and then drenched him with water, his rejoinder was, 'Did I not say that Xanthippe's thunder would end in rain?' When Alcibiades declared that the scolding of Xanthippe was intolerable, 'Nay, I have got used to it,' said he, 'as to the continued rattle of a windlass. And you do not mind the cackle of geese.' 'No,' replied Alcibiades, 'but they furnish me with eggs and goslings.' 'And Xanthippe,' said Socrates, 'is the mother of my children.' When she tore his coat off his back in the market-place and his acquaintances advised him to hit back, 'Yes, by Zeus,' said he, 'in order that while we are sparring each of you may join in with "Go it, Socrates!" "Well done, Xanthippe!"'" (ii. 36–37, in *Lives*, I).

In all fairness to Xanthippe, Plato presents her in a different light just before Socrates drinks the hemlock: "We went in then and found Socrates just released from his fetters and Xanthippe—you know her—with his little son in her arms, sitting beside him. Now when Xanthippe saw us, she cried out and said the kind of thing that women always do say: 'Oh Socrates, this is the last time now that your friends will speak to you or you to them.' And Socrates glanced at Crito and said, 'Crito, let somebody take her home.' And some of Crito's people took her away wailing and beating her breast" (*Phaedo* 59e–60a).

There are many who marry from utter indigence of thought, captivated by the playfulness of youth, as if a kitten were never to be a cat! Socrates was an unlikely man to have been under so sorrowful an illusion. Those among you who tell us that he married the too handy Xantippe for the purpose of exercising his patience,[189] turn him from a philosopher into a fool. We should be at least as moderate in the indulgence of those matters which bring our patience into play, as in the indulgence of any other. It is better to be sound than hard, and better to be hard than callous.

Plato. Do you say that, Diogenes?

Diogenes. I do say it; and I confess to thee that I am grown harder than is well for me. Thou wilt not so easily confess that an opposite course of life hath rendered thee callous. Frugality and severity must act upon us long and uninterruptedly before they produce this effect: pleasure and selfishness soon produce the other. The red-hot iron is but one moment in sending up its fumes from the puddle it is turned into, and in losing its brightness and its flexibility.

Plato. I have admitted your definitions, and now I accede to your illustrations. But illustrations are pleasant merely; and definitions are easier than discoveries.

Diogenes. The easiest things in the world when they are made: nevertheless thou hast given us some dozens, and there is hardly a complete or a just one on the list; hardly one that any wench, watching her bees and spinning on Hymettus,[190] might not have corrected.

Plato. As you did, no doubt, when you threw into my school the cock you had stripped of its feathers.[191]

Diogenes. Even to the present day, neither thou nor any of thy scholars have detected the fallacy.

Plato. We could not dissemble that our definition was inexact.

Diogenes. I do not mean that.

Plato. What then?

Diogenes. I would remark that neither thou nor thy disciples found me out.

---

[189] "He [Socrates] said he lived with a shrew, as horsemen are fond of spirited horses, 'but just as, when they have mastered these, they can easily cope with the rest, so I in the society of Xanthippe shall learn to adapt myself to the rest of the world'" (Diogenes Laertius ii. 37, in *Lives*, I).

[190] Hymettus is a mountain near Athens which is known for its honey and its exquisite marble.

[191] See n. 11 above.

Plato. We saw you plainly enough: we heard you too, crying, *Behold Plato's man!*

Diogenes. It was not only a reproof of thy temerity in definitions, but a trial of the facility with which a light and unjust ridicule of them would be received.

Plato. Unjust perhaps not, but certainly rude and vulgar.

Diogenes. Unjust, I repeat it: because thy definition was of man as nature formed him: and the cock, when I threw it on the floor, was no longer as nature had formed it. Thou art accustomed to lay down as peculiarities the attributes that belong, equally or nearly, to several things or persons.

Plato. The characteristic is not always the definition, nor meant to be accepted for it. I have called tragedy δημοτερπέστατον, 'most delightful to the people,' and ψυχαγωγικώτατον, 'most agitating to the soul:' [192] no person can accuse me of laying down these terms as the *definition* of tragedy. The former is often as applicable to rat-catching, and the latter to cold-bathing. I have called the dog φιλόμαθες, 'fond of acquiring information,' and φιλόσοφον, 'fond of wisdom;' [193] but I never have denied that man is equally or more.

Diogenes. Deny it then instantly. Every dog has that property; every man has not: I mean the φιλόμαθες. The φιλόσοφον is false in both cases; for words must be taken as they pass current in our days, and not according to any ancient acceptation. The author of the *Margites* [194] says,

Τόνδ' οὔτ' ἂν σκαπτῆρα θεοὶ θέσαν οὔτ' ἀροτῆρα,
"Οὔτ' ἄλλως τι σοφόν. [195]

---

[192] Plato *Minos* 321a.   [193] Plato *The Republic* ii. 376.

[194] "Before Homer we cannot indeed name any such poem [satire], though there were probably many satirical poets, but starting from Homer, there is, for instance, his *Margites* [a lost burlesque] and other similar poems.... And just as Homer was a supreme poet in the serious style, since he alone made his representations not only good but also dramatic, so, too, he was the first to mark out the main lines of comedy, since he made his drama not out of personal satire but out of the laughable as such. His *Margites* indeed provides an analogy: as are the *Iliad* and *Odyssey* to our tragedies, so is the *Margites* to our comedies" (Aristotle *Poetics* 4. 9–12, in *Aristotle: The Poetics; Longinus: On The Sublime; Demetrius: On Style*, tr. W. Hamilton Fyfe and W. Rhys Roberts [rev. ed.; "The Loeb Classical Library"; Cambridge: Harvard University Press; London: W. Heinemann, 1960]).

[195] "Neither a delver nor a ploughman him/ The Gods had made, nor wise in aught beside" (Aristotle *Nicomachean Ethics* vi. 7. 2, tr. H. Rackham [rev. ed.; "The Loeb Classical Library"; Cambridge: Harvard University Press; London: W. Heinemann, 1947]).

Here certainly the σοφός has no reference to the higher intellectual powers, as with us, since he is placed by the poet among delvers and ploughmen. The compound word φιλόσοφος did not exist when the author of *Margites* wrote; and the lover of wisdom, in his days, was the lover of the country. Her aspirants, in ours, are quarreling and fighting in the streets about her; and nevertheless, while they rustle their Asiatic robes around them, leave her as destitute, as naked, and as hungry as they found her.

Plato. Did your featherless cock render her any service?[196]

Diogenes. Yes.

Plato. I corrected and enlarged the definition without your assistance.

Diogenes. Not without it: the best assistance is the first, and the first was the detection of insufficiency and error. Thy addition was, 'that man has broad nails:' now art thou certain that all monkeys have sharp and round ones? I have heard the contrary; and I know that the mole has them broad and flat.

Plato. What wouldst thou say man is, and other animals are not?

Diogenes. I would say, *lying* and *malicious*.

Plato. Because he alone can speak; he alone can reflect.

Diogenes. Excellent reasons! If speech be the communication of what is felt, made by means of the voice, thinkest thou other creatures are mute? All that have legs, I am inclined to believe, have voices: whether fishes have, I know not. Thou wouldst hardly wish me to take the trouble of demonstrating that men lie, both before their metamorphosis into philosophers and after: yet perhaps thou mayst wish to hear wherefore, if other animals reason and reflect (which is proved in them by apprehending mischief and avoiding it, and likewise by the exertion of memory), they are not also malicious.

Plato. Having kept in their memory an evil received, many of them evince their malice, by attacking long afterward those who did it.

Diogenes. This is not malice, in man or beast. Malice is ill-will without just cause, and desire to injure without any hope of benefiting from it. Tigers and serpents seize on the unwary, and inflict deadly wounds: tigers from sport or hunger, serpents from fear or hurt: neither of them from malice, neither of them from hatred. Dogs indeed and horses do acquire hatred in their domestic state: they had none originally: they must sleep under man's roof before they share with him his high feeling: that high feeling which renders him the destroyer of his own kind, and the devourer of his own heart. We are willing to consider both revenge and

[196] See n. 11 above.

envy as much worse blemishes in the character than malice. Yet for one who is invidious there are six or seven who are malicious, and for one who is revengeful there are fifty. In revenge there must be something of energy, however short-breathed and indeterminate. Many are exempt from it because they are idle and forgetful; more, because they are circumspect and timid; but nothing hinders the same people from being malicious. Envy, abominable as we call her, and as she is, often stands upon a richly-figured base, and is to be recognised only by the sadness with which she leans over the emblems of power and genius. The contracted heart of Malice can never swell to sadness. Seeing nothing that she holds desirable, she covets nothing; she would rather the extinction than the possession of what is amiable; she hates high and low, bad and good, coldly pertinacious and lazily morose.

Thou, Plato, who hast cause to be invidious of not many, art of nearly all: and thy wit pays the fine, being rendered thereby the poorest I know in any Athenian ambitious of it.

Plato. If the fact be thus, the reason is different.

Diogenes. What is it then?

Plato. That every witticism is an inexact thought: that what is perfectly true is imperfectly witty: and that I have attended more sedulously and more successfully to verity.

Diogenes. Why not bring the simplicity of truth into the paths of life? why not try whether it would look as becomingly in actions as in words; in the wardrobe and at table as in deductions and syllogisms? why not demonstrate to the youth of Athens that thou in good earnest canst be contented with a little?

Plato. So I could, if the times required it.

Diogenes. They will soon; and we should at least be taught our rudiments, before a hard lesson is put into our hands.

Plato. This makes me think again that your grammatical knowledge, O Diogenes! is extensive. The plain and only sense of the second verse . . [197]

Diogenes. What second verse? Were we talking of any such things?

Plato. Yes, just now.

Diogenes. I had forgotten it.

Plato. How! forgotten the *Margites!* The meaning of the words is, 'nor fit for anything else.'

Homer in like manner uses εἰδώς very frequently, to indicate mere manual skill. The spirit of inquiry, the φιλόμαθες, we take upon ourselves

[197] See n. 195 above.

with the canine attributes: we talk of *indagating*, of *investigating*, of *questing*.

Diogenes. I know the respect thou bearest to the dogly character,[198] and can attribute to nothing else the complacency with which thou hast listened to me since I released thy cloak. If ever the Athenians, in their inconstancy, should issue a decree to deprive me of the appellation they have conferred on me, rise up, I pray thee, in my defence, and protest that I have not merited so severe a mulct. Something I do deserve at thy hands; having supplied thee, first with a store of patience, when thou wert going without any about thee, although it is the readiest viaticum and the heartiest sustenance of human life; and then with weapons from this tub,[199] wherewith to drive the importunate cock before thee out of doors again.[200]

[198] See n. 114 above.
[199] See n. 7 above.
[200] See n. 11 above.

Landor concludes the Conversation with a lengthy commentary:

Diogenes Laertius, biographer of the Cynic, is among the most inelegant and injudicious writers of antiquity; yet his book is highly valuable for the anecdotes it preserves. No philosopher or other man more abounded in shrewd wit than the philosopher of Sinope, whose opinions have been somewhat misunderstood, and whose memory hath suffered much injustice. One Diocles, and afterward Eubulides, mention him (it appears) as having been expelled from Sinope for counterfeiting money: and his biographer tells us that he has recorded it of himself [see *Lives* vi. 20. According to Diogenes Laertius, Diocles places the blame on Hicesius, Diogenes' banker-father]. His words led astray these authors. He says that he *marked* false money: for an equivoke was ever the darling of Diogenes, and, by the marking of false money, he means only that he exposed the fallacies of pretenders to virtue and philosophy [Diogenes' own words, as recorded by Diogenes Laertius, contradict Landor. See *Lives* vi. 56]. Had he been exiled for the crime of forgery, Alexander of Macedon, we may well suppose, would not have visited him, would not have desired him to ask any favour he chose [*Lives* vi. 38], would not have declared that if he were not Alexander, he would fain have been Diogenes [*Lives* vi. 32]. He did not visit him from an idle curiosity, for he had seen him before in his father's camp on his first invasion of Greece, where he was apprehended as a spy, and, being brought before the king, exclaimed, "I am indeed a spy; a spy of thy temerity and cupidity, who hazardest on the cast of a die thy throne and life." This is related by Plutarch in his *Ethics* [*Moralia* 606b–c]. Some men may think forgery no very heinous crime, but all must think it an act of dishonesty; and kings (whose moral scale is nowhere an exact one) would be likely to hold it in greater reprobation than any thing but treason and insurrection. Had the accusation been true, or credited, or made at the time [According to Diogenes Laertius, Diogenes was reproached for his exile. See *Lives* vi. 49], the Athenians would not have tolerated so long his residence among them, severe as he was on their manners, and peculiarly contemptuous and contumelious toward the orators and philosophers; Plato for instance, and afterward Demosthenes [*Lives* vi. 34–35]. Here however we may animadvert on the inaccuracy of attributing to him the reply, when somebody asked him what he thought of Socrates as having seen him, *'that he thought him a madman.'* Diogenes was but twelve years old at the death of Socrates, and did not leave Sinope till long after [see n. 32 above]. The answer, we may conceive, originated from the description that Plato in many of his dialogues had given of his master. Among the faults of Plato he ridiculed his affectation of new words, unnecessary and inelegant; for instance his coinage of τραπεζότης and κυαθότης, which Plato defended very frigidly, telling him that, although he had eyes to see a cup and a table, he had not understanding for *cuppeity* and *tableity* [*Lives* vi. 53]; and it indeed must be an uncommon one. Plato himself, the most invidious of the Greek writers, says that he was another Socrates, but a mad one [*Lives* vi. 54]; meaning (no doubt) that he was a Socrates when he spoke generally, a mad one when he spoke of *him*. Among his hearers was Phocion [*Lives* vi. 76. See n. 40 above]: a fact which alone would set aside the tale of his adversaries, a thousand times repeated by their readers, about his public indulgence in certain immoralities which no magistrature would tolerate.

Late in life he was taken by pirates, and sold to Xeniades the Corinthian, whose children he educated, and who declared that a good genius had entered his house in Diogenes. Here he died [*Lives* vi. 29–31, 36, 74]. A contest arose, to whom among his intimates and disciples should be allowed the distinction of supplying the expenses of his funeral: nor was it settled till the fathers of his auditors and the leaders of the people met together, and agreed to bury him at the public charge at the gate of the Isthmus [*Lives* vi. 78]: the most remarkable spot in Greece, by the assemblage of whose bravest inhabitants it was made glorious, and sacred by the games in honour of her gods.

A propos of Landor's reference to the significance of the Isthmus for the Greeks, Herodotus records: "Nathless the Greeks had used every device possible to prevent the foreigners [Persians] from breaking in upon them by land. For as soon as the Peloponnesians heard that Leonidas' men at Thermopylae were dead [August, 480 B.C.], they hastened together from their cities and encamped on the Isthmus [Corinth], their general being the brother of Leonidas, Cleombrotus son of Anaxandrides. Being there encamped they broke up the Scironian road, and thereafter built a wall across the Isthmus, having resolved in council to do so. As there were many tens of thousands there and all men wrought, the work was brought to accomplishment; for they carried stones to it and bricks and logs and crates full of sand, and they that mustered there never rested from their work by night or by day" (*History* viii. 71, tr. A. D. Godley [rev. ed.; "The Loeb Classical Library"; Cambridge: Harvard University Press; London: W. Heinemann, 1961], Vol. IV). According to Pausanias: "There are legends about the rocks, which rise especially at the narrow part of the road [from Megara to Corinth]. As to the Molurian, it is said that from it Ino flung herself into the sea with Melicertes, the younger of her children.... The son, they say, was landed on the Corinthian Isthmus by a dolphin, and honours were offered to Melicertes, then renamed Palaemon [Melicertes was transformed into the sea god Palaemon and Ino into the sea goddess Leucothea], including the celebration of the Isthmian games" (i. 44. 7–8, in *Description of Greece*, I).

See Textual Notes, pp. 251–253, for an addition to the text of "Diogenes and Plato" that appears in John Forster's 1876 edition of Landor's writings.

TEXTUAL NOTES

In the textual notes, the first reference number, preceding the colon, refers to the page in this book, and second number, following the colon, to the line of Landor's text on that particular page, in which the variant occurs. For example, an entry prefixed "3:1" would refer to page 3, the first line of "Boccaccio and Petrarca"; an entry designated "4:18" would have reference to the eighteenth line on page 4. The edition from which the variant is taken is indicated in parentheses at the end of each note. In the edition designations, 29 stands for 1829, 46 for 1846, etc. The texts collated here are:

29. Imaginary Conversations/of/Literary Men and Statesmen/By Walter Savage Landor, Esq./Second Series./The First Volume. [The Second Volume]/London: /James Duncan, Paternoster Row./MDCCCXXIX. Some copies have a *cancellans* at I, 65–66. In this edition all quotations are indicated by italics rather than quotation marks. This variant is not collated in the textual notes.

46. The Works/of/Walter Savage Landor./In two Volumes./Vol. I. [Vol. II.]/London:/Edward Moxon, 44, Dover Street./MDCCCXLVI.

76. The Works and Life/of/Walter Savage Landor/First Volume/The Life/[Second Volume/First series of Imaginary Conversations, Etc., Etc.]/London/Chapman and Hall, 193 Piccadilly/1876.

BOCCACCIO AND PETRARCA

3:1.	amongst (29)	
3:2.	country, as (29)	
4:1.	you. Indeed (29)	
4:2.	writers, and (29)	
4:3.	citizens, lives in exile, from the (29)	
4:4.	thro (29)	
4:6.	honorably: (29)	
4:8.	out to all men by (29)	
4:11.	about this: tomorrow I must pursue (29)	
4:13.	men, altho (29)	
4:15.	produced one equal (29)	
4:18.	them before me, raised (29)	
4:21.	delighted, as you say you have been, at (29)	
4:22.	wherin (29)	
4:23.	Decameron [rom.], (29)	
4:24.	thro (29)	
4:25.	east (29)	
5:2.	reflexions. It shews (29)	
5:5.	messer (29)	
5:8.	powers; if (29)	
5:8–9.	I ever have possessed them. (29)	
5:10.	green walk, (29)	
5:11.	The odour of (29)	
5:11.	altho (29)	
5:12.	are richly so; I cannot say (29); are; I cannot say (76)	
5:12.	resuscitation and revival of (29)	
5:16.	magpie, and (29)	
5:19.	bestrown (29)	
5:22.	rebuke, than (29)	
6:1.	day .. and (29)	
6:2.	sun gives it a yellowish colour. (29)	
6:4.	any thing (29)	
6:6.	the house itself (29)	
6:8.	tho (29)	
6:9.	villas, the (29)	
6:13.	it must lose that cascade yonder, under (29)	
6:14.	villa ... come (29); villa. ... come (76)	
6:14.	off .. the (29)	
6:16.	at this hour of the day ... in (29)	
6:16.	messer (29)	
6:18.	Oricallari. [text] (29); Oricellari. [errata] (29)	

229

230   TEXTUAL NOTES

6:23.	pale, outrivalling her rival. Father, (29)	9:27.	[no ¶] *While father Fontesecco* (29)
6:27.	thro... angel, pleased (29)	9:27–28.	chaunting thro his nose the benedicite, *and* snoring, I (29)
6:28.	such; the (29)		
6:32.	man, of (29)	9:31.	gratitude. Guiberto (29)
6:32.	education, would (29)	9:32.	breaking.. why (29)
7:1–2.	accord .. I (29); however .. but (29); me .. and (29)	9:38.	*Amadeo:* (29)
		10:1–2.	not in these (29)
7:2.	cannot (29)	10:8.	mistress, as (29)
7:7.	Oh that now is impossible: (29)	10:10.	more so than (29)
7:11.	She did so. (29)	10:12.	Profuse in ... Silvestrina, at all times, whenever (29)
7:13.	and, if (29)		
7:28.	stil (29)	10:13.	heart. (29)
7:29.	example, and become (29)	10:15	and, in short, any one but (29)
7:33.	garden-walk, and, (29)	10:18.	any one (29)
7:33.	further (29)	10:19.	and rocks (29)
7:35.	opprest (29)	10:20–21.	times told me so; and I would (29)
7:36.	sundial, and (29)		
7:36–37.	been, on ... day, in the middle of August. (29)	10:21.	fled from them for saying it. Giovanni! *they* could feel it! (29)
7:38.	beyond. He (29)		
8:1.	morning, ere sunrise, did (29)	10:24.	true friend Guiberto, (29)
8:4.	bridegroom was a (29)	10:26.	*first! by* (29)
8:6.	she might be. (29)	10:31–32.	altho ... it: *but* (29)
8:6.	peasant, the labourer of (29)	10:32.	any one, (29)
8:11–13.	He went into ... them. (not in 29)	10:35.	*in this villa, by the connivence of* (29)
8:14.	cried Amadeo. (29)	10:37–11:1	assistence: *you shall* (29)
8:14–15.	*think about it! Bring an old mat* (29)	11:6.	my innermost heart; poor (29)
		11:11–12.	frailties? what ... assistence, (29)
8:16.	*tonight, tomorrow-night,* (29)		
8:18.	illness, by (29)	11:16.	procede (29)
8:19.	day: every (29)	11:17–21.	BOCCACCIO. Guiberto entered (29)
8:21.	after some weeks (29)		
8:23.	grew somewhat calmer (29)	11:22.	from intelligence he had just received, gave (29)
8:28.	wheron (29)		
8:36.	to ascend the (29)	11:24–25.	way to Sienna, (29)
8:37–38.	road. *Amadeo*, said Guiberto, (29)	11:30–31.	kid. After (29)
		11:31.	fell upon him, coming (29)
9:1.	replied Amadeo; *if* (29)	11:38–39.	(Footnote not in 29)
9:5.	Hold! *Amadeo*, said Guiberto, (29)	12:1.	PETRARCA. True indeed! (29)
		12:8.	BOCCACCIO. Ay truly; (29)
9:7.	messer (29)	12:12.	credible; certain (29)
9:11.	invent, than (29)	12:14.	PETRARCA. Not at all, not at all. The (29)
9:11–12.	*Giornata* in my Decameron [rom.] (29)		
		12:14–15.	lover might suffer and act as he did. (29)
9:13.	*forgive me, in* (29)		
9:14.	*be.* He (29)	12:16.	BOCCACCIO. But, Francesco, (29)
9:18.	*stil more so to* (29)		

12:22.	eyes, and threw herself (29)	21:9.	places; since every (29)
12:28.	explane (29)	21:17.	right: for (29)
12:30.	*father . . . he* (29)	21:18.	fact: but (29)
12:32.	PETRARCA. Giovanni, I (29)	21:19–22.	things, because they write more attentively than they examine. (29)
12:35.	BOCCACCIO. Say rather, to (29)		
12:39.	think it so?) (29)	21:22–22:1.	Archimedes, in my opinion, is the only one worthy of the name; for he alone has kept (29); opinion, after our Epicurus, the worthiest of the name, having kept (76)
13:2.	erred! (29)		

LUCULLUS AND CÆSAR

Title. LUCULLUS AND CESAR. (spelled tl is throughout 29)

		22:3.	Science, boasters (29)
18:1.	I am come (29)	22:4–6.	I had forgotten . . . philosophers. (not in 29); goddesses; plagiarists and imposters. . . . philosophers'. (76)
18:3.	hath (76)		
18:6.	dependents (29)		
18:7–8.	affinity (76); him: he (29)		
18:8.	wife, he (29)	22:6.	¶ Let (29)
18:9.	unborn, he (29)	22:12.	lathes (29)
18:9–10.	own nascent love at (76)	22:15–17.	(Footnote not in 29)
18:11.	submitt (29)	23:1–2.	hurry and anxiety had (29)
18:11.	concessions (29)	23:9.	cannot (29)
18:15.	consider, in (29)	23:11.	ceasing: and (29)
19:1.	committ (29)	23:12.	fresh, or (29)
19:4.	triumph; when (29); triumph, when (76)	23:14.	villas because . . . but (29)
		23:14–15.	proportions? surely (29)
19:12.	Caius Julius; and (29)	23:16.	highth (29); height (76)
19:14.	prepossessed in his favour. (29)	23:17.	twentyfive; (29)
		23:18.	quadrangular. Three (29)
19:16.	worthy, whom (29)	23:19.	each; the (29)
19:18.	carcase a (29)	23:23–24:2.	*Lucullus.* Next to it, . . . villa. (not in 29)
19:20.	with wails and dislocations. (29)		
		24:3.	cows: their (29)
20:1.	bring a great deal to (29)	24:9.	leader, from (29)
20:1.	slipt (29)	24:16–17.	whatsoever has attracted so many worshipers: where (29)
20:3–4.	behalf, began . . . permitt (29)		
20:4.	fatigued; which (29)	24:19.	hath (76)
20:6.	alertness. I (29)	24:21.	amongst (29)
20:14.	preferr (29)	25:2.	rites? the first (29)
20:16.	Permitt (29)	25:3–4.	place amongst them, (29)
20:17.	carriage . . the (29)	25:5.	her short slumber, (29)
20:19.	LUCULLUS. Marcipor, let (29)	25:7–8.	houses: the image (29)
		25:9.	cannot (29)
20:19.	again . . no (29)	25:9.	any thing (29)
21:4.	villa; for (29)	25:17.	him; teaching (29)
21:7.	most part (29); straw. Two (76)	25:19.	ceremonies, the (29)
		25:21.	complacence (29, 76)
		26:1.	monarchal; not (29, 76)

232   TEXTUAL NOTES

26:2.	apparitors and (29, 76)
26:4.	The altars (29)
26:4.	and the incense (29)
26:5.	places. It (29)
26:7.	of powerful families (29)
26:11.	the lustre of arms (29)
26:15.	alone. Nations (29)
26:19.	be still distant; (29)
26:23.	lake. It (29)
26:28.	often and (29, 76)
26:30.	twelve constantly in attendence. (29)
27:7.	me! (29)
27:13.	Commentaries [rom.] .. he (29)
27:16.	honey-suckles (29)
27:17.	shew, (29)
28:5.	generous of military men; the (29)
28:6.	judgement (29)
28:8.	Commentaries [rom.], (29)
28:11.	Demosthenes, the (29, 76)
28:13.	defeated, his (76)
28:17.	him: but (29)
29:6.	Cyropedia [rom.]. (29)
29:11.	shewed me (29)
29:19.	reflexion. (29)
29:20.	says *mirari soleo*. (29)
30:1.	any thing, (29)
30:4–5.	I exclamed, *the clown!* (29)
30:7.	believe in it (76)
30:8.	only very possible but very reasonable. (29)
30:9.	*such phrases are common*. In our common and ordinary (29)
30:13–14.	I may be very much ... tatters or slipshod, and, above all, without treading (29)
30:16.	shewed (29)
30:19.	enemies: I (29, 76); country: he (76)
30:20.	it! (29)
30:27.	The apparent blocks (29)
31:1–2.	escape: and the melons are still in the snow; they came (29)
31:2–4.	Luni, travelling by night. CESAR. (29)
31:4.	any thing (29)
31:6.	attendents. (29)
31:12–13.	to equal me in (29)
31:14.	milk. Such, (29)
31:15.	berries*, [footnote:] *The raspberry and gooseberry are not cultivated in Italy, but grow plentifully on many parts of the Alps and Apennines. In one garden belonging to a Florentine are currants introduced by a French family. None of these fruits is known at Rome. Where the climate does much for fruit, the people do little. (29)
31:17.	it: and (29)
32:2.	Gaul. The (29)
32:8.	thro (29)
32:9.	you will look (29)
32:10.	span: here (29)
33:3.	months. We (29)
33:3.	other; and (29)
33:4.	I, even in youth (29)
33:6.	lampries (29)
33:9.	thing: I (29)
33:10–11.	does not now appear [misprint] (76)
34:1.	us, nor any insect (29)
34:16.	cannot (29)
35:13.	CESAR. Its temperature is admirable; its flavour incomparable. (29)
35:14.	thro (29)
36:4.	mount (76)
36:12.	*besides, he* (29)
36:12.	*tho resolved.* (29)
36:17.	descendent. (29)
37:1.	terrour (29)
37:3.	reflexion (29)
37:6.	heavens. I have read the picture; and thus it ends. (29)
37:7.	have shewn me this? you, (29)
37:9–11.	LUCULLUS. This is the only one in fresco; but in the next apartment are seven or eight other pictures from our history ... There are no more: what do you look for? (29)

TEXTUAL NOTES

37:13–14.	remembered: the soul of them is here .. This, (29)	41:6.	Every thing in this world would (29)
37:17.	seasons, a (29)	41:7.	permitt him to shew that (29)
37:20.	any thing (29)		
37:20.	stil (29)	41:9.	foss it and pale it, (29)
37:23.	benefited materially by (29)	41:13.	My very first (29)
38:1–2.	LUCULLUS. I am inclined to think, and my physician (29)	41:14.	you, (if indeed ... me) and, (29)
		41:15.	supprest. (29)
38:6.	Hope better (29)	41:24.	not always in (29)
38:7.	Mithridates: but (29)	42:1.	cannot (29)
38:9.	stil (29)	42:6.	have, and (29)
38:10–11.	his malice (29)	42:9.	in circumstances: (29)
38:12.	cannot (29)	42:15.	you, Cesar; (29)
38:14.	milk, which today is presented me, (29)	42:18.	Those who (29)
		42:20.	city, that (29)
38:19.	not. In (29)	43:3.	weep also at (29)
38:34.	funeral, a (29)	43:4.	cannot (29)
39:3.	any thing (29)	43:6.	cannot (29)
39:6.	any thing (29)	43:8.	one? not you, (29)
39:8.	ropedancer; (29)	43:9.	well. Poetasters (29)
39:12.	yours, for (29)	43:12.	heroes as calm (29)
39:17–18.	prophecy; or rather, accept my assistence: (29)	43:15.	we? or, I [text] (29); we? for, I [errata] (29)
39:19.	Reflexions (29)	43:23.	acknowledged even for (29)
39:24–27.	has, in the natural order of things, its vernal equinox; its first flowers open under fierce tempests: in the autumnal it ceases to follow the laws of the seasons; is exempt from storms, is regular and temperate, looks complacently (29)	44:2.	or the elder Cato with Curius, or the younger with him. It (29)
		44:4–5.	long run. Officers (29)
		44:5.	exclamed (29)
		44:6.	admiration *He fights like Cinna.* Think, Julius, (29)
		44:7–8.	that, among (29)
		44:8.	then [text] (29); them [errata] (29)
39:28.	order, to the solace of friendship, to the avocations (29)	44:9.	one that holds any thing (29)
39:30–33.	Thrown out ... outset. (not in 29)	44:12.	or more so. (29)
		44:14–45:1.	cannot (29)
39:30.	nature, (76)	45:1.	applause (76)
40:5.	before them; in court; defending a client! (29)	45:4–5.	and challenge and game and wager? (29, 76)
40:6.	sate (29)	45:5.	cannot (29)
40:8.	dependant, (76)	45:11.	Cesar, such (29)
40:9.	me, thro his daughter Calpurnia, (29)	45:12.	propell (29)
		45:13.	ourselves, to (29)
41:2–3.	only. She fails to accomplish it. Politically and morally, (29)	45:21.	CESAR. Lucullus, you (29)
		45:22.	cannot (29)
		45:23–24.	you, if (29)

234 TEXTUAL NOTES

45:27–28.	villas of confidential friends. (29)	54:14.	Sir! (29)
45:28.	Tonight (29)	54:17.	reflexion. (29)
45:29.	know .. (29)	54:22.	Pilot. (29)
45:32.	you, then (29)	54:23.	Chancellor or Speaker, (29)
45:33.	confident. (29)	55:12–13.	connexions (29)
45:35.	it. You (29)	55:13.	sympathize. (29)
46:1.	opprest (29)	55:16–18.	that, if the people should ever have strength to rise again, they would crush us: *me* they cannot: (29); dung-cart (76)
46:3.	amidst (29)		

MR. PITT AND MR. CANNING

Title.	M. PITT AND M. CANNING. (29)	55:23.	before. If you go ... manner, your (29)
50:1.	as, your (29)		
51:3.	witholden (29)	55:25.	you shew too much reflexion, (29)
51:4.	do; since (29)		
51:6.	Sir, (29)	56:1.	Sir, (29)
51:9.	light, if (29)	56:1.	my incalculable inferiority. (29)
51:10.	together, and (29)		
52:1.	controul, (29)	56:5.	not, however, think (29); not however think [*cancellans*] (29)
52:7.	these .. I (29)		
52:7.	rich .. they served me .. I (29)	56:8.	hinted, that (29)
		56:10.	Chancellor's (29)
52:9.	degraded, in some way; and (29)	56:16–57:1.	act like a scoundrel, (29)
52:10.	raising their neighbour's hut (29)	57:5–8.	ones. Besides, if you lose the old women, you lose the Heir apparent. He is their champion, and they are his Houris. (29); Besides, * * * * * * * * * * * * * [*cancellans*] (29)
52:11–12.	England. I (29)		
52:12.	will; a (29)		
52:17.	room for them, I (29)		
52:18.	thoroly (29)		
52:22.	but in (29)		
52:24.	it, tho not equally (29)	57:10–11.	conscience, and (29)
52:25.	you. (29); and ... purpose. (not in 29)	57:11.	it, who (29)
		58:1.	adoption: besides, it (29)
52:26.	of prudence may (29)	58:2.	exprest. (29)
53:1.	him; and (29)	58:8.	prest: (29)
53:2.	replies more studiously than any thing else. I had ... owe every thing (29)	58:8.	come come, (29)
		58:9.	plainly ... my (29)
		58:10.	CANNING. How, Sir! what, Sir! pardon me, Sir! (29)
53:4.	altho ... every thing (29)		
53:6.	age .... (29)	58:10–11.	but, Sir! do you imagine, Sir, I ever lied in my life time? (29)
54:3.	condolence .. (29)		
54:4.	fellow, who (29)		
54:5.	half-wit ... Bonaparte. (29)	58:18.	can I alter his belief? What (29)
54:6.	Sir! (29)		
54:7–8.	Cheltenham-water! an (29)	59:2.	minister: you (29)
54:13.	cannot (29)	59:3.	yourself, as (29)
		59:4.	D .. (29)
		59:8.	not, in (29)

TEXTUAL NOTES

59:9.	any one exclames, (29); any one (76)		65:11–12.	selecting, for . . . employments, the (29)
60:2.	receit (29)		65:12.	men; and (29)
60:6.	you: for (29)		65:13.	large and influential party (29)
60:9.	sympathizes (29)		65:16.	altho (29)
60:10.	tho (29)		65:17.	more wisdom than (29)
60:11.	honorable (29)		65:19.	opprest. (29)
60:14.	Now altho (29)		65:23.	declamers, (29)
61:5.	plane: you (29)		65:25.	amongst (29)
61:7.	shewing (29)		65:27.	succede (29)
61:8.	shew, as lady D. did at lady A.'s, while she was arranging the flowers in her bosom, talking to an admirer, and forgetting that she was on the stairs, until she fell down them. (29)		65:31.	any: in (29)
			65:34.	Melville used (29)
			65:38–39.	attribute to . . . himself a thing so much above his capacity or imagination. (29)
			66:3.	that, without (29)
			66:3–4.	it, there . . . country. This (29)
61:10.	Christ-Church (76)		66:4.	embarassing. (29)
61:10.	any thing, (29)		66:5.	all. Oppose (29)
61:11.	hearts! I (29)		66:13.	about our going (29)
61:12.	gifts; the (76)		66:13.	from their sight (29)
61:19.	*gift*. He (29)		66:17.	army-agents, (29)
61:22.	Ah Canning! (29)		66:19.	wheras in fact it (29)
61:24.	was (29)		66:22.	sworne (29)
61:27.	every thing, (29)		67:1.	(but myself) (29)
62:12.	descendent (29)		67:2–11.	It was evident . . . bravely. (not in 29)
62:17.	over-weening. (29)		67:11.	Certainly all appearances (29)
62:20.	Sir? (29)		67:13.	was little likely to (29)
62:21.	addition, to (29)		67:13.	instant, and (29)
62:24.	anxiety, to (29)		68:10.	til (29)
63:7.	declamation, on (29)		68:13.	cannot (29)
63:11–12.	every thing (29)		68:25.	and, when (29)
64:3.	he [rom.] (29)		68:31.	colleagues, if there were: others follow orders: the (29)
64:3.	catholic (29)			
64:4.	reclame (29)		68:32.	succede, (29)
64:10.	*required to . . . might be* (29)		69:2.	cannot (29)
64:13.	*schoolroom*, (29)		69:5.	shewed (29)
64:16.	*Sir! Sir!* (29)		69:6.	corruption*. [footnote:] *It was said to be so in the time of Pitt. (29)
64:22.	any thimg [misprint] (29)			
64:25.	confess however (29)			
64:25–26.	drew all from (29)		69:9.	mandarine (29)
64:28.	rooms. (29)		69:11.	CANNING. We all cease (29)
65:1.	forget will (76)		69:12.	you, that (29)
65:1.	any thing. (29)		69:13–14.	respectability: the (29)
65:5.	Sir, (29)		69:14.	that Melville ever (29)
65:7.	or for their wisdom. (29)		69:15.	a Burdett or (29)
65:9–10.	connexions. A few men of business, and quite many enough (29)		70:4.	shewing (29)

236 TEXTUAL NOTES

70:6.	capacious, the more flowing, and (29)
70:8.	committ (29)
70:9.	any time (29, 76)
70:10.	danger, talk (29)
70:10.	bravely; swear, threaten, bluster; (29)
70:11.	pious; sneer, scoff; look (29)
70:11–12.	gouty; appeal . . . God, that (29)
70:13.	country; that however at (29)
70:14.	present you (29)
70:15.	demagogues; and (29)
70:16.	sovereign, (76)
70:20–21.	read Adam Smith and Emanuel Kent . . . tost [text] (29); Kant [errata] (29)
70:22.	dependants (76)
70:23.	reflexion (29)
70:25.	fists (76)
70:30.	two months' bill. ¶He (29)
71:2.	¶*The greater fool you!* replied I. (29)
71:2–3.	¶*Why, Sir!* said he, opening his hand to shew (29)
71:4.	*any thing?* (29); anything, (76)
71:5.	Kent?" (76)
71:10.	paultry (29, 76); a-day (76)
71:17.	smiled, when people, in (29)
71:17.	hearts, have applauded (29)
71:18.	aggrandizement of my private fortune. (29)
71:21.	dependant (76)
71:23.	Aurunzebe; (29)
71:24.	ayear (29)
71:25.	purse, other (29)
72:3.	Indies and it sweeps (29)
72:5.	dinners; few (29)
72:5.	wine . . . (29)
72:8.	death and (29)
72:10.	madeira (29)
72:11.	effect, the (76)
72:15.	Treasury-bench (29)
72:20.	much another time, (29)
72:22.	mixt (29)
72:23.	cannot (29)
72:24.	party.

Wellesley has a great deal more acuteness, a great deal more perspicuity [perspicacity, errata, 29], than you. Employ him at a distance, and gratify his inclination for pleasure and expense.

Among the whigs, Lord Henry Petty has conciliated many friends, by his good manners, his variety of information, his facility of communicating it, and his sincerity. He speaks well; and tho you have the credit of being a good scholar, he is known to be a better.

These are the only two men in both houses worth noticing: beware of them. Lord Henry would be the worse neighbour to you from the memory of his father, who was liberal in his encouragement to the learned, and indeed to men of genius and science in every department. I am afraid the son partakes of this feeling, which will draw many about him, and obtain him friends and supporters, even among those who have no literary claims and no want of patronage. (29)

72:25–73.	Employ men of . . . exposure. (not in 29)
73:4.	I have no respect for any living author or living genius. The (29)
73:5.	Bolingbroke; who (29)
73:7.	exclusively. Every thing . . . him. Mostly (29)
74:1.	the very thing (29)
74:3–4.	Indemnity; which I am certain (29)
74:4.	can obtain . . . I find (29)
74:5.	may. (29)
74:12.	acclamation! when I (29)
74:12.	deprest! (29)
74:14.	flourishing: I (29)
74:15.	statesmen: I (29)

JOHN OF GAUNT AND JOANNA OF KENT

78:1.	*Joanna.* How is this my cousin,* (76)
78:7.	you. Let (29)
78:16.	him, for favouring the sect of Wickeliff, (29)

79:1.	stair-case, (29)	82:8.	But, if (29)
79:3.	submitt to you. Behold my sword and gauntlet at (29)	82:9.	evil . . but, (29)
		82:12–13.	then, my gentle (29)
79:5.	duke (29)	82:13.	horse and (29)
79:5.	king (29)	82:16.	unkle! (29)
79:8.	did, when (29)	82:18.	rioters . . or amongst (29)
79:8.	fair maid (29)		
79:9.	over! but (29)		

THE LADY LISLE AND ELIZABETH GAUNT

79:13.	battle. We (29)		
79:14.	danger. ¶She weeps. (29)		
79:16–17.	Sir, for no such purpose, as (29)		
79:21.	lately! thy (29)	88:3.	condemned, we (29)
80:2.	cannot! (29)	88:10.	cheerful: you (29)
80:3.	enemy: his innocent child, (29)	88:18.	was so greatly (29)
		88:18.	than myself: I (29); than myself. I (76)
80:5–6.	vizor? Do not expose your body either to (29)		
		88:20.	broken, heart: (29)
80:6.	missiles . . . hold (29)	88:22.	rejoice! let (29)
80:6.	aside . . . I (29)	88:23.	together! we (29)
80:8.	my fair cousin? Speak, and by the saints! (29)	88:25.	pure? have (29)
		88:26.	committed? have (29)
80:11.	below! They (29)	88:27.	relates that he heard from William Penn a narrative of this pious woman's last moments, at which the generous founder of American liberty attended. ¶She placed (29)
80:15.	JOANNA. Away! away! (29)		
80:16.	the oak wainscot. (29)		
80:18.	permitt it: take (29)		
80:22.	forbear! . . . forward. (not in 29)		
		88:28.	¶Lady Lisle (29)
80:23.	skewers, that (29)	88:28–29.	tho sentenced to it, but was only hanged (29)
80:33.	indeed, he (29)		
80:35.	shew (29)	89:2.	sustainer, I (29)
80:38.	you should (29)	89:6.	cannot (29)
81:4.	each. He, (29)	89:7.	now? doth (29)
81:6.	duke (29)	89:15.	wanderer, who (29)
81:7.	thro (29)	89:17.	it. We must bend to the authority of both; but first to the earlier, and most willingly to the better. (29)
81:13.	*him?* an honest (29)		
81:22.	yourselves; were (29)		
81:22.	shew (29)		
81:23.	king, to (29)		
81:24.	stil (29)	89:19.	threatened 'em (29)
81:26.	duke (29)	89:20.	Terrour (29)
81:27.	(*running back toward* JOANNA). (29)	90:6.	altho (29)
		90:14.	cannot (29)
81:28.	thro (29)	91:3.	cannot (29)
81:33–34.	be then if it took its course against it! (29)	91:12.	thro (29)
		91:13.	stil, altho (29)
81:35.	*Gaunt.* Wind: vapour . . . (76)	91:15.	Majesty (29)
81:36.	*Joanna*. . . (not in 29)	92:2.	thro (29)
82:1–2.	above, which can tranquilize and controul (29)	92:8.	heavenly godlike calmness. (29)

238 TEXTUAL NOTES

92:9.	abstain! abstain! it (29)
92:14.	avenue of eternal (29)
92:15.	LADY LISLE. O my angel! that strewest (29)
92:17.	persecuted (29)
92:18.	it! and (29, 76)

CHAUCER, BOCCACCIO, AND PETRARCA

95:2.	Geoffreddo. Welcome (29)
95:3-4.	Decameron [rom.], which I shewed to you in his manuscript, you expressed so ardently your admiration, when (29)
96:2-3.	acquaintance, with . . . me, has (29)
96:4.	Sir? (29)
96:5.	thro (29)
96:5.	*Campo Santo,* (29)
96:9.	heard however some (29)
96:12.	is indeed the most magnificent of (29)
96:15-16.	CHAUCER. The miserable lath-and-plaster white-washed houses spoil entirely the effect of the colleges. (29)
96:17.	BOCCACCIO. Few persons see any thing (29)
96:19.	*The capital of the world,* (29)
96:37-39.	P. Leopold dismantled . . . Italy. (not in 29)
97:1.	any thing (29)
97:5.	altho (29)
97:5.	that they are so: (29)
97:6-9.	most-part in the aggrandizement of families. Messer Francesco, altho he wears the habit of a churchman, speaks plainer on these subjects than a simple secular, as I am, dare to do. (29)
97:10.	preferr (29)
97:10-11.	our scenery, to (29)
97:11-12.	diversified, and less sublime, (29)
97:14.	Florence. Great (29)
97:17.	til (29)
97:20.	cannot (29)
97:21.	the want of laws and civilization* in [footnote:] *The same is the case at present, and has been so for more than a thousand years, and so it will remain, unless the regenerate Greeks shall invade it after a time, and make it again a Magna Græcia. (29)
97:22.	messer (29)
97:22-23.	thro so enchanting a scenery, as (29)
97:28.	hour, when (29)
97:31-32.	glory, in mild translucent clouds, over (29)
97:32.	moon that (29)
97:33.	center of it, seemed (29)
97:35.	thro (29)
97:36.	this! what indeed are the other works of Nature*! [footnote:] *Niagara was undiscovered; and Chaucer had not visited Bellagio on the Lake of Como . . a situation less striking, but probably the most beautiful in the universe. (29)
98:1-22.	*Petrarca.* Ser Geoffreddo! this, which appears . . . abroad. (not in 29)
98:22.	¶CHAUCER. In (29)
99:3.	flanked regularly with (29)
99:6.	descendent (29)
99:12.	inflamed, by (29)
99:13.	Colà Rienzi (29)
100:3-4.	compensations, for lost dignity, lost power, lost independence. We (29)
100:7.	loyalty, with (29)
100:8.	office, and, (29)
100:10-11.	creatures, who would have adored us if we had succeeded. (29)
101:3-4.	or as a churl. (29)
101:5.	messer (29)
101:10.	ser (29)

TEXTUAL NOTES 239

101:11.	Decameron [rom.], (29)	104:25.	thro (29)
101:11.	at the least (29)	104:26.	tenantry (29)
101:12.	courteous with him as (29)	105:13.	befitt him in his expedition; (29)
101:13.	him; if not now, another time. (29)	105:17.	nor even (29)
101:15.	thro (29)	105:19-21.	across. On the third morning he was more than twentyfive miles from home, near a hamlet (29)
101:15.	shedd (29)		
101:16-17.	it; and I will shew Englishmen what the Italians are; (29)		
		105:26.	proceded (29)
101:18.	imagination than (29)	105:29.	therin. (29)
101:19.	cannot (29)	105:32-33.	of those others about him, sprang forward; and (29)
101:22.	ser (29)		
101:23.	melancholic (29)	105:34.	mettle, before (29)
101:26.	me, of (29)	106:9-10.	the only psalms, he assured Sir Magnus, that (29)
101:32.	walks, commanding (29)		
102:1.	ser Geofferi, (29)		
102:3.	may .. the (29)	106:15.	*over, from* (29)
102:8.	Besides (29)	106:15.	*Warwickshire, to* (29)
102:10.	putt (29)	106:16.	*forest, thro* (29)
102:12.	shewed (29)	106:21.	anger grew calmer as (29)
102:14.	wars, under (29)	106:22.	good humour (29)
102:14-15.	fit, or another, had (29)	106:25.	by the people of the hamlet with much (29)
102:16.	justice he (29)		
102:18-103:1.	at cros-staff. He was invited ... Lucies, (29)	106:26.	attendents (29)
		106:28.	*master, Sir Nigel, that* (29)
103:2.	The youth was then (29)	106:32.	altho (29)
103:3-4.	rather more, and a neighbour of about the same standing was (29)	107:2.	*Young gentlemen, I* (29)
		107:4.	*vow, I* (29)
		107:5.	As he spoke, the (29)
103:13-14.	enwrapt in the doublet and under-coat (29)	107:6.	was, lest (29)
		107:8-9.	Disclamed ... Humphrey de Arden* opened [footnote:] *The family of Lucy is as fertile in character and incidents to the comic writer, as that of Thyestes or of Edipus to the tragic. I know not whether my cousins the Ardens will be contented with the part assigned to their ancestors; but I think my old schoolfellow Henry and his brother Humphrey would have acknowledged some likeness in
103:14.	any thing (29)		
103:24-25.	to soften by rubbing, (29)		
104:2-3.	attendents to embrace [text, 29; unbrace, errata, 29; embrace, 76] him, crying, *O Jesu! ... death. Receive* (29)		
104:9-11.	dust and filaments, crying, *Scape-grace! ... splinters! is it thus* (29)		
104:18.	altho (29)		
104:19-20.	him, on the part of the Christian name, which his godfathers and godmothers had given him. This however (29)		

240 TEXTUAL NOTES

	themselves to their elder namesakes. (29)
107:9.	Wherat (29)
107:12.	noble and unextinguished name. His terrours (29)
107:13–14.	*Son Humphrey,* ¶*I grieve that the varlet who promised me those three strong horses, and* (29)
107:15.	*me: for verily we have had hard* (29)
107:17.	*amongst* (29)
107:18.	*til* (29)
107:21.	¶*Whenever* (29)
107:24.	*forthwith twentyfive shillings, due* (29)
107:26.	*meadow:* (29)
107:28–29.	¶The priest took the letter, and (29)
107:29.	¶*Sir Priest, you* (29)
107:30.	*Such, soon afterward, was (29)
107:35.	thirtysix (29)
108:5.	puddings (29)
108:8.	irregular and mysterious in (29)
108:8–9.	¶*O! for the love of Christ! . . . all,* exclamed (29); ¶"O! (76)
108:11.	attendents, and (29)
108:11.	countryfolks, had (29)
108:12.	priest, being (29)
108:13.	suspicions (29)
108:14.	thro (29)
108:17.	amongst them, led him aside, and (29)
108:24.	*attendents* (29)
108:27.	*tenantry: for* (29)
108:28.	*equipt;* (29)
108:29.	or, what he thinks worse, not (29)
108:30.	*villainously mounted.* (29)
109:3.	¶*Ralph!* (29)
109:9.	*mind, there* (29)
109:11.	worne (29)
109:15.	sett (29)
109:17.	much, and (29)
109:18–20.	incontinence, waited, apparently disconsolate, a few paces from the inn. Presently (29)
109:26.	*Honour,* (29)
109:27.	*one, and* (29)
109:32.	*Worship!* (29)
109:36.	answered Ralph dolorously. (29)
109:38.	hang on the (29)
110:3.	shewn to every one (29)
110:4–5.	*Edward à Brockton,* (29)
110:10.	any one; (29)
110:11.	their hands, if [text] (29); their heads, if [errata] (29)
110:18.	under-sheriff, *they* (29)
110:21.	*Sir! good Sir! gentle Sir!* (29)
110:23–24.	canorously, in well-sustained tenour, hymned (29)
110:25.	*Worthy Sir! . . . reason! hear* (29)
110:26.	*faith! hear* (29)
110:34.	laughed aloud and very bitterly, (29)
110:36.	arm, and (29)
110:38.	*betray, if* (29)
111:1.	horses, without a trial (29)
111:2.	his poor master (29)
111:7.	attendents, (29)
111:9.	and commission. (29)
111:11.	culprit; who (29)
111:12.	cannot (29)
111:14.	today, (29)
111:19.	cried Ralph, *I* (29)
111:24.	tho (29)
111:28.	tho it might be the practise (29)
112:3.	sate (29)
112:9.	head, and (29)
112:13.	*it! . . I* (29)
112:14.	*mind . . several* (29)
112:15.	*it . . Well!* (29)
112:16.	you, at this juncture, the (29)
112:25–26.	eyes, to (29)
112:31.	companions quite as little (29)
112:33–34.	meadow-hay at (29)
112:35–36.	and, grieving that the next stage was stil (29)
113:2.	dropt (29)
113:5.	cried *Roebuck! Roebuck!* (29)

TEXTUAL NOTES 241

113:7.	*was, that* (29)		and hesitated. *A good*
113:9.	relenting; *he* (29)		*blazing kitchen fire is*
113:12.	stil (29)		*enough for me*, said
113:15.	*I cannot* (29)		Ralph. *I care neither* (29)
113:16.	therupon. (29)	117:38–39.	*draft of it when it passes.*
113:18.	city, they (29).		*Sack I have heard of* . .
113:22.	altho (29)		*poor* (29)
113:25.	thro (29)	118:3.	table. (29)
113:28.	French, for (29)	118:4–5.	or even a peacock, . . .
113:32.	there, as a judgement (29)		him." (not in 29)
114:1.	tho (29)	118:7.	*til* (29)
114:6.	*must be past, and,* (29)	118:15.	any-body (29)
114:7.	*thro* (29)	118:18.	together, (29)
114:20.	stars have influence (29)	118:21.	knight, that (29)
114:29.	attendent Ralph to explane. (29)	118:22.	*pure sour,* and (29)
		118:27.	*sharp, we* (29)
114:31–34.	water, then a sack of grey peas, then a blackbird in a cage, then a mustard-pot, then a pair of white rabbits, (29)	118:29–30.	them. *The* (29)
		119:1.	Shortly old Ocean (29)
		119:1–2.	powerfullest, not (29)
		119:3.	him, in (29)
		119:7–8.	he, nor any of the sailors, would bring him such a trifle, as (29)
114:37.	stil (29)		
115:8–9.	franticly, *I saw thy shadow upon the wall* . . *No* (29)	119:9.	camomile-flowers (29)
		119:9.	them, and (29)
		119:12.	moon . . the (29)
115:11.	exclamed (29)	119:15.	be very near (29)
115:12–15.	He fell on his knees, . . . hidden." (not in 29)	119:18.	answered Ralph . . crying, (29)
115:16.	altho (29)	119:20–21.	them. *The boat* . . . *daughter: who can keep* (29)
115:16–17.	all hearts are, the (29)		
115:17–18.	said: Humphrey (29)		
115:27.	cried *Matins! matins!* (29)	119:26.	shewn (29)
		119:28.	shewed (29)
116:3–4.	hear all night (29)	119:32.	sailors; *the* (29)
116:4–5.	like king Nebuchadnezzar's, only (29)	120:3.	every thing (29)
		120:6.	tho (29)
116:16.	traveled, (29)	120:9.	stil (29)
116:17.	sixth evening from (29)	120:12.	*with 'em.* (29)
116:21.	king's. On the seventh day, in the afternoon, (29)	120:18.	*Sir!* (29)
		120:21.	hands, to (29)
		120:23.	deferr (29)
116:23.	cried *Master!* (29)	120:24–25.	startled, at dinner-time, when (29)
116:31.	hereabouts, (29)		
116:34–117:26.	"Six pieces of gold!" . . . hundreds." (not in 29)	120:26–27.	offensive. As the ship rolled somewhat, tho (29)
117:4.	moneys, (76)	120:30.	any thing. (29)
117:27–37.	The knight hung back	120:34.	gestures, that (29)

121:2.	*Sir,* (29)	127:3.	shew (29)
121:3.	*altho* (29)	127:7.	was totally changed (29)
121:7–8.	*Sir!* exclamed (29)	127:11–12.	the twenty-five shillings, stil (29)
121:11.	*stil be incog,* (29)		
121:16.	The people were calking a fishing-smack. They (29)	127:13–14.	them, to (29)
		127:18.	stil (29)
		127:21.	bruizes thro (29)
121:22.	attendents (29)	127:24.	shew (29)
121:26–27.	king, *three* (29)	127:28.	tho (29)
121:27.	*beanfield* (29)	127:30–31.	bruizes, . . . Peter Crosby, of (29)
121:29.	*amongst* (29)		
121:32.	shew (29)	128:2.	tho (29)
122:3.	sett (29)	128:11.	*Well-meant,* (29)
122:4.	nodding, *I* (29)	128:14.	*church-yard, among* (29)
122:11.	*Brête.* (29)	128:17.	*Welladay! and* (29)
122:18.	he . . *What* (29)	128:18–19.	*They love us and watch us and* (29)
122:26.	*pot* . . . (29)		
122:30.	*trust-worthy* (29)	128:19.	dont (29)
122:33.	*altho* (29)	128:20.	*any thing. There are chaps too,* (29)
123:7.	*hand-writing.* (29)		
123:10.	*Hei-da!* (29)	128:24–25.	*Gospels, that they closed* (29); gospels, (76)
123:11.	*deliverance* . . *I* (29)		
123:18.	*pomp: vanity* (29)	128:25.	thro (29)
123:24.	*which leaves an* (29)	128:28.	messer (29)
123:26.	*stil.* (29)	128:29.	tho (29)
123:27.	*unsteddy* (29)	128:31.	ser (29)
123:31.	*fixt* (29)	128:32.	except [text] (29); accept [errata] (29)
123:33.	*therefor* (29)		
123:36.	*with them, if* (29)	128:33.	amongst (29)
124:7.	*cannot* (29)	128:38–129:1.	messer Geoffreddo, were not laying (29)
124:9.	*peace* . . *I* (29)		
124:26.	*altho preadventure* [misprint] (29)	129:3.	would even have (29)
		129:6.	messer (29)
124:26.	*thro* (29)	129:9–10.	Italy; amorous poets, stout abbates, (29)
124:31–32.	hands, *and* (29)		
125:1.	*altho he was yet perplexed in spirit, in* (29)	129:11.	halbardiers, (29)
		129:12.	thro (29)
125:5.	Roebuck, on (29)	129:16.	therin, (29)
125:9.	*men, in these parts beyond-sea,* (29)	129:32.	I repeat it, by (29)
		130:5–8.	Beside, he was very handsome; . . . theirs. (not in 29)
125:20.	*admonisheth* (29)		
125:30.	*dispose of.* (29)		
126:2.	*stil* (29)	130:9.	parties: it (29)
126:7.	*monies,* (29)	130:15.	Lord, in (29)
126:12.	thro (29)	130:16–17.	so) of (29)
126:20.	Rufus; above (29)	130:19.	her; and few besides (29)
126:22.	Roebuck: *in* (29)	130:20.	of, among her female friends, as (29)
126:29.	on all sides (29)		
127:1.	altho (29)	130:22.	bishop (29)

130:32.	shew (29)	133:13-14.	which, I confess, are ... and very many others, just as ser Geoffreddo (29)
130:34.	any thing (29)		
130:36-37.	unwieldy with his confinement, and with lying (29)		
		133:15.	assistence, (29)
131:7.	river, he (29)	133:16.	like it, and could not furnish nor hold another such. (29)
131:9.	thro (29)		
131:10.	thro (29)	133:17.	compliments and titles? (29)
131:12.	giving way with her, she fell with him. She (29)	133:22.	audience, for (29)
		133:23.	aisles, and (29)
131:13.	assistence (29)	133:24.	solitariness, at (29)
131:20.	foot, or (29)	133:30.	not quite so (29)
131:25.	poet*, [footnote:] *Many modern critics have believed them spurious, and some manuscripts are without them. (29)	133:32.	favorable (29)
		133:35.	marriage. Nevertheless so (29)
		133:37.	prince (29)
		134:1.	a considerable dowery; (29)
131:28-29.	stout youths, who placed her (29)	134:2.	every thing (29)
		134:3.	prince and the princess (29)
131:34.	monastery, near (29)	134:5-6.	as much so after (29)
132:8.	admittence, (29)	134:8.	ser (29)
132:11-12.	the most lovely of her sex, from the horrours and deplorable consequences of a watery grave; announced (29)	134:13.	him .. Well! let (29)
		134:17.	Altho, to change her (29)
		134:19.	and as villanous (29)
		134:20.	brought with her in her train (29)
132:13.	of an union (29)	134:21.	to spy the motions of the prince. He (29)
132:14-15.	could recommend or countenance it; since such purity ... enfolded, if he might say it, in (29)		
		134:21.	and, calling (29)
		134:22.	[no ¶] *Discreet and fair Jacometta,* (29)
132:16.	to become her (29)		
132:19.	it. Very providential (29)	134:29.	*preferr* (29)
132:21.	proceding (29)	134:37.	*cannot* (29)
132:23.	earlier (29)	135:2.	think that he was offended. After a few more conferences, he persuaded (29)
132:25.	Carpentras* in [footnote:] *Carpentras is about fourteen miles from Avignon. (29)		
		135:3-4.	any thing should occurr, (29)
		135:7.	time, nothing (29)
132:30-33.	bishop, and ... execution: for he had little faith in the waters of the Durance, as (29)	135:9.	would receive her and console her. The (29)
		135:12.	attentent. (29)
		135:16-29.	night. Generally I sleep soundly; (29)
132:34.	whistle more often than (29)	136:8.	now in the (29)
132:35.	amatory songs, (29)	136:11.	tonight. (29)
132:37-38.	*grown correcter and more fastidious,* (29)	136:12.	tho (29)
		136:13.	messer (29)
133:2.	being little so. Unless (29)	136:14.	Italy .. it (29)
133:3.	highths (29)	136:17.	attentent (29)
133:12.	brain, for (29)	136:18.	*Tonight* (29)

244   TEXTUAL NOTES

136:24.	do. Scarcely (29)	142:1–144:2.	*Alexander.* Like my father, . . . another. (not in 29)
136:26–27.	him, *we must submitt.* (29)		
136:29.	bed . . . which, (29)		
136:31–32.	to use whatever violence she (29)	144:3.	point, I (29)
		144:6–7.	PRIEST. Jason fleeced them, and Bacchus (29)
136:33.	inveying (29)		
136:34.	her voice alone was in any degree (29)	144:9.	*Alexander.* Such . . . heads! (not in 29)
136:35.	princessis bed, . . . under hardly less (29)	144:9–10.	ALEXANDER. Such . . . Gods! (29)
136:36.	vexation with (29)	144:11.	PRIEST. Heark-ye, (29)
136:38.	thereabouts, (29)	144:13–14.	Greece, which thou didst deride most biosterously, at least (29)
136:38–39.	to doubt whether (29)		
137:1.	are many malicious (29)		
137:2–3.	within; and, listening attentively, she distinguished (29)	144:18.	blessing . . (29)
		144:18.	acknowledgement (29)
		144:23.	as thou art. (29)
137:4.	*resistence,* (29)	144:27–145:7.	*Alexander.* Discourse upon it . . . proceed any farther, (not in 29)
137:5.	*bliss; denied* (29)		
137:5.	thro antipathy, *not thro* (29)		
		145:7.	Tell me first in what (29)
137:6.	thro any demerits on his part, but thro (29)	145:17.	enow (29, 76)
		145:20.	glory . . (29)
137:11.	tho (29)	145:26.	scorn; but (29)
137:17–18.	vehemence, slipped into bed, and slept (29)	145:28.	ALEXANDER. How! (29)
		145:30.	reflexion (29)
137:20.	that? The reason was, she had learnt (29)	145:32.	care, less (29, 76)
		146:4.	life, in (76)
137:25.	household, in (29)	146:4.	countries, must depend (29)
137:26.	mistressis charge upon her, to (29)		
		146:16–17.	say, when thou begannest, *nothing* (29)
137:28–29.	from a fit, after such exertions and such exhaustion. (29)		
		146:28.	abhorr. (29)
		146:33–147:1.	those, who (29)
137:33–34.	consciencious: at (29)	147:5.	me?) were (29, 76)
137:36–37.	*divine favour has cured my agonized* (29)	147:13.	witty; prodigal (29)
		148:2.	monarch, in Europe . . (29)
138:3.	tho (29)		
138:9.	messer (29)	148:3.	know . . . I (29)
138:9–10.	altar, and (29)	148:6.	excellencies (29)
138:10.	messer (29)	148:7–8.	serpent. We (29)
138:11.	ser (29)	148:10.	around; and, I assure you, neither our records nor those of our brothers in Egypt, ancient as they are, go far enough back, to shew us an instance of any signal politician who was not also a signal
138:15.	messer (29)		

ALEXANDER AND THE PRIEST OF HAMMON

Title. ALEXANDER AND PRIEST OF HAMMON. (29)

TEXTUAL NOTES 245

	cuckold. Thou hast unwittingly thrown in a strong argument in favour of thy divinity. Nevertheless we must ponder upon it. (29)
148:11–12.	serpent! And she was induced . . . (29)
148:13.	ALEXANDER. Induced, fool! Do (29)
148:15.	been very dexterous . . (29)
148:23.	sayest, sirrah! do (29)
148:25.	thou, O Alexander, with (29)
148:27.	Besides, (29)
148:35.	done so, in (29)
148:36.	dutiful: as a husband and a king, (29)
148:37.	deterr (29)
149:2.	one the first time. (29)
149:3–4.	admitt . . . saw nobody (29)
149:9.	priest shews toward (29)
149:14–15.	ALEXANDER. Ask any thing; but do not press me: kings are not used to (29)
149:16.	center (29)
149:16.	Africa; and the (29)
149:17.	adding those of the Hyperboreans: (29)
149:17–18.	of all who officiate (29)
149:18.	world, in (29)
149:21.	cannot (29)
149:22.	therefor (29)
149:23.	so very much (29)
149:27.	little. We are nevertheless as (29)
149:28–29.	dates, the figs, the fresh butter, the antelopes, the kids, the young boars, the tortoises, (29)
149:31.	thro (29)
149:32–33.	evident, you can find (29)
149:34.	PRIEST. Our difficulty (29)
149:34.	this. Our (29)
149:36.	father . . not indeed while he played the dragon, but before and after. (29)
150:1.	another; this (29)
150:4.	stil (29)
150:19.	altho (29)
150:23.	cannot (29)
151:3.	she whom (29, 76)
151:17.	on some still river. (29); dropt (76)
151:17–18.	when a fragment . . . above. (not in 29)
151:20.	they would be (29)
151:23.	heard nothing. (29)
151:26.	together. . . . (76)
152:1.	discreet! restrain (29)
152:2.	horrour! abomination! a (29)
152:4.	*dragon,* (29)
152:5.	abominable the (29, 76)
152:6–7.	again: shew me the way back. (29)
152:8.	such unworthy names? (29)
152:11.	thou doubt her (29)
152:13.	sister . . tho her (29)
152:14.	stil (29)
152:14.	every thing (29)
152:17.	ALEXANDER. Impostor! liar! (29)
152:21.	PRIEST. Temerity! how (29)
152:21.	cannot (29)
152:30.	no! It (29)
152:31.	silence on this. (29)
152:33.	friendship: lead . . . out. (29)
152:34.	altho (29)
152:35.	serve. . . . (76)
153:2.	heart this daughter (29)
153:11.	PRIEST. Alexander, this shews thee (29)
153:13.	proclame (29)
153:16–17.	be, among . . . old, and (29)
153:18.	ofspring (29)
153:21.	confidence; take (29)
153:21.	hand; give (29)
153:26.	*Alexander. Your* (76)
154:2.	family; the (29)
154:4.	His Holiness the Crocodile-god. (29)
154:5.	pedagogues too are (29)
154:9.	neighbourhood; (29)
154:11.	featherbed or barnfloor, (29)
154:15–16.	arms and thy head [text] (29); arms folded and thy head [errata] (29)
154:18–22.	*Priest.* Thou stoppest on . . . Macedon. (not in 29)

246 TEXTUAL NOTES

DIOGENES AND PLATO

159:3.	PLATO. Let me go! loose me! (29)	165:17.	most part (29)
		165:19.	stil (29)
		165:21.	Segments (29)
160:5.	wheras (29)	165:23.	Shew (29)
160:6.	clame (29)	165:24.	warriors or (29)
160:11.	shewn (29)	165:26.	history, when (29)
160:32.	succede (29)	165:27.	poets: for a prudent (29)
160:34.	cannot (29)	165:29.	Keramicus. (29)
161:5.	in shewing how (29)	165:32.	Diogenes, that (76)
161:7.	stabil? (29)	165:32–34.	which wisdom lies amongst us . . . allegory, (29); allegory), (76)
161:9.	sayest: he (76)		
161:10–11.	traveler, he must also be the oldest creature, upon earth. (29)	165:36.	therefor (29)
		166:7.	stil! (29)
		166:8.	you, my (29)
161:14.	peculiarities of the races, and of their neighbours: he (29)	166:10.	DIOGENES. I cannot shew thee (29)
		166:12.	worne (29)
161:23.	starved, if (29)	166:13.	it, and (29)
161:29–30.	*Parts of knowledge, which . . . none perhaps. (29)	166:16.	thro (29)
		166:19.	to shew thee, is (29)
		166:20.	have that intellect (29)
162:3.	philosophers: they (29, 76)	167:5–6.	doubt has he cleared? what fact has he elucidated? Altho (29)
162:6–7.	from the desire of making distinctions and of saying much. They constitute four distinct virtues: (29)	167:6–7.	old, and . . . city, when (29)
		167:8.	him, from (29)
		167:9.	amongst (29)
162:18.	any one, (29)	167:15.	Xenophon offered (29)
162:19.	malice, against (29)	168:3.	PLATO. He had courage at least. (29); I was . . . it. (not in 29)
162:21.	Sicily. There thou (29)		
163:7.	embosments, (29)		
163:8.	sphynxes, (29)	168:5.	¶DIOGENES. His (29)
163:9–10.	singing boys and dancing girls, to whom alone you speak (29)	168:8.	portent and omen (76)
		168:9.	cannot (29)
		168:11–12.	seat rather nearer to the (29)
163:14.	one) but (29)		
163:14.	pots, and, (29)	168:14–172:13.	Plato. Why do you attribute to me . . . Athens, (not in 29)
163:15–16.	generation! Great men forsooth! (29); generation? (76)		
		172:13–16.	PLATO. I cannot be accused of deserting my country in the hour of danger. ¶ DIOGENES. Better hadst thou done it, than praise the tyrant Critias, the cruelest of (29)
164:3.	cannot (29)		
164:9.	glittering, like (29)		
164:10.	reflexion (29)		
164:13.	vile. (29)		
165:7–8.	incontrolable (29)		
165:13.	no; (29)		
165:16.	welded (76)		

TEXTUAL NOTES 247

173:4.	malady? in such torments, (29)	182:2.	connexions, (29)
		182:4.	pleats (29)
173:9–10.	scorn! everlasting reprobation! (29)	182:6.	altho (29)
		182:8–183:9.	Hymen is indeed . . . voice. (not in 29)
173:11–176:5.	*Plato.* Little did I ever suppose . . . better. (not in 29)	182:8.	Hymen is truly no (76)
		183:8.	fifty-fold (76)
175:1.	any one human (76)	183:11–12.	DIOGENES. Ha! ha! thou hast cried *wolf* til thou hearest him. Answer me now one question. (29)
175:18.	mankind: what (76)		
176:6.	you will argue (29)		
176:18.	sincerely . . or (29)		
176:19.	then, your (29)	183:13.	every thing . . . every thing, (29)
176:21.	DIOGENES. I am very much in the right, therefor, (29)		
		184:3–4.	cannot do it by themselves: for, to admitt . . . admitt (29)
176:21–22.	Embrace me: . . . manner. (not in 29)		
		184:5.	chatels: (29)
176:25.	resentments are (29)	184:8.	altho, (29)
176:29.	offense: (29)	184:10.	every thing (29)
177:2.	place: what there is, must (29)	184:16.	shew (29)
		184:17.	every one (29)
177:4.	banks and (29)	184:24.	attendents (29)
177:9.	to shew me where, (29)	185:3.	defendent, (29)
177:16.	thro (29)	185:7.	with the Stoics on (29)
177:21.	any thing (29)	185:11.	Every thing (29)
177:23.	me, to shew (29)	185:15–16.	escaped the perspicuity [perspicacity] of Zeno, that (29)
177:25–26.	matters; first requesting of (29)		
		185:17.	every thing procedes (29)
177:30.	If Minerva or Jupiter (29)	185:18.	choice, or will, must (29)
		185:22–23.	DIOGENES. Be it so! I meddle not with infinity or eternity. When (29)
178:1.	Jupiter or Minerva. (29)		
178:5.	tho (29)		
178:7.	wheron (29)	186:1.	glebe, with (29)
178:8.	it, is (29)	186:4–5.	way beyond the (29)
178:13.	tho (29)	186:13–19.	*Diogenes.* Keep always to the point, . . . within. (not in 29)
179:4.	agony, from (29)		
179:5.	well . . and (29)		
180:2.	chaunt (29)	186:19.	¶DIOGENES. A bladder (29)
180:3.	easily . . and (29)	186:29.	school-room* of [footnote:] *The tub or earthen cask. (29)
180:17.	statute, while (29)		
180:17.	prisons, the (29)		
180:18.	criminal; the (29)	186:30.	proceded (29)
180:19.	tho (29)	186:32–33.	creatures, who . . . palfry, (29)
180:21.	acquitt: (29)		
181:1–2.	it or however the (29); it, however the (76)	186:36.	attendence (29)
		187:1.	wheron (29)
181:5–6.	yet, under thy regimen, they (29)	187:4–15.	I would be servant . . . invitation? (not in 29)
181:7.	bed-cloathes (29)		

248   TEXTUAL NOTES

187:15.	¶Thy (29)
187:21–22.	scourged; for their (29)
187:25.	is very desirable (29)
187:29.	civilization (29)
187:30.	you, about (29)
188:7.	worshipt (29); worshiped (76)
188:15–16.	the very bushes (29)
188:24–25.	A very small ... any thing else, (29)
189:3.	sovranty, (29, 76)
189:7.	towns; first, (29)
189:8.	countries; secondly, (29)
189:10.	poverty; and (29)
189:12.	cowardice or (29)
189:13.	stabil, (29)
189:19–20.	PLATO. Shew me the particular things which thou accusest me of drawing from others. (29)
190:4–5.	informed by you that "the world has no need of eyes; because (29)
190:21.	Asler. [text] (29); Aster [errata] (29)
191:1–3.	religion? No religion will ever last seven years, unless it is well salted with absurdity, inside and out, and hath one immense crystal of it for the center: but (29)
191:6.	conferr (29)
191:9.	altho (29)
191:12.	straitway (29)
191:23–24.	(Footnote not in 29); learnt (76)
192:4.	play with. (29)
192:17.	Yes. (29)
192:18.	The dead. (29)
192:18–19.	The living. Then all things alive spring from the dead. (29)
192:21.	therefor (29)
192:23.	therefor? where it is [text] (29); where is it [errata] (29)
192:26.	Altho (29)
192:27.	any thing, (29)
192:27.	shews (29)
192:31–32.	Thy consequence, (29)
191:32.	can not (76)
193:6.	Diogenes. On my faith, (76)
193:8.	must both be (29)
193:13.	cannot (29)
193:19.	sagacious, not (29)
193:22.	unsteddy (29)
194:1.	¶DIOGENES. Draw thy robe round thee, let (29)
194:3.	then? do (29)
195:2.	similies. Mine (29)
195:3.	humanity and condescension. (29)
195:4.	DIOGENES. I hate those foolish old stories: I hate condescension: a fig for humanity! (29)
195:5.	who have professed themselves (29)
195:8–9.	PLATO. Neither simple (29)
195:23.	steddier. (29)
196:1.	PLATO. Diogenes! thou art the (29)
196:3–198:31.	Diogenes. Thou hast many admirers; ... Diogenes. (not in 29)
196:8.	under-ground (76)
198:32–33.	language the noblest (29)
199:5–17.	Plato. She, like yourself, worshipped ... words. (not in 29)
199:5.	worshiped (76)
199:16.	worshipers. (76)
199:17.	¶PLATO. We know (29)
200:1.	lie, for (29)
200:3.	omitt (29)
200:3–5.	rite that ever was invented, or ever will be, worthy of an honest or a wise man's attendence. It shews us the union of industry and law: here (29)
200:5.	worshipt (29, 76)
200:7.	any one's folly: to (29)
200:7–8.	inhumane, (76)
200:10–203:7.	Must I go on ... advantage, (not in 29)

TEXTUAL NOTES 249

201:4.	than of a beautiful (76)
202:16.	cognisable (76)
203:7.	¶In the name (29)
203:10.	done here) (29)
203:12.	inditement (29)
203:12–14.	distinguished himself repeatedly and signally on the field of battle, and above the bravest and most experienced of the Athenian leaders, particularly at Delion and Potidea, as (29)
203:12.	distinguisht (76)
204:5.	judgement (29)
205:1.	omitt (29)
205:1.	laught (76)
205:11.	bell-weathers, (29)
206:3–4.	it, is, that (29)
206:11.	worse: it (29)
206:15.	sincerity: what (29)
206:18.	can not (76)
206:20.	least sensible, (29)
206:22.	fathers [misprint] (29)
206:23.	tribe: then (29)
206:24.	spectators, for (29)
206:25.	shew (29)
206:26–208:28.	Without the virtues ... people. (not in 29)
208:25.	particularised (76)
208:32.	them, which, (29)
209:2.	Africa, from the remotest parts of Europe and from the nearest, fifty (29)
209:5.	civilization, (29)
209:7.	united ... Athens (29)
209:8–9.	dowery, brought by Liberty, to the only men capable of their defence or their enjoyment. (29)
209:10.	descendants (76)
209:10.	Gods (29)
209:13.	and unambitious of mortals (29)
210:9.	manner, for (29)
210:11.	*thee* (76)
210:13.	firmly-minded. (29, 76)
210:15.	hero, could (29)
210:16.	possest (76)
210:16.	every thing (29)
210:17.	beauty, of (29)
210:17.	cannot (29)
210:21–22.	competitor? (76)
210:23.	proceded (29)
210:24–211:1.	part of it. Archelaus praised Euripidesis poetry: he liked Archelaus for it. The Athenians bantered his poetry: he disliked the Athenians for it. Besides, (29)
210:25.	Euripides's (76)
211:2.	teacher. If (29)
211:7.	choice, than (29)
211:10.	acceptible) (29)
212:2.	those of them who (29)
212:3.	most and (29)
212:5–6.	Diogenes! and have (29); Diogenes? Have (76)
212:10.	counsellor (76)
212:13.	only .. to (29)
212:15.	power *. [footnote:] *Speaking in the language of the Athenians, by *kingly* power Diogenes means *despotic*. The sentiments that follow are suitable to the maxims of his government and the sternness of his character. (29)
212:18.	diadem † [footnote:] † Darius then threatened Greece. (29)
212:18.	victim. All (29)
212:20.	villages, (29)
212:27.	heat. Shew us that (29)
212:28.	Shew us that (29)
212:29.	laws, bear them patiently, deem (29)
212:33.	mind, austerity of life, rectitude (29)
213:3.	sanctioned: impatient (29)
213:5.	inactivity. We (29)
213:13.	it is [misprint] (76)

250 TEXTUAL NOTES

213:16.	to shew them plainly thro (29)	218:14.	cannot (29)
		218:16.	twice? or (29)
213:19.	stirr (29)	218:18.	priests, for want (29)
213:27.	shewing them thro (29)	219:1.	amongst us, prythee take (29)
213:31.	judgement. (29)		
213:33.	judgement. (29)	219:4.	are. He (29)
213:35.	believed. They (29)	219:7.	imps. It (29)
213:36.	teach; namely, (29)	219:8.	sat (29)
213:39.	procedes (29)	219:9.	another like (29)
214:2.	enthralls (29)	219:13.	and so let (29)
214:14.	pandar. (29)	219:15.	Besides, (29)
214:17.	supremacy, than (29)	219:16–17.	hadst shewn them (29)
215:5.	*shepherds*, (29)	219:17–220:1.	Prodicus and thyself, (29)
216:6–7.	thou shewest that *each of us is the half of a man**. (29)	220:2.	explane (29)
		220:4.	any one (29)
216:19.	*obliterated* these *memorable* annals. (29)	220:5–6.	Museus (which are now so totally lost (29)
216:20.	home Solon (29)	220:8.	worshipt (29, 76)
216:23.	Athena, (29)	220:11.	summits (29)
216:25.	Enough to make ... woman. (not in 29)	220:13–14.	tho the earliest and the most universal, (29)
216:28.	* In the Banquet [rom.]. No two things or qualities (29)	221:2.	Minerva (29)
		221:5.	ill suited thy genius: for certainly thou hadst laid (29)
216:29–31.	Shakespear. The idea of the *androgyne* was probably of much higher antiquity than Grecian philosophy or Grecian fable. Whence-soever it originated, we cannot but wonder how Shakespear met with it, or invented it. (29)	221:17.	virtue. (29)
		221:19–20.	it separated (29)
		221:21.	tho (29)
		222:1.	obedient and (29)
		222:6.	the children of (29)
		222:7–8.	those whom their (29)
		222:10–13.	True indeed ... fathers. (not in 29)
		222:14.	introduce him arguing (29)
216:32.	Dauphin— (29)		
216:33.	*she ;—* (29)	222:17.	succeded (29)
216:34.	ACT II. (29)	222:22.	cannot grow so well (29)
216:35–36.	What is beautiful in poetry, is monsterous in physics, and infantine in philosophy. (29)	223:1.	[no ¶] There are many (29)
		223:2.	youth: as (29)
		223:3.	to have ever been (29)
217:6.	theaters (29)	223:15.	selfishness very soon (29)
217:11.	procede (29)	223:18–20.	PLATO. Definitions are safer and easier than discoveries. (29)
217:12–218:11.	I have heard it affirmed ... boast, (not in 29)		
218:1.	art, for (76)	223:21–22.	made. Nevertheless (29)
218:11.	¶Thou stolest (29)	223:26.	stript (29, 76)
218:12.	therefor (29)	224:10.	peculiarities, the (29)

224:10.	or nearly so, to (29)
224:13–14.	*most delightful to the people, . . . most agitating to the soul:* (29)
224:17–18.	*fond of acquiring information, . . . fond of wisdom;* (29)
224:19.	more so. (29)
224:23.	Margites [rom.] (29)
225:1.	higher and intellectual (76)
225:3.	Margites [rom.] (29)
225:5.	quarrelling (76)
225:10.	definition, without your assistence. (29)
225:11.	assistence (29)
225:12–13.	was, *that man has broad nails:* (29)
225:14–15.	contrary. (29); and . . . flat. (not in 29)
225:19.	reason! (76)
225:23.	demonstrating, that (29)
225:24.	wherefor, if (29)
225:28–29.	them shew their (29)
225:30.	ill will (29)
225:32–33.	wounds: the former from sport or hunger, the latter from fear or hurt: (29)
225:36.	feeling; that (29, 76)
226:1.	malice. For (29)
226:4–5.	it, because (29)
226:6.	timid: but (29)
226:8.	recognized (29)
226:10–11.	sadness: seeing nothing . . . desirable she (29)
226:12–13.	good; coldly pertinacious, and (29)
226:24.	table, as (29)
226:25.	that you in good earnest can (29)
226:27.	PLATO. So we could, (29)
226:30–31.	O Diogenes, is (76)
226:35–36.	*nor fit for any thing else.* (29)
227:9.	hands, having (29)
227:10.	thee . . altho (29)
227:11.	life . . and (29)
227:12.	again.

Plato. My presence then may, after so generous and long a hospitality, be excused.

Diogenes. Wait a little yet, to accept a few gifts and gratuities at parting. The *Defence of Socrates* comes out somewhat late. The style pleases me greatly more than in any of thy dialogues: truth is the chief thing wanting in it.

Plato. In what part? For surely the main [*man*] is well remembered by all the city.

Diogenes. Socrates, I am credibly informed, never called Meletus a strange man, as thou recordest, for accusing him of thinking the sun stone, the moon earth, instead of gods; telling him before the judges that such an accusation ought rather to have been brought against Anaxagoras, whose treatise to this purport was sold at the theatre for a drachma. Never did Socrates say that he might fairly be laughed to scorn if he ever had countenanced so absurd a doctrine. Now, Plato, although in thy work on the Laws thou art explicit in thy declaration that the sun and moon are deities, Anaxagoras denied the fact, and Socrates never asserted it. In this misrepresentation of thine, regarding the friend of Pericles, there was little harm beyond the falsehood: for Anaxagoras was dead; and hemlock might be growing on his grave, but could not reach his heart or even his extremities. When I was a youngster I often tried to throw a stone over the moon, unsuspicious that it was a goddess: had it been, she must be the best tempered of all in heaven, or she would have sent the stone back on my head for my impiety. My wonder was, that, although I clearly saw the stone ascend as high as the moon, and somewhat higher, it always fell on this side. The moon seemed only to laugh at me; and so did the girls who were reaping. Had they been philosophers, with any true religion about them, they would have made an Orpheus of me, and have torn me to pieces. But being of Sinopè, not of Athens, they thought about nothing else than merriment at an idle pelter of the moon.

Plato. We may know more hereafter in relation to these matters.

Diogenes. Not, if philosophers are agreed that it is impious to inquire into them, which, as thou relatest, was the opinion of Socrates. Without sun and moon we have more gods than we know what to do with. If the greater are unable to manage us and keep us in order, sun and moon can help them but little. It is long before men apply to any good the things that lie before them. Air, fire, water, have been applied to new purposes from age to age: poets have seen dimly some of them: philosophers would extinguish the little lamps they carry; but not such philosophers as Anaxagoras. Common things, which at present are brought into little or no use, will hereafter be applied to many; above other common things, common sense. Socrates calls that forbidden which, piling up syllogism on syllogism, and exerting the whole length of his tongue, he was unable to reach. Pythagoras, as wise a man, Anaxagoras a wiser, were invited by Nature to investigate her secrets: when they were advancing too boldly, she gently pushed them back, but never threw the door abruptly in their faces; it stands wide open still. Socrates denounced as impious all physical speculations; these the religious man, the only true philosopher, might find manifested to him through oracles and omens. If thy master, among his many acquirements, had acquired the faculty of speaking plainly, he would have spoken like Anaxagoras, whom, at least it must be conceded, he never had, as thou representest, the folly, the disingenuousness, the impudence to decry.

Plato. Did not the priestess of Apollo declare him to be the wisest of mankind?

Diogenes. The priestess was an old woman, and the fumes were potent. I have never been able to find out on what occasion this oracle was delivered. Oracles are consulted by those who are the most interested. Surely not even a philosopher would be so impudent as to ask a god whether he was the wisest man upon earth. Nor are such the matters on which oracles are pronounced; but future results of arduous undertakings. The story carries a falsehood on the face of it.

Plato. You are the first that ever doubted the fact, whatever may have been the occasion: there is a cloud of witnesses to its universal belief.

Diogenes. I never could see my way through a cloud of witnesses, especially in temples. Lies are as communicative as fleas; and truth is as difficult to lay hold upon as air.

Plato. I feel the acuteness of the former simile; and I wish I could controvert the latter.

Diogenes. Consider well the probability of such a declaration from Delphi. Would the people of Athens, religious as they are, ever have ventured to accuse of impiety, and to condemn to death for it, the very man whom an infallible god had so signalised? If fifty ages and fifty nations had taken up this fable, I would reduce it to dust under my feet.

Plato. I dare not listen to such discourse.

Diogenes. Thou shalt; were it only for variety.

Plato. I limited my discourse to the defence of Socrates: with such as Anaxagoras and Democritus we have nothing in common. But censuring Socrates as you do, you must surely want your usual modesty, O citizen of Sinopè!

Diogenes. Praise me then; since, wanting it, I never took anyone's away.

Plato. Little should I now wonder to hear you call yourself as wise as he was.

Diogenes. Could he keep at home as I do? Could he abstain from questioning and quibbling, to win the applause of boys and pedants? Am I not contented in my own house here, over whose roof, standing on level ground, I cast my shadow. I pretend not to know the secrets of the lower regions or the upper: I let the gods sit quiet, and they do the same by me. Hearing that there are three Furies, I have taken the word of the wise for it, and never have carried a link down below in search of a fourth. He found her up here. I neither envy him his discovery, nor wonder at the tranquillity of his death. Wisdom is tripartite; saying, doing, avoiding.

Plato. Mine, I must acknowledge, has been insufficient in the latter quality: but I hope to correct my fault in future.

Diogenes. On this particular I am not incredulous. Thou owest me too much ever to let me smell thy beard again. From this humble and frugal house of mine thou shalt carry home whole truths, and none mutilated; intelligible truths, and none ambiguous. Probably I know not a quarter of thy writings; but, in the number I do know, I find more incongruous scraps of philosophy and religion, sweet, sour, and savoury, thrown into one stewing-pan, and simmering and bubbling, than my stomach can digest or my fingers separate.

Plato. Too encomiastic! If I may judge by the fumes of the garlic, the stomach is surely strong: and, if another sense is equally faithful, the fingers are armed at all points.

Diogenes. Well spoken and truly. I have improved thee already, go thy way, and carry thy whole robe safe back. (not in 29, 46)

227:17–228:24.	(Landor's lengthy note appears at the bottom of the first three pages of the 29 text.)
227:17.	*Diogenes Laertius, (29)
227:17–18.	and most stupid writers (29)
227:19.	No philosopher, or other man, more (29)
227:20.	Sinopè, (76)
227:22.	Sinope, together with his father, for (29); Sinopè (76)
227:25.	words have led (29)
227:26.	money. An (29)
227:26.	Diogenes; and, (29)
227:31.	that, if (29)
227:32–37.	He did not visit . . . *Ethics.* (not in 29)
227:37.	Wise men (29)
227:39.	anything (76)
227:40.	or even made (29)
227:42.	amongst (29)
227:43–45.	the chief orators and philosophers in the city; Plato for instance and Demosthenes. Here however I must animadvert on the inaccuracy, of (29)
228:1–2.	Socrates, as having seen him, *that he thought him a madman.* (29)
228:3.	Sinopè (76)
228:3–4.	[til long after. The answer, I conceive, originated from the description that Plato, in many of his dialogues, had (29)
228:5.	Plato, he (29)
228:6.	unnecessary in themselves, and inelegant; for instance, his (29)
228:7.	$κυαδότης$; which (29)
228:7.	altho (29)
228:8–9.	*tableity* . . and (29)
228:9–12.	Plato himself, . . . *him.* (not in 29)
228:14–15.	their inconsiderate readers, about his public indulgence in certain actions, which no magistrature in the world would tolerate. (29)
228:18.	died; so placidly and calmly, that the friends who usually visited him, found him extinct, his

            head covered with his cowl.
            A contest (29)
228:19.   honour of supplying (29)
228:20-22. til the fathers of his auditors,
            and the leaders of the people,
            met together, and agreed to
bury him at the public charge, near the gate of the Isthmus, as the most remarkable spot in their dominions, or indeed in Greece, (29)

INDEX

Ablett, Joseph, xiii
Academus, 161, 182
Academy (Plato), 21, 161, 169, 182, 219
Achilles, 197
Acrisius, 35, 202
Acropolis, 165
Adriatic Sea, 27
Aeëtes, 38, 144; *see also* Colchis
Aegean, 215
Aeschines of Sphettus, 205
Aether, 151
Africa, 29, 34, 149, 203, 209
Agamemnon, 142
Agathon, 190–191, 201
Agesilaus, 168
Agis IV, 211
Agora, 165
Agriculture, agriculturists, 161, 188–189, 200, 214, 232
Ajax, 197
Alban Hills, 27
Alcaeus, 220
Alcibiades, 173, 175, 222
Alcimus, 189
Alexander of Pherae, 43, 208
Alexander the Great, 43, 141–154, 168–169, 171–172, 194, 199, 227
Alexandria, 31, 145
Algiers, 74
Allegory, 220
Alps, 43, 130, 232
Amalthea (goat), 153
Ambition, 17–18, 44–45, 51, 54, 99–100, 160, 169
America, American, xiv, 33, 54, 74, 167, 237
Ammon, 150, 153–154
Ammon, Oracle of, 141, 145, 150
Amomum, 150
Amphictyonic League, Council of, 142
Amphipolis, 28, 203
Amynander, 183
Amyntas, 189
Anacreon, 220
Anaxagoras, 199, 204, 211, 251–252
Anaxandrides, 228

Androgyne, 216
Androsthenes, 188
Angelus, 114
Anselmini, Brother, 9
Anti-Jacobin, The, 55–56
Antiochia, 31
Antiochus of Ascalon, 21
Antipho, 35–36
Antiquity, 97–98, 215–216
Antisthenes the Socratic, 199
Antonius, Marcus, 44
Antonius, Marcus (Mark Antony), 20
Anytus, 61, 172
Aoudris, 215
Apennine, Apennines, 17, 24, 27, 31, 33, 232
Aphrodite, 25
Apollo, 142–143, 149, 214, 216, 252; Apollo Lycius, 215–216
Apollodorus, 176, 215
Apollonius Molon, 44
Apperley, Charles ("Nimrod"), xi
Archelaus, 22, 210–211
Archetype, 218
Archidamian War, 205
Archimedes, 21
Architects, architecture, 5–6, 21, 23, 96, 145–146
Archytas the Pythagorean, 163
Arden, Forest of, 105
Arden, Henry, 95, 106, 239–240
Arden, Henry de, 106–128
Arden, Humphrey, 95, 106, 239–240
Arden, Humphrey (of Sutton Coldfield), 106
Arden, Humphrey de (son), 106–128
Arden, Sir Humphrey de (father), 107–108, 110, 121
Arden, Maria (Landor), 106
Arden, Sir Nigel de: *See* Lucy, Sir Magnus
Ares, 25
Arezzo, 95, 97, 133; cathedral of, 101, 133, 138
Argos, Argive, 35, 215
Aristippus, 168, 190

255

256 INDEX

Aristomenes, 162
Aristophanes, 211, 216, 220–221
Aristotle, 157, 168–174, 185, 197–199, 209, 214, 218, 224
Armitage-Smith, Sir Sydney, 78
Arno, 6, 32, 96
Arnold, Matthew, xx
Arquà, 95
Arrian, 141, 143, 145–147, 150, 172
Artaxerxes II, 28, 168
Asclepius, 24
Asia, Asiatic, 36, 42, 133, 150, 165, 201, 209, 225
Asia Minor, 20, 22, 36, 166, 197
Aspasia, 199, 204–206, 208–209
Aster, 190–191
Ate, 202
Athena, 177–178, 192, 214, 216–217, 221
Athenaeus, 159, 166, 168, 171–172, 176, 189, 193, 196, 199
Athenodorus, 163
Athens, Athenian, 25, 28, 159, 161, 163, 165, 169, 172–173, 175, 177, 188, 191, 199–200, 203–212, 214–216, 223, 226–227, 249, 251–252
Atossa, 201
Attalus, 215
Attica, Attic, 22, 151, 158, 171–172, 204, 214–215, 220
Attila, 73
Aurangzeb, 71
Austerlitz, 53
Austria, Austrian, 53–54
Authors: *See* Writers
Aventine, 24
Avignon, 99–100, 129–130, 132, 243
Avon, 116, 118, 122
Aylmer, Rose Whitworth, xii–xiii

Babel, Tower of, 95, 113–114, 122, 125
Babylonians, 189
Bacchanals, 201
Bacchus, 56, 59, 144, 177–178, 201
Badoer, Bonaventura, 4
Badoer, Bonsembiante, 4
Bahri dynasty, 52
Baia, 31

Barrow, Isaac, 73
Bastille, xi
Bath, xiii, xv, 53
Beauclerc: *See* Henry I of England
Beauty, 200–202, 210
Beer, 111, 118
Bell, Robert, 57–58
Bellagio, 238
Belshazzar's Feast, 115
Benzoin, 150
Bible: Daniel, 108, 115–116; Ezekiel, 108, 115; Genesis, 113, 127; Isaiah, 108; Jeremiah, 108; Job, 108, 112; Luke, 104; Matthew, 89, 111; Nahum, 108; Nehemiah, 115; I Peter, 115; Psalms, 108, 116, 120; Zechariah, 108; *see also* Gospels *and* Old Testament
Birch, Walter, 49, 157
Birds, 6–8, 26, 113, 165, 168, 172, 190
Birmingham, Warwickshire, 105–106
Black Sea, 23, 38, 166
Blasphemers, blasphemy, 63–64
Blessington, Marguerite, Countess of, xiii, xv, 31, 33, 78, 102, 157
Boccaccio, Giovanni, xiii, 3–12, 95–102, 129, 132–138; *Decameron*, xiii, 3–4, 6, 9, 95, 101, 133
Boeotians, 142
Boileau (Despréaux), Nicolas, 174
Bolingbroke, Henry St. John, Viscount, 73; *The Idea of a Patriot King*, 73–74
Bolsena, Lake, 98
Bonaparte, Napoleon: *See* Napoleon I
Boringdon, Lord, 57
Bourne, Sturges, 57
Boyd and Benfield, House of, 74
Boyle, Mary, 3
Boythorn, Lawrence, xiii
Brasidas, 28
Bresle, 122
Brete: *See* Bresle
Briareos, 44
British and Foreign Review, 50
Brocton, Edward à, 103, 108–110, 123
Brocton, William à, 103, 108, 110, 123
Bromwicham: *See* Birmingham
Bronze Age, 215
Browning, Elizabeth Barrett, xi, xiv

INDEX 257

Browning, Robert, xi, xiii–xiv, xvii–xviii, xx
Brundisium, 44
Brutus, M. Junius, 29, 174
Bunbury, E. H., 32
Burdett, Sir Francis, 235
Burji dynasty, 52
Burke, Edmund, 50, 60, 167
Burnet, Gilbert, Bishop of Salisbury: *Bishop Burnet's History of His Own Time*, 85–90
Burton, James, 85–86, 88, 90–92
Burton beer, 111
Burton-Upon-Trent, Staffordshire, 111
Bury, R. G., 177–178, 183, 205
Bush, Douglas, xx
Byron, George, Lord, xx

Cacus, 24
Caesar, Julius, 17–46, 167, 174
Calcutta, xii
Callisthenes, 38
Callisthenes of Olynthus, 172–173
Calpurnia, 40
Calvary, 96
Camaldoli, 97
Cambridge, 73
Campania, 20, 31, 42
Campo Santo, 96
Campus Martius, 42
Canning, George, xxi, 49–74; "Friend of Humanity and the Knife-Grinder," 56; "Inscription for the Door of the Cell in Newgate, Where Mrs. Brownrigg, the Prentice-Cide, Was Confined Previous to Her Execution," 56; "New Morality," 56; "Pilot that Weathered the Storm," 55; *Poetical Works of the Right Hon. George Canning*, 55
Canning, George (father), 55
Canning, Mary Anne Costello, 55
Canning, Stratford, 50
Cannock, 106, 110–112, 116; ale, 111; forest of, 105–107
Capua, 20
Caricature, 49, 95, 102, 158
Carlisle, Lord, 57
Carlyle, Thomas, xi, xiii, xx, 157–158

Carneades, 21
Carpentras, 132
Carpentras, Bishop of, 130, 132
Carrara, Francesco da (lord of Padua), 4
Carthage, 20, 28
Caspian Sea, 23
Castile, 78–79
Castile, King of: *See* Lancaster, Duke of
Castlereagh, Robert, Viscount, 50, 58, 63
Castor, 150
Catiline, 27, 40
Cato "Censorius," M. Porcius, 34, 44
Cato Uticensis, M. Porcius, 19, 34, 39–40
Caucasus, 23, 38
Celeus, 214
Cenchreae, 165
Ceramicus, Inner, 165
Ceres, 163
Certaldo, 96
Chaldeans, 189
Change, 66–67, 162
Chaos, 151
Chapman and Hall (publisher), 229
Character, 24, 32, 210, 226
Characters, dramatic, 3, 17–18, 49–50, 77–78, 87–88, 95, 141–142, 158–159, 219
Charlecote, 102–104, 109, 116–117, 122
Charlecote, Thurstane de, 103
Charlecote, Walter de, 103
Charles I of England, 86–87
Charles II of England, 90
Chaucer, Geoffrey, xxii, 95–129, 133–134, 136, 138; *Canterbury Tales*, 95
Cheltenham, 54
Cheshire, 113
Chesterfield, Lord, 167
Chios, 20, 197
Christian, Christianity, 26, 33, 55–56
Chryseis, 142–143
Chryses, 142–143
Cicero, M. Tullius, 25, 27, 29–30, 34, 38–40, 44, 157, 174, 219
Cilicians, 35–36
Cinna, L. Cornelius, 44
Cinque Ports, 70
Circassian, 52
Classics, 73
Claudius Quadrigarius, Quintus, 22

INDEX

Clement VI, Pope, 100
Cleombrotus, 228
Cleopatra VII, 24
Cleopatra (Macedonian), 147
Clergy, 52, 56, 77, 97, 99, 130
Clitumnus: *See* Clitunno
Clitunno, 24
Clodius, Publius, 40
Cobbett's Complete Collection of State Trials, 89–91
Colchis, 38, 144
Colefield, 107
Coleridge, S. T., xi
Comedy, 220, 224
Commodus, L. Aelius Aurelius, 53
Como, Lake, 32, 238
Compassion, 11, 100, 132
Consistency, 66, 69, 222
Constance of Castile: *See* Lancaster, Duchess of
Controversy, political, 45
Conversation, 3, 58, 87, 157, 169, 219–222
Corinth, 28, 165, 228
Cornelia (Caesar's wife), 41
Cornelius Nepos, 38, 208
Cosmos, 203, 218
Cottus, 44
Courtenay, William, 77
Crassus Dives, M. Licinius, 18, 39, 41
Crécy (Cressy), 79, 101–102, 104, 107, 127
Crete, 153, 211
Critias, 172, 183
Critical Review, xiv
Crito, 222
Crocus Field, 142
Cromwell, Oliver, 86
Cronus, 25, 153
Crosby, John, 102–104, 128
Crosby, Peter, 102–104, 127–128
Crosse, Mrs. Andrew, 157
Croton, 209
Crow, Martin M., 95
Crump, C. G., xx, 204; *see also* Landor, W. S., *Selected Works*
Culture, 17
Cunaxa, 29
Cupid, 37
Curle, Richard, xviii

Cydnus, 36
Cynoscephalae, 43, 208
Cyrene, 190
Cyrus II, 28–29, 168

Danaë, 35, 202
Danaus, 215
Darius I, 172, 201, 205
Darius II, 28, 168
Darius III, 172
Datis, 205
David, King, 106
Death, xi, xiv, 38, 42, 175, 192–193, 208
Déaulx, Cardinal de, 100
Delium (Delion), 203
Delphi, 142–143, 252
Demeter, 151, 163; Sanctuary of (Eleusis), 151; Demeter Thesmophoros, 200
Demiurgos, 164, 218–219
Democritus, 252
Demosthenes, 28, 217, 227
Dentatus, M. Curius, 44, 98
DeQuincey, Thomas, xiv, xvii, xx
Despots: *See* Kings *and* Tyrants
Destinies, 151
Devil, 64
Devonshire, Duke of, 62
Dialogue, 95
Dialogue (literary form): *See* Landor, W. S., *Imaginary Conversations*
Dicaearchus, 172
Dickens, Charles, xi, xiii; *Bleak House*, xiii
Dicte, Mount, 153
Dictionary of Greek and Roman Antiquities, 151
Dictionary of Greek and Roman Biography and Mythology, 196
Dictionary of Greek and Roman Geography, 32
Dignity, 19, 46, 79, 100
Dinner, dining, 11, 20–21, 27, 30–35, 45, 72, 107, 114–115, 120, 138, 210
Diocles of Magnesia, 227
Diogenes Laertius, 25, 159–164, 166–171, 175–178, 184–185, 187–191, 194, 197, 199–200, 203, 209, 211, 221–223, 227
Diogenes of Apollonia, 164
Diogenes the Cynic, 157–228

INDEX 259

Dion, 162–163, 191
Dionysia, 159
Dionysius I, 162, 168, 210, 212
Dionysius II, 162–163, 168
Dionysus: *See* Bacchus
Diopeithes, 199
Diotima, 202
Discord, 201–202
Dogs, xiii, 5, 37, 71, 105, 114, 128–131, 146, 187, 194, 205, 210, 224–225, 227
Donatus, 167
Dondi, Giovanni, 4
Doni, Father, 12
Drury Lane theater, 60
Duels, dueling, 63
Duncan, James (publisher), 57, 229
Durance, 130–132
Duty, 5, 100
D'Ypres, Sir John, 77

Earth, 216
Easter, 118
Education, 34, 168, 228
Edward I of England, 81
Edward III of England, 77, 79, 101, 108, 118, 121–124, 127
Edward IV of England, 107
Edward, the Black Prince: *See* Wales, Prince of
Edward the Confessor, 105
Egina, 176
Egypt, Egyptian, xiv, 24, 31, 52, 141, 144–145, 153–154, 171–172, 183, 190–191, 209, 214–216, 218, 244
Elagabalus, 53
Eldon, Lord, 56
Eleusinian Mysteries, 151
Elwin, Malcolm: *Landor: A Replevin*, xv
Emerson, Ralph Waldo, xiv, 158, 166–167, 169; *English Traits*, 167, 169
Empedocles, 170
Encyclopaedia Britannica, 221
England, English, xi, xiii–xiv, xvii, xxi, 6, 49, 52–56, 59, 61–63, 66–69, 71–74, 77–79, 82, 85, 89, 95, 97–99, 101–102, 104–105, 107, 111, 113–114, 116, 118, 121, 123–124, 126, 133, 180, 182, 192; "All the Talents," 69; aristocracy, 49–52, 57–58, 62, 69; "Coalition," 60, 72; Constitution, 50–51, 67–68; government, 52, 61, 67, 73–74; House of Commons, 51, 60, 66, 74; Jacobins, 67; national debt, 49, 51, 54–55; Parliament, 52, 54, 58–60, 62–63, 68–69, 71, 78, 81; Parliamentary forces (1646), 113; Parliamentary reform, 54, 59, 66–68; Reform acts (1832), 54, 68; Revolutionary party, 55–56; Seditious Societies, 59; Tories, 50, 72–73; Whigs, xv, 49–51, 62, 67, 72–73, 236; *see also* Great Britain
English Channel, 55
Enna, 163
Epaminondas, 147, 207–208
Epicharmus (comic poet), 189
Epictetus, 167
Epicurus, 25, 167
Epirus, 147, 170
Erebus, 151
Eretria, Eretrian, 203, 205
Erskine, Lord, 67
Esau, 127
Eternity, 185, 191
Etna, 162
Eton, 61, 64
Etruria, 31–32
Eu, 122
Eubulides, 227
Eucleides of Megara, 159, 190
Euclid of Alexandria, 21, 189
Eumenides: *See* Furies
Eupolis, 161
Euripides, 190, 210–211, 220
Europe, European, 53, 56, 60, 72, 148
Eurytus, 189–190
Euxine: *See* Black Sea
Evesham, 105
Examiner, The, 56–57

Faesulae: *See* Fiesole
Fairclough, H. R., 120–121
Fanaticism, 25, 69
Fasces, 26
Fescennine songs, 40
Feversham, Louis, second Earl of, 86
Field, Kate, xi, 33

260   INDEX

Fiesole, xiii, 6–7, 13, 32–33
Fireproofing (ancient), 22–23
Fish, 26, 33, 117, 125
Flasdieck, Hermann M., xix
Florence, Florentine, xi, xiii–xiv, 3–4, 7, 10–11, 33, 95–98, 158, 167, 232
Florus, 32
Flowers, 12, 119, 135
Fontesecco, Father, 9
Food, 11, 17, 20, 30–32, 114–115, 117–118, 149
Formia, 20
Forster, E. M.: *Howard's End*, xix
Forster, John, xiii–xiv, xvii, xxii, 37, 49; *Walter Savage Landor. A Biography*, xi–xiii, 3, 5–6, 37, 50, 54, 58, 69, 96, 99–100, 159, 219; *The Works and Life of Walter Savage Landor*, xx, xxii, 228
Fortunate Isles, 149
Fortune, 18, 23, 163, 177
Fowler, H. N., 173, 195
Fox, C. J., 49–52, 61, 67, 72–73
France, French, xi, xv, xix, 10, 49, 53–54, 56, 67, 71–72, 78, 86, 97, 101, 108, 113, 122–123, 125, 127, 129–130, 174, 232
Frazer, Sir James George, 25
Freedom: *See* Liberty
Free will, 185
French Revolution, 49–50, 66
Friendship, 18–19, 33, 65, 173, 182
Frye, Northrop, xviii
Furies, 151, 173, 201, 253
Fyfe, W. Hamilton, 224

Gabinius, Aulus, 40
Gaeta, Bay of, 20
Gallic War, 29
Games, 102–104, 122, 128
Gardens, 4, 7, 26, 161, 165, 219, 232
Gaul, Gauls, 18, 23, 33, 41
Gaul, Cisalpine, 18, 20, 32
Gaul, Transalpine, 18, 32
Gaunt, Elizabeth, 85–92
Gelanor, 215
Gellius, Aulus, 22, 210–211
Genius, 3, 129, 162, 214, 221
Genoa, Genoese, 96, 101
George III of England, 50, 56, 59, 70–73

George IV of England, 57
Germany, German, xix, 33, 56, 70, 72, 105
Ghent, 79
Gherardesca, Count, xiii, 6
Gherardesca (villa), xiii, 6
Gherardo (Petrarch's brother), 4
Gibbon, Edward, 73
Gifford, John, 55, 59, 66–67, 74
Gilman, William H., 167
Gisors, Tenerin de, 129–132
Glastonbury, 90
Gloucestershire, 54
God, 9, 49, 55, 57, 59, 64, 66, 69–70, 79, 81, 86, 89–90, 92, 98, 100, 109–111, 113, 115, 120, 122–123, 125–126, 128, 130, 135, 152, 185, 188, 203
Godley, A. D., 201, 220, 228
Goethe, J. W. von: *Werther*, *Wilhelm Meister*, 185
Golden Fleece, 144
Gortyn, 211
Gospels, 128
Gosse, Edmund, 220–221
Gothic, Italian, 96
Government: *See* England *and* Politicians
Granville, Lord, 57
Gravel, 9
Graves-Sawle, Rose (Paynter), 31, 37, 221
Gray's Inn, 90
Great Britain, 32; *see also* England
Great men, 4, 43–45, 51, 157, 160–164, 166, 169, 206–208
Greece, Greek, xvii, 20, 22, 24–25, 27–29, 35, 38, 44–45, 73, 110, 142–144, 146–147, 151, 153, 158–159, 163–164, 169–170, 180, 182, 192, 197, 201, 205, 209, 211, 214–216, 220–221, 227–228, 238, 249
Greenough, Horatio, 167
Gulick, Charles Burton, 168, 172
Gyges, 44

Hades, 24, 163, 193, 197
Hammon: *See* Ammon
Hammon, Priest of, 141–154
Hannibal, 44
Hare, Julius Charles, xv
Hastings, Sussex, 104, 116

Hatè: *See* Ate
Hawthorne, Nathaniel: *The Marble Faun*, xiv
Haye, Cyrilla de la, 130, 132
Haye, Egidia de la, 130–132
Haye, Philibert de la, 130, 132
Hazlitt, William, xi, xvii, xx
Heaven, 120
Hebe, 202
Hebrew, 153
Hecademus: *See* Academus
Hecademy: *See* Academy (Plato)
Hecate, 180
Hegesander of Delphi, 176
Hell, 151
Hellas, 197, 200–201
Hemera, 151
Henbane, 179
Henley-in-Arden, 104–105
Henry I of England, 126
Henry III of England, 118
Henry VIII of England, 70
Hera, 202
Heracles: *See* Hercules
Hercules, 24, 150, 166, 188, 193, 197, 221
Hermes: *See* Mercury
Hermias of Atarneus, 197
Hermippus (comic poet), 199
Hermocrates, 162
Hermodorus, 190
Herodotus, 172, 197, 201, 215, 220, 228
Hesiod, 23, 44, 151, 172, 183, 202, 220
Hesper, 191
Hicesius, 227
Hickes, John, 86–87, 89–90
Hicks, R. D., 159, 161
Hindustan, 71
Historians, history, 17, 28–29, 53, 73, 126, 165, 196, 205–207, 215–216
Hoddesdon, Hertfordshire, 90
Holinshed, Raphael: *Chronicles*, 77–79, 82
Holland, Lord, 57
Homer, 142–143, 151, 166, 183, 193, 196–197, 202–204, 214, 220, 224–226
Horace, 120–121
Hortensius Hortalus, Quintus, 44
Horus, 172
Houghton, Richard, Lord, 33, 71

Houris, 57
Houtchens, C. W., xix
Houtchens, L. H., xix
Human nature, 11, 25, 39, 100, 132, 164, 225–226
Hume, David, 73
Humor, 58, 95, 221
Hundred Years' War, 101
Hunt, John, 57
Hunt, Leigh, 57
Hunting, 105–106
Hyksos (Shepherd Kings), 215
Hymen, 182
Hymettus, 223
Hyperborean, 149

Iberi, 23
Ida, Mount, 26, 153
Ihne, William, 196
Illyricium, 18
Imagination, 10, 101, 133, 217
Immortality, 190–193, 207–208
Inconsistency, 70
India, 60, 150, 203
Indies, 72
Inferiority, 56
Infinity, 185, 191
Injustice, 4, 158, 210, 227
Ino: *See* Leucothea
Ion, 214
Ionian, 159, 172, 214
Ireland, Irish, xii, 56, 60, 66–67, 69, 71, 86; United Irishmen, 67
Irreligion, 25
Ishmael, 127
Isis, 24, 172
Ismael (horse), 124, 127
Isocrates, 28
Israel, 125
Isthmian games, 228
Isthmus of Corinth, 228
Italy, Italian, xiii–xiv, xxi, 20, 24–25, 27, 31–33, 37–38, 42, 54, 56, 95–97, 100–101, 129, 136, 153, 163, 166, 190, 209, 232

Jackman, Sydney W., 74
Jackson, Cyril, 72

Jacob, 127
Jacob (horse), 127
Jacometta, 134–138
James, Thomas, xi
James II of England, 85–91
Jason, 144
Jeffreys, George (Judge), first Baron Jeffreys of Wem, 86–87, 89
Jenkinson, R. B.: *See* Liverpool, Robert, second Earl of
Jerusalem, 125
Jesus, 11, 80, 82, 87–91, 104, 108, 111, 113, 116, 164
Joanna of Kent: *See* Wales, Joan, Princess of
John of Bohemia, 101
John of England, 107
John of Gaunt: *See* Lancaster, Duke of
Johnson, Samuel, xi, 73, 180
Jonathan, 91
Jones, Nancy ("Iöne"), xii
Jones, W. H. S., 195, 214
Jordan, John E., xviii
Josephus, Flavius, 215
Jove, 59, 150, 153, 159
Jubilee of 1350, 100
Judaism, 44
Julia (Caesar's daughter, Pompey's wife), 18, 41
Julianus, Antonius, 22
Junius, 36
Juno, 149, 165–166
Jupiter, 24, 35, 141, 143–145, 148–154, 159, 165–166, 172, 177–178, 202; Jupiter Ammon, 153
Justice, 180, 184, 207

Kant, Immanuel, 70
Keats, John, xx
Kenkrea: *See* Cenchreae
Kennington, 77
Kent, 70–71, 77–79, 81
Kent, Edmund of Woodstock, Earl of, 81
Kent, Margaret Wake, Countess of, 81
Keramicos: *See* Ceramicus
Kidney stones: *See* Gravel
King, J. E., 29

Kings, 70, 99, 116, 119, 143, 149, 152, 168, 174, 186–187, 199, 209–210, 212–214, 227
Lacedaemon, Lacedaemonian: *See* Sparta, Spartan
Lamb, Charles, xi, xvii, xx
Lamb, W. R. M., 202
Lancaster, Constance of Castile, Duchess of, 79
Lancaster, John, Duke of, 77–82, 105
Landor, Arnold Savage (son), xii
Landor, Charles Savage (son), xii, xiv
Landor, Diana, 98
Landor, Ellen (sister), 98
Landor, Julia Elizabeth Savage (daughter), xii
Landor, Julia (Thuillier) (wife), xii–xiii
Landor, Robert Eyres (brother), xii, 49
Landor, Walter Savage: "Abbé Delille and Walter Landor," 174; academic career, xi–xii, 58; "Æschines and Phocion," 169; "Alcibiades and Xenophon," 29; "Alexander and the Priest of Hammon," xxi, 141–154; "Archdeacon Hare and Landor," xv; "Aristoteles and Callisthenes," 158, 172–173; birth, xi; "Boccaccio and Petrarca," xxi, 3–13, 95; books, xiii; "Capital Punishment," 174, 181; *Charles James Fox: A Commentary*, 52–53, 60–61, 69, 73; "Chaucer, Boccaccio, and Petrarca," xxi–xxii, 95–138; children, xii; *Citation and Examination of William Shakespeare*, 102; *Complete Works*, xv, 56, 158, 162, 164, 167, 174, 178, 180–182, 185, 212; death, xi, xiv; "Demosthenes and Eubulides," 158; "Diogenes and a Citizen," 158; "Diogenes and Plato," xxi, 29, 157–228; dogs, xiii, 5, 37; "Epicurus, Leontion, and Ternissa," 157; "European Revolutions," 56; female companionship, xiii; financial affairs, xi–xiii; "Francesco Petrarca," 182; *Gebir*, xii, xiv, 185
—— *Imaginary Conversations*, xi, xv–xvii, xix–xx, xxii, 50, 121, 158, 219; composition, xv; criticism, xix–xx; form, xvi, xix–xxi, 3, 17–18, 49–50, 77–78,

85–88, 95, 141–142, 157–159, 177, 195, 219–222; publication, xv, xvii; reception, xvii; reviews, xvi, 50; revision, xv–xvi, xxii
—— *Imaginary Conversations of Literary Men and Statesmen:* Vols, I–II, 1st ed. (1824), xv, xvii; Vols. I–II, 2nd ed. rev. (1826), xvii; Vol. III (1828), xvii; Vols. IV–V (1829), xvii, xx–xxii, 57
—— "John of Gaunt and Joanna of Kent," xxi, 77–82; "Lady Lisle and Elizabeth Gaunt," xxi, 85–92; "Landor, English Visiter, and Florentine Visiter," 174; language, 49–50, 57; laughter, xiii; "Leofric and Godiva," xvi; "Letter from W. S. Landor to R. W. Emerson," 158, 162, 167, 174, 180, 185; "Letters of a Conservative," 162, 164; *Letters*, 31, 37, 56, 221; literary friendships, xi, xiii–xiv, xvii–xviii, 31; litigation, xiii–xiv, 57; "Lord Chesterfield and Lord Chatham," 158; love affairs, xi–xii; "Lucullus and Cæsar," xxi, 17–46, 157; "Marchese Pallavicini and Walter Landor," 5; "Marcus Tullius and Quinctus Cicero," 158, 219; marriage, xii–xiv, 221; "Moral Epistle," 56, 59; "Mr. Pitt and Mr. Canning," xxi, 49–74; music, 37; orthography, xxii, 170; paintings, xiii; *Pentameron and Pentalogia*, 126; *Pericles and Aspasia*, 209; *Poems*, xiv; *Poetical Works*, xx; poetry, xii–xvii, xix–xx; *Poetry, by the Author of Gebir*, xv; politics, xiv–xv, 49–74; "Popery, British and Foreign," 164; prose, xi, xiii–xxii; "Romilly and Perceval," 69; "Romilly and Wilberforce," 69; *Selected Works*, xx, 204; "Solon and Pisistratus," 177; "Southey and Landor," 180, 219; "Southey and Landor" (Second Conversation), 170, 218; style, xxii; "Tyrannicide," 212; tyrannicide, xv, 174, 188, 212–213; "Walter Tyrrel and William Rufus," 126; "What We Have and What We Owe," 174, 178; *Works* (1846), xvii, xxii, 5, 170, 172–174, 180, 209, 218–219;

"Xenophon and Cyrus the Younger," 29
Landor, Walter Savage II (son), xii, xiv
Landscape, 26–27, 97–99
Lanfranchi, Archbishop Ubaldo de, 96
Lansdowne, William, first Marquis of, 59, 62
Larius, Lake: *See* Lake Como
Lascelles, Henry, 74
Latin, 28, 30, 73, 120–121, 203
Laura (Petrarch's), 10
Lausanne, 86
Laverna, 97
Law, lawyers, 4, 60, 68, 73, 87, 91, 99, 160, 174, 180–183, 188, 200, 212–213
Leavis, F. R., xix
Leda, 197
Lemures, 25
Lemuria, 25
Leon, 78–79
Leonidas, 211, 228
Leopold, P., 96
Lesbos, 211
Leucothea, 228
Leuctra, 207–208
Lex Manilia, 19, 41
Liberty, 3, 19, 63, 67, 100–101, 117, 130, 158, 209, 237
Library, 27–30, 158
Libya, Libyan, 141, 150, 153
Lichfield, 112; cathedral of, 113, 115
Lisle, Alice, Lady, 85–92
Lisle, John (regicide), 86–87, 89
Literary criticism, 5, 21, 42, 129, 132–133, 157–158, 170–171, 180, 195, 197–198, 206, 219–222, 227; *see also* Style
Literature, literary, 5, 27–30, 39, 49–50, 61, 73, 220–221
Liverpool, Robert, second Earl of, 57
Llanthony, xiii
Lockhart, John Gibson, 180
Locrians, 142
Logan, James V., xviii
Logic, logicians, 161, 195, 198
London, 50, 55–56, 60, 72, 77–78, 82, 85, 90, 96
London, Bishop of: *See* Courtenay, W.
London Riot (1377), 77, 79

Longcroft, 106
Low Countries, 118
Lowell, James Russell, 3
Lucretius, 39
L'Œuf, Gasparin de, 130
Lucullus, Cn. (Licinius), 38
Lucullus, L. Licinius, 17–46
Lucullus, L. (?) Licinius (son), 34
Lucullus, M. Licinius, 32–34, 38
Lucy, George, 102
Lucy, Joan, 102–103, 112
Lucy, Sir Magnus, 95, 102–128
Lucy, Sir Thomas, 102–103
Lucy, Sir William, 102
Lucy, Sir William de, 103
Lucy family, xxii, 95, 102–103, 121, 239
Luna: See Luni
Lungarno, 96
Luni, 31
Lutheran, 64
Lycaon, 195
Lycurgus, 211, 217
Lying, 56, 58–59, 183, 200, 225, 252
Lyrical Ballads, xiv

Macaulay, Thomas Babington, xx
Macedon, Macedonia, Macedonian, 143, 147–148, 152–154, 169, 171, 210
Machiavelli, Niccolò: *The Prince*, 73
Maeander, 131
Magi, 11
Magliabechian library (Florence), 158
Magna Carta, 107
Magna Græcia, 238
Maidstone, affair of: See O'Connor, Arthur
Maidstone, Kent, 67
Malice, 225–226
Mamelukes, 52
Manes, 38
Manes (slave of Diogenes the Cynic), 187
Manetho, 215
Mantinea, 207
Marcipor, 20, 27, 31
Marie Louise of Austria, 54
Marius, Gaius, 44
Marriage, xii, 3, 8, 12–13, 41, 102, 130, 132–138, 141, 152, 182, 199, 221–223

Mars, 25, 35
Marsic War, 27
Marvel, Andrew, xvi
Massa, 97
Mathematicians, mathematics, 73, 146, 189–190, 200
Medea, 38, 144
Mediterranean, 28, 97, 130
Megara, 190, 228
Megillus, 217
Meletus (Melitus, accuser of Socrates), 61, 251
Melicertes: See Palaemon
Melos, 175
Melville, Henry Dundas, Viscount, 59–60, 65, 69, 74
Menander, 210
Mercier, Vivian, xviii
Mercury, 30, 145, 192
Messenia, 207
Metaphysicians, metaphysics, 158, 161, 185–186, 195, 198
Methodist Church, 52
Methuen, Treaty of, 72
Metroön, 159
Middleton, Conyers, 73
Miletus, Milesian, 36, 159, 172, 199
Military leaders, 41, 43–44, 56, 147, 169, 207–208
Mill, John Stuart, xx
Milnes, R. M.: See Houghton, Lord
Milo (trial of), 40
Milton, John, xvi, 180
Minerva, 247, 250
Misphragmouthosis, 215
Mithras, 153
Mithridates VI, 19, 22–23, 32, 34, 38, 42, 44
Mithridatic War, First, 22
Mithridatic War, Third, 18, 22
Modena, 20
Moderation, 176–177, 223
Mogul, 71
Mohammedan, 57
Molurian, 228
Monalda, Monna Tita, 3, 6–13
Monarchy, monarchal, 26, 51, 60, 77–78, 85

INDEX 265

Monmouth, James Scott (the Pretender), Duke of, 85–87, 89–90
Montfort, Henry de, 103
Moravia, 53
Morning Star, 191
Morrison, Alfred: *The Blessington Papers*, xvi, 102
Moxon, Edward (publisher), 229
Mugnone, 6
Murray, A. T., 143, 204
Murray, G. G., 220
Musaeus, 220
Muses, 27, 197
Music, 12–13, 37, 40, 55, 109, 119, 125, 129–130, 132, 203, 211, 220–221
Mutina: *See* Modena
Myrtilus of Thessaly, 199

Nájera (Najora), 79
Naples, 20, 26, 133
Napoleon I, xiv–xv, 53–54, 72
Nar (Nera), 98
Nard (spikenard), 150
Narni, 97–98
Natural philosophy, 73
Nature, 39, 51, 97–98, 209, 252
Neanthes, 199
Neapolis: *See* Naples
Nebuchadnezzar, King, 116
Necessity, 185
Neithes: *See* Athena
Nelthorpe, Richard, 86–87, 89–90
Neoclassical Age, xi
Neoptolemus of Epirus, 147
Neptune, 216
Nereids, 23
Nero, 31
Newcastle, Duke of, 62
Newgate, 85
Newmarket, 90
Newport, Sir John, 69
Niagara Falls, 238
Nichols, Admiral, 60
Nicoll, W. Robertson, 31, 33, 157
Nicomachus, 168
Nicomedia, 168
Nicopolis, 22
Nile, 25

Nimrod: *See* Apperley, Charles
Ninepins, 128
Norfolk, Duke of, 67
Norman Conquest, 121
Normandy, Norman, 123–124, 126
North, Lord, 72
Northumberland, Henry Percy, Earl of, 77
Numidia, 29
Nyx, 151

Occult, 196
O'Connor, Arthur, 67
Oddi, Friar Guiberto, 8–12
Ode, 220
Odysseus, 200
Oedipus, 239
Œnomarchus: *See* Onomarchus
Old Bailey, 85
Old Testament, 108, 127
Olson, Clair C., 95
Olympia, 168, 200
Olympias, 147–148
Olympus, Mount, 45, 153, 220
Omens, 56, 125, 167–168, 252
Onesicritus of Aegina, 188
Onomarchus, 142
Opinions, 45, 57, 61, 64, 66–67, 165, 176, 199, 227
Oporto, 72
Orators, oratory, 30, 41, 44, 49–50, 52–53, 56–58, 60–63, 69, 71–73, 165, 188, 196, 200, 204–206, 208, 209–210, 227
Orcus, 151
Oricellari, Amadeo degli, 3, 6–13
Oriental, 71
Orpheus, 220, 251
Orphism, 220
Orthography, xxii, 170
Osiris: *See* Serapis
Ovid, 25, 131, 195
Oxford, xii, 57, 64, 96, 120; Christ Church, 57, 61, 72; Trinity College, xi, 58

Padua, Paduan, 4, 95
Painters, painting, xiii, 22, 29, 34–37, 43, 213
Palaemon, 228

266   INDEX

Pallas: *See* Athena
Pammenes, 147
Papacy, 99
Parian, 28, 35, 163
Paris, 54, 130
Parr, Samuel, xv
Parthians, 41
Patroclus, 193
Pausanias, 195, 214–216, 228
Paynter, Rose: *See* Graves-Sawle, Rose (Paynter)
Paynter, Sophia (Price), xiii
Peace, 18, 26
Peasants' Rising (1381), 78, 82
Pedro the Cruel, 79
Peel, Sir Robert, 72
Pelasgi (Pelasgians), 215
Pella, 143, 168
Pelopidas, 43, 147, 208
Peloponnese, Peloponnesian, 207, 228
Peloponnesian War, 175, 207
Penkridge, 108
Penn, William, 86, 88
Percy, Henry, Lord: *See* Northumberland, Earl of
Perdiccas, 175
Perdition, 64
Pergamum, 36
Pericles, 28, 170, 198–199, 204–205, 209, 251
Perjury, 49, 59, 66–67
Perrin, Bernadotte, 17, 36, 40, 141, 147, 175, 199, 211, 217
Persephone, 163
Perseus, 35, 150
Persia, Persian, 28, 151, 153, 168, 201, 203, 205, 209, 214, 228
Perugia, 97
Pesaro, 97
Peterson, Doris E., xix
Petracco, Ser (Petrarch's father), 4
Petrarch, Francesco, 3–7, 10–13, 95–101, 128–133, 138, 182; *De Remediis Utriusque Fortunae*, 5; *Epistolae variae*, 100; *Familiares*, 100; *Metricae*, 100; *Sené nomine*, 100
Petty, Henry, Lord, 236
Phaedrus of Athens, 191

Pharsalus, 34
Phasis, 193
Pherecydes, 191, 211
Philemon, 210
Philip II of Macedon, 141–143, 146–148, 153, 168–169, 171–172, 199
Philip VI of France, 101
Philiscus, 188
Philo (Philon of Larissa), 21
Philolaus of Croton, 189–190
Philomelus, 142
Philosophers, philosophy, 17, 21–23, 25, 44, 157–159, 162–163, 165, 167–168, 171, 175–177, 182–183, 186–188, 190–191, 198, 206, 208, 210, 216–218, 221–223, 225, 227, 251–253
Phocion, 69, 169, 171, 228
Phocis, Phocian, 142
Physics, 216
Picardy, 108, 123, 128
Pileo, Pietro (Bishop of Padua), 4
Pillars of Hercules, 193
Pindar, 147, 183
Pindar, Peter: *See* Wolcot, John
Pindus, 170
Pioppi, Silvestrina, 10–12
Piraeus, 22
Pisa, xi, 96
Piso Caesoninus, L., 18, 40
Pitt, William, Lord Chatham, 50, 53, 61–62, 65, 67–68, 73–74
Pitt, William, the Younger, xi, xxi, 49–74; bill of indemnity, 74
Plants, 5, 38, 161, 165–166
Plato, xxi, 21, 28, 157–228; Platonic, 182
Pleasure, 25
Pliny, 32
Plutarch, 17, 19–21, 23–24, 26–28, 31–33, 35–38, 40–44, 141, 143, 145–147, 153, 169, 173, 175, 199, 208, 211, 217, 227
Poets, poetry, xii–xvii, xx, 21, 37, 44, 49, 55, 58, 101, 129–131, 147, 161, 165, 183, 185, 196–197, 210–212, 218, 220, 224–225, 252
Poictiers, 79
Policastro, Prince of, 133–138
Policastro, Princess of, 133–138
Politicians, political, politics, xiv–xv,

INDEX 267

17-19, 34, 39-45, 49-74, 100, 148, 153, 157, 162, 186, 189, 208, 210, 214, 236, 244; parties, 45, 50-51, 65, 68, 72, 82
Pollis the Lacedaemonian, 162
Pollux, 150
Polybius, 28
Polycrates, 209
Pomero, 5, 37
Pompey, Gnaeus (Magnus), 17-20, 22-23, 34, 39-42
Pontianus of Nicomedia, 168, 176, 193, 196
Pontifex Maximus, 24
Pontus, 22, 32
Popes, papacy, 97, 99-100, 132
Portugal, Portuguese, 72
Poseidon, 214
Potidaea (Potidea), 203
Pound, Ezra, xviii
Power, 19, 39-40, 49, 51, 54, 56, 58, 62, 98, 100, 161, 164-166, 207, 212, 214
Prasher, Alice LaVonne, xix
Press, 63
Pretyman, George: *See* Tomline, G.
Prevaricate, prevarication, 58-59
Pride, 17, 42-43, 98-100, 102, 123, 125, 129
Prince Regent: *See* George IV of England
Princes: *See* Kings
Privy Council, 67
Prodicus of Ceōs, 211, 220
Protestant, 99
Proteus, 35
Proudfit, Charles L., xxii, 57, 170
Providence, 70, 126, 132
Ptolemy I, 24
Ptolemy, XIV, 24
Pucci, Father Pietro de', 6-7
Punic War, First, 28
Punic War, Second, 44
Punishment, 180-181, 183-185; capital, 179, 183-185
Purser, L. C., 151
Putney Heath, 63
Pygmies, 203-204
Pythagoras, Pythagorean, 163, 189-191, 209-210, 252

Rackham, H., 32, 214, 224
Red-Ridinghood, 33

Religion, 24-26, 56-57, 64, 86, 143, 164, 191, 199-200, 215, 251, 253
Rharium, 214
Rhea, 153, 159
Rhegma (Rhegmi), 36
Rhodes, 44
Rhône, 130
Richard II of England, 77-82; Council of Regency, 79
Richmond, Earl of: *See* Lancaster, Duke of
Rienzi, Cola di, 99-101
Righi, Nunciata, 6
Roberts, W. Rhys, 224
Robin Hood, 103
Robinson, Henry Crabb, 135
Robson, E. Iliff, 150
Rockingham, Charles, second Marquis of, 60, 62
Roebuck, Ralph, 103, 108-128
Rolfe, John C., 22, 34, 210
Roman Catholicism, 64, 99-100
Romantic, Romanticism, xi, xiv, xvii
Rome, Roman, xvii, 3-4, 18-22, 24-28, 30-32, 34-35, 38, 40, 42-45, 53, 96-100, 153, 221, 232; Capitoline, 4, 100; Civil Wars, 17, 20, 29, 34; Empire, 20; Forum, 28-29, 40; Republic, 18, 25, 27, 39; Senate, 17, 19, 29-30, 34, 40-42; Senatorial Palace, 4
Romilly, Sir Samuel, 69
Romulus, 44
Rotten boroughs, 68-69
Rubicon, 45
Ruffhead, William, 71
Rufus: *See* William II of England
Rugby, xi
Rugeley, 98, 106
Rumbold, Richard: *See* Rye House Plot
Runnymede, 107
Russia, Russian, 53, 212
Rye House Plot, 90

Sack, 117
Sacred Band, 208
St. Augustine, 64
St. Barnabas: feast of, 107
St. Jude: feast of, 107

268   INDEX

St. Paul, 125
St. Paul's Cathedral, 77
St. Timothy, 125
Sais, 216
Saladin, 52
Sallust (Gaius Sallustius Crispus), 29
Samos, 209
San Domenico, 9
San Marco, 7–8
Sappho, 220
Sardis, 205
Saronic Gulf, 165
Satan, xi
Saturn, 25
Savoy, The, 77–78
Saxon, 105
Schlegel, Meg, xix
Schlegel, Tibby, xix
Science, scientific, 22, 32; civil, 28; experimentation, 190; forensic, 28; military, 28
Scillus, 168
Scipio Africanus Major, P. Cornelius, 44
Scironian road, 228
Scopas, 35
Scotland, 59
Scott, Sir Walter, xiv, 180
Sculptor, sculpture, 27, 35, 43, 120, 212
Scythia, Scythian, 203, 212
Seaford, Lord, 57
Sedgemoor, 85, 90
Serapis, 24
Sertorius, Quintus, 44
Servilia (second wife of L. L. Lucullus), 34
Seven Years' War, 62
Shakespeare, William, 102, 216; *King John*, 216
Shelburne, Lord: *See* Lansdowne, William, first Marquis
Shelley, Harriet (Westbrook), xi
Shelley, P. B., xi, xiv, xx, 182
Sheridan, R. B., 49–51, 60, 67; *Speeches of the Late Right Honourable Richard Brinsley Sheridan*, 51
Showerman, G., 131
Shropshire, 113

Shuckbury, Sophia (Venour), 102
Sicily, Sicilian, 162–163, 168, 171, 209
Siena, 11, 98
Simone, Giovanni di, 96
Sin, original, 11
Sinope, Sinopean, 166–167, 187, 218, 227–228, 251–252
Sion: *See* Zion
Siwa, Libya, 141
Skittles: *See* Ninepins
Slavery, slaves, 20, 31, 178, 186–187, 207, 210, 217
Sloth, 26, 127
Smith, Adam, 236
Smith, Sydney, 58
Smyrna, 197
Social War, 32
Socrates, 61, 166–168, 172–173, 176–178, 189–190, 200, 202–205, 208–209, 211, 219–223, 228, 251–253; Socratic, 177
Sodre, Luisina de, 37
Solinus, 210–211
Solitude, 33–34, 64
Solon, 174, 177, 183, 216
Sophistry, sophists, 157, 167, 169, 203, 220
Sophocles, 220
Soracte, 99
Sorga (Sorgue), 10
Sorrento, 135
Southey, Robert, xiii–xv, 96, 99–100, 158, 170, 219
Spack, Sam, 70–71
Sparta, Spartan, 28, 162, 168, 175, 207–208, 211, 217
Stafford, 60
Staffordshire, 104, 111, 124
Staffordshire Towns and Villages, 111
Stanhope, Earl, 53–54
Sthenelas, 215
Stobaeus, 151
Stoics, 247
Strutt, Joseph, 102–103
Style, xxii, 28–30, 73, 95, 157–158, 182–183, 186, 194–199, 202, 204, 227–228, 251; *see also* Literary criticism
Suetonius, 17, 19–20, 22, 24, 26, 34, 36, 41–44

INDEX 269

Sulla, L. Cornelius, 22, 27–28, 32–33, 42, 44
Super, R. H., xvi–xvii; *Publication of Landor's Works*, xvi, 57; "Walter Savage Landor" (*English Romantic Poets and Essayists*), xix; *Walter Savage Landor: A Biography*, xii–xviii, 102
Superstition, 25, 29, 100
Sutton Colefield, 105
Sweden, Swedish, 53, 70, 74
Swedenborg, Emanuel, 70
Swift, Godwin, xii
Swift, Jane Sophia ("Ianthe"), xii–xiii
Swift, Jonathan, xii
Swinburne, A. C., xi, xviii; *Atalanta in Calydon*, xviii; "In Memory of Walter Savage Landor," xviii; "Song for the Centenary of Walter Savage Landor," xviii
Sympathy, 173–175
Syracuse, 162
Syria, Syrians, 31, 189, 215
Syros, 211

Tamerlane, 71
Tamworth, 108, 110
Tarsus, 36
Tatham, E. H. R., 157
Taurus, 36
Taylor, A. E., 204–205
Tegyra, 208
Terni, 97–98; cataract of, 97–98
Terpander, 211
Terracina, 97
Tewkesbury, 105
Thackeray, H. St. J., 215
Thales, 211
Thames, 82
Thapsus, 34
Thasos, 28
Thatched House Tavern, 59
Thebaid, 215
Thebes, Theban, 146–147, 207–208
Themis, 110
Themistocles, 170
Theodorus of Cyrene, 189–190
Theodotas, 163
Theopompus (comic poet), 189

Thermopylae, 201, 228
Theseus, 214
Thesmophoria, 200
Thessaly, 142, 170
Thibron (Spartan general), 168
Thirty Tyrants, 172, 207
Thoutmosis, 215
Thracian, 220
Thrasybulus, 207–208
Thucydides, 28–29, 173, 175, 204–205
Thyestes, 239
Tiber, 24, 33
Tibur, 98
Tierney, George, 63
Timoleon, 169
Timon of Athens, 166
Timon of Phlius, 161, 196
Timotheus the Athenian, 197
Tinchebrai, 126
Tinia, 24
Tirel, Walter, 126
Titans, 25
Tomline, George, 73
Tomline, Marmaduke, 73
Tooke, John Horne, 49, 59, 67
Totila, 73
Tragedy, 220, 224
Transpadane regions, 4
Treason, 67, 85–86, 89, 91, 227
Trees, 5, 32, 38, 97, 118, 165
Trent, 105
Trial of John Horne Tooke, 59
Triptolemus, 214
Tritons, 23
Triumvirate, the First, 18, 34
Troy, Trojan, 26, 142, 204
Truth, 21, 23, 160, 166, 180, 186, 188, 195, 199, 214, 226, 251–253
Tubero the Stoic, 26
Turkey, Turkish, 33, 36, 52, 74
Tuscan Sea, 27
Tuscany, 33, 97
Tusculum, 27, 34, 43, 98
Tyburn, 85
Tyler, Wat, 82
Typhoeus, 172
Tyrannicide, xv, 174, 188, 212–213

270 INDEX

Tyranny, tyrants, 17, 141–142, 158, 162, 174–176, 187, 214, 249

Umbria, 24
Unitarian, 64
Uranids, 44
Utica, 34

Vanity: *See* Pride
Varro, M. Terentius, 24, 32, 210
Vaucluse, 10, 129
Velino, 98
Velinus, Lake, 98
Venus, 25, 35–36, 51
Vergil, 97
Verres (trial of), 44
Vettius, Lucius: *See* "Vettius affair"
"Vettius affair," 19–20
Via Appia, 20
Victorian, xi, xiii–xiv
Victorian Era, xi
Vienna, 54
Villas, 4, 6, 23–24, 45
Vinum, Arvisium: *See* Wine, Chian
Violence, 26
Virgin Mary, 112, 137
Virtue, 23, 39, 186–187, 221–222, 227; cardinal virtues, 162
Vitoux, Pierre, xix
Vulcan, 201, 216

Wake, John, 81
Wales, Welsh, xiii, 113
Wales, Edward, Prince of, 77–80, 127
Wales, Joan, Princess of, 77–82
Walmer castle, 70
War, 22–23, 25–26, 32–33, 49, 51, 53–54, 62, 71, 100–102, 108, 111, 174
Warter, J. W., 185
Warwick, 98; church of Saint Mary, 114
Warwickshire, xxii, 95, 102–108, 116
Washington, George, 169
Welby, T. Earle, xx; *see also* Landor, W. S., *Complete Works*
Wesley, John, 52
Westminster, 72, 127
Westminster Hall, 69
Westminster Review, xvi
Wheeler, Stephen, xx; *see also* Landor,

W. S., *Charles James Fox*; *Complete Works*; *Letters*; and *Poetical Works*
Whitbread, Samuel, 74
Whitefield, George, 52
Whitehaven Journal, 185
Wilkins, Ernest Hatch, 5; *Life of Petrarch*, 5, 99; *Making of the "Canzoniere" and Other Petrarchan Studies*, 96; "Petrarch's Ecclesiastical Career," 97
William I the Conqueror, 126
William II of England, 126
Winchester, 85
Wine, 9, 11, 20, 35, 49, 56, 72, 128, 144, 177–178, 198, 201, 210; *Arvisium*, 20; Chian, 20; claret, 56, 72; clary, 119; Formian, 20; hock, 72; Madeira, 72; port, 54; Rhenish, 118
Wisdom, 65, 161, 165, 183, 221, 224–225, 253
Wise, Thomas James, 31, 33, 157
Withins, Judge, 86, 91
Wolcot, John ("Peter Pindar"), 51; "Great Cry and Little Wool," 51
Woolf, Virginia, xix
Wordsworth, William, xi, xiii–xiv
Wright, Constance, 5
Writers, writing, 4, 22, 29–30, 57, 72–73, 180, 195, 207–208, 217
Wycliffe, John, 77–78
Wyndham (Windham), William, 59
Wynn, Charles, 72

Xanthippe, 222–223
Xeniades the Corinthian, 228
Xenocrates of Chalcedon, 178
Xenophon, 28–29, 167–168, 173, 203
Xerxes I, 26, 201

Yeats, William Butler, xviii
York, Duke of: *See* James II of England
Ypres Inn, 77

Zama, 44
Zeno, 247
Zeus, 24–25, 35, 150, 163, 172, 197, 202, 221–222; Lycaean Zeus, 195; Zeus Ammon, 153
Zion, 125
Zoïlus of Perga, 199